MODERN ART

MAURICE UTRILLO: *Montmartre Street*

THOMAS CRAVEN

MODERN ART

THE MEN
THE MOVEMENTS
THE MEANING

NEW YORK : SIMON AND SCHUSTER
1934

TO AILEEN

CONTENTS

mianism. Brief periods of work followed by indolence and despair. Drink, drugs, and appalling poverty. Imprisoned by a dealer. Analysis of his art. Neurotic charm, psychological insight. His faithful mistress. A Polish zealot tries to save him. In last stage of tuberculosis, he goes to Nice. Returns to Paris to die in a charity ward at the age of thirty-five. His mistress kills herself on the day of his burial. A royal funeral. All Paris turns out. The last great Bohemian.

x

as an artist. Finds himself as American, then as an artist. The War—boxing and painting. His explorations of American life. His original style. His art—subject-matter and technique. His powers of design. Three major works. The social content of his paintings. No idealism. Assailed by two factions. Represents his period. Our foremost mural painter.

PLATES

ACKNOWLEDGMENTS

For permission to reprint certain passages and chapters, I have to thank the editors of *Scribner's Magazine, Harper's Magazine, The American Mercury,* and *The Forum.* The description of Matisse's early struggles, page 164, is quoted from Gertrude Stein's *The Autobiography of Alice B. Toklas,* by permission of the publishers, Harcourt, Brace and Company. The paragraph on Matisse, page 176, is quoted, by permission of Charles Scribner's Sons, from *The Art of Henri Matisse,* by Barnes and de Mazia. The material on the social life of France, when not based on personal experiences, has been gathered almost exclusively from French sources. I have endeavored in the text to give full credit to the writers consulted, but I must express special indebtedness to Paul Morand's *1900 A. D.,* a brilliant study of French manners. T. C.

MODERN ART

INTRODUCTION

DURING the last generation, the world has been profoundly disturbed by the precipitate course of art. We have seen violence and rebellion, extraordinary personalities, appalling self-sacrifices for invisible ideals, brilliancy of all denominations. We have seen a new art spread like a contagion, infecting young men and women everywhere with wild ambitions and the spirit of discovery. Cults founded upon subtle technicalities have come and gone in swift succession. These cults had their origins in France: they were Bohemian in conception and international in membership. They were born in Paris; they had their day of publicity; they died. They were transported to America where, by artificial propagation, they flowered prematurely and passed away. Today the various sects composing what is known as *Modernism* are officially entombed in the School of Paris, with Picasso as sexton. In that school, one finds the shrouds of the ancient past, the splintered bones of Cubism, salesmanship and the tragedy of the devalued dollar. The new movement is now a subject for the historian. It is one of the most dramatic chapters in the annals of art.

In writing the history of this period, I have considered, first, the background: the conditions responsible for the social and physical starvation of the modern artist—the Left Bank, past and present, and Paris at the opening of the century. Out of this little world where art feeds upon itself, I have drawn, one by one, the leading personalities, presenting them in relation to their environment, to their predecessors, and to the schools they wrecked or founded, and finally, appraising them in terms of intelligible meanings rather than in the flickering light of temporary influence. If some of them come off rather badly, I cannot help it: it is time that criticism took into account the distinction between exhibits of methods—of working tools—which the purists call painting, and the representation of experiences in life, which is the only excuse for the existence of art. My original intention was to begin with the successors of Cézanne, but in order to make this book an independent unit, I was obliged to overlap *Men of Art* to the extent of reviewing again the work of Cézanne, Renoir, Seurat, and the Impressionists.

I have devoted almost half of the book to America. Which is as it should be—for art begins at home. Art is not a philosophical system embracing the whole world; it is the expression of the adventures and discoveries of the human organism reacting to environment, of the perpetual readjustment of habit to the procession of changing facts. Such apprehension of the stream of facts as leaves a mark deep enough to affect the personality occurs within a limited range. The distinguishing, indeed, the inevitable, sign of great art, is the mark of this limited range—the mark of a specific environment, the impress of a special civilization.

Of the Europeans treated at length, I have considered only the leaders, those who stand for some special school or tendency which, for good or ill, has figured prominently in the modern upheaval. There is one exception—Modigliani. I have included this gifted wastrel as a specimen of the effects of Bohemianism on the artist. Modigliani was a real artist but not a great one. He had talent and charm, but was incapable of self-discipline. I have used him as a symbol of the multitudes of young men who go to the dogs in the slums of Paris.

Among the Americans, you will find Frank Lloyd Wright and George Grey Barnard, two men who have done great work and of whom we should all be proud. "These young sculptors are always talking about planes," Barnard said to me. "Look at the head of my bronze Lincoln —there are seven planes in the nose alone! Let them use their planes to some purpose." You will also find a group of younger men who, with the Mexicans, are restoring meanings to art, who are indicative of a new conception wherein form is definitely allied with content, who are going directly to American life for their materials. To these, the future. I have had no room for jury painters, esthetes who sit in studios and nurse their imported illusions, imitations of Picasso and Matisse—the rank and file calling themselves artists because they have acquired abroad a set of painting-habits.

I have considered art as a human activity, as a healthy act of labor proceeding from, and affecting, the lives of people. I cannot, therefore, accept technical experiments in structure as substitutes for experience; nor can I credit the transcendental values read into Picasso's abstract patterns by his hypersensitive stock-holders. Nor can I accept as valid experiences the hallucinations of the Sur-Realists who distort the facts of life to suit their little nightmares. I have no use for an art that is founded upon the limited attention of specialists, or upon the eccentricities of monomaniacs; I ask that art contain meanings which may be verified, shared and enjoyed by a large and intelligent audience. With this in mind, I have had to recognize the fact that a picture is not only a composition, a material thing neatly put together, but a representation of something, a symbol, if you will; and that the art of painting attains to prominence when its symbolism reveals notions, ideas, tendencies, and values rising from the mores of the time. I have used all the resources in my power to drive this truth home: biography, autobiography, description, anecdote, social valuations, and the ruthless dissection of the esthetic claims of the advocates of purity in art.

The question of social content has led me naturally to an extended discussion of the Mexicans and the propaganda artists. In this I have pointed out, by historical examples, the difference between an art dedicated to social interests and an art sold to social ideals, the difference between the free play of individual conviction and the restrictions imposed upon the artist who paints, not what he discovers in the world, but what is doled out to him in verbal form by political zealots. The most hopeful sign in this troublesome issue is that art is beginning to engage the attention of large groups of people who, for a long time, have taken no interest in art for the very good reason that art has taken no interest in them.

The illustrations, for the most part, represent the artists at their best. In fulfilling this office, some of them will be remembered as horrible examples. A few, such as the Utrillo, have been chosen for descriptive purposes, and some of the portraits—the sculptural caricature of Picasso, and the self-portrait of Van Gogh—which some of the experts have declared spurious, have only a biographical significance.

—Thomas Craven

1

BOHEMIA

"THERE is something of Madame Bovary in every French woman," said Taine. There is something of the gipsy in every artist. To these two human frailties, in conjunction, we owe the existence of Bohemia; and to Bohemia we may attribute the popularity of Paris, the ascendancy of French culture, and the tragedy of modern art.

Paris is youth! How often have we heard that enchanting cry! It echoes in the hearts of young and old in every corner of the globe. It is accepted as a universal truth. Bohemia is the artificial prolongation of youth; youth extended beyond its brief romantic span; youth corrupted by that dreadful infirmity of mind which consents to no development and no maturity. The history of Paris is the history of the struggles to preserve the spirit of youth.

I went to Paris in my twenty-first year, drawn there by my faith in the superiority of the French civilization. I went to Paris to drink of the fountain of youth, to get drunk on the wine of culture. I was a believer. I was convinced that to any aspirant of the arts, the experience of Paris and the adoption of French habits were indispensable. The immediate inspiration to the voyage was Balzac, for I believed then, as I do now, that he was the greatest of French artists, if not of all the artists of the world. Out of that monstrous growth on the Seine, the factory of greed and gaiety, of vice and art, he had created a living organism, vast and supernatural, every pore of which he had examined microscopically. I would become a part of that organism. Balzac had survived ten years in a garret to create Lucien and Madame Marneffe and Vautrin. I, too, would live in a garret. Every artist began in a garret. And I carried within me those disturbing words of Flaubert: "A man has missed something if he has not waked in a nameless bed, has not seen lying on the pillow a face which he will never see again, and when he went out from there, has not crossed a bridge and wanted to throw himself into the water." "The voice of the Frenchman," I said, "the confession of the artist."

On my arrival, not finding a convenient garret, I chose the next best thing—a little hotel on the left bank. It was late in the day and I hurried across the Pont Neuf, eager to compass the whole of Paris in one night— as Baudelaire put it, to take a bath in the multitude. At a marble-topped table on the terrasse of the Café de la Paix, I drank, and watched the world go by. I joined the moving crowd which seemed to swell and sparkle as the night wore on. The streets were a fairyland of desire. I saw travelers from all nations, but mostly Frenchmen and the women they have created for their pleasures. I saw bearded men of the world, old boulevardiers seeking the intoxications of the streets; excitable shopkeepers chaffering with cocottes, and a steady current of painted women, slothful veterans of the chase and sly young filles, wearing enormous hats and trailing long lacy skirts by the café tables as they flashed seductive glances at the men. "Here," I said, congratulating myself, "the wits of man are sharpened by incessant competition and stimulated by incessant desire. The satisfaction of the senses liberates the soul. No wonder Paris is the center of art." That was before the Germans had invented inhibitions, but the French, I dare say, have never suffered from afflictions of that sort.

Tired of walking, I climbed to the upper deck of a steam tram. The car rumbled through a series of narrow, poorly lighted streets, passed the Place de l'Étoile, and went on and on. I did not know where I was going, and did not care—the true Bohemian spirit. At last the car stopped—and stopped for the night. A few sleepy passengers disappeared in the trees by the side of a dark station. I walked back slowly towards Paris, walked for hours, and finally arrived at the Arc de Triomphe where I hailed a carriage. The vast organism was beginning to nod; the disheveled cafés were empty; unlucky girls straggled back to their dingy lairs. From the window of my hotel I looked into the Closerie des Lilas. A shabby solitary girl lingered at a table talking with a waiter. From time to time she got up, strolled to the corner, and then returned to the table. I felt very sorry for her. A man came along, young and buoyant, with a wide black hat and a heavy stick. He greeted the drab as if she were a boon companion; they had one more drink; and arm in arm went off into the night. Thus romance was perpetuated. Thus was born the poetry of Verlaine and the decadents. I tried to make a poem about the girl, but it turned out badly. It read like a poor translation from the French.

The first week I went everywhere without plan or purpose, trying to get the hang of the city as swiftly as possible. I watched the crowds at the free Punch-and-Judy shows; I saw pale children in velvet jackets and French socks playing diabolo with uncanny skill; I saw negroes and their French mistresses parading the Champs-Élysées—huge blue-black fellows with chlorotic, doll-like girls locked in their arms. A free country, I mused, thinking of Louisiana. I found a garret on the fourth floor of an old building near the Dôme, bought a stick and a sash, and embarked seriously into the business of transforming myself into a Frenchman. In the mornings when I went down to the court to draw my water, I encountered five girls, more or less undressed, emptying their slops or tugging at the pump handle. They were nice girls—English and American art students—serious, lonely girls who tried hard to be friendly, but I avoided them as if they had been on the register. I wanted a French girl. When a Frenchman whom I had met in Montreal introduced me to a plump blonde, my life was complete.

She was young and strong, not pretty, but attractive enough, with an anti-geometrical face, large blue eyes and banged hair. Her name was Hélène, a perfectly good name—but I had to change it to Coralie in my poems. She had come from Rouen, and was working, so she said, in the shop of a parfumeur. The ideal occupation for a French girl! There was, however, no evidence of her employment—none save that she was

3

addicted to the use of heavy perfumes. She was drenched with perfumes; she always smelt of the bottle. I did not mind; I was delighted. All Paris smelt of perfumes—cosmetics and wine! Perhaps she stopped working when she met me, after the custom of French girls when they meet Americans. On my first visit to her rooms in the Rue des Martyrs, she opened a drawer and exhibited, with a menacing gesture, a tiny, pearl-handled pistol. I smiled: the weapon was suitable for dueling, as the French practice that art, but as an instrument to protect her honor, it was utterly useless. It seemed to me, joining my life with hers and taking into account her sacrifice to love and art, that destiny had placed her in a consummately appropriate street, but I soon discovered that the street was filled with martyrs to less holy causes. Intersecting the Rue des Martyrs was the Rue Notre Dame de Lorette, and I soon discovered, at first hand and in the flesh, the lorettes of history, the lovely little tarts that Gavarni drew.

It was an enthralling life. Judged by the cultural standards of other nations, Hélène was worse than ignorant—she was degraded—but by the standards of France she was a thoroughly representative and desirable woman. For French culture is no longer based upon the arts; it is based upon a certain homogeneous state of mind, an attitude toward life in which the emotional intensity usually bestowed on spiritual things is transferred to physical gratification, to the adornment of sensuality, to perfumes, eating and drinking. From the French point of view, education, in the formal sense, unfits the average woman for her predestined rôle in society. In the opinion of one of the wisest of French critics, "To endow a woman with reason and thought, is to put a knife into the hands of a child. . . . The object of the educational system for girls is to check their growth."

Hélène was not totally illiterate. A little training in a provincial convent; and then the streets of Paris—France's method of bringing up her daughters. She knew the world, or that very real slice of it bordering on Montmartre. Of the grand boulevards and the Latin Quarter she had less knowledge. She was gay and kind-hearted, with an excess of animal

4

spirits, and that incomparable enthusiasm of the French for indulging the same appetites day after day. She did with charm and unfeigned relish what the kept woman of the Anglo-Saxons does perfunctorily and with a rather bad grace. She loved cognac, cheap jewels, a showy frock for the streets, but best of all, she loved to lie in bed in the mornings, exempt from worries, exulting in her freedom from the heart-rending responsibilities of ill-favored girls who had to make an honest living. My money came from home regularly in liberal allowances; regularly she stole a small amount for lottery tickets, and a larger sum for her mother, balancing the budget by ingenious economies; the rest was devoted to my Bohemian education.

It was an enthralling life. We roamed Montmartre from the Place Pigalle to the Butte. I had the good fortune to see Montmartre before the War and the American invasion; when the heights retained at least a semblance of the sequestered atmosphere which endeared that part of Paris to Degas and Renoir. We frequented the Moulin Rouge and applauded the dancers; we enjoyed the Black Cat and the Dead Rat, and the cabarets where Toulouse-Lautrec sketched his Lesbians and degenerates; and in more venturesome moods, visited the vile taverns in the Rue Lepic in the company of pimps, bawds, crooks and obscene working girls in training for the brothel and the jail. I read Villon again and affected the ballade form.

It was worth the price to learn French from the lips of a girl. I never tired of hearing Hélène's strident, sing-song voice as she jabbered over a petit verre, pausing occasionally to loosen her corset or to crunch a loaf of sugar she had dipped in her cognac. With what insane, what ineffable pride I repeated her phrases! She would intone each word slowly, holding it for an instant and then letting it go with a twang, expelling it with a sensual movement of her moist lips. It is extraordinary the importance the world attaches to the French language! Even the reserved Gibbon had to excuse his vanity in being the first English author to write in French. I knew an American painter exhibiting in Paris who was prouder of the introduction to his catalogue which he had composed, all by himself, in French, than of his pictures. I know an American girl endowed with money, a beautiful body and an exquisite face, whose life in New York was miserable in the extreme. She could find nothing in America worth living for, and she had tried everything. She went to Paris, mastered French, and today is completely happy. To learn French is not to acquire a new soul but a new body—to possess the instrument of rejuvenation; to gain access to the kingdom of youth that is Paris. It is not wonderful that other nations look upon French culture with invidious glances, coveting what they cannot create, condemning what they secretly admire, reaching out for the infernal magic of Paris. So the youth of the world, and the old and bored who would be young again, flock to Paris and strive, by embracing her aphrodisiac culture, to be numbered among the devil's chosen people.

From Hélène I learned to eat snails. They tasted like hot worms, but I praised them, quoting the raptures of a Bohemian gourmet: "L'escargot est à nous comme la rose aux fleurs." Who but a Frenchman would compare a garlicky univalve to a rose? Together we rummaged the book-stalls on the quays. Miles of litter and musty rubbish! One day on the Quai de Conti, I happened on an odd yellow-backed volume of *Les Fleurs du Mal* containing Baudelaire's dedication to Gautier. The passionate adoration, the superlatives of affection, the hyperbolical sentiments impressed my young mind profoundly. The French certainly do not disguise their feelings or restrain their utterances. If an American author should inscribe a book in such terms, his friends would call in the psychoanalyst. Hélène amazed me by picking out a volume of Molière—I had a cultivated grisette! She also bought one of Gyp's novels, *Mademoiselle Loulou*. The Molière she never opened; the scented trash of the Countess de Martel she read from cover to cover. Her tastes, I was soon to learn, were typically French: for the security of their reputation and the prestige of their culture, the French talk and write of Molière and Poussin, Delacroix, the Goncourts, and Cézanne; in their hearts they love Sardou and Bouguereau, Pierre

Loüys, Colette and the art of *La Vie Parisienne*. Hélène's conception of high art was fulfilled in the chic dry-points of Paul Helleu; she loved tenderly the virginal lecheries of Greuze.

Once a week, in the hot summer weather, we went to the country, usually of a Sunday when trains, steamers and trams were jammed with sweltering pleasure-seekers. Hélène did not like the country—she enjoyed the excitement of getting there, the thrill of strutting about in her best dress with a lover in tow. Parisians, as a class, do not care for the country; they descend upon it in droves, carrying with them as much of Paris as is portable, and converting parks and riversides into carnivals of vulgarity. Nor is the love for country folk a conspicuously French trait. French novelists, without exception, write of the rustic population with unconcealed contempt, delineating the peasant as an abominable creature by the side of which the American yokel, as described by Mencken, is a scholar and a gentleman. Paris, they say with pride, is the head, the provinces the sluggish body, of France.

Not for Hélène the sheltered copse of Saint Cloud; for her the multitudinous frivolities of Nogent where unlicensed hussies drink and dance and practice al fresco fornication. I journeyed to Nogent in memory of the prince of Bohemian painters who lies buried there—Watteau, celebrant of the melancholia of eternal youth. I also pulled an oar on the Marne until my back broke, inspired by the girl seated before me chattering of things the French love and illuminate, even in decay, her blue plumed hat in her lap, her blonde hair artfully frizzed, her long skirts tucked high around her; inspired by her outstretched legs stockinged in blue lisle, legs many an artist was to paint and caress before they dragged her through the streets to the final degradation of the maison close.

You will have observed that I was doing the regulation things, behaving in the prescribed Bohemian fashion. Strange that Bohemia, named from the land whence the gipsies were erroneously supposed to have emigrated, and implying, by its origin, a little world in which the inhabitants were bound by no conventions, and at liberty to pursue the

7

romance of life, should have become so exacting in its conduct, so thoroughly enslaved to precedent! That its own irregularities should have become as rigorous as the deadly routine of the workaday world; that it should have mistaken physical excesses for spiritual freedom, whimsical indulgences for individuality, and eccentricity for imagination! How well the French understand these matters, and how acutely they have diagnosed the itchings of the Bohemian soul! "France," as the editor of *Le Matin* recently expressed it, "is a nation of small, slow, stingy people—but all these people have at least one virtue—foresight." The foresight consists in maintaining a picturesque background for the universal spirit of youth, in standardizing and exploiting the vagaries of youth, so that, once the victim is ensnared and caught, there shall be no escape.

If one must go to Paris, it is well to go when one is young and susceptible to the fabricated glamor of a prearranged setting. To remain there is a confession of indolence or incapacity; to acknowledge no laws of growth and development; to prolong the gasconading antics of youth into a fixed state of routine pretension. The genius with which Paris has promulgated and made permanent a certain attitude towards life— a joie de vivre distinctly and uniquely her own—is one of the world's great wonders. Historically, Paris, the self-contained metropolis in the most self-contained of nations, is one of the oldest of modern cities. According to the Spenglerian system of mutations, she should long ago have been a graveyard. Yet here she is, in the year 1933, up to her old tricks again, and with only a handful of roving Americans to be fleeced and fed, enjoying life in the grand manner, rehabilitating her time-honored cafés, exhibiting her mannikins of fashion and of art, manufacturing limousines for her choicest cocottes, and valorously preparing for war. More than eight centuries ago Paris was the seat of learning for all Europe, with an established polity and a well-defined culture, when the average Englishman was Gurth, the swineherd. In spite of continual wars, the relapse into starvation and brigandage after the glorious thirteenth century and the temporary triumph of Flemish painting; in

8

spite of the colossal extravagances of the Bourbons, the Revolution, and the recent slaughter, the spirit of Paris has been preserved intact. This spirit, recognized everywhere as the quintessence of refinement, is the Frenchman's most cherished possession—the glory of La Patrie and the basis of his amour propre. "There is always one thing," to quote Stendhal, "for which the Frenchman has more respect than for his mistress —his vanity."

Nothing, as I have indicated, can extinguish the spirit of youth symbolized by the city of Paris. The face of the city has been altered a dozen times, but the temper of the people remains unchanged and unchangeable. Even the oldest structures, which seem to be ancient scars and wrinkles on the face of the newer Paris, are rendered picturesque and inviting by the addition of a cabaret, or shop, and the presence of accessible girls. Even the oldest and most degenerate of vices are rendered tantalizing to youth when practiced by youth in quaint surroundings. Paris is always refurbishing her gaudy charms, scattering perfume on decaying flowers, applying the cosmetics of culture to every form of activity. Against these gay and patriotic rituals I have nothing to say; nor have I anything to say against the morals of Paris, or of France. That France, as Balzac wrote "should be so jealous and proud of the blood of her sons, but should care nothing for the honor and integrity of her daughters," is not my affair. That France should have survived centuries of turmoil and suffering, that she should stand today as the most solidly based of nations, is sufficient proof that she knows what is best for her. No one can honestly say that she has forfeited her old qualities of courage, and foresight, her high spirits and clear intellect, her instinct for decoration, and her peevish hankering for glory and power. My chief concern is with her art and those essentially French characteristics which have identified art with Bohemianism.

Paris owes her supremacy among French cities to a number of causes: her geographical position; the early foundation of the University, with its affiliated unit, the Sorbonne, in the heart of the Capital;

9

her industrial and political life which, after the Revolution had made her the absolute mistress of France, reinforced her leadership in art and learning; her traditional authority in matters of taste and breeding; her women; and her inimitable spirit. Paris is the head of France not only by right of intellect but by right of commerce, a condition which concentrates there the brains and energy of the whole country.

Paris owes her position, as the international center of enlightenment, to her cultural tradition; her polished, but at the same time, realistic and business-like, ministration to the sensational cravings and romantic fevers of man; her women; and her Bohemia—her sacred tributary nourished with profound knowledge of human weaknesses, advertised by sons and lovers the world over. The elements composing the dual supremacy of Paris—the national and international, the economic and cultural, the mercenary and Bohemian—cannot be categorically divided; they mingle and overlap, forming in the aggregate the distinct and seductive organism on the Seine. But from Louis XIV onward, the culture of Paris was gradually withdrawn from works of art—from the objective achievements which normally produce culture —and in the course of time, became a thing apart—a nationalistic religion, an economic asset, a tool for self-glorification. And since the time of Delacroix, certain propensities of France, deeply rooted and productive of her noblest works, have been polluted by Bohemianism, diverted into anti-social channels, debauched by raffish malcontents and wastrels living, for art's sake, in segregated districts of Paris. Before considering the Bohemian incubus, let us glance at the characteristics which do great honor to Paris and the French civilization.

In the infancy of Paris the café appeared, a form of public life destined to become the most popular and influential of French institutions. The café is not of French origin, but in the hands of the Parisians it has developed into a social instrument of inestimable importance to the well-being of the nation. Why it should have taken such firm root in Paris I do not know. Possibly it is part of the classical heritage, a convenient outlet for the old Greco-Roman and Italian impulses to live in the streets, to seek companionship and the discovery of some new thing. Stendhal, a psychologist of social conduct in many nations, gives the reason that "A Frenchman is the most miserable of men, and almost the most ridiculous, if he is obliged to spend his time alone." Taine, the founder of behaviorism, ascribes the café to the absence of a congenial home life, and goes on to say that "otherwise, no Frenchman would seek the compensations and shoddy delights of the bagman." Let us not be mistaken on this point. I do not wish to leave the impression that the French have no home life. The notion that the sacred institutions of home and marriage are treated farcically by the French is the mendacious tattle of Anglo-Saxons who can find no social substitutes for their unhappy homes and their dissatisfied wives. As a matter of fact the institutions of marriage and family are treated by the French with the utmost intelligence and candor. In no other country is family life so strongly entrenched. Marriage, in France, is an economic union devoid of sentimentality and the hysterical mischief of romantic love. The family is also held together by the strongest of all ties—stern economic laws which make dissolution extremely impracticable. Having established his family on a sensible basis, the Frenchman is free to cultivate romance elsewhere: to leave home and wife for the café and mistress. In opposing this arrangement, you may argue your head off, but in France, it works. It contributes to the prosperity of La Patrie.

Whatever its origin, the café is the great, the indefeasible blessing of Paris. From the time of Abelard, cafés, or their equivalents, have abounded: first, the taverns—there were 4000 in Villon's day; in the seventeenth century, taverns and cafés; in the eighteenth, cafés and salons; in the nineteenth, cafés, salons and cabarets; in the twentieth, cafés, night-clubs, bars, and "dancings". There are today, and have always been, cafés for all classes of people: for dilettantes and fashionable loafers, for cosmopolites and expatriates; for scholars and poets, artists and authors, politicians and prostitutes, bourgeois families, crooks, mechanics, jockeys, and scavengers. The effect of these innumerable haunts is to give Paris a color and tone, a unique atmosphere of charm and relaxation. And more; to create within all classes a high degree of sociability, a sense of public spirit and superior civic decency.

Thus the Parisian, molded by public life, sharing from childhood the surprises and enchantments of the café and boulevard, loves his city and takes care that her magnetic brilliancy shall not be tarnished. Thus is propagated a pride that knows no equal, a pride so great that it impels the Parisian, as an Italian visitor remarked, "even to hate with commiseration, to consider his enemies sufficiently punished by the fate which caused them to be born where they were." Maintaining, from her foundation, her countless centers of public life, Paris, in all justice, is entitled to her acknowledged eminence as the most civilized of cities. Her eminence in this particular field, or that, may well be contested, but in those attributes which distinguish man, the sensitive, social animal, from the dull-witted rustic; in all those things which come from urbanity and appeal to urbanity, she is still the mistress of the world. In original ideas, Paris has never excelled; but in borrowing, tailoring, garnishing and adapting; in receptivity to the ideas of others; she has had no rivals. Everything that passes through her fingers bears the stamp of taste and culture, the transmuting touches of inventive magic, the unmistakable trademark of delicacy and distinction. The principal business of Paris is living, not laying up treasures in heaven. And to the adornment of living she transfers the creative fervor reserved by other peoples for the arts alone. In fact, the fine arts, in Paris, are adjuncts of fine living, and are practiced as seriously and with the same intensity as the arts of fashion, cookery and prostitution. All things work together for the enthronement of reason and the civilized gratification of desire. The spirit of Paris, I believe, is the fruit of a highly organized social life in which men and women assemble in public to exchange ideas, to exhibit and compare and discuss achievements, to observe human tastes and needs; in which friends and families of high and low degree drink and dine in public places, and are encouraged to adopt a more civilized decorum, to discard the toothpick, and to relieve the tension of their sordid homes.

Masterpieces of art are conceived and executed in solitude, but the materials composing them are gathered from human relationships. Art is essentially a social phenomenon, urban generally, communal always; and it would be hard to name a French painter of any merit who has not profited by his social excursions. The salon, originally an aristocratic affair, became, in the nineteenth century, an important factor in the appreciation of art. Under the direction of clever and charming women, the salon was the meeting ground of the artist and an intelligent public, according the artist the social recognition denied him by stupid bureaucrats. And every painter and writer was known by the café he frequented. Even old Daumier, by nature a solitary, would wander, after a debauch of toil, to a café to drink a bock with a few cronies. Degas, a confirmed recluse whose studio was impregnable, found the old cafés of Montmartre soothing to his wretched nerves. And Manet, a Parisian of the old school who lived with the most rigid propriety in a house furnished in the Empire style, walked the boulevards daily and was a familiar figure at Tortoni's. The traditional spirit of Paris, her color and charm, her frank acceptance of all good things, and the freedom of social intercourse as prompted by her cafés—these together have brought into French art and letters a celebration of the physical world—a worship of le monde visible—unexampled since the Venetians; have produced such masterpieces of paganism and of simple gaiety as Gautier's *Mademoiselle de Maupin* and Renoir's *Le Moulin de la Galette*.

Bohemianism in art is a perversion of the spirit of Paris. In its remote beginnings it was only a means to an end, and as such a healthy manifestation of social instincts. In its restricted sense it is an end in itself, and so flourishing from the time of Murger, may be held responsible for the disintegration of French art. Bohemianism is a disease indigenous to the Latin Quarter, a term originally meaning only the precincts of the old University entered by the Rue Galande, the ancient Roman road from Paris to Lyons. In the Second Empire the Quarter suffered severe dislocations by the building of the Boulevard St.-Michel and the Boulevard St-Germain, and today, roughly speaking, may be said to extend from the Seine to the Boulevard du Montparnasse, from the Halle aux Vins to the Beaux Arts. The Quarter, in its early history, was called the Pays Latin for the reason that Latin was the language of the class-room—not the pure idiom of Cicero, but an easy colloquial jargon—and remained the official language until the close of the reign of Henry IV. Today the Quarter is a babel of voices, a mixture of all the tongues of the world—except Latin.

At the opening of the twelfth century, Peter Abelard, magnificent in address and in the exposition of his dialectic, attracted the youth of all Europe to the cloisters of Notre Dame. The Cité overflowing, schools and students migrated to the mainland on the left bank, and in 1215, by a consolidation of forces, the University of Paris was founded, and the Latin Quarter became a teeming reality. During the thirteenth century, students of all nations swarmed the Rue St. Jacques and the Rue de la Harpe, drawn to Paris by the great schoolmen of the University and the Sorbonne. Those ancient quarters which seem so quaint and picturesque to modern artists were not regarded with romantic levity by their first inhabitants. The streets were un-drained and unlighted; the houses filthy and disreputable. The students were poverty-stricken and ill-fed; many of them begged for bread, starved, or froze to death in the winter—a form of death threatening most modern Parisians. But they were all inflamed by a common purpose—a zeal for learning—and were willing to endure any privation to attain that end. They made shift to drown their hardships in various diversions. There were fierce rivalries and nationalistic clashes, the French lads being stigmatized as "proud, soft, and womanish"—adjectives not altogether inapplicable today to a large and increasing sect of Parisian males, when contrasted with the strapping matron behind the cash box. They wore berets, roistered in the streets, drank and danced

14

in the taverns. They consorted with harlots, those of more fortunate estate keeping mistresses. Already the dominion of la femme was beginning, and we have the wails of students writing home "of being seduced into pleasure."

With Villon the Middle Ages may be said to have ended. Paris, bled by wars, was desolated, the prey of wolves, plagues, and famines. Tavern life, however, was not diminished; and the University, despite the evil times, boasted of forty-two colleges and 2500 members—tatterdemalion starvelings from France and afar. One of the members, Francis Villon, has been crowned and toasted by each succeeding generation of pretenders as the King of the Bohemians, an insult, I am prepared to say, to his tough masculinity and his poetic powers. If to gamble, drink, and ravish girls, are Bohemian pastimes: if to enter the lowest of occupations, that of the pimp, and to brag about it in verse; and to spend one's time between the hovel and the tavern, and the brothel and the prison—if these are the credentials of the Bohemian, then Villon is the foremost of the confraternity. He was the first Frenchman to win immortality by pursuing, from instinct and choice, the path of crime, and I may add, the last. He was not playing at life, not living by precedent; he was an independent and imaginative rascal with a rapacious insight into the bitterness of hard fact. The taverns he favored—the Fleur-de-Lys, the Swallow, the Golden Lion, and the Scarlet Hat—despite their poetic sign-boards, were dens of obscenity. He did not pretend that they were romantic or essential to his art. The girls with their pretty names, Margot, Denise and Rose, were not fairer than their modern analogues of Montparnasse, Gaby, Kiki and Sporty, who prefer to be whores to artists rather than registered peddlers. He did not pretend that they enhanced his spiritual freedom; he took what he could get from them, knowing that "into the night go one and all." He took and gave, crying cynically, "Tout aux tavernes et aux filles." He saw before him, as the consequence of his actions, not a life fallen into desuetude—not the bleak futility awaiting those who live for art's sake—but the gibbet of Montfaucon.

15

In the fifteenth century the taverns associated with the University began to tempt outside talent—free lance artists and writers; by the middle of the sixteenth, the taverns had multiplied beyond enumeration, spreading from the Latin Quarter to the right bank and to all parts of Paris. In 1635 a group of unattached poets christened their favorite rendezvous—a hillock crowned with inns and windmills—Montparnasse; in 1685, the Procope, the first established café, opened its doors opposite the old Comédie Française. The dirty tavern which drove Erasmus to Flanders with the remark, "I carried nothing but a body infested with disease and a plentiful supply of vermin," gave way to the less pestilent café, and the café was never superseded. The Pomme de Pin, known to Villon and Rabelais, was host to Boileau, Molière and Racine. One could write much of the history of Paris round the old Procope: the erratic Rousseau came there, and Diderot, the preacher; Voltaire, at eighty-two, attending rehearsals of *Irene*, sipped a new beverage called coffee; the leaders of the Revolution foregathered in its dark rooms—Marat, Robespierre, Danton, Desmoulins and Napoleon Bonaparte; in the next century, Balzac, snatching a few moments from his volcanic labors, discussed chastity with Gautier; then the giant Flaubert with his pupil Maupassant; then Taine, Turgenev, Jules de Goncourt and Renan; in the 'nineties, Verlaine, sprawling in Voltaire's chair, drank his wormwood liqueur, and minor Symbolistes droned their bloodless versicles.

In the nineteenth century, from 1830 to 1860, we enter the golden age of the Latin Quarter. The completion of the École des Beaux-Arts in 1839; the prosperity of the University—in 1838 the School of Medicine alone enrolled 4000 students, and an American traveller wrote home that "carts arrived daily, pouring out a dozen or so of naked men and women, as you do a cord of wood, upon the pavement"—and the name and fame of Murger's Scenes de la Vie de Bohème; these, in collaboration, put the Latin Quarter on the map, as we say—the map of Paris. But the most potent agency was Henri Murger, a garret-dweller and journalist of the left bank. Murger's novel and play, extolling the fabulous and romantic aspects of the Quarter—largely imaginary—fixed the name, Bohemia, and its physical background, once for all, and spread far and wide the contagion of gipsy indolence and childish masquerade so captivating to unformed art students. About 1860 European outsiders came to taste the poison, and in the early 'seventies, the first Americans. Whereupon, the more estimable French painters, old conservatives resenting foreigners, declared it was time to get out. "The Latin Quarter," they avowed, "is all right for amateurs and costumed idiots and rabble students, but serious men must work in peace." So they fitted out studios atop and around Montmartre and for many years lived in peace, substantiating their existence by good works.

At present, Montmartre is a pustule on the organism of Paris, but striking and picturesque in its virulent decay. For centuries, Hilaire Belloc informs us, the Butte was the refuge of outcasts and luckless men; and for centuries, in fact, until it was annexed to the city, Montmartre retained its medieval character. Once the site of Roman villas, the old Hill is rich in memories: Henry IV, a true French lover, seduced a nun there and caused her to be appointed Abbess of Montmartre; and Loyola, after a career of riotous living and repentance, sought the contemplative life in an abbey of Montmartre, and conceived the Society of the Jesuits. In addition to its conventual orders, the Hill supported a pastoral life, with flocks and herds, fields of grain, and windmills grinding corn. When Renoir painted the outdoor café at the Moulin de la Galette, in the 'seventies, the mill was still turning and continued to turn for ten years more. In the 'nineties, when Montmartre went Bohemian, the Galette, a symbol and a skeleton of the old days, became a notorious cabaret.

In addition to its holy and pastoral folk, the old Hill sheltered less savory inhabitants. In the eighteenth century it was the auction market for young virgins who were sold over the counter as merchandise; and its vicious taverns, many of which are extant and thriving in their carnal offerings, invited the custom of procurers, vagrant women and drunkards. Rich in memories, the Hill has seen a motley procession pass down its zigzag slopes into history: monks and priests; kings and soldiers; shepherds and husbandmen; poets, artists and assassins, and talented derelicts. Hospitable to spiritual and bestial dissipations alike, it has found room, amongst its nefarious caverns for the Sacré-Coeur, a bastard Roman pile exceeding, in pretentiousness, all modern basilicas with the possible exception of Saint John the Divine, in New York. Since the War, according to André Warnod, Montmartre, reverting to type, is once more the market for girls, not virgins, however, but fallen angels sold into the international trade. But its most lucrative industry was catering to the worst appetites of the spendthrift sons and daughters of the Prohibition Era.

When the separating walls were torn down and Montmartre was incorporated with the city, artists, as I have said, found the streets leading to the Butte an invigorating contrast to the hoodlum romance of the Latin Quarter. They were not, let it be understood at once, Bohemians. There was never a painter less Bohemian than Renoir, never a man more firmly anchored to the sterling simplicities of French life. In his canvases all that is finest in a ripe civilization has its radiant embodiment: the voluptuous woman, undraped and unashamed; the charm of unspoilt children; the sap of the grape and the flesh. And crabbed old Cézanne, awkward in all company, resentful and shrinking, tempered his spiritual rancors in the society of the intelligent men. They were hard workers, the first men of Montmartre, and at the Café Guerbois, in the Avenue de Clichy, they met to talk things over. Far from being Bohemians, they were so sober and conventional that Cézanne, who joined them only occasionally, complained that they took themselves too seriously and "dressed like a pack of lawyers". Manet dominated the group which included, besides the painters Pissarro, Degas, Puvis de Chavannes, Fantin-Latour, Forain, Monet and Signac, the composer Berlioz, and the novelists Hugo and Zola. After the Franco-Prussian War, the Guerbois was abandoned for the Nouvelle Athènes, the renown of which is described by a distinguished

18

writer, then a young and sensual Irishman who tried so hard to be a Frenchman and a painter, and failed in both.

The seeds of Bohemianism were planted in Montmartre in 1881, the year of the founding of the Chat Noir by Rudolph Salis. The expansive Salis undoubtedly had a warm regard for the arts, but he was at heart a showman, and showmanship in art leads to Bohemia. The Chat Noir was followed by the Rat Mort—a dead rat in the beer pump suggested the name—L'Âne Rouge, and other cafés of sinister titles. In its first period, the Chat Noir—the name was taken from Poe's tale, or more likely, from the little beast in Manet's picture of odious memory—was a closed circle of artists and writers, some famous, some on the make, but in a few years, it was soliciting its clientele from the fashionable world. Bernhardt acted all over the place; Catulle Mendès exhibited his empty elegance; and Verlaine unwittingly lent his incorrigible thirst to the prestige of the shop. Poor Verlaine! Everybody pitied him, yet none would have had him otherwise than he was, an inspired sot. The French are not reformers.

By the end of the next decade Montmartre was beyond redemption. The Moulin de la Galette, now a low-class dance hall for soldiers, working men, shopgirls and laundresses—the girls in waists and skirts, hatless, and all under twenty, the men in caps and tight trousers— appealed to dissolute painters on the hunt for color and the coarser forms of sexual commerce. The other Moulin, the Red Mill, was in the heyday of its glory, already the center of lesbianism, as young Will Rothenstein discovered, to his horror. Among the habitués was a descendant of one of the most ancient families of the French noblesse, Henri de Toulouse-Lautrec, of whom we shall have more to say here-after. The Chahut dancers, Jane Avril, La Goulue, and Nini Patte-en-l'Air, split themselves asunder to the applause of artists, homo-sexuals, and sedate fathers out to escape the boredom of home and family. Close by, in his own crowded cabaret, Aristide Bruant, the first of the performing stage apaches, dressed in black velvet with top-boots and a red shirt, shrieked his low songs of the underworld. One of the singers at the Moulin Rouge rose to fame overnight. She was very young, pale and slender, with the breasts of a boy and the chaste, wondering eyes of a child. Her name was Yvette Guilbert; and her songs were lewd and witty. She was a sensation. How the French love the spectacle of children executing salacious dances, or piping the double entendre!

No better proof of the decadence is needed than the jealousy which Montmartre began to arouse among the partisans of the left bank. For a while the rivalry was active and none too polite. Numerically, the Latin Quarter was incalculably superior, but the Butte had a stronger flavor and artists of unquestionable distinction. There was nothing on the left bank to compare with the Moulin Rouge, and every Spring the students of the southern Quarter trooped across the city to the Mill for their annual Quat'z' Arts orgy. The old guard fought a losing fight. The Hill was doomed to Bohemian ruin. In 1913 the last fête was held, and demi-mondaines, grisettes, women of fashion, artists, writers, musicians, and tradesmen, lamented the collapse of the "Independent Republic of Montmartre". During the War, the night life was temporarily checked, but before the armistice was signed, the Place du Tertre was overrun with British and American soldiers, and every aged Frenchman not in uniform opened a wine shop.

Today Montmartre means the Place Pigalle and the Place Blanche, Zelli's—with gigolettes expectantly guarding unopened bottles of poor and costly champagne, and Madame Zelli guarding the cash—and dives for the gratification of every form of iniquitous desire. The last place on earth, we need hardly say, for the cultivation of art. The attitude of the French towards a quarter they had commercialized and debased long before the War is summarized in the following notice taken from a newspaper:

"Two more shiploads of savages arrived at Cherbourg today.
Make ready, Montmartre."

We have reserved for the last the effect of Bohemianism on art. The relation of the true convivial spirit of Paris to its by-product, the juvenile lawlessness of the Latin Quarter, we have shown; the origin, fame, and continued fascination of the Latin Quarter, we have also shown; and we have surveyed the growth of a rival Bohemia on the historic slopes of Montmartre. It now remains to analyze the conditions which forced art into the gutter, or more graciously, which encouraged artists into a way of living least conducive to the health and vitality of the creative mind.

The nature of the romantic movement of 1830 I have examined at length in *Men of Art*. Let it suffice here to repeat that the movement headed in France by Delacroix was part of the world-wide revolt of youth against official tyranny in government and in art. The French Romantics in art and letters—the exponent of free speech embattled against conservatives fighting desperately for academic authority—drew their fire from many sources: from Scott, Byron, Constable and Bonington; from Goethe, Schiller and Beethoven, and from Goya. They were not Bohemians; they were men with a program and a generous philosophy; they were taking the last stand for art—the rights of the individual against political jobbers. But most of them, and three in particular, Byron, Goya and Delacroix, were spectacular figures whose weaknesses were of the sort which inferior minds seize upon as the criteria of artistic behavior. In the end they were triumphant, but their victory was only a moral one. They were the founders of modern art, but officially, and so far as popular suffrage was concerned, they were unmercifully beaten.

It was by no means an accident that Murger's book should have appeared at this dramatic moment. His work is a reflection of the attitude of the small-fry, or Bohemian artists, toward the bourgeoisie whom the big and great men had charged upon without quarter or compunction. For the eternal enemy of art in France is the bourgeois mind—this, in spite of the fact that most of her worthy artists are of middle class origins. In asserting the organic rights of free men, their temperament, and I may add, their genuine sensitivity, the Romantics had attacked the dullness, the porcine complacency—the whole social struc-

21

ture—of the middle classes. It is not hard to see how this gospel of emancipation was welcomed by the artists of the Latin Quarter, little men, but not totally devoid of sensitivity, and eager to uphold the position of intellectual aristocracy attained by Delacroix and the leaders. They had no market for their wares, no money, no official connections, no social co-operation, and they lived in a locality where, as Pierre MacOrlan said, writing of Montparnasse today, it was possible to dwell at ease within certain very loosely defined limitations. Their first and last care—the sum and substance of their philosophy—was to insult the conventions of the bourgeoisie. That was a sign of superiority. Lacking convictions, they affected idiosyncrasies; lacking courage, they shirked the burden of hard constructive toil for the ignominious ease of the mendicant. In short, they became parasites, or Bohemians, using art as an excuse for laziness and incompetence, as a means to pursue the grosser pleasures. And then an ironical thing occurred: the academic painters, the boys from the Beaux-Arts and the schools, succumbed to the Bohemian way of living; and in the course of time, Bohemianism permeated all forms of art and was esteemed by students —and teachers—everywhere as the most essential factor in the training of the artist. At the end of the nineteenth century, the most dissolute and reckless, the softest and most affected of the apprentices of the Quarter, were the pupils of Gérôme and Bouguereau, and that old fraud, Julian.

Hence it came about that when painting lost its social function, the artist, thrown entirely upon his own irresponsibility, retired to the world of Bohemia where he might flaunt his individual conceits to his heart's content, and sport a mode of living every detail of which was calculated to affront the bourgeois society that had cast him out. In the Latin Quarter the field was already prepared; the stage was set. The Quarter was steeped in legends of the old hallowed days when idealists lived together amicably; and the quaint and disorderly surroundings were congenial to the singularities which he fancied his profession demanded. The Bohemia of Murger was probably a gayer world than Montparnasse of the present time: there were not so many outsiders, and the game was newer. The more romantic joys and the lovely grisettes existed only in Murger's imagination, but the irresponsibility of the artist and his contempt for the working classes were faithfully recorded. Murger himself was not a thoroughgoing Bohemian. The moment his position as a writer was assured, he deserted the Quarter and his starving compatriots for the life of the conventional man of the world. "Bohemia," he said, "is the preface to the academy, the hospital, or the morgue."

One of the most persuasive champions of the world of make-believe was that arrant American, Whistler. He was the ambassador from Bohemia to the Anglo-Saxons. In his student days in Paris he was a typical Bohemian: at night he caroused and argued, during the day he loafed and argued, worked fitfully and made himself conspicuous; he kept a mistress, dressed like a fairy, and behaved, in short, as Degas once said to his face, "as if he had no talent whatever". Growing older and perceiving, after it was too late, that he had diligently avoided most of the difficulties of drawing and composition, he went to London where he won inordinate notoriety by his eccentricities and his controversial brilliancy. There was no one in London to take him down, and he caught Ruskin when the old warrior was addled and bedfast from overwork. Whistler had a piercing intelligence, make no mistake about that—as a press agent he was fifty years ahead of his time—and he had, in a certain small way, his own conception of art. But it was a Bohemian art, a thing of compilations, without guts or substance.

As a defence for his limitations Whistler erected one of the most ingenious philosophies ever put forth by a painter, and confirmed his theories by his outrageous behavior. With mutilating wit and disarming cleverness, he exalted, not the free artist, but the snob artist. He pleaded for the expatriate, denied the existence of any national art, abused the British and Americans alike, and placed the artist apart from, and above, the social codes governing ordinary mortals. His pic-

23

tures have faded into indistinguishable delicacies of tone, but his personality is still vividly alive. He set the standard among Anglo-Saxons for the Bohemian artist, the scintillant tramp, the rootless aristocrat of the world, bound by no laws, exempt from human knowledge and human decencies. His example has endured. Practically all artists feel the necessity of proclaiming their business by singularities in dress and by flouting social conformities. So solid a man as Epstein, not content to let his sculptures signalize his individuality, must wear a beret—like the American commercial hack demonstrating his Lincoln—to separate himself from Philistines and shopkeepers who have admitted from the first, with no small anxiety, that he is neither of them nor like them.

"Paris," Elie Faure publicly confessed, "is no longer the center of art, she is the center of the painting industry"—an astonishing statement from a Frenchman, astonishing because it was made in America and aimed at a rich monopoly that Americans have largely supported. Today, in these troubled times, there are 40,000 artists in Paris. Not all, of course, live in the Latin Quarter: some maintain show studios in Montmartre, and a few live in fashionable suburbs and drink at the Ritz Bar. Others, living in the Quarter, waste their time at the old academic charnel houses, or at Lhote's new academy where American girls are taught to draw in the modern manner; that is, to map out the planes of the back and buttocks of a female nude, or to rearrange a French sailor into a little mannikin. But the tone and tendency of modern international art are dictated by the leaders of the left bank, or, more specifically, by the colony in Montparnasse. It is plain that Americans do not go to Paris to see the most significant and original manifestations of contemporary art—if such were their objective, they would go to Mexico. It is equally plain that they do not go to study: they sometimes think they do, but most of them are too young to understand the psychological forces relating technique, or form, to experience and environment; and those who remain never mature. They are lured by the magic spell of Bohemia, by glittering legends of gaiety and romance; in other words, they are lured by the prospect of loose living in a special world created by Paris in the name of art and spiritual freedom, and fostered as a source of revenue.

Life in this world would be insupportable without the women. The cardinal tenet of the Bohemian creed is that men and women should participate in life on the basis of absolute equality: that sexual freedom, or promiscuity, is not only a biological necessity, but a pleasurable stimulus to good work; that only the Puritan is inhibited and the Puritan produces no art; that the artist, being, per se, a more sensitive man, needs a woman as a constant companion to share his sorrows, intensify his moments of ecstasy, whet his desires, and complete his social function; that in a community where the companionship of women is traditional and axiomatic, where all things conspire to the release of his creative energy, the artist begins his career under the most propitious circumstances—unhampered by bourgeois restraints and regulations, a free agent in body and soul. Theoretically, this is fine and sound; in practice it does not work, does not produce art.

I have no moral objections to the system of compulsory cohabitation existing among the artists of Paris; the system is thoroughly democratic and without hypocrisy; it is certainly better and more honorable than the covert habits of the shamefaced artist of New York who, if he keeps a girl, conceals her from the friends and the world in a private brothel, after the fashion of the cheating husband and his stenographer, or the banker and his chorus girl. But as it pertains to art, the effect of the system is to amuse and divert the painter, not to ennoble him; to debase his better impulses; to make him totally dependent on women, and to hold women in the cynical disesteem in which they are held by Frenchmen. For the Frenchmen, let us keep in mind, are turned loose, as boys, on the boulevards to sow their wild oats, with unlimited access to strumpets and every encouragement to live with a woman. It is not strange that they should regard women merely as accomplices in the quest for immoderate and perpetual excitement. "A man of thirty", Stendhal said, "seduces a girl of fifteen, and the girl loses her reputation". Cynical rogues write novels about her, and some charitable artist takes her to his studio.

The girls of Paris have long been famous. Villon penned a ballade to them, and down the centuries, in song and story, their charms have been exposed and magnified. So great is their prestige that men everywhere have a secret hankering for the Parisienne whom they credit with a unique talent for the more mischievous and poignant arts of love. "Whatever may happen to Paris," a French writer said recently, "the woman of Paris will retain her undisputed supremacy. In every class of society she is a hundred times more feminine than in any other city of the world." It is not my intention to dispute her charms; I only wish to point out that the fame of the French girl, as an accessory to the fine arts, is fictional and operatic. It is not beyond belief that in times past she may have been more philanthropical than the modern practitioners of love and selfless devotion. Murger's mistresses, it seems, were content to eat and to run out to Versailles for the day; but their influence on the artists of the time was none the less pernicious— always on the side of frivolity, always in the direction of laziness, cheapness and vulgarity.

The grisette, the delicious little moron, ready for any man's love and any man's bed, whom legend has honored with so prominent a rôle in the lives of artists, has lately been discredited. Indeed, I am sorry to say, French traducers have gone so far as to swear that she was evolved from the libido of sentimentalists like Pastor Sterne, or from the ink-pots of half-starved romancers paid to invest commonplace intrigues with the charm and excitement of devotional naughtiness. The traditional grisette caught the American eye as far back as 1840. "I have seen," wrote our American traveller, "multitudes of bouncing demoiselles, with nymph-like faces, caps for bonnets, and baskets in their hands, running briskly to their work in the morning, and strolling slowly homeward towards evening, with a smile for every gentleman that passes. These are the grisettes. They are very pretty and have the

26

RENOIR: *Le Moulin de la Galette*

laudable little custom of falling in love with one. A grisette in the Latin Quarter is a branch of education. If a student is ill, she nurses him and cures him; if he is destitute, she works for him; and if he dies, she dies with him." This pretty conception, I find, still animates the fantasies of American students who have never seen Paris.

In the present century, shortly after the old habitués had abandoned Montmartre, the raconteur Bayard circulated a questionnaire among the most celebrated Bohemians of Paris for the purpose of gathering historical material on the grisettes. The results were disappointing. The verdict against the grisettes was unanimous. "I have heard of such creatures," was the answer, "but on my honor, I have never seen or known one." From this we are not to conclude that the girls of Paris are incapable of true comradeship, that they have never shown a disposition to suffer, starve, or die for their men. Francis Carco, the best informed of living Bohemians and the most truthful, relates many tragic stories of the insane loyalty of women to poets and painters who were not worth saving. In the low brasseries of the Rue Lepic, with their damp walls, greasy counters and slippery floors, the girls were good sports—they always asked for the cheapest wine and drank it. Sometimes there was but a single room for the whole company, and drinking deeply of bad liquor, they piled into one bed, as many as eight of them, men and women together, to forget their miseries in a drunken stupor. He also describes the end of some of the martyrs in "low, leaky rooms by the Seine, where coughing women, holding dressing gowns tight around them, waited for sailors and sewer cleaners." Carco does not romanticize the life. Nor does he uphold and recommend it. He confesses frankly to certain vicious tastes which he satisfied at a frightful price. But the most heroic example of self-immolation was Modigliani's mistress, the Kidney Bean, whose loyalty bordered on dementia and ended in suicide. Such cases are exceptional, but if they were the rule, and every girl on the left bank a paragon of devotion, my original contention that the system of cohabitation contributes nothing to art would not be impaired.

There are all sorts of girls in the art quarters of Paris: girls from all nations; students, models, and wild Americans—very young and asserting their advanced ideas by running from one man or woman to another; and a sprinkling of demoralized expatriates who hang around artists and sometimes write about them. The French girls, as we should expect, constitute the great majority. They are no better and no worse than girls of the same station in other countries: better companions in indolence, possibly; better harlots, certainly—they have the advantages of traditional culture and training. The supply would seem to be inexhaustible. Continuous streams of girls pour into Paris from the provinces. They do not take kindly to domestic service; they can hardly be blamed for steering away from the deplorable slavery of the factories; they readily lend themselves to harlotry—they like it. Since every artist believes that he must keep an animal even though he live in dirt like the medieval student and his trull, any girl who is personable and a fair animal, is reasonably sure of a roost.

These girls, with their irregular faces and irregular lives, "have never", the French tell us, "the stamp of the proletariat—they are always aristocrats." We grant it. They sedulously avoid work; and their keepers, the intellectual aristocrats, follow their example, persuaded that the world owes the artist a living. It is much more comfortable to sit in a café with one's girl and to talk about art, than to hold one's self to the grinding labor without which no art ever came into being. The girls know this, and craftily they play upon the romantic weaknesses of the artist, relying upon his feeble will to hold him to a way of living, and a profession, that he can neither relinquish nor conquer. The French girls have no greater love for art than other prostitutes, but they give a more convincing imitation of it. Their affectionate prattle is a sham, an incantation; their high spirits a pose, a matter of business. Their main purpose is to lead a lazy, animal existence among more generous and indulgent and playful clients than they could hope to snare, with their nondescript charms, in other quarters of Paris. There are exceptions, of course. Some have an eye

to respectability—to a safe marriage and two legitimate children—
and occasionally are successful in their ambitions. A few, like the insuppressible Kiki, develop unusual talents and become the pets of
celebrities. But the rank and file follow the way of all bartered flesh.

The effect of the Parisian system, in summary is this:

Woman is the curse of the artist. She no longer inspires, she domi-
nates him. The artist, being weak, impressionable, and incapable of
self-discipline, in other words, Bohemian, inevitably acquires the tone
and characteristics of the stronger personality, the prostitute.

The artist is losing his masculinity. The tendency of the Parisian
system is to disestablish sexual characteristics, to merge the two sexes
in an androgynous third containing all that is offensive in both. If you
doubt the growing effeminacy of the artist, you have only to examine
the performances of the modern École de Paris. The school is fundamentally sexless, from Picasso to Laurencin and Dufy. In exteriors, it
often appears harsh and brutal, but the harshness is factitious—the
acid face and dominating toughness of the professional woman. In
essence, it is an emasculated art, an art of fashions, styles, and ambiguous patterns.

That the romantic spirit of youth should have its fling is only
natural; that artists, struggling in a world which neither cares for their
works nor condones their follies, should band together to discuss their
aims and difficulties is healthy and sensible; that artists are entitled to
their fun and to a measure of eccentricity is taken for granted. But the
first has dwindled into a spirit of incurable childishness and sentimentality; the second into an obsessional horror of loneliness and sedentary
application, and into everlasting café chatter; the last into hideous
license and rabid freakishness. The War did not shake the Bohemian
nonsense out of the artists; it served to make them beggars of life more
intent than ever before on the prosecution of their whims. And it
brought to the art colonies an influx of outsiders, nominally artists
and writers, actually the dregs and misfits of disorganized America,
whose presence has aggravated the Bohemian pestilence. We know

them well. Not their own art but the art of Hemingway has made them famous. The ancient mother of the tribe has called them "a lost generation." They have also been called "the children of lost illusions." They are lost beyond reclamation; they will never be anything but children; but they have not lost their illusions. Their sustaining belief is that art is self-generating; that it is produced by art; that it lives and flourishes and flowers in an environment destructive to the sensibilities of the creator. Hemingway is the only one of them, if he may be said to belong to them, who possesses the true spirit of youth. He is filled with health, daring vitality, and the joy of living—but he is less sentimental than Robinson Crusoe. The best of Villon is in him, and more: he is glad to be alive.

They are all alike, these Bohemians; they all gang together in a common effort to get rid of emptiness and boredom, to escape the hopeless uniformity and dullness of their transplanted lives. Appendages to the French cultural tradition, wheedling votaries of French art, they strive to mix art with gayety and convivial rapture. Their so-called gayety is a misnomer, a forced and pitiable levity, the mask of sadness and defeat. Once they contract la vérole Montparnasse—the pox of the Quarter—they are proof against regeneration. Their nerves must be violently shaken, their senses unduly agitated. They crave more spectacular excitements; they become jaded and perverse, and famishing for new stimulants, advance into abnormal lecheries. Eventually they lose all sense of values; and their lives and their art, if distinguished by any one thing, are distinguished by the total absence of good sense. They are now ready for Gertrude Stein, Sur-Realism, and the infinite subdivisions of abstract art. What used to be sensational, or shocking in their art is now only silly; what used to be the innocent fondling of French styles is naïve no longer—it is babyish. Their art having no voice, they are obliged to speak for it over the café tables and in the printed word. Their writings are chuckling tributes to the higher freedom, or meaningless descriptions of their states of mind, never intelligible comments on objective facts. They found magazines in which their insecurity is attested by the continual insulting of America—the cosmopolitan touch—and their originality by incoherent nastiness, hymns to homosexuality, and pleas for miscegenation. There is no evidence that the experiences of any of them are worth mentioning. An immense and vicious sentimentality lies at the bottom of their lives. They profess to be above normal experiences; they are not concerned with the joys and sorrows of humanity. Instead, they exploit, in paint, stolen patterns and futile hypotheses; and in print, their private grievances, envies, grudges and debaucheries. They are avid of French approval, treasuring the venal praise of critics who have never held a brush. In this they are typically French. For all the French, Daumier, excepted, have coveted official decorations. Even Verlaine sought election to the Academy; and foolish Paul de Kock, the favorite of the masses, at seventy-four, weeping over his disappointment, wrote twenty pages to prove that he was not hurt because he had been turned down for the Legion of Honor.

I do not advocate a return to respectability, nor a truce with the bourgeoisie. France is controlled by the bourgeoisie, and the bulk of her art—all that is cheap, and prurient and trivial—is the reflection of the tastes of the petty merchant. Every French artist of merit has been the enemy of the bourgeoisie, and Daumier, forswearing his youthful illusions of popular, or mercantile, sovereignty, smote them, hip and thigh, with his satire. Nor do I advocate the high-toned life of the fashionable faubourgs, a form of social smartness playing into the hands of the dealers and politicians. My point is that the artist, having affirmed his individuality and published his contempt for grubbing merchants, should have the courage of his convictions. If he is truly an individual, as Rembrandt was, and Hogarth, Daumier, Degas, Manet, Cézanne and many others, he should stand alone, capable of social adjustments which would enable him to have his say without sacrificing a single belief. Destitute of convictions and will, he yields to the seductive conventions of Bohemia where individuality is usurped by freakishness, and self-discipline unknown. Misery in art also loves company.

Bohemia has had artists, numbers of them, but they are small and unimportant. The lyric cry of Verlaine is clear and genuine, but most appealing to self-conscious sinners. Verlaine, a truly religious man, was always repenting, always making fresh starts in life, longing for some sylvan, visionary nook in which he might dream of nymphs and sing the virelays of old France. But he was utterly wanting in force of will, and Bohemia was the swiftest road to destruction. The greatest, by far, is Toulouse-Lautrec whom the misfortune of physical deformity converted to a sadistic philosophy. This sinister figure believed in the innate depravity of the human race, a bitter faith in any man, and only possible to the artist whose life is spent in certain quarters of Bohemia. Lautrec's mature life and art were confined to the dens and cabarets of Montmartre, and the depravity of that small, convulsive world which he loved with satanic conviction, he transferred to all mankind. There is no compassion in his art, no posing, no moral sop. It excludes the noble in man, and it excludes the tragic. It deals only with the decayed.

Leaving aside the main body of pretenders and cosmopolitan roisterers, what shall we say of the serious students who are neither dissolute nor lazy, who work day after day, generally under the greatest hardships, faithfully concocting ineffectual studies in the belief that they are making art, or at least learning how art should be made? We shall say that they too are lost, they too are tarred by the Bohemian brush. However earnest and talented they may be, soon or late, they lose their identity. The odds against them are too heavy. They all fall in line, adopt the culture of the Quarter, get themselves in that morbid state of mind which holds them forever to the most useless expenditure of time and talent that has ever been devised—the attempt to make art out of other art. They are all doomed. With the best of intentions, with appalling fixity of purpose, they resign themselves to the life-long occupation of manufacturing pictures that have no reason for

32

existence, no connection with realities and no connection with any-thing save the sources from which they are compounded. The left bank is cluttered with the living tragedies of forlorn souls who can neither make art nor leave it.

The most deadly curse of Bohemia is that it transforms the artist into the stereotype. Instead of being a stage in the development of the artist, it is an end in itself, a career, an isolated world in which men and women are prisoners of art, not conquerors. Living in a vitiating atmosphere of art, breathing and talking art from morning till night to the exclusion of healthy experiences, looking at French art for years, the Bohemian cannot look realities in the face, cannot undergo experi-ences arresting enough to jolt him out of his routine habits into original expression. His habits, in truth, are more conventional than those of the despised bourgeoisie. For the little merchant, trafficking in hard facts, is occasionally confronted with new situations which compel him to revise his routine methods, or perish; whereas the artist, trafficking in theories and abstractions, encounters no situations in real life which make the slightest impression on his mental processes. He will starve rather than alter his old habits. His life is formed entirely on precedent, not guided by experience. His habits of thought become hardened beyond repair, his approach to art a conventional procedure. In body and mind he behaves exactly like his fellows. In Paris he does the expected thing: paints like this man or that, picks up a set of painting tools, becomes a painting machine, nowadays, a Modernist machine. He spends the rest of his life exhibiting borrowed tools under the delusion that he is using his technical implements for an expressive purpose. There are perceptible variations in the painting habits of the Bohemians, but they are largely mechanical. Schools are founded on these variations—vanity, as well as youth, must be served. Schools are also founded on incompetence. It is told that a young student, having difficulty in learning to paint like someone else, asked this of Picasso. "I do not seem to know how to draw. Should I go to school?"

"No," answered the master, "you should not go to school; the thing for you to do is to found a school." The Spaniard had tried both.

It is this sort of life that transmits modern art to the rest of the world. Every new idea, to gain the allegiance of artists, collectors, critics and dealers, must be ground through the Bohemian mills of Paris. Even Cézanne who loathed Bohemia, whose art is a mighty protest against Bohemia, has been ground into harmless patterns, sterilized and softened for universal consumption by the mills of Paris. It is this sort of life that captures American youth and emasculates American art.

Paris is youth, Bohemia the artificial prolongation of youth. There is nothing on earth more pathetic than the behavior of artists who persist in being young, unless it is the bleat of expatriates too proud to return home.

It has been said by one of them that the artists of Paris are willing to sacrifice their lives for spiritual freedom, to die for their ideals. It is remarkable that no signs of this mysterious freedom have appeared in their art! It is hard indeed to be a martyr to one's own ideals, but to be a martyr to second-hand ideals, to sacrifice one's life to borrowed habits, is the crowning humiliation imposed by Bohemia on the prisoners of art.

"Bohemia," Murger said, "exists and is possible only in Paris."

2

THE NEW CENTURY

AT THE opening of the new century, we find France vehemently engaged in remodeling her insular soul. The old century had not died peacefully. It had died in agony, in a commotion of antipathies. Since 1871, the country had been controlled by the bourgeoisie—the small, stingy people with pockets full of money. Snug in their security; hoarding and hiding capital; ignorant of the outside world; they took for granted their superiority. They acknowledged their pre-eminence, in unguarded intervals of magnanimity, not to annoy less civilized competitors—that were an unworthy condescension—but as a spur to their acquisitive talents; to keep the national machine functioning smoothly. Their superiority extended in all directions: in commerce, in ships and soldiers, in accumulated culture, and, of course, in art, though their art had descended to the lowest form of driveling mediocrity. Paris was the capital of the world; La Patrie the most glorious of modern nations.

But in one year, the very last of the century, a succession of extraordinary events occurred. The little people were shaken with terrors. Their security was disrupted; "the Republic imperiled." They were not, I need hardly say, obliterated, for they are the bone and muscle of France; but their materialistic ideals, their provincial legacy of isolation and selfish toil, were unexpectedly assailed. They beheld, all too suddenly, the dawn of a new age, an age heralded by thunder and trouble. And they were to see cruelties and uprisings, the encroachment of foreigners, the miracles of industrial genius brought to their doors by the great Exhibition; they were to sacrifice their last drop of

blood in universal war, before they were finally to adjust themselves
to the new age, and to restore France to her customary position at the
head of the bourgeois nations of the world. In the year 1899, there
were strikes everywhere and troops quelling militant workers; the
socialist masses were organizing for action, the Nationalists plotting
and screaming, the anarchists behaving badly; there were the scandals
of the curés, the ursine shadow of the Russians, the return of Major
Marchand to Paris, and the war in the Transvaal; there was the death
of Felix Faure and the election of President Loubet—and "the smash-
ing of the President's top hat, under a rain of eggs, at the Auteuil
races"; and most turbulent of all, the revision of the Dreyfus case. We
must admit that the little people who wanted only peace and the continuation of the status quo, had cause for their terrors.

The year ended with the Right Wing, the conservatives, in power
since 1875, "suddenly awakening to find itself disarmed and at the
mercy of the Left, the radicals." The rising new party, so Paul Morand,
who was born into it, informs us, "was a bourgeoisie which, though
radical in its views, was comfortably installed in the midst of extraordinary contradictions: anti-militarist and yet jingo; believing in the
equality of races, yet coveting colonies; sympathizing with Dreyfus, yet
shutting its doors against Jews more firmly even than the Faubourg
St. Germain; its men, atheists; its women, devout Catholics; a reserve
of upright functionaries, not rich, yet not poor; it was a bourgeoisie
of the Left Center, a race of clear-headed counselors who hated the
Nationalists and the party of the Right, were faithful to the memory
of Gambetta, travelled as little as possible, played no games and though
they read little, knew their classics."

The little people, though frantically unsettled, were not dispos-
sessed. Ostensibly France was governed by politicians and parvenu
agitators: they made the noise and the gestures—the declamatory outbursts and the theatrical display. The actual work, the business of
administration, remained in the hands of the bourgeoisie. Since the
invention, by Bonaparte, of the permanent civil service, France had

gradually constructed the most elaborate and efficient governmental machine in the history of western polity. Wheels within wheels; levers, cogs, and alarms; a clocklike mechanism comparable only to the bureaucracy of old China. "The machine," as a writer of 1900 expressed it, "like the corset, is indispensable to the figure of France." Ministries might be wrecked; the cobblestones of Paris piled up in barricades to demonstrate minute animosities; but so long as the machine remained in gear, the safety of the people was not jeopardized. You will remember that Murger's Bohemian poet ordered the concierge to wake him by calling through the keyhole "the day of the week, the date of the month, and the government under which we live." The wrecking of ministries had its humorous side. Whatever happened at Paris or Versailles, the prefects in the provinces were always at their posts. Governments might change each day, but the machine went on forever. Thousands of provincial mayors, each a little president! The mayor made the commune; the commune the canton; the canton the arrondissement which, in turn, made the department. Wheels within wheels! The revolutions were schemes to control the machine, not to change the course, nor to tamper with the mainspring. The bourgeoisie constituted the mainspring. The fundamental labors were in their jurisdiction: they collected taxes, educated the masses, looked after the health and death of all. First the citizens—the hoarders of money; next the soldiers, the defenders of the hoarders of money; then the cocottes, the safeguards of the homes of the hoarders; and last, the artists—useless, except when trained by the academy into purveyors of glory. Such was the hierarchy of bourgeois France.

To write of the social and economic functions of the machine would be to condense French literature from Balzac to Zola, from Maupassant to Gide and Morand, an impossible task. Balzac, with his prophetic mind, got at the root of the matter when he made the hero of the Comedy the five-franc piece. He has been severely censured for his mundane discovery, but the present stability of France bears out his deduction; and his hero was certainly the lord and master of the

37

Versailles Treaty. In Balzac, in Rolland's description of Paris in *Jean-Christophe*, in a dozen other French writers of the first rank, we have the desperate and concentrated assertiveness of the parvenu spirit; not the brutal, speculative mania of the Yankee plunger, but the possessive instinct carried to the extremes of esurience where every action is the result of design, where not a muscle is moved without some end in view; the laying up of franc upon franc for security, advancement and purchasable pleasures. We have it in the sock-stuffing provincials, the descendants of old Grandet; in the multitude of Parisian clerks returning to their shabby barracks at night, racked with schemes for getting money and renown; in lawyers and politicians climbing at the expense of women, or sitting in cafés hatching conspiracies for profit; in the political ambitions of writers and the underhand campaigns of artists for official ribbons and honors. And we have it in the patient, laborious housewife and the fat madame of the shops with their national passion for order, method and thrift. To insure the tranquillity of the republic the hoppers of the machine must be filled with francs.

Politics was a national game in which every one participated. "It was a pure art," Morand assures us, "indigenous to the soil. It permeated everything, was everywhere, colored all and gave to the Paris of 1900, a slight air of comic opera, smacking of a San Domingo Revolution, while the sittings in the Palais Bourbon recalled a parliament in the Antilles." Politics was a cultural fetish. It had severed relations with the business of governing; it was an independent art. Like culture, which had lost connection with objects of art and had become an art in itself, it was a popular instrument for personal and national aggrandizement. It might assume any form of radicalism and intemperance with no perceptible difference to the workings of the machine. It was the medium of exchange for hatreds. "If the Théâtre Francais burnt down, it was because the Director was a notorious partisan of Dreyfus; if the fire was not put out, it was the fault of the Municipal Council who had organized a strike among the firemen. If a bull-fight was authorized, the Dreyfus party sympathized with the bull, while the anti-Dreyfusites sang a hymn glorifying bloodshed."

Each faction had its paid scribes and orators, and the press was drunk with invective and denunciation. In their extravagant use of insult the journalists were not surpassed by the old school of Tennessee editors described by Mark Twain. The Right went for the Jews; the Left defended Dreyfus but opposed the Army and the Church, denouncing one as "the gold-laced rabble," the other as "the clerical vermin"; Jean Lorrain ridiculed "the anarchist riff-raff, the dregs of the prisons, the scum of the reformatories, their faces ghastly and greenish, their lips dry and pinched like those of submissive old maids, their cheeks as yellow as those of sick soldiers or greasy dishwashers." It was all vanity and invective. None of the parties bothered to develop a social policy, and as a consequence, the Socialists increased enormously, inciting the workmen to rebellion, and producing, in Jaurès, the greatest orator of the day. On one point alone were the French in harmony: their hatred of England. They insulted the senile Tory queen in dreadful caricatures; "England's business," they said, "is the blood of other peoples"; they went wild over the reverses in the Transvaal, and welcomed Kruger with a brilliant—and slightly fatuous—hymn by Rostand. Only the French tastes and ingratiating Bohemian habits of the Prince of Wales averted serious complications.

The anti-Semitic feeling raged like a medieval plague. The cause of this malignant hatred of the Jews has not been satisfactorily explained. French doctors fighting the evil attribute the madness of 1900 to wounded pride—the reaction of France from external humiliations. "Mutilated and insulted by Germany; a butt for Crispi's hostility beyond the Alps; robbed and despised by her ally Russia and slapped in the face by the English at Fashoda; she was, therefore, obliged to work off her irritation on something within reach, on whatever most resembled the foreigner, on that oldest of all foreigners, the Jew." The root of the evil, I think, is to be found in the aggressive xenophobia which has always characterized France. Her prestige depends upon the

39

inviolability of her little ideals. She welcomes foreigners, but the basis of her hospitality is economic. You are expected to pay your money, enjoy yourself—and get out. You may remain on only one condition: that you continue to pay and extract nothing except a faith in French superiority. Hemingway, a partisan of France, puts it in this way: "Everything is on such a clear financial basis in France. No one makes things complicated by becoming your friend for any obscure reason. If you want people to like you, you have only to spend a little money."

The Jew remained, but committed the unpardonable crime of becoming a citizen, a thoroughly assimilated, exemplary citizen. He did not pay. On the contrary, accepting the tripartite guarantee of the French republic at its face value, he opened shops and banks, and made money. More than a citizen, he was the best of patriots. He even became an artist—the last insult to French vanity. He wrote profitable plays; he was part-owner of Proust and Bernhardt; he became, later on, the wealthiest and most influential painter of the modern École de Paris.

The revision of the Dreyfus case hurried the phobia into a crisis. France was divided into two camps; the enlightened Left, reinforced by literary notables such as Zola and Anatole France, demanded justice; the Nationalists, supported by gilded bigots like Barrès and Gyp, clamored for the blood of an innocent officer. "The Semitic race," Barrès wrote, "may be recognized almost uniquely by its negative qualities; it has neither mythology nor epic, neither science nor fiction, neither philosophy nor plastic arts." He calmly considered extermination. When Gyp was asked her profession by the Court of Appeals, she answered "Anti-Semite." In his Montmartre studio, Degas, intolerant of outsiders, piled imprecations upon the Jews as he scolded his unwashed models. They were worse than Americans. Forain devoted his lacerating talent to illustrations for a popular anti-Jewish song called "The March of the Yids," and to dastardly caricature in which he pictured the Republic as "a fat Jewish Baron, wearing a Phrygian bonnet or a Dreyfus cap, who was responsible for the failure of banks, for schools without God, and a subsidized Parliament."

With the acquittal of Dreyfus, Jew-baiting, on a grand scale, went out of fashion. But the anti-Semitic fever breaks out from time to time in politics, society, and in letters. In art circles there is a strong under-current of hostility against the Jews. When Cubism was successfully floated by Apollinaire, Salmon and Max Jacob, the more conservative Frenchmen, fluttering on the brink of spiritual bankruptcy and pro-tecting the old boudoir tradition of nudes and daring Impressionist landscapes for gullible Americans, denounced the whole Modernist movement as a premeditated outrage, the invention of shifty Israelites seeking pecuniary rewards. When they were convinced of Picasso's Jewish blood, their suspicions hardened into confirmed and eternal enmity. Similar charges have come within my own experience. Several years ago, I happened, in print, to notice favorably a modern French painter of considerable prominence. To my surprise, he wrote me a letter; no, not a letter, an epistolary brochure, a grand document. These Frenchmen are masters of casuistry.

He began with a note of appreciation, delicately phrased, graciously tendered, but with the unmistakable insinuation that I was an excel-lent critic because I had recognized his ability. Having wrenched that courtesy out of his ego, he proceeded to excoriate the Jews. The exco-riation consumed eleven pages. The Semitic element had ruined French painting, destroyed the great tradition, besmirched art with vulgarity. That the Jews should try to paint was another proof of tribal insolence. It was impossible for them to create anything; they had no imagination and no culture. They were all bad, but the Central-Europeans were beneath contempt. He insulted Modigliani, Pascin, Kisling, Soutine, Epstein, and twenty puny Cubists not worth mentioning. Picasso was a Jew—he forgot his own debt to the Spaniard—and therefore not an artist. Picasso was backed by Jews: the dealers and the critics were Jews. He made a pogrom of Modernism. The Jews had too much of medioc-rity—they were worse than Americans. Was I an American? He could not bring himself to believe it. I had too much of style to be an American, too much of the esthetic dignity of the Frenchman. It was my turn to feel insulted. I answered his blasphemies and he wrote to me no more.

The ferocious bickerings and blown-up animosities were buried in the Universal Exhibition. The French are easily distracted. They will laugh and clap for hours at the plight of a station guard whose cap has fallen on the rails. The discovery of a new toy like Cubism will amuse their artists for a quarter of a century. A group of oriental belly dancers at the Exhibition precipitated their deep esthetic emotions, and turned the impending catastrophe into an international side-show. In April, 1900, *La Vie Parisienne,* the organ of popular French taste, appeared with a picture of Paris, the mother, instructing her daughter, the Exhibition, in matters of etiquette. The title line read: "Monsieur Emile is to inaugurate you, my dear. You must behave prettily." Monsieur Emile did the honors with traditional solemnity, attended by the Ministers of State, Monsieur Bouguereau, deputy of the Beaux Arts, and Academicians plodding with difficulty to the measures of Massenet's March, their toy swords dangling against arthritic legs and green palm leaves embroidered on their coats. The President was not insulted. The approbation was general, but in the gleeful hubbub one heard the croakings of sceptics. The custodians of culture feared the contamination of foreigners. They called the Exhibition, "a cardboard cosmopolis." Boni de Castellane remarked, "The impression it makes on me is that of a great sore on our poor Paris, which is attracting the nasty flies from all the corners of the earth." The little people grumbled, "They've been too ambitious; it will be a failure; our wines don't sell; foreigners won't come because of the Boer War." And Anatole France's heroine, in *l'Histoire Contemporaine,* speaking in what Morand charitably calls very queer English, said, "I think that the Exhibition will be a silly humbug and a crash." But their apprehensions vanished when they beheld the plastic art of the belly dancers.

What did the French, a nation of stay-at-homes, see at the Exhibi-

CEZANNE: *Still Life with Primroses*

tion? They saw the great blue arc of the Seine flanked with gorgeous palaces in which the wonders of the outside world were presented. Exotic delights! For the French, untraveled as they choose to be, are not incurious, and have always thirsted after exotic stimulants. They saw the cages of the Eiffel Tower ascending to the clouds, and in the Place de la Concorde, the monumental gateway. This entrance, I am grieved to say, was France's conception of the beautiful in art. It has gone down in history as the symbol, the monumental proclamation, of French taste. I am familiar with the horrors erected in America in the name of art—exposition architecture; war memorials; the sculptures in Washington; the Flatiron Building; the Greek garage of the Phila-delphia museum; the ramshackle Modernism pitched on the Lake front by the architectural bandits of Chicago; the old residence of Senator Clark on Fifth Avenue; the Foshay Tower in Minneapolis; Grauman's Hollywood theatre; the domed houses of Atlantic Beach, New York; and the façades of Coney Island—but such blemishes are masterpieces of classical sobriety, if we think of them in connection with the French arch with its polychrome statues and minarets, and the idiot siren, the personification of the City of Paris, at the top.

They saw the Rue des Nations, the meeting place of the world: the Palace of Electricity and the marvels of science and invention—the phonograph, the automobile, and a flickering instrument named the cinematograph; they saw German laboratories and the beginnings of German industrialism; the Great Wheel; the moving sidewalk; Swiss villages and Senegalese huts. In the Rue de Paris, in the Cours-la-Reine, they reveled in the exotic; they watched the masked actors from China, and the jugglers from Japan; they examined the handicraft of Arabs and Africans; and in the Trocadero they saw strange fetishes in wood, the carvings which, a few years hence, were to reform their Bohemian artists into negromaniacs and worshippers of the by-prod-ucts of savages. In the Palace of the Dance they were fascinated by the sinuous rhythms of dark females—Javanese, gitanas, with amber skin and bluish hair, Hindu bayaderes and contortionists from Egypt. They

43

saw an elderly and erotic bookworm, known to letters as Anatole France, smacking his lips over a performance by the illustrious courtesan, Cleo de Mérode, who, in an attempt to rival the Javanese, "was dancing with golden serpents around her wrist and golden bands in her hair." They entered the Cabaret Artistique where they stared at long-haired intellectuals from the Boul' Mich' and minstrels who came down from Montmartre to recite their verses. At every turn they bumped into Germans; they saw huge Grand Dukes, forerunners of the Russian menace; the King of the Belgians, the King of Sweden, the King of Ethiopia and the Prince-Royal of Greece; they saw Guitry, Bernhardt and Rostand: Henry Irving, Ellen Terry and Lord Alfred Douglas. Oscar Wilde, diseased and in rags, languished in a cheap hotel in the Latin Quarter.

The Americans had not yet discovered Paris and made no impression on the French. Their pavilion, built in the style of the Capitol at Washington, attracted only Yankee visitors. The French were ignorant of America: if they thought of her at all, it was as a nation of inglorious bullies who had thrashed the poor Spaniards in a trumped-up war. Culturally she was lower than the Igorrotes of her new colony in the Pacific. All that she had done to enrich France was to send over poor art students, the cocktail, and false teeth. In their excitement, the French forgot that the Idol of Paris, Loie Fuller, was an Illinois farm girl. They prized her as their own special creation, so perfectly did she express their conception of the beautiful. She was the first of the sensational American dancers to win the heart of Paris. After her came Isadora Duncan, jazz, and Josephine Baker. Loie Fuller was taken seriously by the French highbrows. She was regarded as esthetic, and so she was—in the sense that the monumental gateway was esthetic. She introduced into tripping modern art the spectacular effects obtained by projecting incandescent light through colored slides. She was the "Incarnation of Light," the "Electric Fay," the "Goddess of Electricity." Her Fire Dance at the Exhibition inspired this from Jean Lorrain: "Outlined in ardent flame, Loie Fuller is not consumed. She filters and reflects light. She is the flame itself. Her robe is agitated and undulates round her like the smoke of a volcanic fire." The erotic bookworm wrote, "She evokes the lost movements of Greek music, voluptuous and mystic, interpreting the phenomena of nature and the metamorphoses of being."

The Exhibition did more than reduce the tension of a fidgety nation. It brought the little people face to face with a new age. It acquainted them with the terrifying march of science, with the turmoil and mixing and expansion of the outside world. To survive they must adjust their insularity, their medieval machine, to the trend of industrialism. That they have done so, without collapse or surrendering their identity, is a tribute to their courage and tenacity. The Exhibition did not diminish their hatred of foreigners—it taught them to control that hatred. It was a financial success. Millions of foreigners came to their doors, paid their way, and departed with the conviction that France, in the fine arts and the arts of pleasure, was without a peer. They would return. Happy thought! A new industry was born, a new article of commerce, not merchandise, but actual people! For ages Paris had attracted students and specialists, but they were poor souls: now she had captured travelers with money in their pockets. Let them come! Let everybody come! She would entertain them, but on a clear financial basis. And they would not regret the travelers' cheques which she would redeem in gold. Another staple was added to the French system—the dealing in people.

Apart from the Exhibition, a co-operative affair in which France was the stage manager, how did the most civilized nation of 1900 repay the prying foreigner? In her most distinguished commodity, you will say, her taste. Let us examine that taste; first, as it relates to styles for women. It is easily remembered, for it was exported to America in wholesale lots and copied by dressmakers in every part of the country. Visualize the styles of the mail-order catalogues of the year 1905, and you have a literal picture of the smart Parisienne of 1900. Nothing so intrinsically hideous was ever devised to cover and adorn the body of

45

woman. Enormous flat hats pinned to mountains of dead hair; long skin-tight sleeves or mutton-legs slashed and embroidered; the neck choked in high fantastic collars; every square inch of bust concealed by straps, fichus and rosettes; a low, constricted waist line set at an angle of forty-five degrees; trailing, bell-shaped skirts with lace gores, flounces, frills, and knotted ribbons. Underneath were creamy lace petticoats, cambric drawers cut very full and elaborately ruffled, be-jewelled garters, cotton stockings and the straight-front corset. The body was so villainously laced, artists have confided to me, that before a model could be appraised, it was necessary to undress and untie her, and to wait for the liberated form to resume its natural proportions.

The French monopoly on women's wear dates from the middle of the nineteenth century when Worth, an English draper, went to Paris and became a famous dress designer. Originally, Worth's designs were approved by the court and the grandes dames and displayed at the opera, the salon, and the races. Competition soon changed that policy. Today designs are arbitrarily cooked-up, displayed by paid models, and sold on the ground to representatives from foreign shops. The result is the abolition of class distinctions in styles, with the American shopgirl, as a rule, better dressed than the Parisian lady. In the first years of the present century, French creative genius rose to its highest esthetic level. I shall leave to a French writer the description of this fascinating achievement, for none but the French can approach the subject with appropriate ecstasy. "It remained for France," writes Uzanne, "to create the last mythological expression of woman—filmy, beautiful underclothing. Centuries were required to develop the deli-cate tastes of these coverings of modesty." In other words, the destiny of France was to manufacture lingerie. I am reminded of Stendhal's observation: "Try as they may, the French will never get beyond the pretty." I have it on French authority that Madame Récamier and the haughty princesses who wore the Empire gowns designed by that pseudo-classical monomaniac, Louis David, "knew not the luxury of underwear." Nor were the fair duchesses of Balzac more fortunately appareled. They wore smocks of coarse and unclean linen, and no drawers. The effect of the last mythological expression of woman on French culture and commerce—and on American morals—is a study for the social historian. It is characteristic of the French that they advertise their filmy creations in seductive terms, such as "chemise d'amour." The best the Americans can do is a stupid trade coinage signifying utility.

The well-dressed gentleman of 1900 was stilted and ridiculous. He wore his hair—when he had any—long in the back and parted in the back; he affected high, stiff collars and Ascot ties; and his street clothes looked for all the world like the styles I used to see in the charts of country town tailors in the Middle West. But the Frenchman on the boulevards carried himself with the pompous elegance of the dummies in the charts, whereas the American, in clothes of identical cut, was altogether different. He was never the imposing gentleman of the chart—somehow or other he was touched by local seediness. Dress clothes, made under English direction, were more personable. There were French dandies who employed English tailors exclusively, and others who were arrayed like negro minstrels. When Count Boni de Castellane arrived in New York, "the reporters were stupefied by his wardrobe—his brown sack-overcoats lined with green silk, his trousers without a crease, but so wide that they showed only the tip of a small foot." The laboring classes, on duty, dressed becomingly, as they are inclined to do everywhere. The members of the latest economic order, the chauffeurs, resembled explorer Peary in his Arctic uniform.

In 1900, the French had not begun to bathe. There are records to prove that in early times, when France was imitating the Italians, once the best tubbed people of Europe according to Burckhardt, bathing was a sumptuous amusement of the Court. Primaticcio designed and decorated the bathroom of Francis I, and was in charge of the adjoining boudoir in which the King, after his dip, contemplated his finest pictures—masterpieces by Leonardo, Raphael, Michael Angelo, and Titian. "Primaticcio also fitted up and decorated a fantastic grotto in

47

the gardens where," Wilenski writes, "the ladies of the court were wont to bathe and where by an ingenious arrangement of mirrors the King could observe them."

But that was long ago, and bathing, an aristocratic sport at best, was superseded by the use of cosmetics. The uncleanliness of Lenclos, Maintenon, and Pompadour is not a subject for pleasant speculation. If the famous courtesans were anointed with oils and perfumes, what of the masses who could not afford the luxury of fumigation? Returning to modern times, we have the testimony of Gertrude Atherton that bathing among the French noblesse of 1900 was an infrequent and rudimentary practice. When I first went to Paris there was not a bathtub in the Latin Quarter. The best hotels, catering to eccentric Americans, boasted of "a bath for every floor." The last thing the Frenchmen would undertake was a bath. It is true that girls of polite breeding were taught, at an early age, the value of certain sanitary rites, but complete bathing was confined to demi-mondaines and women who were likely to be investigated. And most of them resorted to perfumes and disguises. If America has to thank France for styles and beautiful coverings of modesty, she has reciprocated by bringing to the French the love of cleanliness. The American girl has practically cured the Parisienne of aquaphobia. But not the provincial. I heard a malodorous peasant girl of Cassis exclaim that "she was not like those Paris girls— she never washed herself." From the Americans the French girl has learned not only to bathe but to walk and to love sports. To the Americans she owes her independence—the gradual dissolution of the fool's paradise in which she used to be reared—and the tendency to think of something besides sex.

The prying foreigner must have been dazed by the architecture of Paris. Collectively, in a setting of bridges, boulevards, plazas and fountains, with the gayety and excitement of the Exhibition, Paris was splendid and effective. The architecture seemed to be very artistic. Examined closely, it was ruinously inartistic; it was banal, conglomerate, profuse; in official structures, overdressed and self-conscious—the public expression of a proud people without reticence in their classical derivations. The old quarters of the city, transfigured by decay and musty sentiment, were picturesque to outsiders not constrained to inhabit them. The pretentious buildings—the works of art—aiming at the glories of antiquity, announced a genuinely classical spirit garbled by a genius for trumpery decoration. There was the Pantheon, a parody of St. Peter's; and the Bourse, a Greco-Roman temple; there were little rococo theatres, and innumerable monuments and fountains dripping with nymphs and goddesses. The taste of 1900 is illustrated by the permanent eyesores erected to house the collections of bourgeois art— the Grand and Petit Palais designed by inmates of the Beaux Arts. Forty-five weak-minded Academicians, working like drunken couturières, were paid by the State to embellish the surfaces of these buildings. They did so, defacing domes and cornices, and every square yard of wall space, with the kind of sculptures and jigsaw ornament that Americans, trained in the Beaux Arts, have smeared on our public buildings and, with less intelligence, on our skyscrapers.

If the scrupulously accredited American entered the bleak mansions of the elite, he retreated as soon as possible to the buzzing warmth of the café. He found himself in one of those dreary Versailles interiors hung with tapestries and salon pictures, lighted by crystal chandeliers, and furnished in the finest period style with spindling tables and bow-legged chairs. There was no comfort anywhere, except in the bedrooms. The servants were huddled together on the top floor under the eaves, to the great detriment of their morals. In the houses of refined Parisians —those who went in for l'art nouveau—the American was thoroughly at home. He saw, if not the same objects, the same travesties of nature, the straining after deformities and senseless patterns. He looked twice at the pewter bowls and vases. He was not aware that pewter was fashionable: when he returned home he would hunt out those dull Colonial pieces he had relegated to the attic. Instead of cut-glass and hand-painted china, he saw the stamped wares of the Sèvres factories— the finest porcelain twisted into absurd figurines, plaques, and fruit

49

dishes encrusted with scarved dancers. He saw sagging furniture carved to death, or painted with dying swans; pictorial wallpaper; what-nots and mantel-pieces strewn, not with shells and starfish, but with strange imitations of marine fauna. His sharpest esthetic desires were satisfied by the beautiful specimens of the newest of the arts—pyrography. It remained for French genius to discover the ultimate possibilities of burnt wood and leather. There was little to choose between French and American styles of the period. French vulgarity was somewhat relieved by an exotic fancifulness; American vulgarity was substantial and undefiled.

Lodging with the little people, the American visitor was initiated into the sordid processes of French thrift. By experience he learned, as one poor traveler remarked, that the bourgeoisie "do not take you in to make you comfortable, nor to give you value received, but to get all they can out of you." The bourgeois home was operated on the principle of acute miserliness and self-denial. The floors were uncarpeted; the rooms unheated; the chairs worn and painful. There was no linen or silver, no flowers, no shining glasses. The napkins were old and patched, and a coarse sheet served for a tablecloth. The kitchen was a cubby-hole and the cooking was poor: cold vegetables, stale cheese, bad wines, and a yard or two of bread soaked in greasy water called soup. The only comfortable room in the house was the bedroom. The beds in all French houses, high and low, were an outstanding satisfaction. Katherine Mansfield suggested that the prevalence of adultery in France was caused by the general discomforts of the furniture. The bedroom alone was well appointed and attractive, and the beds were deep and tempting.

The writers of the new century, reflecting social disturbances, were involved in political and economic controversies. Taine and Renan were dead, with none to take their place; but powerful extraneous influences contributed to the formulation of social concepts. Nietzsche, who died in 1900, was claimed alike by reactionaries and radicals; the Russians arrived with Tolstoi as deity; Ibsen, the grim home-wrecker of the North, terrified the bourgeoisie with his dramatization of the new woman; the Germans were read; d'Annunzio and Maeterlinck appealed to exotic tastes; Kipling had crossed the Channel; and Wells captivated the nation that had produced Jules Verne. The great body of writers, if not directly attached to political parties, were directly concerned with social issues, a fact that should gladden the hearts of untrained American intellectuals who have suddenly become economists. Before the War, a French critic counted "no less than fifty-five schools, groups, or coteries, chiefly made up of young writers, but including not a few who had already won their laurels." Romanticists, classicists, and naturalists wrangled and fought side by side, but their grievances were forgotten in the new nationalism—"the renaissance of French pride." These schools, for our purposes, may be reduced to two groups: the social historians; and the neurasthenics, or apostles of art for art's sake.

The first group includes the men who were largely formed in the old century, but who contrived, by means of political sympathies, to prolong their reign. The school of naturalists, derived from Balzac, Flaubert and Maupassant, was declining. Zola, the chief, before his death in 1902, revived his following by his noble stand in the Dreyfus case, while Huysmans, repudiating the master, wound up in unintelligible mysticism. Bourget, after deflecting the naturalist current into the psychological channel, veered into social propaganda for "the needs of France," and returned to Romanism. Barrès, nostalgic dilettante, roused by political turmoils and the Panama scandals, interpreted the cult of energy and heroism; and Prévost turned from the analysis of feminine passions to studies of anarchists. Brunetière, out-moded in his prejudices and great learning, condemned everything new, took refuge in the Church, and railed like one of the little people against the enemies of France. Faguet, by nature academic and duly received by the Immortals in 1901, renounced the criticism of literature for social philosophy. Anatole France, a mixture of virtuosity and sensual-

51

ized erudition, came down from his ivory tower to defend Dreyfus and to join the demonstrations of the Socialists.

The second group, though not less nationalistic, represents the tastes and ideals of a new generation of pure esthetes. It is permeated through and through by Bohemianism, by the exotic and perverse, the affirmation of individual languors carried into the abnormal—the avoidance, at any cost, of bourgeois sentiments. The high gods, Verlaine and Mallarmé, were in the grave, but the spirit of Bohemia in its various deviations—Parnassianism, Symbolism, Decadence and what not—was kept alive by older poets such as Mendès, Sully, Prudhomme, Coppée, and Armand Silvestre; and by the new recruits—the Americans, Stuart Merrill and Francis Griffin; Henri de Regnier; Jammes, Klingsor; Paul Fort and Jules Romains, masters of vers libre; and more recently by Fernand Divoire, champion of Cubism and the technique of the dance. The English member of the firm, the author, with the help of Schwob, of Salome, died in 1900.

"On a November morning," Morand relates, "Oscar Wilde, the prince of the Black Irises, the precursor, dies in a little hotel in the Rue des Beaux Arts, a ruined man, fallen and forgotten. The cheap hearse in which lie the remains of the former King of Piccadilly, is followed to the cemetery by a handful of writers of the Left Bank, who repeat as they go these lines from *De Profundis*: 'Something must be paid for everything that one has done.' If Wilde had lived today, he would have died a glorious death, in full apotheosis, President of the International Society of Inverts."

A later, and decidedly more vigorous, manifestation of Bohemianism appears in the apache authors: the writers of crazy adventure, such as Pierre Benoit, Pierre MacOrlan, and Maurice Renard; and those finding inspiration in the dregs of the underworld—Cyril Berger, Maurice Dekobra, André Salmon, and most talented of all, Francis Carco. But the distinguishing characteristic of the new age is the perversion of the exotic into the neurasthenic, a tendency continuing to the present day, and so sickly and repugnant in many of its aspects as to fill critics, both French and foreign, with alarms for the virility of French art and letters.

The love of the exotic seems to be bred in the French people. Gautier, Delacroix, and all the Romantics have it; nor is Balzac immune; nor Flaubert, nor any of the Naturalists; nor indeed the social historians and the authors of *Sappho* and *Thaïs*. It is the basis of Bohemianism, and the stock in trade of Gauguin; and only the other day it broke out afresh in Matisse, Rousseau, and the Modernist schools. In 1900, the cult of the exotic flourished as never before, in art, letters and high-life. We have it in Loti, Loüys, and in the cabalistic metaphors of Paul Adam; in Gourmont and Gide; in the detestable plays of Henri Bataille; in the impressionism of Jean Lorrain; in Schwob, Debussy, and the neurotic Proust.

High-life, in all its phases, was marked by the cultivation of degenerate pastimes and the feverish pursuit of forbidden thrills. The aristocrats, to exhibit their absurd costumes and have their nerves set on edge by Bernhardt, endured the performances of *l'Aiglon*; to flaunt their intellectuality and to enjoy a new shudder, they attended Lugne-Poë's productions of Ibsen, Hauptmann and Strindberg; for the satisfaction of their vicious tastes, they flocked to Bruant's cabaret. They took drugs, went into esthetic fits over negro entertainers—the first to arrive—and experimented in unmentionable intimacies—anything to uphold their superiority. The arbiter of this world was Count Robert de Montesquiou, who had the arrogance and effeminacy of Oscar Wilde, but none of the talent. But he had a title. He was a real aristocrat, feared by all, envied by all—including Anatole France. An invitation to his infamous parties was a passport to the voyage across the border. He tried to write poetry, but even his favorites were not fooled by his sonnets "written in red ink and powdered with gold." He is remembered as Proust's Baron de Charlus. Of this creature, Francis Porché said: "In a prosopopeia now celebrated and indeed magnificent, Proust evoked an immense sect with its ceremonial, its emblems, its secret language, its physical stigmata and its moral blemishes, its notes of infamy and its marks of honor, its eternal inquietude, its boundless pride, its incurable bitterness, Charlus was no longer alone— an entire species, to which he belonged, surrounded him: it comprised several races, numerous classes, a multitude of varieties."

Proust crosses the border. He carries the exotic into the realm of the psychopathic, which is to say, he develops the esthetic ideals of the aristocrats and Bohemians to their logical termination. His following today is large and curious. In his own immense sect he is the object of whispered worship; most of his admirers, unable to read him and un-conscious therefore of the meaning of his black philosophy, accept him as the modern symbol of the intellectual aristocracy of art. The man himself with his padded cell, his veronal, and his morbid nerves, is accepted as the supremely sensitive soul. To mention his name is to remove one's self from the ruck, to be identified with an esoteric cul-ture. In similar fashion, the Bohemians of Paris, by their ghastly Sur-Realism, their subservience to Picasso, their preoccupation with things which can hardly be discussed with decency—by their scornful abdica-tion of the every-day world—imagine they have made themselves artists.

Paris, in 1900, was the charming hostess to all nations, but what was she doing for the artists? This question will be fully answered in subsequent chapters, but it is fitting at this point to enumerate her heroes and record her official attitude toward the men whom she dis-obligingly neglected. At the Exhibition, contemporary art was lavishly displayed in the Grand Palais, occupying ten rooms. Knowing the tastes of the time, one may easily guess the prize-winners and medalists. The honors went to artists glorifying bourgeois ideals in saints and nudes of sham-classical purity; in moral studies; heroic portraiture; "imaginative pieces"; and in grandiose historical scenes conducive to patriotic tears. The populace stood in reverence before the auburn-haired and unquestionably chaste beauties of Henner; the rustic poetry of Henri Martin; the life-like portraits of Bonnat; the battle pictures of Detaille; the death beds of Jean Paul Laurens; and the romantic Arabs of Benjamin-Constant. More educated taste was centered on

54

Besnard and Carolus-Duran; while the critics voted for Bouguereau, Dagnan-Bouveret, and Gérôme, the grand old man who asked nothing for his criticisms at the Beaux Arts—except the honors of the Republic. Not a single artist of real merit was invited: not Renoir, Cézanne, Degas, Monet, Gauguin, Lautrec and Seurat; not Vuillard, nor the inoffensive Puvis de Chavannes, nor any of the Impressionists. These men were suspect—they were supposed to hold subversive opinions and dangerous sentiments. Official France could not appreciate the simple posters of the Impressionists. She cannot appreciate them today. She judges artists, not by their pictures, but by their morals and their politics.

The sculptors fared no better. Falguière, his pupil, Mercie, and the bric-a-brac school, came off in triumph, with the bust-makers a close second. But Maillol was ignored. There was plenty of room for Dubois, Fremiet, and the Jeanne d'Arc sculptors, but no room for Rodin. The last, however, was too big to allow himself to go unnoticed. At the Place de l'Alma, in a special pavilion in which he had collected his drawings and all his important sculptures, Rodin blew his own trumpet. It was believed at the time that the city of Paris, to do honor to Rodin, erected at its own expense a separate building for the exhibition of his works. This belief has persisted among historians, and France, after the great success of the sculptor's exhibition, has not discouraged it. The truth is that the scheme was conceived and executed by Rodin. He persuaded three Paris bankers to finance the pavilion at a cost of 80,000 francs; he obtained permission to build on ground close to one of the entrances of the Great Exhibition, overcoming the hostility of the Municipal Council; and he repaid his backers from moneys taken in at the gate. And he reaped a harvest of fame.

The academic mills produced pictures quantitatively in the mercantile spirit of Worth, the manufacturer of gowns. The Impressionists, snubbed by the State, sold out to farsighted dealers like Durand-Ruel through which agency the poorer works of Monet and the specialists in sunlight dribbled slowly into America. The best canvases, like wines, were put away against a rising market. Cézanne, slandered beyond endurance, his masterpieces in storage, retired, in 1900, to Aix, and died in 1906, to the great relief of the peasants. Van Gogh, one of his few supporters, shot himself, in 1890; and in 1903, Gauguin's miseries were ended. Toulouse-Lautrec, the devil's advocate, concluded his Bohemian passage in 1901. Among his last works was a series of panels painted for the caravan of his old model, La Goulue, the dancer who went on the road as a lion-tamer. A year before his death, he was being imitated by a young Spaniard on his first visit to Paris. The young Spaniard was Pablo Picasso.

In the new century, Sarah Brown, the former Queen of Bohemia, taking her Last Bath in the manner of Daumier's character, threw herself into the Seine—and cynical Paris laughed. Degas was in the green-room of the Opera, studying the ballet dancers and scowling at the old roués who tottered in to claim their girls. Degas, Renoir, and Monet lived on for nearly a score of years, productive to the last and minding their own business. Sem, the wicked caricaturist, was feared and admired in fashionable circles. He was compared to Daumier: one might as well compare the Broadway columnist to Theodore Dreiser. Mucha, the Moravian, was famous for his posters of Bernhardt. I remember Mucha well: about 1908 his covers for American magazines were framed and displayed in drawing rooms by art-loving ladies dressed in the styles of French ladies of 1900. He exerted a profound influence on the commercial artists of the Chicago Art Institute; and today enjoys a conspicuous place in the annals of modern Czech art. Matisse made his modern bow at the Independents in 1901, and two years later at the Salon d'Automne. Whistler, victorious over the British in his Bohemian warfare, died in London in 1903. Toward the end of his life, a London newspaper, informed of his illness, published an account of his career. Whistler wrote to the editor: "May I acknowledge the tender little glow of health induced by reading, as I sat here in the morning sun, the flattering attention paid me by your gentlemen of ready wreath and quick biography?"

56

The bourgeois machine was busily turning; wines were selling, money piling up; the horrible Impressionists and allied menaces were properly put down; the safe and stupid artists won all the laurels—the Exhibition was a huge success. But revolt was in the air. The little people and their claptrap painters did not know what was in store for them. New ideas were generating; young men were organizing and conspiring, eager for vengeance and official blood. Up in Montmartre, in a long, rambling wooden shack, a band of guttersnipes, vagabond poets, apache authors, and wild, waylaying painters, prepared for battle. The fat Apollinaire, poet and merry-andrew, established an auxiliary base in Montparnasse, uniting the insurgents of both banks. In the company, marching shoulder to shoulder, were Picasso, Braque, Derain, Van Dongen, Utrillo, Modigliani, Gris, Salmon, MacOrlan, Carco, Jacob, Dufy, Friesz, and Galanis. We shall hear more of them.

By this time you will have perceived that French taste, in all its departments, was the reverse of the artistic, and that French art was unworthy of the name. This fact, recognized by the younger men, constitutes the most legitimate excuse for the upheaval known as Modernism. But the world at large was not conscious of the inferiority, so charming was Paris, so gay, so like a great bazaar, and so wise were the French in ministering to individual needs. French taste, in essence, consists in putting ugly things together with distinction; in combining odds and ends so that the total effect is one of charm and pleasurable surprise. Picasso, under Parisian influence, gives style and distinction to such barren things as naked cubes. With a row of consumptive trees, a little gravel, a few nude statues, and a strumpet, the French make a boulevard that fetches the world. With a theory they make a new school in art. With appointments that would disgrace a Third Avenue eating-place, their cafés become the rendezvous of connoisseurs from all nations. They are a nation of artists in little, the only people in whom the art impulse is universally distributed, who, in their relations with outsiders, transact their business with the grace and distinction born of a ripe—or over-ripe—culture.

57

American artists and expatriates talk continually of France's liberality in all things pertaining to the arts. What they really mean, I suppose, is the personal freedom which France generously bestows on artists and visitors. France does not care what an artist, or any one else, may do so long as his conduct does not touch the safety of the State. But let him voice an opinion, or paint a picture, at variance with bourgeois ideals, and she bears down upon him without mercy. Courbet was not exiled because of his pictures, but because he was believed to be a Communard. Daumier's political convictions sent him to jail; and Cézanne's enemies, seizing the most effective weapon with which to ruin an artist, charged him with Communard sympathies—this against a man who, politically, was a rank conservative. All that Manet's honest conception of the nude brought him was a life of persecution. Let all American painters who howl—and justly howl—against the indifference of our government consider these facts: "None of the pictures by the Impressionists, Post-Impressionists, and by Cézanne and Seurat now in the Louvre and Luxembourg museums has been a purchase. Manet's Olympia, offered by subscription in 1890, was at first refused and only accepted after protracted negotiations. When the whole of the Caillebotte Collection came to the nation by bequest, in 1895, the Administration des Beaux Arts refused two pictures by Cézanne, one by Manet, three by Sisley, eight by Monet and eleven by Pissarro, and accepted the remainder under protest."

What does the presence of an art colony mean to Paris? It means more color, more revenues, and the perpetuation of French prestige in the fine arts. But the average artist, let us keep in mind, has no convictions of any sort. His esthetic squabbles do not interest, much less irritate, the guardians of the machine. The Modernists, at first, were viewed with some anxiety, but once it was evident that their uprising was only a technical restlessness, they too were allowed to fume and suffer. And they were officially ignored. If one of them should tamper with the national machine, he would be immediately taken care of. Much has been said—and to an extent, rightly—of French liberality in the publication of books. Let us not be confused on this point. Take the case of Joyce's *Ulysses*, a work printed in Paris, and stupidly confiscated in the Customs House of New York. The publication of a book which English readers cannot decipher without an exegesis is as harmless to the French public as an edition of Rabelais, brought out in old French by a New York publisher, would be to the American public. Baudelaire, you will remember, was first published in Brussels; and *Madame Bovary*, a noble and moral book, was regarded as dangerous to the bourgeoisie, and was pounced upon by the authorities—all of whom kept mistresses—with the ignorance and bigotry of Bostonians.

France is perhaps the most realistic of nations, and the most sensible in matters of individual behavior. She does not legislate against organic impulses and desires, nor does she throw her citizens into jail for innocent ideas and diversions. She recognizes the polygamous nature of man, the looseness of most women, and the vicious cravings inherent in all human beings. She faces the inscrutable ways of prostitution frankly, registering and inspecting girls, and systematically working to prevent the spread of disease. She loves her vices, and succeeds in making the rest of the world like them because they are French. The notion that the French do not enjoy dirty shows; that they stage them for foreigners, and attend them, if at all, only to be convinced of their worthlessness, is nonsense. The French originated and applauded this form of amusement long before the Americans arrived; and if, of late years, they have somewhat abandoned their lighter recreations, it is because they are more interested in saving money. In no other nation is the spirit of self-preservation so highly developed. The French will tolerate, if not foster, any form of amusement, any irregularity, any art, so long as it does not injure the spirit of self-preservation.

France, or Paris rather, indulges the artist, smiles on his childish follies, encourages his Bohemian customs. She knows the secret in his heart. In the late 'nineties, Sarah Brown, the beautiful model who was mobbed when she posed at Julian's, appeared at the Quat'z'Arts Ball completely nude, as Cleopatra. A social reformer named Berenger,

59

a rare nuisance in Paris, announced his intention of suppressing the Ball. The students of the Quarter marched into the Chamber of Deputies and demanded an apology; marched to Berenger's house, smashed the windows and yelled, "Come out and be slain! You must and you shall be slain." The Ball was not suppressed. Paris, a wise old strumpet, invests personal freedom,—the joys of the flesh, the full play of the senses—with the romantic lure of art and culture. And the young man who goes to Paris for art's sake, goes for the personal freedom of which art has been made the symbol. That freedom, and not art, shall remove gnawing restraints, satisfy unfulfilled longings, and enable him to live as every young man burns to live, and cannot live anywhere else. That is the secret in his heart.

3

TWO KINDS OF ART

WISEACRES tell us that a nation gets the kind of government it deserves. I do not know whether the law of compensation is binding on large social groups, but I do know, from my own experience, that individuals get what they deserve. I know, too, that painters get what is coming to them: exclusive of a few brave souls, they give nothing to society and receive nothing in return. A cruel reflection perhaps, but art in the modern world is a cruel business. The reflection on government may also seem uncharitable in these hard times when national woes and the appeals of the unemployed are answered by the apologetic bawlings of the party in power, and by the political tears and promises of the opposition; when the government bestows its remaining millions on the assassins who cling desperately to the economic corpse. But I was not thinking of the Americans—I was thinking of those indomitable bourgeois Frenchmen. The French have the government they deserve, but they differ from the rest of the world in being satisfied with their political machine. I wish other nations were so sensible and so easily contented. The ideals of France are not very lofty, but they are positive and attainable. The aim of the French civilization is essentially materialistic: national security, the solidarity of the family, a job for every man and every harlot, and the methodical satisfaction of physical desires—these things progressively from generation to generation, but added to them, reverence for the dead and the right to wear mourning, and the freedom to invent the insignia of culture.

It is also true, I think, that a nation gets the form of art which it deserves. The French do not love art, but they are not unique in this respect—neither do the Americans, nor the British, nor the Spaniards, nor the Italians, nor any other modern people. The Americans do not deserve any art. We entrust the manufacture of our art to the French: intimidated by French culture, the legend of French supremacy in the fine arts, and the apocryphal gospel of French taste; and remembering the good times we had in Paris—the wine, the girls, the wild parties, the anonymous and unrestrained revelry—we accept French painting, both original and imitation, at the valuations put upon it by dealers who are also diplomatists, and by critics who have never written an intelligible line. We sell our sons into Bohemian slavery, and when they return from Paris, demoralized, their talents corrupted, broken in will-power and altogether unmanned for their struggles in a grim, and to them, semi-foreign environment, we kick them into some small interstice in our business civilization where they remain till they die, crushed and forgotten. If we should attempt to produce novelists by this system, we should ship our promising youths to Paris, compel them to write in French and to devote themselves exclusively to French subject-matter—and we should breed a colony of indeterminates, a lot of lesser Julian Greens, or, if possible, more effeminate Jean Cocteaus. The Americans do not deserve any plastic art.

In normal times, when the machine is running smoothly, the French do not need art. When the citizens of the State are perfectly adjusted to their environment; when business is thriving, money piling up, and the frontiers unassailed; the leaders of France do not call in the artist, that is, the artist who is more than a docile sycophant paid to lay an appropriate wreath on an old glory. For the genuine artist, more often than not, is a disturbing and rebellious fellow whose comments on bourgeois society are not likely to be compliant or flattering. The notion that the arts are born of the union of peace and plenty had its origin in the philosophy of academic retirement, and is merely a defence for the ineffectualness which, in modern life, the professional thinker shares with the artist. To wait for the marriage of peace and fat is a poor excuse for impotence. Real art, like thought, is born of turmoil and violence. Real art is born in periods of nervous forebodings and restless strivings—when the future is uncertain. When society calls on the artist for the objectification of its ideals, you may depend on it that its ideals are in danger: the old order is tottering, and art is the last line of defence. The great religious art of Italy reached its highest expression in times of corruption. France, however, with her tight conservatism and the tested satisfactions derived from purely material comforts, is afraid of her original artists, and instead of using her best minds, insults and persecutes them. If you think that I am exaggerating the case, I ask you to examine the career of every French artist of merit from Delacroix to Cézanne; and I am willing, in the definition of merit, to include all the Impressionists. It is true that France produces more pictures than any other nation, but not, I assure you, for esthetic purposes.

About 1900, as I have shown at some length, the neatness of French ideals, and the security of the little people were violently unsettled, and the ministers of state, with their immortal juries, called on the artists for propaganda. The move was not only good politics, it represented the tastes and preferences of bureaucrats when they go in for art. Bourgeoisie themselves, they had only to exercise their own judgment in pictures in order to kindle the torpid imagination of the masses. This official maneuver was not an innovation in France. As a matter of fact, since the breaking-up of the early guild system, the French artist, in official capacities, had no choice but to glorify sovereign ideals. You will recall the flamboyant mural orgies commissioned by the minister of the Grand Monarch to decorate the vanity of the State, and to symbolize the fantastic belief of the French in their mythological lineage; you will recall that in the most dramatic moment of French history, the blood-stained republicans fighting for the rights of man, retained their classical superstitions, revived the toga, and posed for the painters as surly old Romans. And Bonaparte, the incarnation of bourgeois ideals, demanded the same heroic paraphernalia for the Empire. "Give them glory," he shouted to his painters, "and more glory!" Always it was the academicians who captured the jobs. One could not go wrong on the academicians—they could be counted on to do the expected thing. They believed in the antiquity of the French people, and in the antiquity of draughtsmanship: one system, immutable and intact.

The call, in 1900, was answered by a group of old men—complete academicians, dependable, heavy with medals, convinced of their own greatness. The fruits of their toil were first displayed at the Exhibition to reassure the world of the superiority of French painting and the nobility of French ideals, and then, by an admirable system, farmed out to provincial museums. I have seen provincial families standing before these canvases, awed and overcome, gazing at obvious moralities with the same blinking stupefaction that distorts the dull faces of the admirers of Picasso's latest things. The pictures embraced every variety of conventional sentiment: there were huge battle pieces to amaze the multitude and to extol the bravery of the soldier; there were substitutes for patriotic speeches, and for the narcotic effect of the Mass; there were romantic conceptions in which the weaker side of Delacroix was played up in the grand style, and oriental dreams to satisfy exotic tastes; there were scenes inculcating the dignity of dirty labor; and of course, the Maid of Orleans.

I have no quarrel with the subjects of the pictures—any subject is valid in art, if it is not an "invisible substance," or an abstraction—my quarrel is with the sentiment which was cheap and shallow, and with the drawing which was the worst sort of sham-classicism. The men who painted these pictures were fundamentally stupid—in any department of life calling for the exercise of intelligence they would never have been heard of. They thought they were classical—they were only trained in the Beaux-Arts. They drew by precedent and rigid prescription, by a scheme of arbitrary proportions supposed to be pure Greek, but actually handed down from Greco-Roman copies by the academic tradition, and authorized by Poussin and David. On this arbitrary

64

method they grafted the faked, naturalistic values of the photograph, and the mixture precipitated the most degraded form of art that ever pleased a jury. The leaders of this dreadful group are now forgotten, but in their day they were famous. Gérôme, Bouguereau, Bonnat, Benjamin-Constant, Carolus-Duran, Dagnan Bouveret, Henner, and the elder Laurens; and Henri Martin and Besnard who robbed the Impressionists of a few tricks and sold them to the State. What a crew! And how does it happen that such mediocrity always triumphs in painting? I enumerate them for several reasons: they were typical of the taste of the period; they and their successors are responsible for the vulgarity that passes for art; the young Modernists hated them so thoroughly; their sons are the official pets and prize-winners of to-day; and we shall have this breed in art as long as the old system of patronage endures.

We need not pursue them further except to point out their relation to society. Though called to the service of the State in their old age, they were outcasts whose art performed no honest function. They too lived in the Latin Quarter, using Bohemianism to compensate impotence and to strengthen self-assertiveness. Taine, who knew them well, has described their wretched lives. In their youth they lived in a state of poverty that would break all but the most conceited of men. At forty they got into the papers; at fifty they earned a little money and suffered terribly from rheumatism; at sixty, or later, they won medals and with the proper political backing, official jobs at an age when the springs of their energy, all but dried-up, leaked out, at long intervals, in miserable drops. Married or single, they lived with old actresses, broken-down models, or superannuated grisettes who had shown their legs in public halls. We need not waste any sympathy on this type of painter. He does not belong in art, and he and his women, and his promoters are the curse of art. He thinks he is a hell of a fellow, and he is the artist who gets on in the world, slowly but surely.

There were other artists in France who, whatever their limitations, were so far above the bemedaled hacks impaneled to soothe the embarrassed vanity of the State that we should not mention them in the same breath. They have been variously lumped together as Impressionists, independents, unofficial artists, and, in the words of the astute critic Wilenski, "gentlemen fanatics," an excellent designation though there was not a gentleman among them save Toulouse-Lautrec who had repudiated his birthright; nor had there been a gentleman in French art since Delacroix. They were all boors—plain and earthy, as painters should be—willing to bury individual grievances in common cause against officialdom. The most convenient classification, it seems to me, is Impressionism, if we construe that term to include both the realists—the followers of Courbet and Manet—and those painting, or trying to paint, atmospheric effects, "the air we breathe" as Degas expressed it, and the things of which the eye alone is conscious. I have analyzed Impressionism from one end to the other in *Men of Art*, but it will be necessary to review the movement briefly in order to explain the attacks made upon it by the Modernists.

The movement which, in the 'Seventies, infuriated press and public alike and which was still in bad odor at the close of the century, was not the unexpected spasm of a few fanatics; it was the culmination of a chain of influences, social and technical, in operation since the decline of the Italian Renaissance. When art, any art, has an honest position in society; when people need and demand it, enjoy and welcome it as an emotional necessity and a stimulus to richer living; when the competitive spirit runs high and exuberant, and honors and rewards are abundant; when people are able to talk about it in sensible human speech, without the aid of critics or without resorting to mystifying terminology invented by the esthetes; the chances are that the artist, being a genuine practitioner and as estimable as any other business man, will break his back to do great things and to ennoble his profession. When art loses caste, or more exactly, when its rightful function has been usurped by another art; when it cannot adapt itself to changing social conditions; when it becomes a luxury or a vestigial organ kept alive by artificial nourishment; the artist, forced into isolation or Bohemianism, is relegated to the cultivation of individual caprices, abstractions, technical sleights and introspective agonies which he magnifies and worships and into which, with the assistance of literary charlatans, he projects absurd and psychic meanings. The history of Impressionism is the story of the errant struggles of an art that had lost its function, of the path of painting from the church and the public to the dealer and the museum.

The movement, step by step, is the descent of painting, once the glorious art of the imaginings and co-ordinated experiences of the thinking mind, to the flat impressions of the recording instrument. The theories and speculations from which it developed had been known to artists for ages. The Orientals had proved that the maximum of intensity is gained when colors are placed in juxtaposition with their complementaries; Leonardo da Vinci, with characteristic thoroughness, had formulated laws of coloration and fully investigated atmospheric phenomena, noting the division of tones and the fact that shadows are not black but filled with color; but he had rejected his discoveries on the ground that they dissolved form and wrecked design. His famous Chiaroscuro, as Wölfflin has observed, was not a step toward Impressionism, but a means to obtain bulk form and greater relief. The first artist to deal practically with the analysis of natural light was Titian when, as he approached the grave and peered at the world with half-closed eyes, he discovered that light falling upon objects breaks up the surfaces into patches of tone. Accordingly, he began to paint broadly, with touches of color in the shadows, to coax into pigment the vivid illumination of nature.

Titian's methods were studied in Madrid by Velasquez, the most marvelous eye in painting. Velasquez, painter to the king and limited by his office to the portrayal of decaying royalty, had but one aim: verisimilitude, or the illusion of the appearance of objects from a single point of focus and under natural lighting. Together with the Dutch, extraordinary craftsmen with no higher ideal in art than the making of little substitutes for nature, he brought to perfection the technique of the imitated tone, that is, the rendering of objects as the eye actually sees them in the clear light of day. But the Dutch, like Velasquez and Goya, were indoor painters: the exploration of outside illumination began with Claude Lorrain, and was carried forward by Watteau, Corot and the Englishmen, Constable, Bonington and Turner. It becomes apparent, as we proceed, that the direction of Western painting was towards the problems of light and atmosphere, a tendency in itself legitimate enough had not the higher functions of art been ignored.

In France, throughout the whole of the nineteenth century, the painters, as I have said, were arrayed in two factions—the lackeys of the Academy and the Impressionists. The Academics we have already disposed of; the good men, in one way or another, were all affiliated with Impressionism. It also happened that the good men—the list includes most of the illustrious names in modern French painting, Delacroix, Géricault, Corot, Courbet, Manet, Degas, Seurat, Lautrec, and Cézanne, were in possession of independent incomes. Their financial security had its advantages and drawbacks: they were free from the temptation to compromise with official juries and to pander to rabble passions; they were free, as some of them said, "to please themselves"—to paint for art's sake—and to live decently without sacrificing their best years to Bohemian squalor. On the other hand, while professing to ignore the juries, they were continually wrangling with them and seeking to undermine traditional authority; and like the Bohemians, they forgot that the function of painting is not complete until a picture has won a responsive audience. In their opposition to bourgeois ideals, they deflected painting from the larger centers of human interest, concentrating on technical experiments, theories and novel processes. It was not an accident, I think, that Daumier, the one man who had to paint for a living, the one genuine practitioner, was the greatest artist of the century. Many tears have been shed over Daumier because he had to work for his bread and wine; but it was the blood and fury of social combats that raised

68

his art to an eminence beyond the reach of any of his contemporaries. His lot was not altogether enviable; he paid a heavy price for his convictions; but in the end he was happier than the gentlemen who offered him the admiration which he accepted shyly, and the sympathy which he did not need.

The others, wiser from experience, found out that a man does not paint merely to amuse himself, nor for art's sake unless he is a failure or a fairy. Denied a public and as useless as astrologers or necromancers, they endeavored to fight their way into the sanctums of the academic corporation. They were rebuked, repulsed and beaten; instead of recognition they won notoriety and execration. Delacroix, an importunate aristocrat, applied five times for a seat in the Institute, and finally, in his last years, was admitted—an empty and unworthy honor; Courbet, rejected by the Salon, unsuccessful in his efforts to exhibit his pictures without the imprimatur of the dealer, and accused of Socialism because he painted strapping plebeian women, was arrested, ruined and chased out of the country; Manet, the most calumniated of all, was charged with pornography and died a nervous wreck; Degas gave up the fight and spent the last thirty years of his long life in seclusion, a lonely and disagreeable old bachelor; and Cézanne, his morbid touchiness exacerbated by ignorant juries and lying journalists, retired to Aix—to the peaceful world of vegetables and peasants.

These painters, in company with others who were neither practitioners nor men of independent means, carried French Impressionism to its conclusion. Delacroix, by his great gifts, his gallant leadership in the revolt against academic tyranny, and by introducing the broken-color procedure of the English painters, left his mark on every one of his successors. Courbet, crying blatantly in behalf of realism, that is, realism as opposed to religious imagery and allegory—contemporary events instead of romantic fictions—hurried painting towards the photographic reproduction of nature. Let us never forget that the direction of Impressionism was towards the literal image of the sensitized plate.

Much has been written of the influence of the Japanese color-print which came into French painting about 1860. It would be unwise to deny this exotic influence; for it is plain that Manet, Degas, Lautrec and Whistler were affected by the flat patterns of the Orientals. But a much more significant factor in the art of this group was photography, not only the photographic vision as it had steadily risen to prominence since Velasquez, but also the curious and striking effects registered on over-exposed plates. The ambition of Degas, in his own words, was "to observe his models through the keyhole," which incidentally is almost a perfect definition of Impressionism: a view of nature through a peep-hole; an eyeful of nature; a snapshot of a little fragment of the visible world. Degas made snapshots of his models, catching them in eccentric poses, and emphasizing in the manner of the camera dislocated lines and bizarre effects of light and dark. His pictures have many of the characteristics of stunt pictures. Toulouse-Lautrec was of a different stripe. He too was an Impressionist snatching at fugitive poses and positive colors—the grotesque beckonings of the obscene, and the rhythms of dancers reared in impudicity. But he was much more: he was a man of convictions—of character, if you will—deeply moved by degenerate things, and one of the best artists of the century. He had a fine sense of design, and by design I do not mean the fiddling with lines and the juggling of planes to make a Cubist poster, but the controlled thinking and ordered experiences which went into the making of his own posters—the best that France has given us—and into all his conceptions of inhumanity.

The arch offender was Manet. He was by no means unintelligent; he again painted "life"—occupational scenes and current events—and his influence on modern art cannot be overlooked. But Manet was a sight-seer; he had no convictions, no preferences, for one thing above another. His sole aim was to paint well in the manual sense —to record what the eye could take in at a glance; and within his own terms no man ever painted better. He was a painting machine whose last pictures, *The Bar of the Folies Bergères*, for example, were actually copied from photographs. He was absorbed in processes, in tones and values—not in any light that tones and values might throw on the riddle of living. Like Daumier, he broke the academic mold, but when we compare the work of the two men and follow the Manet tradition to its logical conclusion in Sargent and the horde of despicable portrait painters, the vast divergence in their approaches is at once apparent. Daumier was profoundly affected by life—by living people, social disturbances, human complications; and he, in turn, moved the stationary world of traditional practice, creating new forms. Manet was a painter of surfaces; his art was ready material for shallow imitation. And by the close of the century he had begotten a school of flashy painting machines who needed for their mechanical transcriptions of nature neither mind nor imagination.

In the popular mind the term Impressionism refers to Monet, Sisley and Pissarro, and their innumerable imitators. The term suggests immediately the exercises in granulated nature which, I am sorry to say, still crowd the exhibition rooms of America. This branch of Impressionism, however, was only a more pronounced technical manifestation of the debased tendency of modern painting, and in its creative aspects has even less to recommend it than the naturalism of Manet and Degas. The men who rallied round Monet and Pissarro laid the greatest stress on "the innocence of the eye," the eye that registers nature impartially like the lens of a camera, and is not hampered by the action of a critical and inquiring mind. They invented a code for the transcription of natural statistics, a scientific recipe arrived at by observation but corroborated later in the laboratory. They made a chromatic formula the aim and end of art and perfected a method, which, being scientific and mechanical, was proof against all error.

They were outdoor painters determined to transfer to canvas the vivid contrasts of sunlight and shadow. Observing that the values of natural light, when literally copied in pigment, lose their original life and brilliancy, they began to enliven their canvases by injecting complementary tints into the shadows. Next, they indicated not only shadows but local colors by facets of pure pigment varying in tint and hue, which, when recomposed by the eye at a distance, produced the vibrant animation of nature itself. For example, in painting grass, they did not use a prepared green, but stippled the canvas with little touches of blue and yellow, leaving the blending process to the spectator. The purpose of all this was to compel the painter's colors, which are mud and oil, to serve as light, which is clean and pure. In other words, they were color photographers.

This was a fine way to enjoy nature, a jolly outdoor sport—but it had little relation to art. In time the sport became popular the world over among painters who had nothing that could be called a mind; and it is popular today in America, especially in California where sunlight is plentiful. Daumier has a cartoon of a couple of these sportsmen, master and pupil painting the beauty of nature, one sitting directly behind the other. The title line reads, "The first copies nature; the second copies the first."

Impressionism signifies the victory of technique over the creative spirit. Seduced by playful mechanics, its devotees forgot all about art as an expressive medium, painting nature exactly as seen, recording visual sensations, and dissolving the substance of things in floating veils of atmospheric iridescence. It is an art without design, if such may be called art, since design is not a formula but the fruit of controlled or directed thinking—nature modified by the mind, the imposition of the will on the elements of experience. It reveals, instead of new meanings, and new kinships in the details of the world, new aspects of nature, resembling in this respect the incandescent lamp of the theatre which, by slides of different colors, suddenly changes the appearance of the stage. Like the camera, it reduces nature to an apprehensible scale and discloses a number of interesting facts overlooked by the dull eye of the layman, but the reduction, call it whatever pretty name you wish, is only a piece of nature.

At the end of the century, after an ignominious beginning and many years of vicious opposition, Impressionism was a firmly established school, numbering among its adherents not only the founders, several of whom were bigger than the movement, but also a young brood of artists who could not tolerate the Academy, yet who needed someone to tell them what and how to paint. In its restricted sense, Impressionism produced nothing more creative than a large stock of very real and convincing representations of sunlight. With this fact in mind, and in full knowledge of its innocent intentions, we may well wonder at the indecent and unrelenting protests which it aroused. Like the descriptive painting of the little Dutchmen, it should have been a popular bourgeois art; it brought a well-chosen, expertly embroidered piece of nature into the drawing room, fulfilling the office of cut-flowers and chintzes. It had charm and color, asked nothing of the mind, and its rather novel technique, I am certain, would never have excited the suspicions of the little people, if they had not been told that it was the handwriting of communards.

The reasons for the slow growth of Impressionism are twofold. In the first place, it threatened to take the bread—such as it was—out of the mouths of the academic painters, and those terrified wretches, backed by the State and by the lowest of critics, attacked the new school in the most cowardly fashion, deterred by no considerations of honesty or fair play. Second, the movement was underwritten by dealers who monopolized the best painters, gave them a pittance, put their pictures in storage, and gradually converted them into collectors' rarities. The result is that today, after sixty years of exploitation, the best examples of Impressionism are controlled by the original underwriters, Durand-Ruel, which firm slowly releases its enormous stock—the Impressionists, remember, were very prolific, a pile of straw or a pool of lilies affording Monet material for innumerable paintings—at propitious moments. These pictures are sold and resold by dealers and collectors in a veritable merry-go-round of market rigging. Actually they are worth from twenty-five to fifty dollars, but they are sold in terms of old masters—according to scarcity values. I should like to own one—to look at on dark winter days when I cannot go to Florida, and to remind me that the Modernists had just provocation for their revolt—but like most people entitled to pictures, I cannot buy any. America is full of Impressionist pictures of the well known garden variety, and the stock is augmented annually. There are enough, as our politicians say, for every man, woman, and child. No one need go hungry. But they are stored in the stock rooms of dealers, in studios, lofts, barns and cellars. Our painters, bred in an iniquitous system, had rather starve than sell a painting for what it is worth. Occasionally an American like Childe Hassam makes a handsome living by his art, but that is because his pictures are indistinguishable from the French originals.

The condition of French art and culture, in 1900, may be summarized as follows:

Popular taste in every department was abominable, so thoroughly corrupted, in fact, that I can sympathize with the Futurists, when, somewhat later, they issued a manifesto demanding that all the art of the world be scrapped, and that the artists take a fresh start relieved of the heavy burden of traditional baggage.

The popular artists were the submissive sheep of the Academy—Bohemians by necessity and called upon in emergencies to glorify bourgeois ideals.

Impressionism, though running out as a movement, was the fixed creed of all painters at war with the official system. Its leaders were not Bohemians but men of independent means or nurselings of the dealers. On the surface, it appeared to be radical and invigorating; at bottom, its radicalism was only technical—an exploration of photographic processes. Impressionism carried on the healthy realism of Courbet and Manet by dispensing with conventional subject-matter, drew attention to the artistic material in the nooks and corners of

GEORGES SEURAT: *La Grande Jatte*

the everyday world, eliminated quantities of ugly mud from the palette, and codified the relation of light-values to color. But it had the defect of leaving the mind unemployed.

Out of Impressionism came three men, Seurat, Renoir and Cézanne, who sought to temper its excesses and correct its errors; and two others, Van Gogh and Gauguin, who prepared the art of Cézanne for the Modernists. Seurat and Van Gogh died ten years before the close of the century but their influence was not felt until later.

In the background lay a band of young Bohemians, violently anti-bourgeois, anti-Impressionist, and ready to toss a load of explosives into both camps. We shall soon bring them forth, one by one, and investigate their ammunition and their motives.

Seurat, a name heard more frequently these days than of yore, died in his thirty-second year, leaving only a small body of work to a generation that could not follow him. But it was work of exceptional quality, painfully premeditated, scrupulously thought out, and pieced together with an infallible sense of placement. He esteemed the outdoor Impressionists as purveyors of fuzzy photography, and Degas and Lautrec as no better than skilful reporters. His plan was to select materials of which he had intimate knowledge, generally plebeian pastimes—circuses, cabaret scenes, picnic parties, and the like—to preserve the essentially French characteristics of his subjects and at the same time to strip them of superfluous trappings; and to provide an architectural framework for his experiences. In a word, he sought to restore to French painting classical decorum, formal order and monumental style. He succeeded: as designs, his pictures could hardly be improved on, but, as I have written elsewhere, his art is labored to death. He developed the granular method of the Impressionists into the molecular method of the Pointillists, binding his powers to the most complicated and nerve-racking technique ever wished upon himself by a man of superior intelligence and sound convictions.

It has happened that whenever the French artist attempts to be classical, he loses his vitality and produces inert, still-life forms or bloodless abstractions. There is the example of Poussin, Ingres, Puvis de Chavannes, Cézanne, in most of his work, and Picasso in his whole oeuvre, as the English critics say. Seurat was no exception. His figures are frozen in space, flawlessly mummified; his scenes are constructed on the dead level of perfection, without dramatic accents or variations of emotional intensity; his canvases look as if they had been stamped, screened and sterilized. Naturally, his exasperating technique has had few imitators, but the architectural elements of his art were closely studied by a rising generation of painters leagued against the thoughtless, hit-or-miss style of the Impressionists.

Renoir is a fine painter; so fine indeed, so easily understood, so perspicuous and enjoyable, that I am loath to subject him to analysis. For a certain kind of criticism—the surgical incisions of the esthetes —implies an autopsy. Let us keep this man off the operating table: he is certainly not a corpse. He is alive, and he will continue to live, I think, for many a day. His pictures, like those of all good painters who make themselves clear, need not the words of doctors to keep them alive—they need only to be seen. If Renoir's paintings were properly dispersed and circulated, men, women and children everywhere would enjoy them, spontaneously exclaiming, "How rich and fine!"—and let it go at that. Participation is the law of survival. But it is talk that keeps Picasso's pictures alive; and when the talk ceases, his art will cease to exist. Its vitality is verbal.

I should like to own a good Renoir, but for obvious reasons, I cannot. I should like to hang one in my study to freshen my faith in art when professional duties oblige me to write of the cranks and failures who have made modern painting a blunder and a shame. Renoir was on good terms with life, and his happiness in living is communicated by his art. He was rooted to the simplest things in life —pagan, animal joys which never degenerated into Bohemian lecheries—the things which make life bearable in any age and at any time. If he was unmoved by the tragedy of man; if he pretended to no deep philosophies, and refused to concern himself with thoughts of God and destiny, he never stooped to the base, the empty or the absurd. He painted trees and sunlight, fruits and flowers, bourgeois recreations, children, and above all, the female nude. His nudes are among the few in modern art that have any meaning. His women are not studio exhibitionists; nor are they distorted geometrical assemblages; nor harlots. Out of the naked women whom all men love to embrace and enjoy he created a type—a symbol, if you care for the word—adding to the natural fact his own voluptuous appreciation. There is no fake emphasis on biological accessories; his nudes stand as the highest symbols of his delight in living, his satisfaction in God's handiwork. It is hard to paint a naked woman in that way. The average painter, when he tells a woman that he wishes to paint her in the nude for "spiritual reasons," or because she has "such a beautiful body," is not telling the truth. He is only trying to use his art as a means to more amorous business—and the woman knows it. In consequence, he produces only a carnal engine, or a detailed piece of flesh containing no traces of the honest joy or exhilarating life which Renoir put into his nudes. Few artists ever paint the nude for spiritual reasons—few artists have sufficient detachment. Rembrandt was an exception; but he chose some soiled remnant of humanity which he used as a receptacle for emotions quite the opposite of those aroused by splendid nakedness.

The nude was as natural to Renoir as a bowl of fruit was to Cézanne. He could not paint a man: his men are all bearded women. I should like to own a Renoir nude for associative reasons (among others) : to bring home again my first days in France when I experienced without shame or espionage the pleasures of a world which the French admit and cultivate more gracefully than any other modern people.

Because Renoir is so direct and unconfused, his owners and admirers have labored hard to endow him with a massive intellect, great subtlety and all sorts of monumental virtues. They cannot believe that so extraordinary a talent should have had only one idea

77

in his head—the acceptance of nature and the rendering of the sensuous aspects of the world. So they dig and delve into his art, collecting scraps of technical matter, analyzing his designs, and tracing his descent from the immortal gods. What really amazes them is his craftsmanship, but I know several painters with an even more involved craft who have absolutely nothing in their heads. Renoir used a modified form of Impressionism: while following the values of natural light, he avoided the flatness of literal rendering by manipulating the illumination to his own ends; that is, he focussed the strongest lights on the crests of his forms, using light where it was needed to accentuate mass, and not where it would naturally fall. His pictures, composed on a basis of highly saturated tones and naturalistic values are simple patterns out of Watteau and Fragonard—obviously more sculptural, but modeled in relief, not in the full round. Too much fuss has been made over the huge nudes of his last years, the boneless tubs painted loosely by paralytic hands and drenched in hot colors. It would seem that Renoir hoped to rival the opulence of the Venetians by effacing the physical characteristics of his women, and expanding their bodies into geometrical volumes. These nudes are said to be rich in plastic values. Undoubtedly; but I know a painter, a marvelous craftsman, who turns out every year a number of nude torsos which are much richer in plastic values, but nevertheless without meaning. Plasticity in the abstract is no virtue.

Renoir has exerted only a moderate influence on modern painting. His art, unlike that of Cézanne, is not instrumentally fertile, does not lend itself to new developments. To be sure, he has had plenty of imitators, but none worth mentioning. His imitators would do better to emulate his example as a man. Renoir faced the difficulties in the way of the modern artist with infinite forbearance, never whined, never expected too much of the world, and was uniformly happy and productive to the end of a long life. He was a simple man—simple in the best sense of the word—but not so sweet and childlike as he has been painted. His gentleness and rather harmless exterior were balanced by the shrewdness and spice of the practical son of a French tailor. In his last years he was a rheumatic cripple, but he continued to paint seated in a wheeled chair with his brush strapped to his hand. Frank Harris tells the story that Matisse, visiting the old master, found him at work, painting slowly and with great pain, each movement of the brush abrading his paralytic hand.

"Why do any more, master?" asked Matisse. "Why torture yourself?"

"The pain passes but the beauty remains," Renoir answered.

In 1861, a young man of twenty-two came up to Paris from a southern province with ambitions to be a painter. He was poorly equipped for Parisian life: he was underbred, ill-natured, and inhibited, with an unpleasant dialect and an ugly face. But he had the qualities of courage, patience, great humility in the presence of great art, belief in himself, and uncommonly good judgment of the merits of his contemporaries. Excessively shy, he would disguise his fears by sudden eruptions of temper; lonely and lacking in social graces, he affected a rank Bohemian swagger that betrayed his boorishness and made him a joke. He was a problem to the few painters who slowly learned to believe that there was something to him; for he was by starts over-bearing and ridiculously self-effacing, and he was entirely too free with his criticisms. He had an allowance from home, and never at any time painted to please anyone but himself. Fortunately his ideals were high.

Rejected by the Beaux Arts, he attended in desultory fashion one of the more liberal academies and copied in the Louvre. For ten years he worked but he did not seem to get anywhere. There was, however, merit in his abortive trials; he was never banal and he was a colorist by the grace of God. He tried to be a Delacroix, but he could not paint imaginary subjects; he tried the vein of Courbet and Manet and failed in both, as much from want of sympathy as from want of superficial competence. When the Salon turned him down, he naïvely appealed to the jury to reconsider its decision. Paris hurt him, but could not weaken his resolution; and every year he returned to the South to re-cover his faith and to paint landscape.

In 1867, he married a plain and rather stupid country woman who made him a good wife, letting him alone, and sitting like a graven image when he needed a model. A brave woman indeed to endure not the one but the hundred sittings he required for a portrait; and to put up with those misshapen masks which he slowly fashioned from her homely face! During the Franco-Prussian War he evaded military serv-ice and went on painting. Led into the study of natural light by Pis-sarro, and encouraged by Renoir, he exhibited with the Impressionists in 1873, and again in 1877. From all the exhibitors he was singled out for the worst drubbing; and to make matters more painful, as he rose above Impressionism, his friends held no very high opinion of his efforts. He went back to the farm and thereafter was seldom heard of in Paris. Returning to the Capital in 1889, he allowed Tanguy, the benevolent old color-man, to show some of his canvases and to offer them for sale. The prices ranged from 40 to 100 francs, according to size, but even at that price no one would take a risk, neither dealer nor collector.

In 1895, the dealer Vollard exhibited a number of his pictures, but nothing happened save a titter of scorn from the artists and a few published gibes from the gentlemen of the press. In 1899, he retired permanently to his estate in the South. In that year, and in 1901 and 1902, he exhibited with the Independents, but recognition came too late to do him any good. "He was sick of Paris," he said, "and the whole damned art racket." In his last years he painted alone in his studio or in the open air, growing more nervous and exacting, destroying can-vases, throwing them out of the window, abandoning them in the fields, and giving them to the peasants who smiled behind his back and called him a crackpot, or worse, meaning an artist, but who could not refuse the favors of a man of property. He died in 1906 from a fever con-tracted while painting in the rain. Such in brief was the life of the man who set the world of art on fire.

RENOIR: *Bather*

I was about to repeat the asseveration of the Modernists that Cézanne is the most influential painter of the last hundred years, but historical facts restrain me. There is Delacroix to be reckoned with; the world is littered with Impressionist pictures which owe their existence to Monet; the Manet tradition, commercialized by Sargent, has produced legions of shoddy portraitists; and the influence of French academics like Gérôme and Bouguereau is beyond calculation. But it is not presumptuous to say that on the present generation of painters in Europe and America the influence of Cézanne predominates. Looking back on the condition of French art at the close of the century, one would have said that Daumier, by his practical stand against Impressionism and by his dramatic attack on the fundamental malignities of the human race, was the rightful prophet of the new age. But Daumier, being primarily a cartoonist, was not eligible to a seat in the sacred temple erected by the gilded fanatics of High Art. Such praise as he has received in the present post-Cézanne period has been the trifling recognition of his cubic structure expressed in the rigmarole of pure esthetics. Cézanne, in his fumbling, devious attack on nature, left the Bohemians something to play with, and the sharp-eyed playboys converted his "little sensation" into novelties and jigsaw nightmares.

Despised and slandered at every turn of his career, Cézanne, after his death, was sanctified, and for some years reigned in the world of art with the authority of an old master. So absolute was his position that artists and critics alike lost their heads in doting worship, a British jackanapes declaring that "if the greatest name in European painting is not Cézanne, it is Giotto." Today the reaction is beginning: the tendency among painters, especially those reared in the Cézanne tradition, is to challenge his authority, and to underestimate, I think, the value of his art. As an illustration of this change of heart, I need only point out that his influence on the leading American painters of today is imperceptible. The scope and character of his influence will be fully considered as we trace the course of the various Modernist cults. For

81

the present it is enough to look into the nature of his aspirations and achievements.

To the general public Cézanne is still something of an enigma—volubly accepted in many quarters, suspect in others—and among painters trained in the academies he is regarded as a bungler and a sham pushed into prominence by one of the most aggressive uprisings in the history of art. This strange situation calls for comment. The case of Cézanne is incontestable proof of the total estrangement of the modern artist from the public. When the work of a contemporary painter cannot speak for itself; when it is inaccessible save through chambers of metaphysical horrors; when it has to be fed forcibly, like medicine, to a refractory public—plainly there is wrong somewhere. And the wrong is not wholly on the side of the public. Against society may be charged ignorance and misunderstanding, but to the earnest souls who have tried so hard to care for art we must accord at least a measure of forgiveness. For a long time they had been offered a cheap substitute for art and had been instructed to like it; and when, at last, they had acquired a taste for poor painting, they were suddenly presented with another brand, a form of art which seemingly bore no relation to anything they had ever encountered. And they were told in the most defiant language to like that too, or be known as morons and clodhoppers.

The painters are the most culpable—the little, unsuccessful fellows who fell back on Modernism in the same spirit that has driven our bankrupt literati into the Communist fold. In default of anything to say in their own right, they fastened upon Cézanne; erected philosophies round his imperfections; aped and exploited his most trivial things—his water-colors; devised preposterous creeds to explain away his clumsiness; restricted the significant factors in the production and appreciation of art to those whose understanding rested upon special training or unusual experience, thereby ruling the layman out of court; described minor technical processes in the terms of physiological mechanics and psychology, making the simplest exercises enormously impressive; went generally mad and shocked the bourgeoisie as they had not been shocked since Manet painted his naked demirep.

Of Cézanne's aims there can be no doubt: they were identical with the aims of the greatest masters. Awkward and incomplete in paint, he was capable, at moments, of extraordinary verbal lucidity; and he has expressed his intentions more succinctly than any of his critics. He said that he wished "to do Poussin over again from nature"; and "to make out of Impressionism something as solid and durable as the paintings of the museums," meaning the Renaissance masterpieces. In other words, he was tired of the shallowness of Impressionism—the trick-shots of Degas, the Japanese novelties, the photographing of appearances as practiced by Monet and the connoisseurs of sunlight—and he addressed himself to the problem of correcting current evils with the patience and courage of a religious martyr.

Cézanne admired, and to a certain extent understood, the "classic organization of things"—the various schemes or systems employed by the old painters to correlate their knowledge of humanity. He deplored the fact that the modern artist, when he is a thinking man and not a painting machine, is obliged to devote the better part of his life to the forging of tools—and to apologize for his labors into the bargain, whereas the old painters, as boys, had something to work with—living precedent, a point of departure, a set of expressive instruments, a method of correlation enabling them to proceed immediately to the business of adapting and modifying established procedure to the needs and situations of their own time. Cézanne admired Poussin's organizing ability and his laudable ambition to recover the classic style; but his admiration did not prevent him from recognizing the lifelessness and immobility of the old Frenchman's pictures. Wiser than his disciples, Cézanne well knew that a painting may be a perfect architectural unit and yet be dead and academic.

Poussin loved and worshipped the classic organization of things, but was unable to separate the technique of procedure from the things affected by procedure, unable to dissociate the organization from the

83

materials under its control. That is a tough sentence and we shall have to translate it. Art is produced by the reciprocal action between experience—the self in contact with environment—and the instruments of expression. This is true even for the very limited experience which makes for whatever is good in decorative and abstract, or non-representational painting. You will have noticed that there are variations of form among the Cubists; that exponents of pure form, or structure in the abstract, like Picasso and Braque, exhibit slightly different approaches to the modern environment. With the majority of artists the making of forms is a mechanical exercise, a servile habit acquired from the imitation of the works of other men. They will never learn that true creation consists in the modification of traditional styles and methods under the pressure of living experiences. This modification, as I have said, cannot be gained by the study of processes or traditional achievements alone. It is the result of new interests and convictions which inevitably call for new instruments of expression. The technique of painting is a vastly complicated affair. No man can escape or destroy it; and no man, by an act of will, can transform himself into a savage and begin all over again. Nor can anyone recover the classic style by affecting antique subject-matter. We do not expect the artist to work miracles any more than we expect the American writer to destroy the structure of the English language and invent an entirely new idiom. But we have the right to demand that he enrich established speech by local variations.

Poussin, living in Rome among tombs and excavations, fondly imagined that he was one of the old Romans in daily converse with gods and heroes, but unfortunately the environment which had produced the classic forms had passed into oblivion. In consequence, he was left to deal, or elected to deal, with dead things. Inasmuch as the subjects he meditated—Vergilian heroes, Roman gods, nymphs and Sabine women—were vicariously experienced, that is, through the classic structures, they could only be employed academically, as scholarly facts. And scholarship of this sort has no place in creative art which, whatever its subject may be, is occupied wholly with the organization of experienced things. When knowledge is divorced from current activities, from new needs and new experiences, it becomes the tool of the historian and the archeologist. Cézanne, whose tastes and experiences were those of a French peasant, had no interest in Poussin's false gods; he hoped, by digging in Poussin's neo-classical cemetery, and by analyzing the works of Rubens and the Venetians, to build up a new and valid method, a modern organism sufficient for his own perceptions and direct contacts with life. Surely no one can complain of his ambitions, and I may again add that if art had not strayed into the byways of photography, had not been overborne by bastard issues, he would have been spared the protracted labors and discouragements which eventually laid him low.

Cézanne did not set at defiance the discoveries of the Impressionists. He approved of the light palette of the tone painters, and of their direct concern with natural subjects; for repeated failures had convinced him that he could not construct imaginary situations. But instead of confining himself to the analysis of the appearances of things, he set out to achieve the monumental in a modern language of glowing, vibrating tones; to reveal and compose forms in their material and rhythmical aspects by the juxtaposition of colors; to retain the local color of an object and to harmonize it with the various influences of light and shade tending to destroy it; to work out, in each instance, a scale of tones expressing the mass and character of the form. Thus he slowly evolved a technique of agonizing complexity. He submitted objects to a series of color-divisions, his purpose being to unite form and color, an intricate business demanding rigid attention to tones and planes. To gain solidity and deep space in a scheme where darks vibrated and were as colorful as lights, he was impelled to a profound study of geometrical formation and cubic structure. From his experiments and occasional utterances arose all this talk about planes, cubes and cones, plastic form, dynamic organization and functional color; and upon his experiments in method were erected the numerous Mod-

85

ernists cults which shrieked their way into the limelight and enjoyed a brief moment of notoriety.

Cézanne's goal was reality—to make things real and true by loading them with his own perceptions and first-hand experiences, to create a full, rich, three-dimensioned world in the mass and depth of which one might undergo experiences comparable in force to those of practical life. His purpose was as rare as it was lofty; he was on the road leading to the land of the masters. But, the impatient observer will ask, is there not an appalling discrepancy between his aims and his achievements? There is indeed, and no amount of special pleading can remove his deficiencies nor distract us from the rudimentary nature of his perform-ances. In the first place, he was compelled to remake the tools of his trade, resembling, in this, a traveler who, having an important mes-sage to carry, is compelled, before setting out on his journey, to con-struct his own conveyance, or means of locomotion. The result was that the greater part of his groping labors went into technical proc-esses. Second, he was committed to a sketcher's technique. Third, he was a man of limited intelligence.

It is an open question whether the technique of Impressionism, essentially a flimsy contrivance to ensnare effects of natural light in pretty webs of complementary colors, is compatible with an art involv-ing the experiences of a thinking mind, an art envisaging a world of depth, bulk and substantial form—symbols used by imaginative paint-ers in correlating their knowledge, their emotional clashes and adven-tures, and all the basic factors of their daily lives. In my opinion it cannot. It has been tried again and again and been found wanting. The present reaction against Cézanne may be attributed to the inability of his successors to carry his art forward to a more complete expression. And let us remember that it was his incompleteness—the potentialities of further development—that won him the allegiance of the younger generation. He expanded Impressionism to its uttermost boundaries in his efforts to rival the museum masterpieces, but the best he could do was to paint almost entirely in patches; and his color-divisions, too

86

small and fragmentary to function as distinct parts of design, exhibit the planes of objects instead of their mass.

I am aware of the hundred and one theories put forth to explain the finality and indefectibility of Cézanne's art: the crooning praise of his plastic form, his functional color and his logical consistency—as if these abstract properties were the end of art; the strange descriptions of his little world as a microcosm in which every patch and particle, every distortion, plane, and indefinite contour, was preordained by the omniscient creative wisdom of God Almighty; the comparisons of his worst things—those "figure compositions" of deformed, slanting females differentiated from the other sex by the ungainly prominence of buttocks—with Raphael's *The School of Athens*. I can only account for such aberrations by mentioning once more the muddled condition of modern art: originality in painting is so rare an article that the presence of a little of it in a slow-witted French provincial is enough to cast a spell over artists and critics and to deprive them of all sense of values.

Setting aside his own confessions of failure, which his idolaters ascribe to humility and bad-temper, we have, in the pictures themselves, the most damaging evidence of his meager and unfulfilled art. Cézanne employed all the knowledge at his command to construct pictures as substantial and finished as those of his beloved masters: he was at infinite pains to establish the planes of his pictures in depth; he set objects at sharp angles, one defined against another, to trap the eye and lead it back into deep space; in modeling, or modulating, as he called it, his forms, he strove to bring the component planes into perfect relationship in order that the forms might be as solid as the mind, through all its experiences, knows them to be; to gain relief he used the device as old as Masaccio—the superimposition of forms. One cannot doubt that he was reaching for the bulk, weight, and amply dimensioned bodies of the old painters. He spoke constantly of "realization," by which he meant the complete development of his forms; not simply geometrical volumes, not crude wooden images for faces, not

87

those thick clubs standing for arms and legs, but figures carried out in full detail, convincing as masses and containing all the human implications. But he was not big enough for the job—did not know enough. On his home ground, in landscape, still-life, and his own head which he studied minutely, he came within striking distance of realization; of the human figure, of which he was practically ignorant, he made a sorry mess.

If Cézanne had been a mere decorator in the flat, a rug maker like Matisse, we should have nothing to say against him as a designer of richly tinted patterns. But no one ever pretended that he was a rug maker. We know his ambitions and we have his pictures to confirm them. We used to think of his art as strong, but we know now that it is faint, and that it seemed strong by contrast with the spineless art of the Impressionists. But knowing too the resources of painting; in possession of the thousand complex and perfect harmonies wrung from this instrument by master hands; it is not sensible to ask us to accept the tentative labors and uncertainties of a man who but rarely finished a picture as worthy of a place among the great compositions of the world. Nor is it sensible to ask us to forget what has been done, and becoming children, to revise our judgments of painting to fit the unfinished conceptions of a limited mind.

Cézanne, in part at least, remained an Impressionist. Determined to master the structure of objects, he was nevertheless dependent on knowledge gathered on the spot in a given circumstance. He had terrific concentration but little imagination. He understood that to paint without knowledge was to dabble in surface effects; but he was incapable of studying objects in all sorts of conditions and circumstances, and then, from his studies, of constructing a new form revealing, not a natural fact, but the sum-total of all his experiences and the tenor of his mental habits. I must qualify this statement. Some things he learned to know pretty thoroughly—the landscape of Aix, for example. Van Gogh, roving the landscape remarked, "I wish I knew this country as old Cézanne knows it." The remark is significant in that it indicates the distinction between the superficial records of the Impressionist, or camera eye, and the accumulated knowledge of the thinking artist. In landscape, and in still-life, which he observed with an intensity that has never been equaled, Cézanne exhibits profound knowledge of the anatomy of natural forms. But even his pictures of hills and fruit and flowers impress us as raw studies in structure, as solutions, or attempted solutions, of the technical problems of modeling and composition. The man's intelligence was narrow and inflexible.

The creation of a new vehicle of expression is not simply a laboratory experiment in trial and error; in last analysis, it is the force and depth of an artist's experiences which break old molds and arouse him to the making of new things. Cézanne was pathetically lacking in knowledge of the implications of things, the representational attributes which fix a work in time and place by revealing racial traits, historical tendencies, environmental peculiarities, and individual opinions. This is essentially the human or symbolical element of art, the enduring emotional content with its various meanings and its unlimited capacity to induce feelings of pity and terror, joy, pathos and tragedy. He learned to his everlasting torment that the museum masterpieces were the fruit of a much greater knowledge than he could ever acquire: a knowledge of mankind, of the ways and habits of people, the character of events and the significance of action. He attempted to gain such knowledge by regarding human models as pieces of still-life, by isolated studies as concentrated as they were mortifying.

Cézanne was incredibly timid, bound to a narrow routine, out of joint with life. He had an erotic passion for the nude, and his lifelong desire was to pose a nude woman in the open air. He never did; nor did he paint more than two or three in his studio. He was afraid. He was afraid of women and afraid of life. As a result, he withdrew to the vegetable kingdom, transferring his secret passions to inanimate forms. It is no wonder that his studies in still-life are his strongest and most satisfying, his most complete and dramatic contributions to modern painting.

The influence of Cézanne, his limitations notwithstanding, has been nothing short of enormous. He brought back into art at the proper moment, at a time when painters were preoccupied with appearances of nature and the transitory effects of light and shade, two indispensable factors: first, the necessity for knowledge, the *knowing* of things, their structure, density, and mass—all their material qualities; second, the necessity for correlation, that is, for formal order, for conscious planning, for a scheme of relationships by means of which forms may be brought together in a rhythmical unit. His influence then has been purely instrumental, and can only be measured by its effectualness as a foundation for or inspiration to further discovery and invention in the unceasing evolution of what artists call "types of form." Its immediate result was to plunge artists headlong into the consideration of problems of structure and organization. But instrumental knowledge, unless vitalized by human experiences and social relationships, leads to sterile intellectualism and abstractions. Thus it came about that the pioneering work of Cézanne was snapped up by rabid little Bohemians who not only ignored but denied the representational, or human element of art, and, posing as intellectuals, swiftly reduced the art of painting to bleak abstractions and the manipulation of particles of dead matter.

In all enduring art, I need hardly say, the two characteristics—the formal or instrumental, and the emotional or human, are inseparably united. Happily, artists are at last waking up to this elementary fact; and today, after some thirty years of experimentation, some of which has been healthy and instructive, some vagrant and silly, painters everywhere, especially in America, are turning from "pure form" and "abstract organization" to the study of social and economic conditions. When the proper balance between instrumental and social knowledge has been struck, we may hope for a new orientation of painting.

Before Cézanne's art was butchered by the Cubists, two men appeared, Van Gogh and Gauguin, who are interesting as intermediaries between Cézanne and the present Ecole de Paris, and as examples of the fanaticism into which the artist is frequently driven by modern society.

VAN GOGH: *Self Portrait*

FROM THE CHESTER DALE COLLECTION

4

VAN GOGH

THERE was the town with straight narrow streets and rows of little houses, all clean and bright; then the farmhouse and fruit trees leading back into flat meadows; and further on, the dunes, and dismal canals moving slowly to the sea. The wind chased black clouds across the low wide sky, and swept the steaming meadows where fat cattle were lying down by pools of fresh water. The plastered farmhouse, with its sagging roof and dark green shutters, was old and mossy, but the hedges enclosing it, the berry bushes and gardens, were trim and flourishing, and the flower beds in full bloom. The house was the rectory of Pastor Van Gogh.

In the front garden a brood of young Van Goghs were playing in the afternoon sun. They played together happily, shouting and laughing, but at intervals they stopped of one accord, and led by Theo, a boy of thirteen, ran to the outside hedge and looked down the highway. They were waiting for Vincent to come home. Vincent's school days were over and he was returning to his father's house. He was born lonely, but born with great affection in his heart, and the two opposites had already filled him with aches and pains. His life in the boarding school of a neighboring town had been miserable and hard, but he had not complained—he was a boy of incredible courage and forbearance, fearing no one, regretting nothing. He wanted most of all to play, but he never played. His vehement enthusiasm and his outbursts of uncouth affection were really terrifying and boys shrank from him as from a savage beast.

His appearance also was against him. I doubt if nature in her most audacious moods had ever before planted so unselfish a spirit and so many heroic impulses in such a repugnant carcase. It was a tragic experiment from the beginning. Cézanne was as homely as they come, but harmless looking; the face of Vincent Van Gogh was a thing to turn one's soul—it was gruesome and holy, the composite of peasant, convict, and Christ. His angular, mattoid skull was crowned with short red hair; his nose was huge, his mouth fierce and set like a trap; his cheek-bones stuck out, and his greenish eyes, deep-sunken beneath enormous brows, stared at the world, now with the gentle blankness of an infant, now with the ghastly brilliance of a religious lunatic. Vincent was innocent and untidy, and hungry for human companionship; but no one would suffer him—no one but his brother Theo—and the boarding school was a painful experience. Here he read deeply but indiscriminately, for he was destitute of critical sense; and here he collected plants and insects, lavishing upon nature the abnormal affection which he would gladly have given his fellows.

At night in his dreary cubicle, after a debauch of books, he lay awake, thinking of home and Theo. He was extraordinarily impressionable, and his visual powers were nothing less than phenomenal. His mind was a repository of images, each crystal clear, but the whole an untidy jumble without sequence or connection. Things trooped before him in the dark, clear and sharp like living presences. He saw the town with its straight narrow streets and the pollard willows in the old Dutch meadows; he saw the little house with its dark green shutters, and every room in the house; every plant in the garden, marigolds, mignonettes, and rows of dried pea-vines; the clothes-lines hung with snow-white linen, the fields of rye, the neighbors, the church, and even the jackdaw's nest in the tall acacia tree in the cemetery. He saw his mother at the window; and his father, a good man in a small way, but living in deadly reserve and constant fear lest an incautious word or misunderstood smile should convict him of sin in the eyes of his Lutheran flock. And he saw Theo at the gate, ready to shake his hand—dear Theo who answered his long letters and always welcomed him home.

Vincent walked along the road toward the rectory. He looked old for a boy: his eyes were sad, and there were lines in his brow, and he walked like an old man, stooping over, his head bowed. Passing the houses of his father's parishioners, he saw women and children grinning and tittering at him from behind the curtains. "Why did people laugh like that, and mock him behind his back?" he wondered. "People hadn't much love for one another in this world." Vincent was coming home! The young Van Goghs ran forth to meet him. He kissed his sister, pushed her gently aside, and shook Theo's hand. The brothers were silent, but as Vincent tried to speak, the door opened and he saw his mother and father approaching. The scene was too much for him, and without a word he turned from the family and fled, running through the orchard and across the meadows to the dunes where he remained alone in the wind and sun until he had got his feelings under control.

The boy was not only a problem but an object of humiliation and shame, and Pastor Van Gogh decided at once that he should be put to work. Vincent had no objections; anything would be all right—he was not afraid of work. Had he not advised Theo that "the first duty of man is not to be happy but to be honest"? Unduly religious, he would gladly have entered the Church, but he was so ugly and awkward and inarticulate before men that he doubted his ability as a preacher. Psychoanalysts, who know all about the workings of exceptional minds, have told us that Vincent had an inferiority complex. Perhaps, but if he was so afflicted, then Christ too had an inferiority complex. The two had much in common.

In the autumn of 1869, at the age of sixteen, he went to the Hague to become an assistant in a branch of the famous Goupil Galleries of Paris. The post, an important one for a poor rustic, had been obtained through the influence of his uncle, the manager of the gallery. Vincent was industrious and intelligent, and having no taste in pictures, a model salesman. He entered upon his duties with the same inflammable convictions that had driven him to the collecting of insects, and more recently, to the literal acceptance of Christianity. Before this he had never thought of pictures; nor had he, like most boys destined to be artists, made sketches

93

and filled his copy-books with drawings. But now, all of a sudden, he recognized the nobility of art, and saw, with the clairvoyance of a fanatic, the inseparability of art and religion. Naturally, then, he turned to pictures which seemed to him to bind mankind together with the sentiment of universal love: to Rembrandt, but also to Breton; to Corot, but also to the poorest members of the Barbizon school; to Millet, and the lowly painters of Dutch genre. However maundering and commonplace the sentiment of the picture, he filled it to overflowing with the philanthropy of his own soul—and the Dutch burghers were persuaded to buy.

At the end of four years he had acquitted himself so honorably that he was promoted to the London branch of the firm in Bond Street. A year of happiness awaited him. After the custom of the more estimable clerks of the day, he wore a top hat and morning coat; and with the full confidence of his chiefs, was a thoroughly contented and successful young man. "This is a fine business," he said. He smoked his pipe and read poetry, and wrote gushing letters to Theo in praise of Constable and Turner—and the paint-sick Pre-Raphaelites. He was acknowledged to be the best man in the gallery; his salary was raised, and he sent money home. Pastor Van Gogh was delighted—blessed are they which do hunger and thirst after righteousness. Then the whole thing went to smash.

His landlady had a daughter named Ursula who kept a shop in the suburbs where she sold dolls and took care of children in a small kindergarten. Vincent fell in love with Ursula. He thought that she was the most beautiful girl in all the world; he worshiped the ground she walked on, her name, her children; and called her, privately, the Angel of the Dolls. After months of repressions he finally got up the nerve to declare his passion. The angel was outraged and coldly British. Fancy marrying that ugly mug! When she informed him that she was engaged to another, he grew more importunate, begging her to break her pledge. She laughed in his face, and ordered him to be off about his business— and the laughter nearly killed him. He did not blame Ursula, did not reproach nor hate her, but he could not understand that love sometimes

must be wasted and unreturned. He gave himself over to mystical speculations, and his years of sober industry ended in bitterness and ruin. At
the gallery he was arrogant, quarrelsome and ridiculously pious; and, as
one suddenly beholding a great light, he exclaimed, "Art is made for
the glory of God, but dealing in art is a form of organized cheating!" His
superiors, taking into account his excellent record, transferred him to
Paris in the hope that he might cool off and recover his balance.

In Paris Vincent sank to the lowest depths of despair. He lived in
Montmartre but the peaceful, picturesque life of the Butte could not
divert his ardors. At the gallery, instead of trying to sell pictures, he
talked religion to Goupil's smart clientele, pouring out, in bad French,
a flood of unintelligible philosophies on the brotherhood of man and
the sublime artistry of the Son of Man. At night, in his loneliness, he
smoked incessantly and read the Bible. He also read Longfellow, Harriet
Beecher Stowe, and Eschylus; Renan, Michelet, Heine, and Hans Christian Andersen. Next to the Bible he loved Dickens and Zola. He was
struggling to find a way into his true vocation which, he warned his
father, was that of "a fisher of men." But he remembered that honesty
was the first duty, and accordingly, sent in his resignation to Monsieur
Goupil. Pastor Van Gogh was furious and rushed over to Paris to dis-
suade his incorrigible son. A preacher himself, he was afraid of his son's
practical notions of Christianity. But it was no use—Vincent had made
up his mind. He was determined to pay for his theological studies by
teaching; in fact he had already applied for a post in an English school
and had received a favorable answer.

In the spring of 1876, in his twenty-fourth year, he returned to
London, this time as teacher of French to a class of twenty young hood-
lums in the East End. For a while all went well: he was a poor teacher,
but he kept his pupils interested by telling them stories of Holland.
Then a longing to see Ursula obsessed him, and he hunted her out, only
to find that she was married and her door closed against him forever. He
threw up his teaching job, and prayed for guidance, and was immensely
comforted when a Methodist minister offered him employment as a sort

of chaplain and charity worker in the slums of Whitechapel. His new
duties brought him into direct contact with the terrible poverty that
Dickens had described so trenchantly, and affected him so profoundly
that he felt, for the first time, the need of expressing himself in pictures.
To his innumerable letters to his brother—letters which were in themselves vividly, and sometimes brilliantly, pictorial—he appended drawings as supplementary descriptions. His first efforts with the pencil were
not intended as exhibitions of skill; indeed they were utterly wanting in
skill—they were poor, childish, labored things, but not without signs
of a strange and sensitive vision. Theo, now in the service of Goupil,
was overjoyed. He had long suspected the artist in Vincent, and urged
him to study painting. But art was not yet to claim him.

His work in London barely paid him enough to live on, and one day
in the Christmas season, without notice, he turned up at Etten, the new
parish of his father. He was ragged and broke, but his spirit was on fire.
Have you ever gone out into the world as a youth, with hope in your
heart and your mind colored with dreams of mighty accomplishments?
And have you returned home, beggared and ignominious, with nothing
to show for your foolhardy flight, to face a weeping mother and the
awful glances of a father who wishes you had never been born? It is an
ordeal—and no mistake—but Vincent bore it beautifully. He was a
beggar in Christ. He said good-bye, as if nothing had happened, and went
to Amsterdam to prepare himself for the ministry.

A long-suffering uncle gave him lodging, and with the fortitude of a
dozen saints he plunged into a seven-year course in theology. For fifteen
months he stuck it out, denying himself all worldly compensations,
stuffing himself with dogmas, syllogisms, and scholastic rot. "Taking
lessons in Greek," he wrote his brother, "in the heart of the Jewish
quarter in Amsterdam on a very hot summer afternoon, with the dread
of many difficult examinations before very learned and wily professors,
is quite different from a walk in the fields of Brabant, which must be
beautiful just now—but I am fighting for my life." He was always fighting for his life.

The strain told and his nervous system collapsed. "I had hoped to get closer to Christ," he cried, "but what has all this to do with the Gospels? This bargaining in divinity—it is worse than bargaining in art! The curse of God on all your stinking subtleties!" His mind lost its moorings, and he was found on the outskirts of the city preaching to soldiers and peasants. In a calmer mood, he turned to Rembrandt and Bruegel for nourishment and sketched a little. But when Theo pressed him to continue his drawing, he replied that, "it might keep me from my real work, and it is better perhaps not to begin this sort of thing. When I got home I started a sermon on the barren fig tree. Luke XII; 1-9." And then he added, for there was a streak of fun in him, "The symbol of St. Luke, the patron saint of painters, you know, is the ox."

If he had failed in his plans for ordination, he had not surrendered his convictions. He would be a lay-preacher, or missionary, and in the summer of 1878, he put his Christianity to a practical test. He had read of the sufferings of the coal miners in the Borinage, near Mons, and armed with the authority of the Society for Evangelization, of Brussels, departed for the black country. Conditions among the miners were insufferable, and with his appalling love for humanity, he set out to remedy them. Vincent won the hearts of the miners, not by preaching, but by good works. They were a rough, illiterate lot, but they were real, and they believed in him. He took care of the sick, nursed the injured at the infirmaries, taught the children to read, comforted the old and helpless. And that he might live as meanly as the worst of them, he gave away his money, his blankets and his clothes; and lodged in an old floorless hut, sleeping on a bag of straw. He was happy; but the hypocrites at Brussels heard of his scandalous conduct and revoked his authority. They said that he was cheapening his calling, that he had no dignity. "Whoever told you I had any dignity?" Vincent retorted.

They might remove his authority, but they could not drive him out. He remained in his black hole, and his family gave him up for lost. Even Theo's faith was shaken. "You ask me why I didn't stay at the University," he replied to his brother. "I can only answer that I prefer to die a natural death than to prepare for it at a University. When you have attended the free lectures of the College of Misery, you will reap a firm faith, and learn more than you can express in words. Many a man has a bonfire in his heart and nobody comes to warm himself at it. The passers-by notice only a little smoke from the chimney, and go their way. I am drawn more and more to the conclusion that to love much is the best means of approaching God. I am trying to save my soul. I love these poor miners. Disdaining marble, clay and color, I work in living flesh and blood, as did Christ, the greatest of all artists."

Vincent reaped the faith that he could not express in words, but the free lessons in misery multiplied daily, and pressed him into the service of art. It was a decisive step—one that took all his courage. He was twenty-seven years old, none too strong physically, and in technical matters, an untutored child. He went to work, slowly and methodically— it was serious business now. If he should fail, it would be the end of him. He had premonitions of an early death, and he must reach the house of art before nightfall. He began by copying prints after Rembrandt, Millet and the moping Dutchmen of his day; he spent his last pennies for a worthless treatise on charcoal drawing; he sketched unceasingly from nature. The second winter of his life among the miners was the coldest ever known, and he was reduced to vagabondage. He roamed the country, sleeping in barns, begging his bread, but always sketching. He made studies of landscape and of coal diggers—dirty men wielding pickaxes and shovels; women in black kerchiefs, old and ugly. Having gone forward a little, he thought it would be a good idea to take his drawings to Jules Breton, whom he regarded as a great master, for criticism. After eight days of tramping, he arrived at his destination, hungry and foot-sore. But the sight of Breton's studio, a handsome new structure of shiny red brick, disheartened him, and he went back to the miners.

He encountered technical difficulties which he could not conquer alone, and began to feel the need of the companionship of artists. There was an academy in Brussels, a famous place, where, it was said one might learn to draw and paint in the most approved style. He wanted to go there, but he had no money, and a diet of chestnuts had weakened his stomach. His brother, the most promising assistant in the Goupil's of Paris, financed the journey, and bought him a decent suit of clothes. Henceforth he was entirely dependent on Theo for support. "Dear Theo," he wrote in gratitude, "I have hopes that my thorn tree will flower with white blossom in due time, and that these seemingly sterile contests are only the sorrows of fruition."

The thorn tree flowered slowly. The famous academy was not for Vincent. With that strange mind of his, sometimes so muddled, again so illuminating, he penetrated at once to the basic evils of the academic system. In all Europe, he observed, there was not a single school where one could learn to paint a man digging, or sowing seed, a woman hanging a pot over a fire or doing needle-work; but in every insignificant town there was an academy with a whole selection of models for historical, Arabian, and, in short, all kinds of figures which did not exist in the everyday world. He visited the museum, but the old Italians, in spite of their religious subject-matter, did not please him. "The figures in the old masters," he said, "are all idle. They never work. I want my peasants to be peasants, my beggars to beg. I don't want them to stand there like imitation saints, or ideal images, too proud to soil their hands." He learned the rudiments of perspective from an artist poorer than himself, borrowed books on anatomy, light and shade, and design, and studied day and night. He went into the streets and the fields for his models, his aim being to depict a real workman, his clothes, his expression and his soul. Daumier had the right idea—he did not pose models—he caught men and women in their routine occupations.

Vincent worked hard that winter, and under trying circumstances. The immeasurable discrepancy between the objective fact—the drawing —and the sentiment informing it, saddened him but could not weaken his purpose. Heretofore he had not looked at pictures as an artist looks at them, with an eye to their structure and the solution of technical problems; it was the subject-matter that had drawn him to Rembrandt and Millet, and those humanitarian motives which, he was convinced, were the springs of all art. Now he was an artist in the making—he must improvise a structure for his own unbridled imaginings. The first results were pitiful in the extreme; infantile; to tell the truth, and enough to daunt the hardiest of men. No other artist destined to such original utterances was ever so unpromising in his first efforts. But he pegged away, and at the completion of each drawing, consoled himself in the thought that he was slowly going ahead. Theo sent him money regularly, but the allowance, while sufficient to keep him alive, left nothing for clothes and materials; and during most of the winter he was ragged and underfed.

In the spring he returned to Etten to visit his parents. No fatted calf was slain for the outlandish tramp with a new passion in his breast. Vincent was home again, the unlovely son, darkening the family hearth, deliberately going from bad to worse, from steady employment to vagrant preaching, from evangelism to a vocation for which he had no qualifications. The parishioners gossiped and whispered insinuations to Pastor Van Gogh. Vincent was unrepentant but amiable, and with proper food and a real bed to sleep in—the first since his top hat days in London—was soon in fine fettle. He rigged up a studio in the barn, smoked his pipe, and worked ten hours a day at his art. Theo came home for a holiday, and remarking his brother's steadiness and abounding enthusiasm, made his visit the occasion for general forgiveness and rejoicing. The pastor was relieved, and hearing that his stubborn offspring might conceivably grow into an artist, actually charitable. There was money in art—that is, if one painted nice, marcel-waved sheep like Cousin Anton Mauve. Vincent laughed boisterously—the world was looking up.

The Pastor's niece, a prim widow and mother of a small child, came to stop with the family. Vincent's starved emotions fluttered incontinently. He accompanied the widow on long walks in the country, played with the child, made himself agreeable, and held himself together. But not for long. All too soon he idealized the woman, fell in love with her, and asked her to be his wife. The affair was almost the exact repetition of his experience with the Angel of the Dolls: the widow refused him peremptorily, but he would not take no for an answer—he would wait until she came to her senses. She fled to her home in Amsterdam; he pestered her with infatuate letters, and getting no response, followed her to her father's house. She told him to get out of her sight, that he disgusted her and would always disgust her, that he was a presumptuous fool and a churl.

Once more he concluded that God's purpose had somehow gone wrong. The blow deranged him, but fortunately, he now had his art to comfort him, and he retired sadly to his barn to draw pictures. But he found, on his return to Etten, that the little town was a pig-sty of scandal. The Pastor's shiftless son was not only a mad loafer, but since the escapade with the widow, a seducer posing under the name of artist. That misbegotten idiot an artist! He was a menace to public morals! His father and mother turned upon him with the bitterness of back-yard crusaders, and Vincent, hot and overwrought, answered his accusers in loud hysterical language. "I have had enough," he cried, "of your bourgeois religion. Your cheap, cheese-paring Christianity! You are sour-bellied hypocrites, all of you! I am through with your church business forever! If this is what you call religion, I wash my hands of it—I will now follow the decent gospel of art." Having thus delivered himself, he lit out for the Hague.

Old Mauve, the smug purveyor of studio sheep, received him kindly for the sake of the family, and gave him his first lessons in oil painting. Vincent was thankful and obedient, religiously copying flowers and old shoes, and trying to get the hang of a new medium. The association prospered until Mauve, having decided that his pupil was an ignoramus, ordered him to draw from casts. The pupil thought differently about it, and promptly smashed the casts to pieces. "You are not only ignorant," howled the old ram, "you are vicious." Vincent laughed gruffly and went on his way.

Back again in his garret in the suburbs of the Hague, he sat at his easel alone. "I want to paint humanity," he wrote to Theo, "and again humanity." But humanity, apparently, would not come to terms with

him, and he was seized with a desperate loneliness. Privation he had
endured and could endure again, but man, he reflected, especially the
artist, was not meant to live alone. He longed for a wife and children—
"the white blossoms of matrimony"—but there was no woman anywhere, he had had reason to believe, willing to tolerate him. At a public
soup-house he fell in with a prostitute who was good to him, but who
deserted him the moment she discovered that his intentions were serious.
He visited the brothels seeking companionship, hoping that he might
find a woman as miserable as himself, one whom he might lead to a better
life. Sometimes the girls were kind; more often they snickered at his
notions of regeneration.

One evening, in a bar-room, Vincent met a woman as miserable as
himself. For a small consideration she consented to be his model, and he
took her to his garret. She was a low creature in the last stages of drunken-
ness and destitution: dirty, pock-marked, foul-mouthed, mother of one
child and pregnant with another. The prospect aroused his finest compassion and revived his dreams of an ecstatic married life. This diseased biped was the symbol of his own hapless struggles, his spiritual
sister, his angel of sorrow. They would climb the golden stairs together.
He made a drawing of the fallen one, a drooling, naked woman in profile,
which he called *Sorrow*, and beneath the maudlin image he inscribed
these words from Michelet: "How is it that there is in the world a woman
alone and deserted?"

It is not recorded that his tippling consort repaid him in any shape or
form for his tenderness and self-sacrifices, but it may be truthfully said
in her behalf that she lived with him on a basis of equality, pretending to
no false pieties, and that, in some strange manner, she solicited his purest
devotion. Vincent planned to marry her as soon as he had saved a little
money, but she stole his savings and got drunk. The birth of her child
involved an operation which he paid for out of money set aside for food
and paint. "How can I call her bad," he wrote to Theo, "when she has
never known goodness?" Theo increased his allowance and hoped for
the best. Vincent installed a cradle in his studio, bathed the baby when

the mother was tight, and cared for it as if it had been his own child—all the while trying to paint. The ménage lasted twenty months and might have been the death of him, had not his brother arrived on the scene. Theo found Vincent ragged and broken in health—starving himself for the sake of humanity—and on the verge of another nervous fit.

"I confess freely, brother," Vincent said, "that I am not good according to the standards of the professional moralists; like them, indeed, I condemn the dissolute, but I feel true humanity in the dissolute in spite of everything, and this keeps me from having any scruples in holding intercourse with them."

"Never mind that," answered Theo. "You're going home now to get well and to do your work."

Vincent consented—perhaps it would be better for the woman if he left her. "Good-bye," he said to her. "I don't suppose that you will be able to go straight, but be as honest as you can. I'll try to be as straight as I can myself—but I know that I shall never go through life as I should like. Even if you are only a poor woman and a prostitute, as long as you act so that your children will find a real mother in you, you will be good in my eyes. I must work hard and so must you."

The woman went back to the brothel.

Vincent spent the next two years in the province of Brabant. His parents had moved to Nuenen, a village in the weavers' district, but he contrived to keep away from them as much as possible: his unseemly behavior made him, as before, an unwelcome guest, and he had no will to hurt them. He roamed the moors, painting peasants; sketched the weavers at their looms; and worked in his studio, a room in the house of a Catholic priest. His sojourn in Brabant is memorable for two events— his last venture in love, and his first picture of importance. Love, this time, came to him. The woman was much older than himself, not very personable, a little off, and given to spells of mystic swooning. She saw a kindred soul in Vincent, and he reciprocated valiantly. They were happy, for a moment, in their spiritual delirium; but her parents intervened and hustled her away, complaining that he "awakened her dead melancholy." The woman took strychnine, and Vincent killed his sorrow in overwork. He painted *The Potato Eaters*, a group of peasants at their evening meal, a remarkable picture right from the heart of rustic life, and smelling, as he said, of dirty potatoes. This sooty monochrome, besides being the summary and the culmination of his work as a peasant painter of the Dutch school, marks the beginning of a style which was soon to develop brilliantly, and in the few years remaining to him, to make him one of the most original of modern painters.

The wandering fever was upon him, and he decided to go to Antwerp to see the museums, and to have another try at an art school. His father was dead; he said good-bye to his mother and sisters—and they never saw him again. In Antwerp he created a riot among the students—a wild man indeed with sad blue eyes, cropped red hair and a red, straggly beard. He came into the classroom smoking his pipe and wearing the fur cap and blue smock of a cattleman; he used an old box for a palette and astonished teachers and pupils alike by his insane rapidity of execution. They were painting from a cast of the Venus of Milo, and Vincent endowed the goddess with the capacious hips of a Dutch matron. His instructor objected, and taking a brush, pared down the hips to the classical proportions. Vincent stood on his box and shrieked. "So you don't know what a woman is like! A woman must have hips, buttocks, and a pelvis that will hold a child!" They showed him the door.

He worked incessantly at the expense of his body and suffered another breakdown. The doctor told him he had symptoms of typhoid, and that he would die if he did not take better care of himself. Vincent was frightened out of his wits: he did not want to die; he was only thirty-three and he had just begun to paint. He would go at once to Paris and place himself under the protection of his brother. The next day, when Theo arrived at his office in the Goupil Gallery, he found a telegram from Vincent. "Meet me at the Rembrandt in the square room of the Louvre."

Nine years had gone by since his first visit, and Paris was strange to him, magical but over-stimulating. He was wiser now, but at bottom the same old Vincent, ungovernable, yet as gentle as a lamb, harshly self-assertive, and yet the meekest of men, always ready to listen and to learn. In one respect, however, he was a different being: the evangelist had given way to the artist, and the artist was now absorbed in mastering the instruments of his craft without which he never would have amounted to anything, for all his depth of feeling and his purity of spirit. He approached Paris cautiously, with diffidence even, conscious that he was only a self-taught novice among the most accomplished painters of the world. With the best of intentions he enrolled in one of the studios—but it was the same old story. He attracted the attention of everybody by his eagerness and naïve determination, but the academic routine revolted him, and at the end of three months he gave it up. "I still believe," he told his brother, "that in studios one learns next to nothing about painting, and certainly nothing about life, and that one should do all one can to learn to live and paint without recourse to those old fools and wiseacres."

Theo understood, and moved to a more commodious apartment in Montmartre, still a wild and rustic spot, in order that Vincent might work independently in quiet surroundings. Theo was kindness itself, the prince of good fellows, the manager of the gallery, and one of the two or three dealers hospitable to the Impressionists. He had not, as yet, the temerity to admit the new men into the main gallery, but he tactfully displayed their works in an ante-room and made them personally welcome. It was here that Vincent met Pissarro, Lautrec, Seurat and a cynical, overweening rascal named Gauguin who dominated him from the start. His immediate impressions of the groups were disquieting: they were a funny lot, always joking about art, taking nothing seriously, making sport of sacred things—Gauguin particularly, with his brutal mocking laugh, and his blasphemous cracks at Israels, Meissonier and Millet. "How can you call yourself a painter and stick up for a tin soldier, a lousy button-maker like Meissonier? Answer me that, Redhead." Vincent was bowled over with embarrassment. None the less, Gauguin became his hero, his evil genius. How wise he was! He could do anything—a man of the world! Infallibly, with a wicked stinging quip, he put everything in its proper place. The others, more charitable, soon saw that Vincent was more than Theo's unsightly dependent, that he had qualities of mind and heart that could not be acquired in Paris, and that he had it in him to go beyond any one of them. At times he bored them with the twaddling sentiments of the yokel fresh from the polder; and then again, he talked like one inspired, ineffably clear, and profound, with a far-reaching, prophetic vision, an all-encircling humanity which put their own studio concoctions to shame. And he was so guileless, so ardently disposed to be friendly, signing his pictures simply *Vincent*, as man to man, as one would say John, or Jesus.

He looked at their canvases and rubbed his eyes. What were they driving at, these manufacturers of a new ism, with their cold-blooded method, their streaks and spots of pure color, their calculated avoidance of all human complications? Loyal to his old favorites, he fought shy of the new-fangled style—his Dutchmen couldn't be wrong. But he was open-minded, and in time began to recognize the relation of his own lashing strokes borrowed from Hals, and the pastels of Millet, to the direct attack of the Impressionists. He worked slowly towards the modern style, first clearing the palette of Dutch filth, painting in soft quiet grays and half-tones, and proving to the satisfaction of Theo's friends that he was no fool. At the end of a year, to the great delight of Theo, he was an avowed Impressionist. Brilliant, vibrating color, applied in the fever of excitement, was the only way in which he could get his sensations into paint. He discovered Japanese prints and his head was in a whirl. The sharp linear draughtsmanship of the Orientals pinned him down to the consideration of design, a factor he had neglected in his mad pursuit of color, and for a while he floundered between the consciously planned silhouette and the effusive color of Monet and Pissarro. The Cézannes in old Tanguy's shop pointed the way to the reconciliation of structure and color, and helped him to build up a firmer, stronger form, to preserve his Dutch individuality in a new dress of blooming tones. In two years he had made astonishing progress and was well on the road to his glorious final period. He painted his famous *Flowers*, now in the Louvre,

VAN GOGH: *A Woman of Arles*

a fierce conjunction of frenzied sensibility, hard, wiry drawing and molten color. He painted a portrait of Tanguy, the color-man, which the artists around Montmartre pronounced stunning; and shrewd old Tanguy, who knew a good thing when he saw it, began to exhibit his pictures, and to hold on to the best ones in payment of debts. There were no buyers, but Vincent was confident. "As to the market value of my pictures, I should be very much surprised if, in time, they did not sell as well as other people's."

He was right, but he would, I think, have been very much surprised if he could have foreseen the day when one of his canvases should pass into the hands of an American collector for $85,000. That was the irony of it: he painted for humanity, for the homes of Tolstoy's disciples—and his pictures were gobbled up by dealers and hoarded by rich esthetes.

But he was not, by nature, a city-dweller, and Paris was wearing him out. He was losing himself in an atmosphere of big talk, glib theorizing, and professional romanticism. He longed to return to the moors of Holland, to live again among simple people, and to work out his salvation in solitude. His buoyancy changed to surliness; his frankness to arrogance. He delivered moral lectures to Toulouse-Lautrec; and meditated on a universal brotherhood of artists, a fantastic scheme whereby painters might pool their pictures, sell them like hot cakes, grow prosperous and make the world happy forever and ever. He wanted Theo to resign his job and organize the brotherhood, but when Theo declined, pointing out the loss of bread and butter to both, he flew into a passion. He spoke of going away and Theo did not discourage him. But he did not go.

"The house becomes almost uninhabitable," Theo wrote to his mother. "I hope that it will not be long before he departs. He himself broached the subject not long ago, but as I agreed with him, he deliberately takes no further steps. There are two different beings in him, one gifted, sensitive and sweet, the other insensible and harsh. There is no doubt that he is his own worst enemy; it is not only the lives of others, but his own, that he makes intolerable."

Another winter came on and Vincent lapsed into melancholy. He was in wretched health; the years of starvation in Holland had drained his vitality, and chronic drinking in Paris had not helped matters. His friends were alarmed. Lautrec advised him to pull up stakes and go down to Provence, tempting him with a graphic account of the sun and color of the South. Theo, who was engaged to be married and eager to bring his bride to the apartment, pledged more money. Finally, Vincent came to his senses.

"Theo," he said with overflowing humility, "I must start all over again; I must go down into the earth, naked, once more—only for three or four years—that's all I have, but one more effort I must make. Somewhere, beneath an open sky, I must find it at last. There is wind down there which I long for. I must feel it on my skin—and the warm sun, and the sweet smell of the ploughed field. In Paris I have lost my sense for the wind altogether, in fact I am losing my very skin by degrees."

The two brothers went out to a Wagnerian concert, and the next day Vincent scrubbed the studio, tidied up, nailed his canvases to the walls, and set out for the South, leaving an affectionate note of farewell.

The South was white with snow, but spring came suddenly, the wind blew warm and strong, and the valley was filled with the voice of running water. It was a rich country, ancient and cultivated, the long slopes shining with the green and silver of olives, the roads lined with plane trees, and the red uplands planted in vine. There were wild, barren stretches, ravines piled with rocks, and tall cypresses on the hill-tops; and in the background mountains washed with purple. And woven into all things, shining down from a sky of green and blue, was the sun. Vincent was intoxicated, a pilgrim arrived in the promised land. "Behold the kingdom of light!" he wrote to Theo. "How wonderful is the golden sun! How lovely the yellow corn and the sunflower!" His letters were shrieks of exaltation.

He lived in a little hotel in the town of Arles and was soon a public character. He painted with stupefying rapidity, ten canvases at once—flowers, landscape, and such local folk as were not ashamed to sit to him. The last dead grays, the heritage of his Dutch period, disappeared, and along with them the tentative half-tones of Montmartre. His pictures were painted in fury and signed with fire. "I paint scenes of monstrous gaiety," he cried, "lashing the canvas with irregular strokes and letting them stand—and they are irritating to people with preconceived notions of technique." He painted straight from nature, but treated the color in an arbitrary fashion. "The important part," he explained, "is the wilful heightening of the color scheme. Blonde hair is raised to orange, then to chrome, or even pale lemon color. Then the stupid wall behind the head is taken away and a simple background of rich blue extends to infinity. And with a simple combination of two rich colors it is possible to give luminosity to a head, as mysterious as a star in the azure sky." He painted those immortal sunflowers, their faces of greenish gold against a yellow ground, bringing into dizzy harmony colors no one had ever before dared join together. He staked everything on the first impassioned attack, win or lose, and his pictures became symbols of the flaming combustion going on within him, the collision of an abnormally sensitive mind with the most powerful stimuli of light, color, and living forms.

Vincent worked mostly in the country, not from choice, but because the people of the town, save and except his landlady, and the old postman and his wife, set him down as a freak to be avoided. If he had painted prettily, he said, like Bouguereau, people would not have been ashamed to let themselves be painted, but they laughed at his portraits, thinking them "badly done"—"only pictures full of painting." "Nevertheless," he wrote, "they soak me for food and clothes and materials, because I am an artist." He journeyed to Marseilles to see the bull-fights and found the arena superb when crammed full of men and sunshine; he talked with "heart-broken Christians with large beautiful eyes like old cab horses"; he saw dear narrow old women, like his mother. He loved the people of Arles, despite their hostility. He loved them all, from the babies in long clothes to the old women with faces like dusty blades of grass; from the women with black hair and white skin to those with golden hair and brick-red, sunburnt faces.

He saw shy little Arlésiennes going to their first communion, and the priest in his surplice, who looked like a dangerous rhinoceros. He saw "a very quiet and lovely thing, a girl with a coffee-tinted skin, ash blonde hair, gray eyes, a print bodice of pale rose under which the breasts were visible, shapely, firm and small. This against the emerald leaves of some fig trees. A girl as simple as the fields—every line of her virgin." He hoped to get her to pose in the open air, but she earned a few pennies by going gay, and had something better to do.

Such frenetic concentration could not last, and by the end of the summer he gave signs of exhaustion. Loneliness haunted him, and he tried the three-franc brothel, only to afford the girls a new form of entertainment. They giggled and joked and called him the nutty red-head. In a letter to Theo, he diagnosed with remarkable insight the ills of the artist. The modern painter lived too much the life of art which, do not fool yourself, was not the real life, and in consequence suffered from a neurosis that grew worse from generation to generation. But he did not lose courage, and though tormented by insomnia and toothache, continued to paint as one in a trance. Banknotes came punctually from Theo, but he was a poor manager, and always in debt. To clear himself, he cut down his rations, subsisting on ship biscuit and coffee for days at a time. Theo too was ill and dispirited, and this time it was Vincent's turn to play the comforter. "O Theo, if you suffer because you think you have no power of creative work, how much more should I be unhappy, for I can do nothing without your help! Smoke your pipe in peace, and do not fret yourself; for we accomplish together, and with less suffering, work that neither of us could achieve alone. Before another year has passed you will see our efforts crowned with victory."

To escape public curiosity he rented a little house of his own, which he proceeded at once to furnish, fussing, like a woman, over beds and curtains. The move cost him more than he had figured on, and poor Theo had to divide a legacy from his uncle to foot the bills. Vincent repaid him in pictures that would not sell. He felt snug again and his courage rose. "I have had the little house painted yellow," he said, "because I want it to be for everyone the House of Light." For everyone? For whom? The situation awakened his old dreams of a community of artists: he would make his house the stopping-place for painters; he would establish his brotherhood with headquarters in the South; he would begin by inviting Gauguin to share his fortune. Gauguin was in Brittany sulking in his penury, grumbling continually about his bowels, their cursed civilization, and about money. Joyfully Vincent fitted out a room and made ready to receive his guest. Gauguin had to be coaxed: he was evasive and disobliging—waiting to see exactly what there was in it for him. At last, after long negotiations—and after Theo had dug into his legacy again and sent him the money—the great man conde-scended to move, and in October, 1888, arrived in Arles.

Gauguin took possession of the place immediately, and the glory of the House of Light faded into gloom. Far from being run down, as he had described himself, he was strong as a bull, large, athletic and master-ful, with a sneering superiority that shriveled Vincent into insignifi-cance. There were quarrels and truces: Vincent was not the easiest person to live with, and Gauguin must be top dog in everything. He mentioned the financial career which he had forsaken for art—he had made 40,000 francs a year in the stock exchange—but he was very proud of that career. And he was proud of all his minor talents. Nothing pleased him, and Vincent's domestic incompetence brought roars of laughter. In a jiffy he put the house in order. "You eat this rotten café grub and pay three prices for it. Let me show you how to cook." He was an accom-plished chef, and Vincent marveled, never having tasted such food. "You buy those commercial colors—they cost money and they're not worth a damn. Let me show you how to grind colors." He knew all about the grinding of colors. "Those gilt frames you use are for bourgeois paintings. I'll show you how to make frames." He was an expert car-penter. He made fun of Vincent's friends; and when anything seemed to be right, claimed all the credit for it.

Thus they lived in increasing discord for two months. Vincent's forbearance was running out, his mind dangerously close to another breakdown. Gauguin robbed painting of all its joy: he was jealous of Vincent's art and of his intense devotion to his work. "It's quality that counts," he said. "You paint with a fool's recklessness—it leaves you no time for thinking. You paint from nature like an Impressionist. You should use your imagination." He gave a demonstration, and his talents never showed to better advantage.

"Didn't you learn anything from the Impressionists?" Vincent asked innocently.

"I have forgotten more than they ever knew."

Gauguin talked learnedly of synthesis. A painter must have synthesis, in other words, intelligence. Without synthesis there could be no art.

"And is there no synthesis in my *Sunflowers*?" Vincent inquired.

"I can't deny it. And in your *Old Woman*, and maybe a little in your *Chair*. My compliments! My example has not been in vain."

"Everything, then, is nonsense except what you produce?"

"Right for once, Redhead."

The inevitable break occurred in the Christmas season. They were walking in the park and Vincent, in one of his finest moods, launched into his pet subject—the brotherhood of artists. Gauguin replied with a tremendous laugh, a prolonged roar that almost stopped Vincent's heart; but he quickly changed his tune when he saw the look of horror in his companion's eye.

"Forget your stupid artists," he said quietly. "This is the season of rejoicing. Let us call on the girls."

They entered the brothel together and the girls crowded around them. Gauguin was the center of attraction. He was handsome and strong and the girls fought over him; each hoping to get him for her lover. He knew how to handle women—he had been liberally educated in the brothels of many lands. He received their blandishments roughly, laughed, sang, and told stories of the Brazilian putas. The laughter sank deeper and deeper into Vincent's soul. The crazy Redhead hadn't a chance with the girls when the romantic housemate was with him. A wheedling little brunette took pity on Vincent, caressed and teased him, and begged him to give her a five-franc piece. "And if you can't do that," she cried, pulling his ears, "you might at least give me one of your big ears for a Christmas present." The kindly Madame came in and the room shook with laughter.

They went home again but Vincent was unable to speak. He could not get that laughter out of his system—it was a mockery of everything he had striven for. He could not eat, nor sleep, nor paint, and Gauguin was prepared for trouble.

"Come out of it, old boy. This is the time to be merry. Let's have a drink."

While they were drinking together in the café, Vincent, still silent, suddenly threw an absinthe glass at Gauguin's head. Gauguin, a trained boxer and fencer, ducked and the glass crashed against the wall.

"Your marksmanship is poor," he said, as he slowly stood up. "But mark my word, Redhead, if you should happen to hit me, you must be ready to take the consequences."

He seized Vincent by the neck and threw him into the street. The next morning Vincent broke silence and begged Gauguin's pardon—he didn't know exactly what for—his mind somehow had gone blank, but for whatever had happened he was very sorry. Gauguin accepted the apology, but informed his friend that it was time to dissolve partnership. He put his decision in writing and sent the letter to Theo. Vincent was stricken with remorse: he still believed that Gauguin was a great painter, a master, and he was only trying to do him a good turn. He begged a thousand pardons, wept, and implored the master to change his decision. Gauguin finally consented, but made certain reservations: he would not eat at the same table, and with the caution of a man who had been in dangerous situations before, went to the hotel to sleep.

About midnight there was great excitement at the brothel. The porter brought in a package for the little brunette, a Christmas present delivered at the door by Monsieur, the nutty Redhead. The girls gathered in a circle and the package was opened. One wrapper after another, and the last, a blood-soaked piece of canvas containing a large human ear. The brunette fainted and the Madame notified the police.

The following morning, when Gauguin returned to the yellow house, he found a mob at the door. The police conducted him upstairs and there, on the bed, lay Vincent, unconscious and under the care of the doctor and his friend, the postman. His head was a mass of bandages, but he was out of danger, the doctor said. Suspicion fell upon Gauguin, but his alibi was perfect; and it was subsequently discovered that Vincent had gone completely out of his senses, had cut off his ear with a razor, and had carried it over to the brothel. Theo arrived the next day, and Vincent, regaining consciousness, apologized for spoiling his brother's Christmas. He was removed to the hospital, and Theo returned to Paris, accompanied by Gauguin.

He was discharged early in January and went to work as if nothing had happened. He asked forgiveness of the Madame and the girls, and wrote a friendly letter to Gauguin, but the master's only reply was a curt note asking for his foils. He finished his picture of the *Woman Rocking a Cradle*, which, he explained, was intended for sailors on the high seas. But Vincent was no longer to have any peace in Arles. People intercepted him in the streets, insulted him as he passed, and prowled round his house. One day he counted as many as fifty idlers below his windows— men, women and children. He asked them to disperse, but they hooted him, crying in one voice, "Redhead! Nutty Redhead! One-eared Redhead." He lost his reason and attempted to preach to them; but they yelled the louder, and he hurled canvases down upon them. The town authorities dragged him into an india-rubber cell and padlocked the House of Light, but two months later, at Theo's request, he was sent to an asylum at Saint Remy near Arles.

Vincent remained in the asylum of Saint Remy for a year, first in solitary confinement, then among howling lunatics whom, for some unknown reason, the keeper had insisted on over-feeding until they had grown sleek and fat like demented swine. Some one visiting the asylum has told the story of the red-headed inmate who worked all day long covering canvases with thick streaks of color, while close by sat another lunatic patiently scraping the paint off the finished pictures. There was an admirable freemasonry among the lunatics, and some, as Vincent wrote "were very distinguished, always wearing a hat, spectacles, cane and traveling cloak." But he bore his lot cheerfully and sometimes with humor. "After all," he said, "there are so many painters who are cracked in one way or another, that little by little I shall console myself." He kept in mind an epitaph graven on an old tomb near Arles: "Thebe, priestess of Osiris, who never complained," and wrote to Theo, "If you see Gauguin you should tell him that."

During this period he enjoyed intervals of profound self-mastery and penetration—the unnatural poise, the terrible lucidity that precedes death—and he produced several of his greatest pictures. He painted, in his own description, "A night sky and a moon without radiance, the slender crescent barely emerging from the opaque shadow cast by the earth—a star with exaggerated brilliance, a soft brilliance of rose and green in the ultramarine sky across which are hurrying some clouds. Below a road bordered with tall yellow canes, behind these the blue Alps, an old inn with yellow lighted windows, and a very tall cypress, very upright, very somber." He painted, from the garden of the asylum, a landscape "to call forth the feeling of fright which often seizes my fellow sufferers; to give the impression of fear without going direct to the historical Gethsemane." He painted the *Ravine*—one of his masterpieces—in which the earth lifts itself in hurtling agony, and mounts higher and higher in a convolution of forms. These pictures are not the disordered litter of a lunatic's mind; they are the compacted symbols of the life of a painter who was also a poet, the symbols of his love, his agitations, his sunshine and his sufferings—of the terror and tragedy of his superhuman effort and sensibility.

In better control of himself, Vincent was allowed more liberty and to paint abroad; but late in February, 1890, while on the road, he was overtaken by a fresh attack, and was carried in an ambulance to the asylum where he lay for two months in a state of prostration. Theo arranged at once to find a home for him at Auvers, near Paris; and in May entrusted him to the care of Dr. Gachet, a specialist in aberrations and a great lover of art. In two years he had painted more than two hundred pictures!

Vincent was pleasantly lodged in a small inn not far from Dr. Gachet's house, and here, in surroundings celebrated by many painters, made a final effort to save himself. Daumier had once lived at Auvers, and the memory of that master, blind, paralyzed, and uncomplaining, gave him courage. He went up to Paris to visit his brother, was filled with anxiety over Theo's poor health, and with affection for his little nephew who, he said, "might grow up to be a Courbet, to judge by his big voice." But it was plain to everyone that his condition was critical. "My life is threatened at the very roots," he said, "and my steps are wavering. I must work hard, or I shall never finish my job." He worked hard, but the sunshine was gone. Darkness came into his pictures, and a lurching dramatic energy too intense for contemplation. Flying blackbirds crossed his mind, like the crows of the South, and he painted *The Rooks over the Cornfield*. He grew more nervous and suspicious, and had difficulty with the simplest things. He painted Dr. Gachet—the good Doctor who called his pictures the songs of heroes—"with the heartbroken expression of our time."

One afternoon, as he was sitting under a tree by the inn, everything suddenly became clear to him. Behind him he saw his father's rectory, the flower beds, the white linen, the grinning neighbors, the church and the tall tree in the cemetery; he saw Ursula, the coal-miners, Montmartre, and Theo shaking hands with noisy painters; he saw the South and the House of Light, and all the pictures he had painted there; and he saw Gauguin and the girls—and he heard again that dreadful laughter. Ahead, he saw only one thing: the asylum and himself the maddest of the lot—permanently mad.

"It is impossible!" he exclaimed. "Impossible!"

With true courage he pulled a revolver from his pocket and fired a bullet into his stomach. Then, very calmly, he gathered up his painting gear and walked into the inn, just as he had always done after a day's work.

"I have been shooting," he said gently.

The Doctor said that death was only a question of a few hours, but he lived for two days more. He was pale and the pain was hard to endure, but he uttered no word of complaint. He smoked his pipe and talked quietly of art to his brother.

"O well, I risked my life for it—not once, but many times—and my reason foundered. I suppose I made a bad job of it."

Vincent died on the twenty-ninth day of July, 1890, at the age of thirty-seven. They buried him at Auvers, in the cemetery between the cornfields, and Dr. Gachet planted sunflowers round the grave in honor of the great soul that rested there.

5

GAUGUIN

G AUGUIN was born with a grievance against the world. There was bad blood in his veins, and in his soul a splenetic grudge which, in his swift erratic youth, ripened into an active contempt for modern civilization. Essentially practical and endowed beyond the average in small talents, he derived no comfort from his material victories; and having proved his competence in the economic struggle, renounced his worldly successes for the fugitive satisfactions of art. He turned to art as the ordinary ill-adjusted weakling turns to drink or to drugs, as an escape from life; and when his hatred of humanity had rendered his own countrymen intolerable, he escaped to the dreams and primitive sensualities of the far South. But he was not a weakling: he was a mixture of the conqueror and the coward, and his life was a series of sudden abdications. He had plenty of physical courage, but of moral courage very little; and when life bored him or repressed his savage itchings, he bolted without compunction, leaving his friends and his family to take the consequences. But no Frenchman can despise his own people and get away with it; and in the end he reaped the harvest of ruin which, one might say, he had deliberately invoked. A half-breed and a half-artist, he carried the exotic element of French painting from Montmartre to the unexplored lore of the tropics; but the reward which he expected for his services was denied him, and the fame he coveted was, with true Gallic irony, withheld until it was known that the missionaries had gleefully taken charge of his corpse.

Eugene Henry Paul Gauguin was born in Paris, in 1848, the son of a small-fry journalist from Orleans, and a Creole mother of eccentric stock. His maternal grandmother, a Peruvian by birth, was descended on one side, from Aragonese nobility, and on the other, from the darker strains of the Arabs and Africans. At the age of three, the boy was taken to Peru; but his father died on the voyage, and the sorrowing family, consisting of himself, his sister and his high-born mother, settled down at Lima in a hot country of ancient races and strange customs. Here he lived for four years among wealthy nobles of the highest social standing— a proud people accustomed to luxury, sensual pastimes and cultivated indolence. Chinese and negro servants waited on him; a mulatto girl trotted along when he went to church, bearing a rug for him to pray on; and on the roof of the house a pet lunatic was kept in chains, after the fine old Spanish custom, for his amusement. In this atmosphere of laziness and torrid color, he acquired, in his earliest childhood, a taste for brown skins and semi-barbaric splendor; and reminded continually of his superior lineage—the sun-lovers of old—he acquired naturally the hidalgo manner which was, throughout his life, to make him sinister and detestable wherever he wandered.

When Gauguin was seven years old, his mother returned to France and entered him in the Jesuit Seminary at Orleans. Speaking only Spanish and averse to discipline, he distinguished himself in nothing. He could learn anything—when he cared to—but he showed no disposition to learn; and was remembered as a snarling, disobedient boy who looked like a Creole and took whatever pleased his fancy. "At school," he said, "I picked up that spirit of Jesuit casuistry which is a force not to be despised in the struggle with other people."

At the age of seventeen, inclined to no profession and filled with exotic memories, he shipped as a pilot's apprentice on a boat chartered in the South American trade. In his *Intimate Journals*, he tells us with a vainglorious chuckle, that on his first voyage he carried with him a letter of introduction to a woman in Rio; that the woman, to his astonishment, proved to be the prima donna of the Brazilian Opera Company; and that she accepted him as her lover in preference to her local admirers. The liaison spurred him to further conquests, and on the return voyage, in defiance of ship's discipline, he clapped up an affair with a Prussian woman and foregathered with her in the privacy of the sail locker. These, he assures us, were not his maiden efforts. He boasts of unmentionable prowess at the age of five, and of his first satisfactory sins committed in the dives of Havre. He was an excellent sailor, tough and pugnacious, capable with his fists and tricky with the sword. But the merchant service began to bore him and in his twentieth year he enlisted in the French navy as a stoker. Loving authority and uniforms, he was ambitious to become an officer, but he soon discovered that an illiterate could hope for nothing better than a berth with the blackgang. Three years later, at the end of his term, he deserted the sea to embark on an altogether different career.

Gauguin's deviation into the financial world was purely accidental. He was tired of life in the stoke-hole; his mother had died in poverty; and through the influence of his guardian he obtained a clerkship in the offices of a stockbroker. He entered upon his duties with no special enthusiasm, but once he put his mind to work, the business came easily to him, and he was soon a brilliant figure in financial operations. He wished to shine in all directions, and with his boundless self-confidence and his sharp intelligence, mastered in no time at all the intricacies of the Stock Exchange. His career as a broker lasted for eleven years, during which he married, had five children, speculated shrewdly and made a lot of money. In the opinion of his associates, he was the most enviable of men: a completely successful Frenchman, a bourgeois trader with wife, children and mistresses, growing richer day by day and accumulating interest for the security of the nation.

But it must not be supposed that Gauguin was a contented man. He was by nature incapable of contentment, and though he was proud of his sagacity in stock gambling, the very ease with which he had mastered the game filled him with contempt for his confrères and for the stupid monotony of their transactions. Nor are we to suppose that his life in this period was that of the exemplary French money-grubber. He was restless and disagreeable, with a mind accustomed to translate desires and ideas into actions. He learned to play the guitar and the organ, and a fine game of billiards; under professional instruction he became an expert boxer and fencer; he taught himself to carve and to paint, and his command of the French language indicated a remarkable style; and he bought pictures—not the popular academic brand, but Manet, Daumier, Renoir, Pissarro and Cézanne. His marriage was a prolonged failure. His wife was all that he disliked most: very respectable, a Dane, a Lutheran and a prig. Gauguin should never have married, for he acknowledged no fidelities and no loyalties, and by his own confession, "cared only for women who were fat and vicious." In his letters he refers to his wife as "the bourgeois sow." His tastes ran to prostitutes and negresses. But he loved only himself; and his children, with the exception of his eldest daughter, made no impression upon him.

Gauguin sought in art an escape from the rancors of practical life. At first he painted only on Sundays and holidays, but when his trials had vindicated his belief in himself and established his talent, he devoted every moment of his spare time to his new passion. He came to art rather late, his first signed picture bearing the date 1875. It was an Impressionist work, executed with some skill, but without distinction. He soon found out, in spite of his nimble talents, that good painting was a slow and complicated attainment; but the exasperating dullness of the workaday world impelled him to seek, with increasing ardor, the compensations of art. Ignorant of the history of painting, he joined the Impressionists for temperamental reasons: he admired their color and their stand against the drudges who lived and died in the museums; and he was influenced by the tonal exercises of his friend and counselor, Pissarro. He exhibited with the Impressionists in 1880; again in 1881, showing a nude and a painted carving; and again in 1882. His work received some critical attention, especially the nude which was extravagantly praised by Huysmans. The praise was consoling, but Gauguin was too intelligent a man to be misled by emotional palaver. He knew that his painting, thus far, was only Pissarro at second-hand; but he also knew that within him, somewhere, there was an original artist. Impressionism no longer satisfied him—it was a convenient formula, showy and effective, but he wanted something spectacular and effective on a big scale. There were grandiose visions in the back of his head. But painting had seduced him into a curious situation: he had gone into art as an escape from life, and he now found himself in a way of life from which there was no escape. In January, 1883, he made his decision. "To hell with all the brokers!" he exclaimed. "I am an artist, and henceforth I will paint every day!" His wife was horrified.

But he was not to paint every day, and henceforth was to follow a lonely road leading him farther and farther from the civilization which he could not tolerate and yet could not eliminate from his system. The malady of art had caught him, and painting was the only enduring loyalty of his life. He sold his collection of pictures at a loss, gathered together his convertible possessions, and departed with his family for Rouen where, he had heard, living was cheaper than in Paris. After eight months of domestic brawling, he moved on to Copenhagen, to him the most hateful of places, trusting that his wife's respectable connections might find him a sinecure which would enable him to paint without interruptions. But his unconventional habits and his promiscuity brought down upon him the enmity of the cantankerous Lutherans. Their suspicions were confirmed: the man who had sacrificed his business and his family for a fool's dream was not only a shameless egoist but a Bohemian reprobate. Gauguin's relations with women, as I have already intimated, were not characterized by any sentimental delicacy; they were the casual bouts of the sailor, entered into without regard for public opinion and immediately forgotten. An artist must be free, he said, and having gained his freedom, he was in no humor to be restrained. He took French leave of his wife and children, and returned to Paris, morose and penniless.

He lived on next to nothing, working at times as a bill-paster and a hack scenic decorator. He was no stranger to hardships and he had the groveling instincts of the gipsy; but his life, in contrast with the aimless sallies of his youth, was burdened with an artist's ambition. Living was

GAUGUIN: *Self Portrait*

less important than painting. He submitted to poverty, not exactly with courage but with obduracy, railing against society and posing as a martyr. He was not above playing on the sympathies of his daughter, to whom he wrote occasionally, bragging about his fortitude and "the suffering that sharpens genius." Unlike the gipsy, however, Gauguin was a hard worker, and during his hand-to-mouth existence, painted nineteen pictures which were exhibited with the Impressionists in 1886. He was still a pupil of Pissarro, but in several of the canvases one could see that a new style was evolving. But the squalors of Paris, after his years of opulence, wounded his pride—he was now playing the role of the unrecognized genius—and destroyed his spirit for work; and in a profound huff he suddenly went off to Pont-Aven, in Brittany.

Gauguin was called to Brittany, he explained, by the desolate landscape, and by the elemental character of a people who had not been corrupted by civilization. He needed solitude—or thought he did—for the development of his dreams, but in the starkest isolation he was never alone; he was haunted by that elusive spectre called fame, and for five years vacillated between the Capital, which afforded, at best, an enervating notoriety, and the sobering environment of the province and the colony. He passed a year in Brittany, surly and unapproachable, supported by a group of young painters over whom, with his hidalgo arrogance, he had quickly gained ascendancy. In 1886, he was back in Paris again, strutting in the cafés and talking himself into considerable prominence. In Montmartre he met the Van Goghs: Vincent, the painter, ingenuous and extraordinarily impressionable, whom he bullied into pathetic hero-worshipping; and Theo, the prince of dealers who undertook to sell his pictures. The pictures would not sell. They were the best things he had done—the first, in fact, to contain anything that might be called design—but in his efforts towards a decorative style, he had put aside, for the moment, his strongest asset—his color, and the results were bleak and unappealing. He howled with indignation, damned everything and everybody, sold his last Pissarro, and accompanied by a young

123

artist named Laval, took ship for the island of Martinique, where, he swore, a man might paint in peace.

Exposed, once more, to the luxuriant slothfulness and color of a hot country, but this time with a fixed purpose in life, Gauguin, it seemed, was at last where he longed to be. The women were not only fat and vicious but black and accessible; living was cheap, and civilization unnecessary. The color returned to his canvases, a crude, sweeping, flagrant color reflecting his moods and his surroundings. But there was a flaw in his paradise—the climate. In the winter it had been bearable, but the terrible summer came in with poisonous heats; and his comrade, less rugged, succumbed to a fever, and in a delirium, attempted suicide. Gauguin, in a bad way himself from an attack of dysentery, managed to save him; and the two painters, abandoning their black paramours, set sail for France.

His third attempt to conquer Paris was the same old story; a brutal assertion of his superiority, a thankless acceptance of charity, and a departure. Reduced to the lowest stage of indigence, he was given food, shelter, and working quarters by a retired stockbroker and collector. In return, he sneered at his benefactor's tastes, took possession of the house, and declaimed against the effete society which refused to pay homage to his genius. At this time he learned the technique of ceramics, and struck up a friendship with the painter Daniel de Monfreid, his most generous admirer and the only man with whom he never quarreled. And then, having arranged with Van Gogh for the first individual exhibition of his works, and having borrowed a little money, he retreated to Brittany to await results. Nothing much happened—only a few pictures were sold; his pottery attracted scant attention; and the critics were either dumb or indifferent. The failure of the exhibition inflamed his irascibility—the more readily since he had not fully recovered from the dysentery; and in the autumn of 1888, at the most urgent request of Vincent Van Gogh, he journeyed to the south of France to share the Dutch painter's House of Light.

The gruesome consequences of Gauguin's sojourn in Arles I have already related in the chapter on Van Gogh; and it is enough to repeat that the partnership was abruptly terminated at the end of two months, with Vincent deprived of one of his ears and locked up in an asylum. Gauguin was not wholly to blame: Vincent was abnormally excitable and predisposed to madness, and excessive stimulus of any sort was dangerous to his reason. But Gauguin was aware of this condition, and instead of making allowances for it, seemed to take a diabolical pleasure in tormenting his friend and slowly extinguishing his enthusiasm. He has given us his version of the affair in his journals, making himself, needless to say, the hero of the drama. "Van Gogh has drawn fruitful lessons from me," he writes. "When I arrived at Arles, he was a groping child seeking a way out of Impressionism, while I was a full grown man. It was from me that he learned the principles of Synthesis." The truth is the other way round: assuredly it was not an accident that Gauguin's best European pictures should have been painted directly after his intercourse with Van Gogh. It was not to his discredit, of course, that he learned from Vincent—an artist picks up a good thing wherever he finds it—but he was too conceited to acknowledge indebtedness to anyone. His attitude toward Van Gogh is best illustrated by his callous reply to the committee which, in 1890, solicited his co-operation in organizing a memorial exhibition of Van Gogh's paintings. "I have no interest," he said, "in bringing before the public the abortive works of a lunatic."

He hurried to Paris to exhibit with a group of outcast painters in a café near the grounds of the Universal Exhibition of 1889, got nothing for his pains, and retired again to Brittany. His last residence in Brittany is memorable for the foundation of what is known historically as "The Pont-Aven School." Gauguin was not the sole founder of the school but he was the outstanding personality, and the only man in the movement worth mentioning, with the exception of Maurice Denis who is not remembered for his pretty decorations but for his excellent critical writing. Pont-Aven was now an artist's colony; in one camp, the academic students, in the other, the scurvy radicals dominated by Paul Gauguin. It was an interlude of glory for Gauguin. He removed with his subjects to Pouldu and ruled them as if they were the dirt under his feet—and sometimes they were. They fed and quoted him, aped his affectations and advertised his genius; and he, like a true despot, took their grub and their theories, browbeat and ridiculed them, and went on his way com‐plaining. A deformed Dutchman of unusual self-abasement installed him in a large studio the walls of which he covered with decorations in paint and wood, and the lintels with obscene inscriptions. Gauguin was in his element. He let his hair grow, wore a beard, and dressed in the Breton fashion; in short, he behaved like a little Bohemian lord, a superman, an enemy of the people.

The atmosphere at Pouldu was charged with esthetic speculations: there were schisms and defections, and angry debates on the question of who stole from whom, who invented this theory or that, and who discov‐ered Synthesis. The school, which owed its existence to the reaction against Impressionism, was united on one point—the soul of art was Synthesis. The term Synthesis was a pedantic label chosen to announce the return to the essentials of painting—the simplified decorations of the Italian primitives and the flat designs of the makers of stained glass and cloisonné enamels, in contradistinction to the cubic structure of Cézanne. Gauguin, no mean theorist himself, controlled the contro‐versies and came off victorious. He was neither vague nor long-winded, and his hard practical experiences made him suspicious of the transcen‐dental equations so solemnly mouthed by his henchmen. The egregious wrangles over the meaning of art afforded him many a laugh, and his laughter was more deadly than his sarcasm. "Art for art's sake? Why not?" he roared. "For life's sake? Certainly—and for the stomach's sake! What does it matter?" He even went so far as to burlesque the sacred word Synthesis in one of his decorations. But he was more than a cynical wit. Half of him was a serious artist of exceptional strength and resolution. And when he repudiated Impressionism, he may be said to have read the obituary of that precious mechanism:

"The Impressionists kept searching round the eye and not in the mysterious center of thought, and thence fell into scientific reasoning.

126

They are the conventionals of tomorrow, and worse than those of yester-day. The art of the latter was carried to its end, produced, and will yet produce masterpieces, while the conventionals of tomorrow are in a tossing, ill-starred and unfinished craft. When they talk of their art, what is it? Purely superficial, coquettish, materialistic art, wherein Thought resides not."

The accusation that Gauguin stole his stuff from Emile Bernard will not hold water. It is perhaps true that his progress was somewhat facili-tated by the experiments of that insignificant painter, but to charge one man with plundering another of his originality is nonsense. Artists are entirely too sensitive in such matters, and seem to believe that originality is a transferable secret. I know a painter whose work is an undigested mixture of a dozen modern styles, and yet who will not admit another painter into his studio for fear that he may be robbed of his originality. With a much better show of reason did Cézanne insist that "Gauguin had stolen from him his little sensation in order to cart it round in every tramp steamer." In his last year in Brittany, Gauguin was beginning to find himself, to work out an appropriate instrument for the objectifica-tion of his grandiose dreams. In his march toward a personal style he had drawn from many sources, mostly contemporary; for he was in no sense a scholar, and if it is true that he was influenced by designs in stained glass and enamels, the influence was transmitted to him by his diligent satellites. In his use of line and silhouette he owed something to Ingres, but much more to Degas; he should have thanked Van Gogh for his powerful colors and his heavy unbroken contours; and there can be no doubt that he adapted Cézanne's planes to his own conception of art—an art of fantastic symbols and flat patterns which Cézanne de-nounced unreasonably. Since his break with Impressionism, despite his rather shaky attempts at modeling in the manner of Degas, he had traveled steadily toward the organization of surfaces; but he was not, in the true sense of the word, a composer—he was a maker of panoramas, a distinction we shall analyze in the next chapter.

During this period Gauguin painted two pictures, the *Yellow Christ* and *Jacob Wrestling with the Angel*, which proved to his bickering disciples that he had formed a style of his own. The first is a sensational tour de force, a premeditated shocker that gave rise to the most indignant protests, not because of its formal distortions, but because of its distortion of a conventional idea. The second is a very clever conception, a biblical episode converted into genre, a supernatural wrestling match as he imagined the Breton peasants would visualize it. In neither work is the religious feeling of any consequence—Gauguin had no religious feeling. But in subject-matter, and in treatment, both pictures mark the beginning of the last phase—the Gauguin as he is known to the world, the fabricator of grotesque symbols, of striking decorations in which patches of vivid color are sharply contrasted and defined by long, undulating contours.

His authority in Brittany was absolute, but his kingdom was small and his subjects stupid. He could not keep Paris out of his mind, and late in 1889, made another attack on the Capital. Penniless, but full of his own importance, he walked the boulevards, wearing a Breton costume and clogs of his own carving. The retired broker put him up again, but he soon parted company with his keeper for the more congenial studio of his friend, Daniel de Monfreid. His fame was growing, and a cult of young writers, the Symbolists, discovering an affinity between their own aims and struggles, and those of the Synthesist painters, welcomed Gauguin to their metaphysical pow-wows at the Café Voltaire. He was conscious of the literary element in his art, often referred to it, and more than once wrote of the suggestive power of his paintings—but that was as far as he was prepared to go. For the Symbolists as a sect, and for their elaborate theories, he had nothing but contempt. He allowed them to celebrate him, and even to call him one of their own, hoping for material rewards; but their patronage resulted in nothing more substantial than Bohemian flattery. So he dropped them and nursed his grievances alone. "If my works do not survive," he said to Monfreid, "there will survive the remembrance of an artist who freed painting from many of its academic bonds and from its Symbolist absurdities."

A confirmed misanthrope, **Gauguin** cut his friends and spent most of his time in a disreputable bar, sulking like a fallen monarch. Paris had never inspired him to paint, and now she offered him—the hungry master of a new school—not food but the cadenced flattery of her little poets. His imagination dwelt on things remote; a land of blazing suns, mountains rising from the sea, and soundless nights; an escape from incestuous schools and yapping hounds of fame; a new kingdom and himself the ruler, his subjects bound to him by no motives of self-advancement but by a spiritual allegiance, and at his side his dusky consort, naked and unacquainted with sin. A booklet describing the tribal charms of Tahiti determined his course, and he acted promptly. Selecting a number of his paintings, thirty in all, he offered them for sale at the Hotel Drouot. The auction was well attended, thanks to the blurbs of prominent writers, but the proceeds amounted to less than 10,000 francs— which he pocketed with a bad grace. The Ministry of Public Instruction handed him an engraved document "entrusting him with an art mission"; there was a farewell dinner at the Voltaire, with speeches and verses by Mallarmé; and a benefit performance at one of the theaters, the profits to be shared equally by Gauguin and Verlaine. There were no profits; and on April 4, 1891, he departed, in the words of Mallarmé, "for exotic lands that lie afar."

Gauguin's invasion of Tahiti is revealed to us in full detail in his *Noa-Noa* and in his correspondence and *Intimate Journals. Noa-Noa,* in the Maori tongue, means any form of scent, but a more appropriate rendering, in this case, would be the word *smells*. The book, in essence, is a tract, a clever bit of special pleading from the pen of an artist of fortune who saw what he wanted to see, and lived, or pretended to live, up to his reputation as an esthetic savage. He planned his effects like the born writer that he was, and with an unexpected command over the poetic resources of the French language, succeeded in convincing the Bohemians of Paris that he had at last entered the magic circle of contentment.

Gauguin was in difficulties from the moment of his arrival. He made a grand show of himself; the black governor received him as an important personage, not as an artist; and he was soon the talk of the capital. But when he presented his papers accrediting his "art mission," the governor sized him up as a spy, and ordered barefooted sleuths to report on his movements; and when he lived openly with a half-caste girl, in contrast to the covert practices of the hypocrites of the town, the bishops and ecclesiastical snoopers pronounced him a public nuisance. Life in the capital sickened him, and naturally, since it harbored, in a shabbier and more venereal form, the very elements he had sought to escape. European civilization among the Maoris—hideous paradox! A princess, niece of the king, called on him, displaying he said, "the insolence of a European." He was suffering from nostalgia and bronchitis but she showed him no mercy. "Shall we drink an absinthe together?" she asked at once. They drank, and the princess was a brave tippler. She rolled a cigarette and talked in French of the fables of La Fontaine, and having finished her discourse, removed her mother hubbard and from force of habit, slid into his bed. Her body he could stand—he had stood worse—but French fables on the lips of a princess who should have spoken the metaphors of an ancient race revolted him. His half-caste wench with her casino harlotries revolted him: she was neither European nor savage, neither wife, nor animal; she was not even a good model—her figure was hybrid; and pulling up stakes he fled to the farthermost part of the island, a distance incidentally of less than thirty miles from the seat of government.

Here he purchased a hut and a piece of ground, and as swiftly as the tropical sun dips down into the sea, he discarded the rags and memories of his past life. Gauguin went native without effort, he informs us, in obedience to some powerful atavism in his blood. Shoeless and naked to the waist, he dwelt among the unspoilt children of nature; ate their yams, shrimps and breadfruit; mastered their language; drank of their wisdom and absorbed their superstitions; and at night listened to the beating of drums, the love march that warmed him through and through; or sitting alone in his hut looked from an unglazed window into a procession of his people, each bearing a lantern to ward off the spirit of the dead which came down from the wall of mountains, as from the black skyline of death, to claim its victim. "I begin to think quietly," he wrote, "to entertain but little hatred for other men; nay, to love them. I am in possession of every joy of life, animal and human, in my freedom. I have escaped from the false, and enter into Nature with the certainty that the morrow will be as today, as free and as fair. Peace wells within me; I am developing normally and am rid of empty cares." That speech was written to make the anemic Parisians turn green with envy.

But his life was not complete. He lacked joy, he said, meaning sexual excitement, and one fine morning set out to find a mate. He had not to travel far; the woods were full of women—it was a question of plucking the most luscious fruit. Marriage in Tahiti was as simple as that. He picked a girl of thirteen: "a large child," he said, "slender and strong and wonderfully proportioned; her skin was golden and two swelling buds rose on her breasts." After listening to her mother's recommendations, Gauguin, by way of courtship, cross-examined the girl.

"Are you in good health? Are you clean? Do you love me?"

Tehoura was the immaculate flower of health—free from white man's disease—but the answer to the third question would have to wait. "The question was born of ignorance," he observed, "for no Maori girl could love a man unless his nuptial addresses had proved satisfactory." In such circumstances a ceremony seemed superfluous, but he heard it with a straight face, and promising to return Tehoura to her mother within eight days, if he had not won her love, led his bride back to his hut.

Eight days passed; she said that he was good; and they lived on together in a profound and dreamy peace that evoked the best that was in him. A superman, he astonished Tehoura by his physical talents—his educated fists, his mountain climbing, his swimming; and he astonished her still more by his carving and painting for which she could see no necessity. If he was contented with life and not afraid of the evil spirits, why should he paint images of people? He could not answer her, could not explain the ego of the white man. He swam across a black volcanic lake, a prodigious feat of strength, frightening his child-bride into a tantrum. When he made light of her fears, she asked if he too had not been afraid. "The Frenchman knows no fear," he replied. He was a little annoyed by her craving for hard liquor, occidental dishes, and the cheap trinkets peddled by the Chinaman, but he forgave her these unnatural desires for the sake of her savage love. One night, at the end of the sixth month, Tehoura confessed innocently to numerous infidelities, and stood before him, with bowed head and naked back, ready for the beating he had promised her. But he could not bring himself to beat her, not, at any rate, for so conventional a lapse. Gauguin, for the first time in his life, was in love, and love had made him over into a gentleman. Thus ends the story of *Noa-Noa*.

The book, whatever its effect on the fin-de-siècle esthetes of Paris, reads today like so much provender for the mills of Hollywood. Compared to the psychological studies of Conrad, it is shallow stuff rising only occasionally above the miasmatic trash of the Sunday supplements. There was, in truth, much of the Sunday journalist in Gauguin: he was always on the hunt for sensational copy, like the red-blooded lads who go adventuring among blackamoors and witch doctors and return with argosies of bogey lore. The mythological blather of *Noa-Noa* will deceive no one; nor did it deceive the author. Gauguin was primarily concerned with color and sex; and the Polynesian religion was no longer a thing of beauty. Debauched by the sins of the French traders, and by the hocus-pocus of the missionaries, it was either a lascivious ceremonial or a cringing attempt to elude nameless terrors and to propitiate the biblical witches. Gauguin employed all his craft to make it beautiful and moving, but he was an outspoken rogue and shamming was not included in his long list of talents. The book of many odors is redeemed here and there by pictorial passages composed with poetic fervor and inserted to clarify the literary allusions in his paintings. But even his most poetic writing is tinctured with hatreds and brackish disappointments from which there seemed to be no escape.

132

For a true account of Gauguin's experiences in Tahiti we must consult his letters. In these the heroic mask of savagery is discarded, and the half-breed malcontent stands before us in all his barefaced ugliness: Gauguin of the enlarged ego, coarse, candid, witty and cruel, but sharp of eye and very gifted. He went to the island as one, sick of civilization, "turns to live with animals" in a state of continuous placidity. And what did he actually find there? A handsome people with the grace and elasticity of wild animals, the men effeminate, the women large, sculpturally formed and virile. He found disease grafted on indolence, and indolence steeped in sin. A race famed for light-heartedness was now only frivolous, behind every traditional courtesy lurked a subtle deceit; and the old spirit of generosity had given place to cruelty and wanton disregard for property rights. The noses of children were broken, and their bodies steamed and fattened to enhance their sensual charms; wives were systematically exchanged; and the women suckled puppy dogs in preference to their own offspring. None of these customs offended his sensibilities, and some appealed to him strongly. His main grievance was against the European evils which had contaminated the promised land.

Tahiti was a small place and the ways of the white man had permeated every corner of it. There was no escape. He was reminded of his native country not only by experiences and memories which were a part of him, but by the grosser customs and insufferable vulgarities which the islanders so eagerly adopted. In reality, Gauguin had no desire to forget. Being an artist, he worked, as all artists do, with an audience in mind—only the audience was in France and communication difficult. Had he reverted to true savagery, as his Tehoura had sensibly observed, he would have had no need to paint, or for that matter, to work—and no thoughts of fame and money. He would have been happy to sit and sin— to enjoy complete physical freedom, to indulge his sexual cravings to the limit of his endurance, and to appease the vindictive gods with lunar rituals of frenzied intimacy. I do not mean that savages have not produced art. They have—and in forms which have made monkeys of jaded Parisians—but not as a commodity, not for fame and money. Normally,

133

savage art is inspired by tribal fetishism; its significance is wholly religious; and its forms, from the polished sculptures down to personal ornamentation and the abstract designs on pots and utensils, are of symbolical origin. Gauguin, devoid of religion and working for money and renown, painted to astonish Parisians for whom he had no respect. In his inordinate vanity, he also painted to astonish the Tahitians. The French were but mildly excited; the Tahitians not at all; and he was left to publish his sacrifices and nurse his self-inflicted hurts, a reviling sentimentalist playing at savagery.

Gauguin went to Tahiti in the expectation of extending his sexual freedom. In this he was not disappointed, and for a while, enjoyed his freedom. But he was soon surfeited—a man cannot live on sex alone. The absence of barriers, the lack of challenge, robbed the game of its excitement, and he began to complain of the very conditions he had hoped to encounter. He remembered his escapade with a servant girl, at Pouldu, whom he had seduced by climbing over the roof to her room; and he longed for a tussle with the tough girls of Paris. He had no love for children, and the birth of Tehoura's man-child moved him to unfeeling wrath. This event was followed by a letter from Juliette, the mistress he had left behind him, informing him that her baby was doing well, and begging for money. "I have lost a mistress and acquired a dependent," he said. He was beginning to reap where he had sown.

From his letters one would think that his life was a succession of calamities. He could no longer stomach a diet of shell-fish and wild bananas; he longed for a hot ragout and French service; he wanted to come home—but he was strapped. The burden of his correspondence is a fulsome whining about money.

"I have not had a penny for my work in months, which means I have sold nothing. My money is gone—and how am I to pay for my colors? I shall have to give up painting." Or this: "I understand that a whole band of my imitators is bustling round and making money. I shall be dropped by the way." And this: "All these young fellows who are making money owe me at least this much—the sale of one of my large things to some rich man—but they won't take the trouble, the bastards! But for Gauguin they would not be in existence; but for him the world would not accept them." The wonder to me is Daniel de Monfreid's patience with the ungrateful beach-comber. Monfreid, his Paris agent, never lost heart, and contriving to sell a few pictures, sent him the drafts. The only thanks he got was a tirade against the wretched mail service.

But despite his bellyaches, he found in Tahiti the stimulus to his best production; and during the more tranquil days of his first visit, painted the pictures upon which his fame rests today. His mind on Paris, he had visions of a grand exhibition which would bring him the rewards he coveted most; but with characteristic egoism, he believed that the success of the affair would depend on his personal appearance. He had no money, and the natives with their inverted sense of humor rejoiced in his misfortune, passing the word along that the maker of images had put on his shirt and gone back to his people. His dear friends of the capital had the pleasure of refusing him passage money, and of citing him as a horrible example of profligacy. He combed the beaches alone, begging from the Chinaman, and eating raw sea-food and mangoes. A check from Monfreid put him in funds again, and he was off. He arrived at Marseilles, on August 3, 1893, and immediately dispatched a note to his friend. "Got here today with four francs in my jeans. Good Lord, what a rotten passage!"

Gauguin's return to France was followed by a lucky break in his misfortunes. A forgotten uncle conveniently died bequeathing him 13,000 francs in cash, and he swaggered into Paris anticipating a triumph. His time had come—he would make a killing. The august house of Durand-Ruel agreed to exhibit his art, and with the industry of a man fertile in the tricks of publicity, he conspired to take the public by storm. His friend Morice, a poet-journalist, prepared the catalogue, playing up the sensational life of the artist, and defending the unpatriotic behavior of the renegade who had voluntarily gone into exile. The pictures, many of which were soaked in an unintelligible mythology, bore strange Maori titles; and Gauguin himself, in a bantering style, "for the benefit," he said, "of those who always insist on knowing the whys and wherefores of everything," undertook to explain the genesis of one of his most famous paintings, *The Spirit Watching*. The analysis, as the French biographer Rey points out, recalls the ex post facto quackery submitted by Poe to explain the genesis of *The Raven*.

Nor was the artist less singular than his works. Gauguin, a superb decorator in paint, had, in other things, a low order of taste. His studio, equipped to exhibit the personality of the artist-barbarian, was worthy of the Emperor Jones. Here it is, as described by one of his friends.

"Many a painter, many a writer has visited the place. Everyone remembers the small door, the panes of which, adorned with paintings by the Master showed the characteristic motto, in Maori, 'Here one makes love.' The room was large and painted all over in chrome yellow. On the walls, plastered with barbarian paintings, were hung trophies and military weapons: knobkerries, boomerangs, hatchets and lances, all brightly colored and in foreign woods. On the mantelpiece stood shells and mineralogical specimens. A primitive doorbell tinkled faintly, and the visitor saw approaching him a splendid mulatto woman with shining eyes, the Javanese mistress whom Gauguin had picked up in Paris. A shivering monkey snuggled among the bed-clothes, and in this exotic setting one felt very far from Paris. There came and went an incessant stream of idlers. Gauguin, now a swell, had a day on which he received callers, just like a candidate for the medal of honor. He gave parties, had tea served and cakes passed round with silent dignity by the somber rival of Tehoura."

In this jungle Gauguin should have worn at most a loin-cloth; but it was November in Paris, and he went to the other extreme, getting himself up like a nigger minstrel. He wore a sky-blue frock-coat, long and close-fitting, with mother-of-pearl buttons; a magnificent blue waistcoat, buttoning down the side, and embroidered, on the frilled collar, in green and yellow silk; his trousers were yellow; his gloves white; his gray felt hat wound with a bright blue ribbon. And he carried a large stick, carved by himself and set with pearls. The savage on parade!

136

The exhibition opened and closed, and Paris managed to survive the shock. She had seen exhibitions before, and Gauguin was just another artist—more picturesque than most, but only an artist. To give the old girl a lasting thrill he should have been a German soldier or a Yankee debt collector. But as shows went, it was fairly successful, eleven paintings out of forty-three selling for small sums, and celebrities dropping in to be amused or affronted. To the academicians, his art was ignoble and out of drawing; and the director of the Beaux-Arts, who had pledged an official purchase, unctuously refused to be party to "so revolutionary an art." Degas liked it—he recognized the drawing; Puvis de Chavannes liked it—those poses looked familiar; Renoir was for it, although he could not understand why anyone should go to the end of the earth to paint; and the erotic bookworm, Anatole France, seriously considered the extension of his own sexual freedom. But the rich buyers were repelled by the pretentious symbolism; and the general public, which Gauguin, like all artists, hoped to capture as Zola had captured it, was not even aware of his existence. So Gauguin was a failure and his return to Paris was an expensive error. "I gave them a new art, but they turned away. It's no use."

Careless of money, he had wasted his inheritance, and for the purposes of economy as well as to forget his failure, he went back to his old stronghold in Brittany, taking his Javanese girl with him. One Spring day, accompanied by the girl and Seguin, the painter, he was strolling along the quay in a coast town when a drunken sailor reeled by.

"Hell's bells, men!" sang out the drunk, signaling to his mates, "Do you see what I see? There's a circus in town."

The sailor had some cause for his confusion. Gauguin, in his blue and yellow costume, carried a monkey on his shoulder; the Javanese wore the loudest orange; and Seguin looked like a freak. The drunks closed in screaming threats and insults, their eyes on the ravishing mulatto.

"The black bitch is mine!" one shouted. "She looks like good ——"

Gauguin, swinging from the ground up, knocked him cold with a

137

blow on the chin. Seguin, pursued by four blue-jackets, ran for dear life, dived into a basin, and swam to safety. The mulatto prayed to an unknown god. Gauguin, cool under fire and an old-timer at gang-fighting, stood his ground alone, beating off his assailants with the skill of a finished workman. He dropped three more, and nerved to victory, had the others on the run, when a powerful roughneck, attacking from the rear, kicked him with a clog in the ankle. The bones cracked and he went down and out. When he came to, the drunks were gone and the girl was gone. He rolled a cigarette and waited for the stretcher.

"I never saw the black bitch again," Gauguin said. "She caught the first train to Paris, went to my studio, stole everything she could lay hands on, and disappeared."

The broken ankle was not properly treated and he was a cripple for the rest of his days. While waiting in Brittany for the wound to mend, the bandaged monarch pondered his disaster. His grudge against the world racked him far more than his injured foot, and he wrote to Monfreid of his next and final move. "Sell everything. Get what you can for it, but sell it. I'm going away—back to the hot country. I'm not licked—I'm sore. But it doesn't matter. The opinion of the world no longer interests me. It's adieu this time; I'm going for good—and it's farewell to painting."

The sale was held in February, 1895, and was the occasion of his famous brush with Strindberg whom he had asked to write the introduction to the catalogue. The melancholy viking declined the honor in positive language, but not without civility and intelligent respect for Gauguin's fortitude. The painter, with his flair for publicity, printed both the letter of refusal and his own reply, and the catalogue became historic. Strindberg wrote:

"You have created a new heaven and a new earth, but I find no pleasure in your creation; there is too much blaze of sun for one who loves subdued light. And in your paradise dwells an Eve who does not conform to my ideal—for truly I also have an ideal, or two, of woman. You, Gauguin, are the wild man who hates a hampering civilization;

GAUGUIN: *Spirit of the Dead Watching*

you have something of the Titan who, jealous of the Creator, knocks together a little creation of his own at odd times; a child who takes playthings to pieces to make different ones out of them; a man who braves opinion, preferring to make out that the sky is red instead of blue, as most of us believe."

Gauguin replied:

"Your civilization is your disease, my barbarism my restoration to health. The Eve of your civilized conception makes us all misogynists. The old Eve who shocked you in my studio will perhaps seem less odious to you some day. I have perhaps been unable to do more than suggest my world, which seems unreal to you. . . . Only the Eve I have painted can stand naked before us. Yours would always be shame-less in this natural state, and if beautiful, the source of pain and of evil."

The sale netted him a round sum, but he was in no condition to celebrate. The white man's disease, which he had guarded against in the tropics, had been given to him by Strindberg's civilization: in a misadventure with an unscrupulous street-walker he had contracted syphilis, and his rage was worthy of a suffering Titan. He named the loyal Monfreid administrator of all his affairs, and embarked for Tahiti, to return no more.

Gauguin's second descent into savagery is the story of slow dissolu-tion. Age had not sweetened his temper, and his physical afflictions diminished his exceptional energy. He was soon in want and his letters are "one long monotonous grumble." In April, 1897, he wrote, "I have just received a note from my wife, very brief and very terrible. She brutally tells me of the death of Aline. I have lost my daughter. I no longer love God!" His old habitation had been sold, and to build elsewhere he was forced to borrow from a local bank. At the end of the year he wrote, "Nothing but death can free me. I owe 1800 francs this month, and I have no more credit. A wild but sad and wretched business my coming to Tahiti!"

His will to live kept him going—his insolent creative vigor, and the irresistible appeal of burnt women. Notwithstanding his disease, he

139

visited Tehoura. "My old sweetheart got married in my absence," he reports, "so I was obliged to fool her husband." He played mournfully on his little organ; cultivated his dahlias and irises, the seeds for which he had brought with him; painted and made love. But the obstacles were too much for him. His ankle grew worse; eruptions appeared on his legs—the effects of his gift from the street-walker; and he could not sleep. His life was a running sore. "I have not even a crust of bread; I live on a little water, and a few guavas and fresh-water prawns." In 1898 he decided to follow Van Gogh's example—the final escape—and hobbling off into the hills so that the ants might devour his identity— he still had his pride—he swallowed arsenic. But he took an over-dose, and in the agony of recovery, finished his large canvas entitled *What Are We? Whence Do We Come? Whither Are We Going?*, one painting, at least, in which he comes within striking distance of an intelligible symbolism.

The painting, one of his best, revived his will to live. The bank renewed his note, but in order to live, he was forced to work as a government clerk for five francs a day. Temporary relief came when Vollard, the cunning dealer, sold nine of his pictures. Gauguin, now fifty years old, settled his debts, left the capital and crawled back into his hut. His woes increased, but the artist in him was not dead, and he must give expression to his hopelessness. "I am going to the Chink's to beg bread," he wrote to Monfreid. "I haven't a penny to my name." His legs were killing him; he lost all control of himself; and his letters overflowed with the meanest sentiments. "Let us leave the dirty bourgeoisie," he counseled his agent in Paris—"even if they are our children—in their dirty places, and finish the work we have begun." When his kindliest disciple, Maurice Denis, invited him in 1900, to participate in a large group-exhibition, he replied by piling insult upon ingratitude, with a few digs at Cézanne and Van Gogh for good measure.

The French Colonials called him "the fool who paints pink horses"; and the frivolous natives, exulting over his fall, teased him and pilfered his meager stores. Insisting on prosecutions, Gauguin published open letters in a local newspaper, execrable screeds that moved the apathetic Colonials to laughter; and having worked himself into a fever of vituperation, he founded a little paper of his own—*The Smile*, he named it—which he multigraphed and circulated among the riffraff of the Island. Again he was rescued by the enterprising devotion of his agent. Monfreid forwarded him the sum of 1200 francs, and by an arrangement with his dealer, promised him a monthly allowance of 350 francs. Gauguin hurried to the hospital for treatment, and somewhat relieved, laid plans to sail to the Marquesas Islands. He gave three reasons for his decision: the natives were no longer willing to pose for him; the market for Tahitian pictures was declining; and his imagination was beginning to cool.

It was all over but the dying. Civilization had corroded his heart and a plunge into pseudo-savagery could not cure him. The Marquesans, singled out by Melville as "the fairest of men, surpassing all in beauty of form," were, in Gauguin's time, a dwindling stock, ravaged by leprosy, consumption, elephantiasis, and syphilis. Living was cheap there, and Gauguin was now in possession of a regular income, but he was beyond redemption. He continued to paint but his work was done, and his thoughts elsewhere. Nothing remained but his diseased body and his irascibility. He wanted to go home—to France, and he thought of Spain, "of bulls and Spanish women with hair plastered down with grease." He had a little house and a servant and endeavored to create the impression that he was a man to be feared and reverenced. On either side of the door were carved inscriptions, one reading, "Love and you will be happy," the other, "Be mysterious and you will be happy." Near the entrance stood a large clay idol on the base of which he had cut the words, "Te atua," or "God." It was said—and he allowed the tale to spread among the bishops—that it was his habit to kneel before this statue and to pray aloud to the sun-god. The mumbo-jumbo antics persisted to the end.

Here Gauguin painted his last picture, a snow scene reminiscent of Brittany!

In his lingering misery, doping himself with morphine, he lifted his voice in terrible wrath against the colonial régime. On behalf of the brown people, with unabated fighting spirit, he publicly denounced the gendarme for accepting bribes from foreign traders. Charged with defamation of character, he was fined 1000 francs and sentenced to jail for three months. He appealed the case, and while awaiting the verdict of the higher court, wrote to Monfreid, in April, 1903, "These worries are killing me." A month later the missionaries claimed him, and with a touch of irony, buried the heathen painter in their own cemetery. Gauguin had escaped at last.

6

WILD ANIMALS

THE conventionality of the average person shrinks back appalled at the lives of Van Gogh and Gauguin. Judged by the standards governing the conduct of normal members of society, these two men were anarchists of the most subversive type; judged by the frivolous excesses of their followers, they were heroic souls. In contrast to their uncivilized assault on Philistine ideals, the spectacular campaign of Whistler was only a form of jittery egoism, the artful flutterings of the butterfly. It has been submitted that society has no right to expect, or even to tolerate, such fanaticism in art; that the painter is not called upon to devote his talents to an ideal which is not only a prolonged agony and a preparation for suicide, but a brutal flouting of the established canons of human decency. The answer is that society did not take Van Gogh and Gauguin into its bosom; that it tolerates, yes, even admires, fanaticism in high finance, but deals pitilessly with the same intensity of purpose when it happens to animate the painter. I am not advocating madness in the arts, but as long as the painter is denied any considerable audience, as long as there is no intelligent social check on his wildest impulses, just so long shall we continue to deliver one of the noblest of the arts into the clutches of strange beings who translate the common circumstances of life into vindictive singularities expressing emotional tortures and feral despairs.

No one can deny that Van Gogh and Gauguin paid the highest possible price for their loyalty to art; nor can it be said that they were wanting in ability or courage. But in reasserting the fundamental right of the painter to use his medium as an emotional language, in their vehe-

ment attack on Impressionism, and the photographic transcription of
nature, they pushed personal expression to the utmost verge of eccentricity and thence into the realm where madness lies and the artist is
left to traffic in lyrical deformations and enigmatical symbols. In destroying Impressionism, they destroyed themselves, and their immediate
effect upon art was to embolden the Bohemians to destroy everything in painting except the pattern basis. Cézanne, the preceptor of
both, could not endure their aberrations, calling Van Gogh an idiot and
Gauguin a charlatan. Neither was a great artist, but both were bigger
than their successors. The first was a painter of genius; the second an
extraordinary creature of vicious talent.

While engaged in painting, Van Gogh was the servant of a terrible
afflatus which demanded for its embodiment contorted forms and smit-
ing colors inconceivable in artists of more equable temperament. It is
true that after he had sacrificed his life to his convictions, more rational
and far more ingenious painters, affecting his madness and profiting
by his painful forms, invented various kinds of pictures in which the
relation of art to nature, and to humanity, is totally obliterated; but
these pictures, which have come to America by the shipload, are superficial and, for the most part, worthless. It needs no deep perception to
appraise them for what they are: the studio contrivances of Bohemians
not one of whom is blest with the powerful, if unbalanced conviction,
and the vitality which make Van Gogh the most trenchant voice in
modern art.

But in calmer moods, when the spasm of paint had passed, Van
Gogh was capable of remarkable reflections on art. His philosophy
of painting, in many of its aspects, is profound—vitiated here and there
by the worst of Tolstoy, and shining out with humanitarian sentiments
at variance with the realities of life as he had faced them. But how much
nobler and more intelligent than the narrow esthetic of those who have
converted his pictures into senseless diagrams and rebuses for which
none but the maker holds the key! He believed that art should have a
purpose—a message, if you will; and if, in his early evangelical days,

he confused this purpose with a moral code, he rose above the homiletic as his knowledge increased through practical experience; and in the final period looked upon art as a spiritual necessity. He believed also in the universality of art—not as the connoisseur to whom the art of China, let us say, is only an archaeological toy or a formal curiosity, notwithstanding his high-toned jargon—but in the sense that the art impulse is implanted in every human being and that the proper nourishing of the impulse would, like true religion, bind social groups together into spiritual units and thus make the world a better place to live in. A humble man and well acquainted with the lowest orders of society, he conceived his pictures for uneducated emotions; he thought of them, so he said, as singing into the hearts of sailors or quickening the pulses of peasants. By the irony of fate, they have, every last one of them, become objects of speculation, traveling from the auction room to the collector, as useless to the humanity he had hoped to touch as the cryptograms of James Joyce.

The most familiar things in life—the sun, a pair of shoes, a baby, or a tree—transported Van Gogh into a state of ecstasy which can only be compared to that of the religious fanatic beholding the crucifix. It is hard to believe that the mind can work itself into the extremes of exaltation over objects which, to the generality, are commonplace facts, but there are the pictures as evidence—the most purely autobiographical records of nervous excitement in all painting. To appreciate the pictures some knowledge of the mental condition of the artist is required; otherwise one might think that Van Gogh could not see straight, or that he attempted to reproduce what met the eye, and made a bad job of it. It is important to remember in this connection that abnormal sensitivity is not needed for the production of art; that it leads almost invariably to fatuous symbolism; that, in recent years, under the names of Expressionism and Sur-Realism, the cult of sensitivity may be held responsible for the subjective manias that have made painting a detestable business. Van Gogh, like Blake, was an exception —both were men of tremendous conviction. The inflammable temperament of the Dutchman was quenched and beaten back by practical difficulties and acute hardships, or it would have driven him into a world of hallucinations at the beginning of his career; the visionary mind of the Englishman was sobered by his daily work as a commercial engraver. But sensitivity, as exhibited by playboys, and as the defence mechanism of cowards, has become a universal nuisance in art.

Beholding a bunch of sunflowers or a cypress under the moon, Van Gogh lost his head and was soon in the throes of a spiritual intoxication. At the mercy of the scene, or object, before him, like the Impressionists, he was, at the same time, too genuine an artist to regard nature as an assemblage of surfaces absorbing or reflecting light. A painter of emotions, he discovered in his first trials that the emotion could not be communicated by the simple process of reproducing the object which had, as a match to an explosive, touched it off. The object, then, served as a scaffold which he loaded, in the broadest definition, with his great love for humanity. This love was no ordinary passion; it was ferocious and all-absorbing, but thwarted, pent-up, denied practical satisfaction. When released by art, it gushed forth in a torrent of energy which he was powerless to hold within reasonable bounds. As a receptacle for his love and the particular mood it assumed under the stimulus of the moment, no conventional illustration of affection would do—no sterile concept or listless academic symbol out of Puvis de Chavannes, no Pre-Raphaelite dream fabricated from old ballads, but something staggering and supernatural. Working at white heat; lashing the canvas with irregular streaks of heavy pigment; unhampered by the burden of traditional knowledge; he painted with the directness of a primitive and the simplicity of the child. With heavy contours, with colors of undiluted intensity, with strained and crackling silhouettes, he transformed nature into emblems of his own agitated feelings. He was an inspired painter, if ever one lived.

Van Gogh's pictures must be accepted as interpretations of extraordinary conflicts—he saw, felt, and burst into paint. Considering his pathological afflictions and the disadvantages of his training, we can scarcely account for the amazing lucidity of his accomplishments. His work, taken as a whole, is definitely bound to actualities; to the last he remained a painter, occupied, to the best of his ability, with problems of design, and with subject-matter directly experienced. He is remarkably free from the nonsensical visions and infantile sentiments characteristic of unbalanced minds held captive by art. That he should have believed in the synesthetic properties of color was consistent with his curious temperament—he said that "yellow was a color to delight God," that blue "expressed infinity," and he associated the green tones, which Toulouse-Lautrec brushed into his shadows, with bitterness and despair; the marvel is that he should have succeeded in weaving his colors into glorious harmonies and in relating them to an intelligible context. Sometimes, in the heat of an uncontrollable passion, he deformed nature into fabulous conceptions which have no meaning to most of us; again, he was no better than a demented child; but he never produced a photograph or a platitude.

Out of Impressionism—an indirect method of recording direct sensations of light and color—Van Gogh forged a technique perfectly adapted to his own ends. He set the rigid procedure of Monet and Pissarro in motion, elongating dots and dashes into whirling bands, and making them serve as units of rhythm. Against a background composed of tones of striking yellows or somber blues, he placed his forms—faces reflecting his own stinging affections, deranged houses, violent trees— all strongly outlined but with only a suggestion of relief. Gradually he eliminated shadows and local colors, and in his best canvases, applied color without reference to natural truth, but for decorative purposes and for the emotional significance he fancied it contained. His practice was to paint the whole canvas at one sitting, even if it killed him, and he was never able to improve upon the initial effort. That was the strength and the weakness of his art. He confessed his limitations frankly, as the following letter shows:

"When Gauguin was at Arles I allowed myself to be led into working from imagination. But it is an enchanted land, and suddenly one finds oneself confronted with an insurmountable stone wall. Maybe after a life spent in manly effort and endeavor, and after a hard struggle shoulder to shoulder with nature, one might venture to try it; but for the present I shall not crack my brains over it; and I have slaved all the year round painting from nature."

It would be a waste of time, I think, to speculate on what Van Gogh might have achieved, if his struggles with society had been less strenuous and his formal knowledge more extensive. In its own sphere his art is perfect—the complete and piercing expression of the soul of a fanatic reacting to environment. But the appreciation of his genius does not absolve us from the obligation to define his limitations and to analyze the nature of his influence. His meager technical equipment was sufficient for his needs, and he managed, by means of heart-breaking exertions, to bring out all that was in him. More cannot be asked of any artist. As concerns design, he departed from the co-ordination of forms in three dimensions—the Renaissance method revived by Cézanne—and strove for linear balance and harmonious areas of color in the manner of the Japanese print. He achieved a unity of surface that is more than an agreeable pattern; it is a device to convey with the utmost force and clarity the psychological state induced by his contact with nature. He seems, with his summary drawing and his rapid-fire brushing, to dispense with previously acquired knowledge and to abandon himself to an overpowering impulsion. To a certain extent this is true: the self-discipline and vast formal knowledge of his hero, Rembrandt, would not have helped him.

Van Gogh's art is flat—the proper form for the manifestation of his fiery moods. His paintings burn; they have the restless vitality of the flame, but like the flame, they are wanting in substance. They appeal to our rarer moods, and unless one is capable of those moods, they are interesting only as specimens of abnormal mortification. In the first years of the century, Van Gogh was hailed as a prophet, the leader of the younger men in their escape from academic bondage and in their mad propensity to scrap the representational elements of painting. But today, with the return of painting to more realistic issues, with the rise of the mural and the tendency of artists to consider the social habits of the race, the flat art of Van Gogh has fallen into disrepute. The man's courage, his strength of character, and his verbal ideas are still commended, but his fitful surrender to fragments of nature offers little to sober artists engaged in building a logical structure to carry their complex experiences in the modern world.

Gauguin was an animal of different breed. While Van Gogh modestly endeavored to woo the world, Gauguin took the opposite course —Nietzschean castigation and flight. He succumbed to the sultry lure of the far South through the same weakness that sends the American artist into the Bohemian quarters of Paris—to sidestep the complications of modern life. That, in a word, explains his popularity among minor artists. There is, of course, in almost every one, a degree or two of the romantic fever, a yearning, when times are hard and tribulations abundant, to escape to the enchanted isles, to the life of fragrant slothfulness and cosy sin which philosophers call the state of nature and which the steamship companies exploit with snapshots of grinning naked girls strumming the jazz lute between assignations. That explains such popularity as he has enjoyed with the public. Tahiti was his Bohemia, his land of make-believe. The true artist, however, as Balzac observed, is not a turncoat but "the conqueror of difficulties." Gauguin was hardly that; but in justice to his brute strength, it must be said that of all the Bohemians who talked of exotic climes and drugged themselves with exotic vices, who complained of the sickness of civilization and bourgeois impediments, he alone had the guts to get out, to forage among the garlanded wenches of the tropics. In vacillating between civilization and savagery, he mastered neither; and his influence on painting has been more sentimental than structural.

Gauguin, by training and temperament, was more liberally equipped than most artists for a reversion to the primitive way of living. That his experiment ended in disaster is only another proof of the inability of man to slough off, by an act of will or a change of scene, his whole inheritance—his fixed mental habits and conditioned responses. He boasted, you will remember, that immodesty was foreign to his paradise, that his Polynesian Eve "stepped forth naked and unashamed, an unspoilt child". Let it be granted, for the sake of argument, that his Tehoura was as he described her, an unspoilt Eve; there remains the insuperable fact that he was no unspoilt Adam. On the contrary he was a man of the world, a globe-trotter, a sophisticated Parisian with the civilized vice of painting for exhibitions. There was no way in which he could live with his Eve on terms of equality, no access to the secrets, of her soul, no real participation in the life of her people. He could not drive out the snake of civilization he had brought with him. As a matter of truth, he did not try very hard; for a while he derived some satisfaction from the novelty of pretending to, and from the savor of dark meat, but soon he was writing home for money, and crying for French mistresses, French food, and French praise. His going native consisted in taking off his clothes and despoiling his Eve—the rest was scene painting and play acting for the Parisians. The superstition of the unspoilt Eve, as created by Gauguin, has inveigled many painters into a search for her paradise, but I have noticed that they do not thrive on a primitive diet; that one and all, however feebly conditioned they may have been by civilization, come wandering back again, with a batch of trumpery pictures done in the style of the master, to join the bread-line leading to the door of the dealer and the museum.

Gauguin's art is a French instrument cunningly tattooed with the insignia of savagery. As a reflection of life—which all art, however individualized in its form, must inevitably become—it is less illuminating than a newsreel or the jungle melodramas of the motion pictures. As an interpretation of his experiences in an unfamiliar world, it is vague and disingenuous. He tries to persuade us that he has got under the skins of the brown people, that he is one of them, a sharer in their inmost secrets and superstitions. We know from the pictures that he was nothing of the sort. If, like Conrad, he had been content to remain a white man, and to deal with the psychology of the white man in savage environments, and had left the myths to the anthropologists, he might have won legitimate honors in an untilled field, for he was intelligent and very talented.

An air of mystery hangs over Gauguin's conceptions, as if something profound and soul-stirring had been in progress. But what it is his pictures do not say. There are portentous hints, suggestive titles, and heathen imagery—but no tangible meanings. The reason is that the subject-matter was not truly felt; that Gauguin, after all, was a disgruntled sight-seer; that he did not know, from the depths of his experiences, the things he painted, and all their implications; that he resorted to makeshifts to conceal his ignorance, and to mumbo-jumbo properties to gain picturesque effects. One would think that his luscious subjects, which, at first, filled him with sensual delight and later with organic revulsions, would have aroused him to dramatic utterances and self-revelations of a high order—but he was hell-bent on playing the bogey-man.

As a consequence, his pictures are fantastic illustrations. I use the word illustration, not to reproach representational painting—all painting, when it is not mere ornamentation, is an illustration of experience—but in its popular meaning: to describe the work of those artists who attempt to translate verbal ideas into paint, to recast in pictorial form the organized experiences of others. Gauguin seeks to defraud our emotions; instead of scenes and figures sufficient in themselves, he offers us weird allusions to a world beyond our ken. The ruse is cleverly arranged. The symbols—the brooding figures and magical gimcracks—when not obviously counterfeit, indicate a superior knowledge on the part of the painter. We are led to assume that he knows more about the primitive spirit and the significance of its ceremonials than he discloses; we need a literary explanation to finish the mood—to complete the meaning.

Van Gogh, on the other hand, is a real painter. His art is self-explanatory; it tells its own story by the sheer expressiveness of the medium. He writes in the language of paint, and if you cannot read him,

it is because you do not understand that language, or because he sometimes uses a shorthand that is too personal to be deciphered. But it is
the shorthand of paint, and if you are unable to construe it from within
yourself, no literary explication will help you. Gauguin tries to speak
two languages at the same time—but the arts do not mix very well.
The longer he lived in the hot countries, the more dependent he became
on allusions and verbal supplements; and in the Marquesas Islands,
diseased and weary of his tropical playthings, he produced stuff that is
not much better than eccentric magazine-illustration.

Gauguin's technique is a calculated method, an artifice imposed on
various kinds of subject-matter—not a traditional instrument modified
into new forms by the pressure of new situations. It comes as a shock
to those acquainted with the sources of his forms to see how little he
was actually influenced, as a creative artist, by his adventures. Even his
color, which seems to be a tropical efflorescence, has its origins in the
bright palette of the Impressionists. He began as a pupil of Pissarro
and for several years persisted in the method of divided tones. A shallow
soul in many ways, he was too sensible and full-blooded to spend his
life embroidering the face of nature, and he stumped his fellow-dab-
blers with a discovery: "If it's greenness that you're after, why a metre
of green is more effective than a centimetre." An elementary observation, but when painters are absorbed in technical minutiae, they forfeit
the habit of thinking. Straightway, he expanded the precious little dots
into large patches of color. Then he was crowned king of the Synthesists,
a dubious honor which he wore with his tongue in his cheek.

In searching for synthesis, Gauguin was merely searching for design,
the backbone of art overlooked by the Impressionists. There was, he
reasoned, somewhere in art a precedent to guide him, a scheme for
holding areas of color together. He found it, or his henchmen dug it
up for him, in the earlier periods—in stained glass, enamels, and the
simplified decorations of the Byzantines—and he was not unaware of
the Japanese influence on Degas, Lautrec and his friend, Van Gogh.
From these sources, he worked out his plan for surface organization,

binding together, by means of heavy, unbroken contours, patches of color vividly contrasted, or figures which functioned in design as flattened masses. In Brittany, and more particularly in Tahiti, pretending to look at the world from a primitive point of view, he made the most of his borrowings, adapting strong outlines and also the surface characteristics of Cézanne's canvases—the planes and distortions—to negroid figures for which they seemed to be singularly appropriate.

Gauguin's Maori figures, strange to say, were all posed in pseudo-classical attitudes, an absurdity he attempted to disguise by the use of distortions, by brilliant color, and by the appeal of the subject-matter. His most original contribution is his color, which is truly magnificent. A fine color sense is not uncommon in literary men, and Gauguin had it in the superlative degree. His sensual nature reveled in the strongest pigments—yellows, deep blues, scarlets and vivid greens—which he placed in unexpected juxtapositions. But he did not apply color with the chromatic violence of the savage; the dominant hue is compounded of many tones, subtly interwoven, the effect of which suggests the rich texture of an Oriental fabric. His drawing, though far inferior to his color, was not less deliberately contrived. A poor draughtsman with small knowledge of the human body, he steered away from three-dimensional form and the difficulties of structural composition. He made an effort at modeling, but his forms seldom arrive at the thickness of the bas-relief and hence do not interfere with his surface arrangements. His figures, save for their sour faces signifying the approach of death or something inscrutable, are only units of decoration. He worked, so he told Van Gogh, from imagination, boasting that he never changed a line. By imagination he meant memory—and he had a good one—the memory of Puvis de Chavannes and Degas—but even so, he could not conceive a figure that strikes us as a fresh construction, or one that has the power of movement. The thick unrevised contours, he fancied, helped to create the impression of deep inspiration and spontaneity which he associated with primitive forms. Thus he made his synthetic art.

Gauguin's skill as a pattern-maker cannot be questioned. He has an excellent sense of placement, of mapping out a flat surface into partitions of color which are justly balanced both spatially and in black and white values. But he can hardly be called a composer, an artist who correlates his knowledge of life, whose conceptions are free from enigmas and subterfuges, whose experiences, large or small, simple or complex, are definite, firmly embodied, and presented in a completely unified structure. His talent belongs in the field of utilitarian craftsmanship—among the potters and textile designers. His best pictures are panoramas, or more precisely, sections of scenes decoratively rendered. Carry his art a step farther and you get a Matisse; and after Matisse, the interior decorator. Gauguin appeared at a critical moment, and with ruthless energy misdirected, turned the course of painting into the elaboration of pattern. He excited the popular imagination by the Byronic vigor of his personality, gained posthumous fame, and swiftly passed into legend. But it is possible, in this demoralized world of absconding bankers and jobless millions, that his indictment of civilization may be revived as the cry of the prophet; that men and women seeking escape from the capitalist ruin may find comfort in his romantic art.

In the first years of the century, there were, as I have pointed out, premonitory symptoms of a sensational uprising in art. Many forces, some of which we shall enumerate, had been working toward that end, and the time was ripe for revolution. As early as 1903, the igloos of Bohemia were humming with incendiary talk, and the talk was of three men, Van Gogh, Gauguin, and Cézanne. Vincent's bones lay among the sunflowers at Auvers, but his pictures kept his memory green; the complaining savage, crucified by his ego in his own private Bohemia, had just expired, vicariously atoning for the weaknesses of his followers; and the old Master of Aix was stumbling through the fields, still trying to realize his little sensation. These three, an odd combination of courage, hatred, and patience, filled the starving young painters of Montmartre with joy. For the Bohemians, being parasites by profession, sit in their igloos and talk, watching and praying for a man of genius; and when, at length, one does appear, they tear his art limb from limb, and spend their silent moments fining down their individual portions into arresting novelties which, soon or late, will bear the label of a new school. In 1906, when the death of Cézanne was announced, the critics of Paris surpassed themselves in those obituary defamations which make the decent French artist afraid to die. But in this case, the insults were answered by an insurrection known historically as the stampede of the Fauves, or wild animals.

In the historical sense, the Modernist upheaval was the culmination of anti-bourgeois tendencies in operation since the time of Delacroix. The direction of those tendencies in the nineteenth century we have already considered; and we have looked into the social life of France at the opening of the Universal Exhibition, in 1900. The Exhibition, it is well to recall, made the aristocrats, social and esthetic alike, conscious of the sordid ideals and abominable tastes of the bourgeois artists and politicians whom we have affectionately named the little people. The social lords—the high-life crowd—revolted in an orgy of exotic fripperies which were, if possible, more ludicrous than the tastes of the tradesmen. This exotic mania, fomented by the oriental and Ethiopian wares at the Exhibition, infected every department of art and letters and soon became the staple of Modernism. The young painters, the intellectual aristocrats, nursed a double grievance against society: first, the juries representing the little people had refused to sanction the work of a single contemporary artist of merit; second, the standards of French taste, from the highest to the lowest social order, were an affront to the national honor. There was but one solution— to scrap everything and create a new style.

The new movement in painting was anti-bourgeois and anti-social, in a word, Bohemian. Locally it was born in Montmartre, high on the old hill, not far from the Moulin de la Galette on one hand, and the sacred Roman pile on the other. Here, shoulder to shoulder, lived a colony of young men and women—the women, alas! unremembered— many of them in the Rue Ravignan in an old bathless building shaped like a washerwoman's barge, with a row of cubbyholes for studios. Here lived Pablo Picasso, of the unruly forelock, and Max Jacob, André

Salmon, Juan Gris, Kees Van Dongen, André Derain, Georges Braque, Pierre MacOrlan, Pablo Gargallo, Raoul Dufy, Francis Carco, André Warnod, Amedeo Modigliani, and Maurice Utrillo—poets and painters who had chosen Bohemianism as a career. They were young; they were poor; and they had nothing to lose. Their aims were not very clear, but their hatreds were emphatically defined: they would have no truck with Impressionism, or Neo-Impressionism, and academic training was the darkest blemish on the fair name of France. They would all be mad like Van Gogh, all enemies of society like Gauguin, and patient scholars of form like Cézanne.

Their madness was an affectation. Actually, they were a light-hearted crew, content to dine now and then, happy to barter a canvas for a bottle of wine, or to hang an inchoate masterpiece in the shop window of a mattress maker. They were all talented—some prodigiously so—but they were frustrated by the Bohemian conception of art. I record this fact with diabolical pleasure as a corrective to the calamity howlers who are continually bemoaning the frustration of American talent. You have heard their tale of woe: American produces a crop of fine young men, idealistic, gifted, potentially capable of great things, but their promise is never fulfilled—they are baffled, stunted, crushed into the habits of money grubbers by our brutal civilization. Shall we ship them to France? Well, we have tried that experiment on our painters. I shall have more to say of this hereafter; for the moment, it is enough to call attention to the Bohemians of Paris. Not one of them grew up; not one matured into a first-rate artist—I will not say of the stature of Daumier, that were asking too much, but of Cézanne or Van Gogh; they all followed, as André Lhote put it, the path of the merchant. There are the two leaders: Matisse, an old man now, who has been repeating, for lo! these thirty years, the bright patterns of his youth; and Picasso, in his fifties, slyly revising his juvenile Cubism for profit. The frustration of talent is not confined to America.

About 1905, having drafted a line of attack, the aforesaid painters were divided into two cults: the emotional expressionists—those professing to portray, in its original purity, the effect of a given experience on their sensitive souls; the intellectual abstractionists—those believing in pure form, that is, form as an isolated phenomenon living its own life and independent of human implications. At first there were no hard feelings between the two factions. Whatever their temperamental divergences, they were united in the common determination to wallop the bourgeoisie. The dividing lines were by no means absolute; and painters tactfully shifted from one cult to the other, some for honest reasons, others to bask in the limelight. Out of the two primary groups, there emerged in rapid succession, as we shall see, a profusion of diminutive sects which, at the hour of their birth, seemed to be of eternal importance. Today nothing is left of them save their sonorous classical trade-names. The whole Modernist movement—the mother cults and all the children —was of Bohemian origin. In the light of historical significance, the aims of the various denominations were identical: consciously or unconsciously, the painters of Paris completed the separation of art from its basis in the real world; they made living one thing and painting another; they made art a studio performance, a stew cooked up from the canvases of the past. As precipitately as might be, they carried art into the elaboration of pattern.

In 1906, a delegation from Montmartre including Van Dongen, Derain, Braque and Dufy, reinforced by Matisse, Marquet, Vlaminck, Rouault, and Friesz, exhibited their samples together, and the new art became a public problem. If those outcast painters intended to give the tastes of the little people a terrific clout, they achieved their purpose— their pictures shocked an audience that had hissed Van Gogh and Cézanne. Indeed they fetched an indignation so continued and vociferous that the politicians called to investigate the scandal. Discovering nothing in the pictures that could possibly affect the State—or anything else—the deputies sensibly withdrew, leaving the matter to the tender mercies of the press. The critics, not being paid—French critics are notoriously venal—did their worst, referring to the new art as "the wild colored shrieks of brutes." Thus Fauvism, the first of the Modernist schisms, was christened.

The Fauves traded in sensitivity. They regarded as of supreme importance the emotional flurry aroused within them by a piece of still-life, a perfunctory model, or the naïve expressions of the primitives. They would go Van Gogh one better; they would go him ten better; they would paint thrillers which would make his spiritual orgasms look like conventional illustrations. Fascinated by the simplified forms of the ancients, and following Van Gogh's practice of using color for its symbolical properties, they violated natural shapes and appearances, and visual truth, in the interest of emotional purity. They painted lemon yellow skies, red trees and green physiognomies. Why? To effect the direct transfer of their experiences; to concoct the diagrammatic equivalent of their agitated sensibilities. Pursuing their theories, they soon encountered a rather embarrassing critical objection. The average person, suffering no such agonies in the presence of simple things, found their pictures empty of all human values. Whereupon the Fauves, primed by enterprising literary friends, proclaimed the esthetic emotion, a psychological invention indispensable to the appreciation of art. Unless one were fortunately endowed with this peculiar emotion, one could not respond purely to the beauty of formal relationships. To such benighted souls, the Fauves recommended Jeanne d'Arc illustration and all subject-pictures, except, of course, the Renaissance masters who were out of favor at this period, or admired for qualities beyond the grasp of the average man. Aided by the introspective psychologists, especially the Freudians, the Fauves had professional justification for anything they might produce; and in a remarkably short time the art of painting was dragged into the imbecile medleys of pure Expressionism.

Esteeming themselves as far more important than their subjects, the Fauves rendered nature with unrestricted freedom, subordinating formalistic accuracy of drawing, tone, perspective, and verisimilitude to a whimsical delight in pattern-making. Technically they owed much to Gauguin's flat designs and to Van Gogh's clear streaks of color, but the elliptical style of the mad Dutchman, by comparison, was as compact as a Holbein. Though they boasted of their sensitivity and the direct transfer of their feelings before nature, the main source of their inspiration was the museum. Unable to find, among the bigger figures, precedent for their calculated vagaries, they rummaged the lesser masters of the far past: the primitives of every land, the Egyptians, Cretans, Byzantines, Persians and the negroes. To the layman, their archaeological plunder, whipped into wild, eclectic combinations and sizzling arabesques, though unintelligible, seemed to indicate some fierce turmoil of the spirit. But the wildness was only technical—only the manner of infants and savages. After the excitement of floating the movement had subsided, the Fauves were as tame as lambs. Today, thanks to the American market, they are prosperous business men. Let us examine the career of one of them more closely, that eminently successful Frenchman, Henri Matisse.

7

MATISSE

In the month of May, 1933, a French liner discharged at the port of New York, a ruddy little gentleman of international fame in the arts. He was a painter but he did not look the part; he had the personal appearance and the manner of a successful merchant, and fellow passengers unacquainted with his fame mistook him for a Polish Jew who had prospered in America. In many respects he was a merchant—and a very shrewd one; he had grown rich in American gold by supplying unsuspecting and snobbish business men with a commodity the possession of which, they fancied, not only endowed them with the finest elements of French culture, but also expressed their own personalities, thus making them creative artists. He had come to this country to further his investments. But gold and renown had not given him arrogance; nor filled him with that sniggering superiority which European artists habitually affect when they condescend to visit American customers. He charmed every one by his modesty, his cordial decency and his tactful silences—qualities distinguishing him from the French bourgeoisie which he represented. He brought with him some of his precious merchandise, but at this particular moment, his pictures seemed as empty of significance as a bolt of dress goods; as distant from the turmoil of contemporary affairs as those fragile things put under glass in the far corners of museums for the feeble delight of senile experts.

In normal times Matisse would have been good for a column of copy. But the times were far from normal: May was as cold as March, and the depressing weather increased the apprehensiveness of a nation which the President was swinging headlong into the New Deal; and in New York

City, for the first time in history, art was on the front pages of the newspapers. Art, for once, was a living issue, a social problem, a political weapon aimed at the heads of panic-stricken capitalists. It was all because a Mexican painter had been deposed from his mural throne in Rockefeller Center. But the issue was much more serious than the expulsion of one painter, or the fate of his fresco: to many it indicated the overthrow of political dynasties and the consolidation of the proletariat by the insidious power of art. Even the hard-boiled editors admitted that esthetic considerations had nothing to do with the case. In this alarming situation, Matisse, with his modiste's talent and his bundle of innocuous rags, was practically ignored. The press had no other interest in him than to solicit, for a brief news item, his opinion of Rivera and the action of the Rockefellers.

The question was embarrassing. Matisse was puzzled and discreet; he shrugged his shoulders and wisely reserved judgment. There was no precedent for such an action in France; in his country an artist did not dare to harbor political convictions, or to air them in his work. If he did, he went to jail like Daumier, or, like Courbet, into exile. Not anywhere in the whole of France was there a mural which did not glorify the status quo and testify to the inextinguishable grandeur of la patrie. A painter should be an artist, not a propagandist. He, himself, in his younger days, had been the victim of ignorant persecution; but once it was plain that his art was quite traditional and a tribute to bourgeois well-being, he became the idol of the masses. "Was Rivera paid for his services?" he inquired amiably. "He was paid handsomely and in full," was the reply. Matisse smiled jovially—the smile of the canny shopkeeper who has driven a good bargain—and spoke cautiously but to the effect that the incident had been satisfactorily closed.

But the incident was not closed and will not be closed for many a day. Far more important than any question of the artist's Communism, or the right of the Rockefellers to confiscate public property, was the social interest aroused by Rivera's murals. Here was painting that brought into the market-place the deadly issue between the academic

artists—the die-hards of the old school and the upstart Modernists alike
—and those whose work was inspired by living subject-matter and expressive of social values; here was painting that was nothing less than
a declaration of war against the shifty dealer, the reign of the useless
easel picture, and the partisans of pure form; painting that could be
understood without the aid of psychological manuals translated from
the French. The opposition was not confined to the capitalists and their
subsidized critics: the neurotic pattern-makers also read the handwriting
on the wall and circulated ugly stories about Rivera, whispering that he
was a mountebank and a big noise; that his work was all sound and fury
and ballyhoo. In this atmosphere, Matisse was uncomfortable; and departed immediately, with his son, an art dealer in New York, for a suburb
of Philadelphia where he was trying to compose a mural for a costly
mausoleum. Being essentially a miniature painter, he has had great
difficulty with wall space which the huge Mexican would have polished
off in a couple of weeks.

Henri Matisse was born in the north of France, in the year 1869, the
son of a small grain merchant. He came to Paris in his early twenties to
study pharmacy, but soon turned to painting, a decision which caused his
people the sharpest annoyance and no little shame; for they believed,
with the prejudice of their class, that art was a low and unmanly business
—the refuge of vicious beggars. Of a methodical turn of mind, he entered
his new profession in a business-like manner, worked hard, and managed
to make a living. For ten years he copied dead masters in the Louvre—
copied them patiently and photographically, and sold them to the
government for distribution among provincial museums—exhibited
occasionally with the Beaux-Arts academicians, and won some notice
as an extremely skilful executant of the most conservative type. During
this decade he formed certain mental habits and submitted to certain
influences which contributed largely to the development of his art as it
is known today. He was profoundly influenced by his first teacher, none
other than the great Bouguereau, the people's choice; not technically but
spiritually—by his master's celebration of the cult of prettiness which

Stendhal had churlishly prophesied the French would never outgrow. In the studio of Moreau, where he met Raoul Dufy, Rouault, and Marquet, he learned the value of exotic themes, and how to dress such themes in the styles of the past. And in these years he acquired the museum habit: the tendency to go to other artists for his materials, to separate painting from living, to make pictures by the tactful revision of old forms. This habit persisted and eventually became his stock-in-trade, his point of departure at every phase of his career. He admitted that "on entering the Louvre, he lost the sensation of the life of his own time," but nevertheless, the museum remained for him, as he put it, "the native land."

Matisse, however, was no ordinary copyist. Working daily in the museums, he kept his wits about him, studied the styles and methods of the men of every period, and acquired extensive knowledge of the technical history of art. But it was true, as he said, that he painted just as every one else painted, and he was very unhappy. He felt that he was not honest with himself, that his diligence was getting him nowhere. He was conscious that he was exhuming corpses and copying them for money; that what he was doing had no connection with the life of his own age. Whereupon a change came over him. Slowly, and with the caution for which he is famous, he moved toward the stormy centers of radicalism. First, he introduced into his copies his own emotional impressions; but the Government refused to buy, and his troubles began. He joined the Impressionists and painted canvases that were no better and no worse than those of Bonnard; he went into Divisionism but soon turned his back on that quasi-scientific recipe. He applied his inventive talent to Cézanne, then to Gauguin and Van Gogh; and from Van Gogh he hurried to negro sculpture and the flat designs of the Orientals. From these sources he compiled an elliptical style of expression which gained him the derisive title, "Leader of the Pack of Wild Animals"; but which, after the unpleasant notoriety had died down, rewarded him with a large and steady income.

During this transition Matisse had a tough time of it. In his twenty-fourth year, he had married, bringing into the household, according to

Gertrude Stein, a natural daughter "by whom Madame Matisse did more than her duty because, having read in her youth a novel in which the heroine had done so and been consequently much loved all her life, she had decided to do the same." There were two legitimate children, both boys; and the family lived on the left bank, in a small apartment by the river.

The family endured the most painful poverty in that little apartment. "The year after Matisse's success at the salon," Gertrude Stein writes, "he spent the winter painting a very large picture of a woman setting a table, and on the table was a magnificent dish of fruit. It had strained the resources of the Matisse family to buy this fruit. Fruit was horribly dear in Paris in those days, even ordinary fruit; imagine how much dearer was this very extraordinary fruit, and it had to be kept until the picture was completed, and the picture was going to take a long time. In order to keep it as long as possible they kept the room as cold as possible, and that under the roof and in a Paris winter was not difficult. Matisse painted in an overcoat and gloves, and he painted at it all winter. It was finished at last and sent to the salon, and there it was refused.

"And now Matisse's serious troubles began; his daughter was very ill, he was in an agonizing mental struggle concerning his work. Every morning he painted, every afternoon he worked at his sculpture, late every afternoon he drew in the sketch class from the nude, and every evening he played his violin. These were very dark days and he was very despairful."

Madame Matisse will go down in history as the rival of Catherine Blake for the honor of being the perfect wife to an artist. "She was an admirable housekeeper," to quote Miss Stein again. "Her place was immaculate. She kept the house in order, she was an excellent cook and provider, she posed for all of Matisse's pictures." And, I may add, she did not have a lunacy commission appointed when her husband bought a Cézanne—Cézannes were cheap in those days, but the purchase strained their resources much more severely than the purchase of fruit. "She opened a little millinery shop to keep them going in their poorest days.

She was a very straight dark woman with a long face and a firm, large, loosely hung mouth like a horse. She had an abundance of dark hair."

Matisse's rise from the hack copyist to the wildest of the wild animals was not a parvenu flight. Nor was it the result of any inner compulsion of the spirit; nor was it guided by a strong central conviction such as drove Van Gogh onward in his rapid career. It was a premeditated advancement, every change deliberately outlined, every consequence shrewdly anticipated. It was not determined by his experiences with living, but by his experiences with pictures. He had the intelligence to understand that Cézanne, Van Gogh, and Gauguin, must have successors, that a new tendency was forming on the struggles of those pioneers: and with admirable foresight, he believed that he had an excellent chance to become the leader of a school of emotional Modernists. Matisse knew the French: how they howl down each new thing and how, in the end, they rejoice in its possession, if it is traditionally rooted and decoratively presented. He also knew that in the wake of French recognition came the American buyer; and that ultimately life would be rosy. He loved his creature comforts.

In 1905, at the first autumn salon, his pictures and those of his confrères, Derain, Rouault, Vlaminck, Manguin, Braque, and Marquet, so incensed the public that the term "Fauves," as I have already recorded, was applied to the authors, and a new school was born. One of his exhibits was the famous *Woman with a Hat*, a portrait of Madame Matisse. I say famous because this canvas was thought to be particularly hideous, and angry spectators who cast their spleen on inanimate objects tried to scratch off the paint. But the picture was responsible for his first patron. Gertrude Stein thought it quite natural, liked it and bought it—after Madame Matisse had stubbornly held out for a price which her husband insisted was prohibitive.

The following year, a large individual exhibition at Druet's brought him more patrons and indisputable leadership of the pack of Fauves. In 1907, he painted *Joy of Life*, and on the strength of his growing reputation, undertook to instruct young artists in the principles of sound draughtsmanship. He was a hard taskmaster, laying down the law of tradition to his pupils, and counseling them not to imitate him but to learn to draw "correctly," as he had drawn in his youth. He had now arrived at his mature style, and his work since 1907, while it has added materially to his fortunes, has added nothing to his position as an artist. What has been called the continuity of his art is no more than the repetition of a successful method. Matisse was introduced to the American public in 1908, by Alfred Stieglitz, at the historic shrine known as "291." Stieglitz tells many amusing stories about that exhibition to illustrate changing fashions in art. The following is typical. An ostentatiously cultured lady, the wife of a prominent curator, came into the gallery, peered at the Matisses, held her turned-up nose with a gloved hand, and exclaimed, with the audacity of the uninformed, "Mr. Stieglitz, these pictures are decayed! They make me feel unclean. Remove them and have your gallery disinfected." Stieglitz, a fanatic himself and indulgent with cranks, replied agreeably, "Things are happening in art. Go home and take a bath, but don't repeat what you have said here. It might be used against you." A few years later, in Paris, when Matisse was having things his own way, this same lady fell on his neck, pestered him with flattery, and confided that she had adored his work from the moment she had first seen it. "There were many others who were disinfected by familiarity," Stieglitz said.

Exhibiting at the riotous Armory circus, staged in New York in 1913, Matisse was treated to a provincial drubbing that was truly Parisian in its malevolence. He was classified as an aboriginal and an impostor; he was called incompetent, indecent and depraved. The protracted ridicule aggrieved him sorely, and he begged an American traveler to vouch for his character. "Do tell the American people," he said, "that I am a normal man; that I am a devoted husband and father; that I have three fine children; that I go to the theater, ride horseback, have a comfortable home, a fine garden that I love, flowers, etc., just like any man." Current opinion has swung to the other extreme, and today Matisse is accepted as a conventional gentleman of the old school. Unlike most Frenchmen, he is not afraid of water and has traveled in many parts of the world—in Russia, Italy, Morocco, Tahiti, and America. On a trans-continental journey across the United States, viewing at first-hand the untouched materials awaiting the painter, he expressed surprise that the American artist should go abroad to paint. Since 1917, he has lived in a villa at Nice where he has painted his most popular pictures. He lives, not luxuriously, but with the measured gaiety and wine-sipping satisfaction of the bourgeois who has attained security. He has a weakness for the movies and nude models.

Matisse's art is all on the surface, and it is impossible to penetrate very deeply into a superficial art. There are three aspects of his work to be considered: his technique; the content, if any, of his painting; and the reasons for his exaggerated reputation.

His technique is a synthetic method arbitrarily compounded in the studio by exhaustive research into historical examples of balanced decoration. Primarily devoted to surface arrangements, he has extracted little from the great occidental masters, scarifying the lesser men and burrowing among the Orientals. The Impressionists and the photographers had ruined the picture space; Cézanne undertook to restore it in three dimensions; Manet, Whistler and Degas, and then Lautrec, Gauguin and Van Gogh, all influenced by the Japanese print, were concerned with surface unity—the organization of representational subject-matter in the flat; Matisse carried painting forward, or more precisely, backward, to the drastic simplifications of the primitives. He practically abolished representation, mutilating his figures into conventional diagrams, reducing the means of expression to the minimum so as to convey the emotion, he explained, directly. By emotion he meant the clear apprehension of the organized picture space; he sought to eliminate disquieting objective characteristics, to avoid every element of surprise or dramatic emphasis, everything that might interfere with the immediate grasp of the pattern. It seems never to have occurred to him, as he sorted his studious scrapings into logical combinations, that the artists he admired were not purposeless mechanics; that the art of the Byzantines, before it had withered into abstractions was religious ideography; that the art of the Persians and the Japanese was symbolical; that negro sculptures were fetishes designed to terrify evil spirits, not forms put together for art's sake; that Van Gogh's frenzied abbreviations expressed his battles with the real world; that even Gauguin's aboriginal pretensions were intimately related to his experiences. He was interested in formal relationships; he wished to have no commerce with reality, and said so, quite candidly.

Matisse has defined his technical procedure clearly. "Expression for me," he wrote in his *Painter's Notes*, "is the whole disposition of my picture—the place occupied by the figures, the empty space around them, the proportions—everything plays its part. Composition is the art of arranging in a *decorative manner* the various elements used by the painter. In a picture every separate part will be visible and will take that position, principal or secondary, which suits it best. Everything which has no utility is harmful, for the reason that every superfluous detail will occupy, in the mind of the spectator, the place of some other detail which is essential."

This, needless to say, is a definition of pattern-making, an art in which the size, position, proportions and colors of forms are not authorized by visual truth, nor by the artist's experiences in the world, nor by human meanings, but solely by precedent and his skill in improvising new arrangements. Every one of Matisse's pictures appears to be, and in fact is, a studio set-up, a posed and languid affair, and artificial in the sense that whatever meaning it may have lies largely in the ingenious solution of a technical problem. Let us put the case more concretely. His favorite subject is "the odalisque in the hotel bedroom," a theme he approaches with the physical enthusiasm of the Frenchman, thus saving his design, as we shall see, from the vacuity of the stenciled fabric. The odalisque, wearing red transparent pajamas, reclines somnolently upon a Moorish divan. Matisse contemplates the scene with satisfaction, his purpose being to produce, he says, "a harmony corresponding to his own feelings"—to his nicely regulated sensuality. How to proceed?

He might render the lady anatomically, and with a certain amount of verisimilitude, but this would never do. It would convey the flabby carnality of his favorite, but not his own feelings—himself and his emotion; and his efforts to construct a solid figure were as academic as those of the Beaux-Arts students. His head is filled with oriental matter— he will do it in the Persian style! From the storehouse of his memory he conjures up a particular design to serve as a working graph, a decision which takes the edge off his sensual enthusiasm, and transforms the interior into a cold technical exercise. Swiftly he sketches the scene, preserving as much of the general characteristics as is consistent with flat oriental decoration. This done, he bids his fleshly assistant goodbye—for the time being—and returns to his studio.

His task now is to scheme out a combination of balancing colors and harmoniously related lines. He paints the tone of pajamas, establishing a relation between the red of the garment and the white of the canvas; he paints the yellow of the floor and the green of the shutters, establishing further relations which, in turn, are complicated by other tones as he puts them down—the patch of sky in the background, the flowered divan and the light wall paper. "These different tones," he says, "diminish and tend to destroy each other. I must put them into a relationship that builds them up instead of knocking them down." Gradually he substitutes a new combination of colors with green as the dominant tone instead of red. The floor comes out a dark reddish brown, the shutters light yellow and the pajamas a brilliant green.

Similarly he proceeds with the drawing. The right posterior cheek of his model is flat and billowy but, even so, much too meager to counteract the bulge of the bed. He doubles the natural expanse of the contour —it is bad for the figure but good for the design. Adhering to his principle that "it is better to modify proportions than to invalidate compositional balance," he enlarges or diminishes the outlines of all the properties in the room; and when he has finished the job, he has evolved a pattern "to appeal to our esthetic sensibilities." During the process the intrinsic character of the scene has been altered beyond recognition, and his little emotion dissipated—but the loss does not disturb him. He has achieved a balanced decoration, all the parts of which, and the empty spaces between the parts, are in just relationship.

There are no rules for design of this sort. The free or proportional pattern, borrowed by Matisse from the Asiatics, completely ignores the symmetrical motif which most occidental artists consider indispensable to non-representational schemes. The free pattern, in contrast to the symmetrical, lends itself to endless variation, its successful use depending on the artist's feeling and his ability to hold lines and colors in equilibrium. Matisse has said, "While working, I try never to think, only to feel." We have no evidence that he has gone very far in either direction, but we have proof enough that his wits are sharp and that he knows what he is driving at. He has taste, tact, certainty of spacing, and a genius for adaptation. His whole decorative scheme is based on the re-proportioning of objects. His design, such as it is, is not the result of the analysis and organization of planes, as with Cézanne, but of the artful shifting of the proportions of the silhouette. Nature, in this process, is not reconstructed, but tastefully distributed for the sake of balanced expression. And the artist who sacrifices realism to decorative motifs, who merely changes the proportions of silhouettes to attain balance, binds himself, emotionally and spatially, to the limitations of a flat mechanism.

At one time, pursuing his theory of a logical art, Matisse committed the grossest violations of natural forms. In the interest of a balanced ensemble, he would distort parts of the human body—the curve of the hip or the length of the leg—many times beyond the natural proportions. He had historical precedent, I shall not say for distortion, but for radical departures from the norm: Michael Angelo's Adam has the neck of a bullock, and the frame of a giant, and El Greco's figures are elongated into supernatural effigies. But these departures are harmonious throughout; they do not impress us as bodies wilfully pulled out of shape but as new and more powerful constructions. Nor did Michael Angelo and El Greco—nor the Persians and Africans for that matter—modify their forms for the sake of decorative neatness; they created figures for dramatic purposes, as parts of a spiritual context. Matisse simply took the

HENRI MATISSE: *The Hat with Plumes*

easiest way out, producing freaks and eyesores, deforming the figure and allowing the pattern to consume the subject. His pictures were logical— and also ridiculous. Imbecility may be balanced and eccentricity may be logical, but art has no need of either. Yet they might not have been ridiculous if he had made them very small—as illuminations for books, or designs for textiles. Reluctantly, he abandoned his glaring deformities for a more seemly approximation of nature; but not before his example had done its worst. A few years hence, the little Matisses in Europe and America filled the show rooms with logical monsters. Sensitive souls expressing themselves!

A leader in the revolt against the camera vision in art—the literal duplication of nature—and influenced by Gauguin's creed, and by his own excursions into the methods of the Asiatics, Matisse endeavored to get himself into an unsophisticated state of mind, to make pictures charged with "primitive emotion." "I try to see as my little boy sees," he said. Strange that so sensible a man should have been duped by the philosophy of childishness! A man cannot become a primitive by an act of will; and to see as a child sees is an impossibility, unless one remains, like the infantile Rousseau, in a state of arrested development. Gauguin put that foolish notion to a practical test, hoping, by a change of environment, to divest himself of civilized habits—and we know what happened to him. There is a vast difference between the simplified art of the educated adult and the simple expressions of the child. Children and primitives are not devoid of knowledge; they do not draw with absolute innocence; they know their world, only their world is small and their knowledge limited. Their art is interesting because they do not exceed their capacities; they work directly from experience, and their technique is sufficient for their emotional needs. When a child sketches a locomotive, he does not attempt to photograph the engine, nor to make it mechanically plausible; he is satisfied with a diagram, a form which shall stand as the equivalent of his own little experience with an instrument that has touched his imagination. This is art of a kind, arresting in its logic, perfect, if you will, in a small way, but relatively unimportant.

171

Too much fuss has been made over children's drawings by artists who cannot draw, and who hope to advance themselves by exploiting the nursery.

For a sane adult whose experiences with the locomotive are many-sided, who not only knows its organic structure, but its workings and implications, and its effect on the modern man's ideas of speed and space—for such an artist to attempt to see as the child sees is a pose or a delusion. Matisse, of course, never descended to the driveling stuff put forth in the name of "purity of vision." What he actually did, as far as it was humanly possible, was to keep his daily experiences from interfering with his preconceived notions of logical decoration. To do this, he regarded his odalisque as a piece of still-life, an isolated form, an object bearing no relation to the world outside his studio. Whereas the child was held to the end by his interest in and experience with the subject, Matisse was sustained only by his interest in the method. On this account, his pictures; the best along with the worst, are more or less abstract; and in abstraction there is no vitality.

I have, I fear, given the impression that Matisse's art is empty of human significance. This is not altogether true, but his art is so predominantly a matter of technical dexterity that his own son, on being respectfully requested to tell what manner of man his father was, answered curtly that it was nobody's business. This would appear to be the case; for his son, an art dealer now handling Matisse's pictures as if they were cosmic particles dropped down from heaven, evidently regards the artist as a kind and loving father who works all day in his studio, and at nightfall, closes his shop like a merchant, to return to his family and a life which has nothing to do with his pictures. But in the last judgment, a man's art—and this is as true of the abstractionist as of the Communist—is a reflection of his mental and physical habits; and Matisse, in spite of himself, has allowed something of the warmth of life to enter his studio. Better than anyone else has he defined his purpose.

"My dream," he wrote, "is an art of balance, of purity, of tranquillity, without disquieting or preoccupying subject—an art which shall be to everyone who works with his brain, to the man of affairs as well as the man of letters, soothing and calming in its appeal, something comparable to a friendly armchair which rests him from bodily fatigues."

An art for the retiring business man! A suggestion of nudity to soothe him, and not enough reality to excite him!

Matisse's dream has been nicely realized. Surely no one familiar with the true nature of painting will complain that his art is burdened by strong convictions or powerful feelings; that it springs from a deep interest in mankind or an original view of the world. It is a mild and lethargic art, containing at best a pleasing savor of the sensual aspects of things. We behold no transformations of nature to serve an ideal purpose, no dramatic sequences born of an active imagination; we find, instead, traditional knowledge and consummate taste—in a word, nature, le monde visible of Gautier, presented in terms of flat pattern. He is saved from total electicism, from the meaningless devotion to academic processes, and from lifeless abstraction, by his joyous response to nature. Though preoccupied with pure design, he manages, nevertheless, to preserve his direct contacts with the living model, and to express those contacts with ease and remarkable fluency. To an extent he achieves a harmony corresponding to his own feelings—to his first sensual vision of the nude woman in an exotic setting. His work is finely tempered and exquisitely poised; in it we feel something of the gaiety and color of life, and the enthusiasm born of good health. Matisse once said, "If one feels no emotion, one should not paint. When I came to work this morning, I had no emotion, so I took a horseback ride. When I returned I felt like painting, and had all the emotion I wanted." When we say that his emotion is but another name for bourgeois well-being, and that a fraction of it, equally distributed, informs his designs, we have said all that can be said of the content of his painting.

It is obvious that an art composed mainly of traditional methods offers little to the student and less to the layman who does not use painting as a sedative. It is also obvious that such an art runs inevitably into conventions and pattern-making for its own sake. By long practice and scholastic knowledge, one may erect an imposing shell round museum deposits—but the substance of art comes from experience. One cannot ensnare reality by rearranging contours and surfaces. It is fairly easy to devise a balanced decoration, if the artist avoids the world of fact—the strong preferences and recalcitrant experiences which play the devil with logic and which, for successful co-ordination, call for dramatic centers of interest, exciting contrasts, and powerful variations in size and type.

Matisse proceeds on the dead level of uniformity. He allows the pattern—a traditional and abstract scheme—to modify and devitalize the subject; the more original artist is forced by his interest in the subject, and by fresh situations in life, to create a new design consistent with his experiences. His art, therefore, is stationary; it has neither rhythm nor movement—only color and equilibrium. His closest approach to animated forms is to be found in those large unsightly foetuses, which, posed in dancing attitudes, seem to possess, if not the power of motion, at least the property of elasticity. Matisse, I repeat, would be most useful in the field of book illumination or textile designing. His motifs should not be framed—they should be stamped on cloth and sold by the bolt. But he has no sense of scale, and for some reason, probably because he imagines that mural decoration consists in spreading small and harmless ideas over a big space—and it does, in the hands of the academic space-fillers—he considers himself a wall painter. His trials in this department reveal nothing but his poverty of imagination. His elastic nudes, when stretched all over the wall, become grotesque and silly.

The world of art is wide and its jurisdiction infinite. Any work, I suppose, involving skill, precision, proportion, and a modicum of organizing ability, to which charm has been added, and the personal touch, no matter how faint, may rightly be called art. Matisse has worked faithfully for a minor aim; he has produced a form of art—but let us not overestimate its significance. In demonstrating the manifold variations inherent in the free pattern—his experiments have brought color and fresh vigor to costume designing and household ornamentation—he has exerted a salutary influence and deserved his reputation; for deflecting the Modernist current into the sleazy boudoir tradition of France, he will not soon be forgiven. His reputation is the natural consequence of a movement in which painters, discovering the compositional basis of pictures, lost their moorings and proclaimed the aim and end of art to be the exhibition of structure. He superseded Cézanne as the tribal deity. He was, and is today, the ruling spirit among those painters who have no business in art; who mistake a method for an emotion; who believe that painting is music; who pretend that their little technical interests reflect their experiences; and who, with a smattering of psychology to strengthen their impudence, try to persuade us that their random blobs and aimless disfigurements represent profound states of the soul.

Matisse's position has been fortified by dealers and laggard critics. The criticism of his work, for the most part, is a collection of clinical notes which, when sifted out, disclose but two intelligible statements. First, Matisse is ninety-nine per cent pure, that is, pure tradition, and perforce a great artist. Second, to appreciate him, one is obliged to swallow the fallacy that abstract balance, or harmony, is not the accompaniment but the end and purpose of art. To illustrate the clinical operations that have been performed on the Frenchman, I quote a passage from *The Art of Henri-Matisse*, by Barnes and de Mazia, page 373. The picture referred to is the celebrated *Joy of Life*, a large and vacant picture built round a naked triangle. There are no hidden meanings in the picture. In the center of the triangle is a cluster of leaping foetuses; on the right side, smudges and some irregular patches attached to stems— presumably trees; along the base and in the lower angle at the left, nudes are strewn. The nudes are vague, amphibious space-fillers—nothing more. The proportioning and spacing are novel and excellently managed; there is no drawing whatever. The design would be appropriate and pleasantly inconspicuous, if woven in wool for an antimacassar; in its present dimensions it is a vapid tour de force. I should like to reproduce it, but it is interred in the Barnes Foundation and may never be seen again. Here is the quotation:

"The design as a whole represents an organic fusion of derivations from Greek and Hindu sculpture, mosaics, the forms of Andrea del Castagno, Giorgione, Tintoretto, El Greco, Rubens, Renoir, Gauguin and the Impressionists, all of which, because of the exotic color and the decorative pattern of intertwining arabesques, are dominated by a quality fundamentally Oriental."

This utterance will go on record as the most preposterous elegy ever delivered by a plastic surgeon over the dead body of his patient.

Matisse himself is a modest person. To my knowledge, he has never claimed to be a great artist; and he has never said that the close study of traditional practice is an indication of originality. He remarked recently that the purchasers of his paintings did not always understand them: "How could they, when I don't understand many of the paintings myself?" He meant, I take it, that he sometimes wondered whether there was any meaning to be gathered from elaborate and recondite dabbling. He also remarked that "art is an escape from reality"—the truest thing ever said of his own work. And it is because of this very fact that a comfortable bourgeois gentleman has become the idol of the Bohemians. Matisse, the leader of a modern school, has kept his art aloof from modern life. He is contemporary only in the sense that he is connected with a movement in painting which, though opposed to any participation in the real world, happens to be in existence at the present time.

Caricature of Picasso by Gargallo

8

PICASSO

PICASSO is the most fortunate of modern painters. It has been his happy lot to be judged, as artists wish to be judged, solely by esthetic standards; to win universal recognition; to enjoy and utilize a fame that may not survive him. He has been canonized during his own lifetime. This small, sly, uneducated Bohemian is the king of modern painting; by common consent the master of the modern School of Paris. And a master he is—but not of art. He is a master of methods.

Picasso's career is a masterpiece of strategy. He has not taken his art too seriously—that remunerative ritual he has entrusted to his literary friends, and to his imitators. Only once has he committed the tactical error of talking about his work and revealing his mental limitations; of the thousand and one egregious philosophies projected into his vacuous contrivances, he has signified neither approval nor resentment. Instead, he has maintained an oracular reticence, pluming his genius lock, cocking his dark eye, and conjuring up further mysteries. Bothered by no deep convictions which try the souls of bigger men, he has patiently cultivated the enigmatical. He has faced adversity with a light heart; he is companionable in a small circle of miscellaneous refugees; and in his enormous mercantile success, he has remained immune to the usual vanities and self-laudations of the brotherhood. He has stubbornly resisted his experiences; he has no interest in life; he is interested only in art—in the mechanical formation of pictures. He has used his nimble intelligence to complete the withdrawal of art into the inorganic world; like the monastic logicians, he lives in the cells of method. His art is perfect because it offers nothing; pure because it is purged of human

177

content; classic because it is dead. By converting the personality into a process, Picasso has become the leader of the methodists.

He was born in Malaga, in 1881, of Spanish, Jewish, and Italian stock. When a small boy, he displayed prodigious skill as a copyist, and, in 1900 was sent to Paris by his father, an art teacher in the academy of Barcelona. He saw at once that Paris was the place for him, and, in 1903, settled there permanently. By second nature, he joined the quacking indigents of Montmartre; and his life has followed the conventional pattern of the Bohemian careerist. He lived with various women, was never without a practical joke in his lean years, and rose swiftly into prominence. Perceiving, as a youth, the trend of modern painting towards an abstract basis, and ably seconded by poets and eccentrics hungry for notoriety, he took the bold but quite obvious step, of denuding art of its representational vestments. The effects of his wily operations are known to every one. Latterly, rich and respected, he has lived with his wife and son in a more fashionable quarter of Paris, close to the big dealers and the smart international gamblers whose tastes and ideals his art so accurately reflects.

Picasso is generally presented as a creature of many modes and skins, an unaccountable fellow who is likely, at any moment, to astonish us with some new and insoluble rebus, some baffling, diabolical invention. On the surface, this would appear to be the case; but on closer inspection, it is plain that he has adhered, from the outset, to one inflexible principle. He believes that art is a purely material thing; that is to say, a picture is a composition in the same sense that a pile of neatly arranged bricks is a composition; that its value is measured simply and solely by the skill, the orderliness and the novelty of the arrangement; that the unity of a picture is the unity of a chain of sausages, or a crystallized mineral; that art is an independent entity, governed by its own laws; that a picture represents nothing; that even when dealing with the human figure, it does not communicate emotions inseparably connected with the figure; that it is not a symbol charged with human implications, an instrument employed by artists to express their experience with life; in short, that the material constituents—the actual mud and oil—when arrestingly consolidated, contain the true esthetic values.

Following this principle, he is absolved from all commerce with reality. He is under no obligations to his experiences; he has no need of a point of view; nor of any knowledge of the world of affairs; nor does he need beliefs, faiths, doubts, and reflections. He has no use for nature, nor for living models. He is above responsibilities; a completely detached organism, an esthete pure and simple. Why should he fret his soul to create new forms when the stuff of art lies ready-made in the museums? Why should he go to the trouble of making the preliminary selection from nature when the work has already been done? The world is full of perfectly good forms. He has only to despoil them, to obliterate the vulgar human characteristics, and despoiled them he has, one after the other, like an omnivorous beast: the forms of Steinlen, Forain, Whistler, Lautrec, Gauguin, Van Gogh, Puvis de Chavannes, El Greco, the negroes; Cézanne, Ingres, Corot, the Greeks. Whenever Picasso tackles a real problem in art, his failure is monumental. Years ago, when he was on the climb, he attempted a portrait of Gertrude Stein. That uncouth spinster was collecting geniuses and he was willing to be collected. She professed to admire his pictures, and was patronizing him for all there was in it. He had never drawn from life and was ignorant of the structure of the head; but he pegged away at the job for nearly a year and finally called it finished. And there it is, a lifeless old squaw; something between the living and the dead; the celebrated carcase of Stein! Since that fiasco, he has let nature alone, except for an occasional school-piece for the American juries.

During his first years in Paris, Picasso's master was Toulouse-Lautrec. But the abstract mania was already upon him, and though he painted recognizable subjects such as harlequins, absinthe drinkers, and emaciated beggars, his subjects have only the faintest connection with the environment in which he lived. They are artificial forms manufactured in the studio; they are devoid of vitality and meaning; they have no basis in the observed facts of life, or in the behavior of man. He uses a stock expression for all his faces; his figures are all alike—all concepts, curiosities, isolated trash. There is not, in the whole lot of them, a single convincing human being; not one created from the specific situation which gives to art—to the face, figure and attitude—its peculiar character and distinction. In his blue and pink periods, Picasso demonstrated his remarkable craftsmanship and his ability to manipulate the technical implements of other artists; but it was his Cubism that made him famous.

In 1907, influenced by the simplified carvings of the negroes, he made drawings in which the human head approximates an abstract design; and some three years later, pursuing his natural inclination, he went completely abstract. First, he blocked out an object in planes and angles—the head, for instance, though still recognizable, being reduced to an assemblage of geometrical fractions. In the next phase, the head was hacked into sections which were arbitrarily shuffled together so as to bring into a single focus aspects observed from several points of view. Or, as his satellites put it, "moving round an object, he seized several successive appearances which, when fused into a single image, reconstituted it in time." The head is now only an eye, a nose and an ear scattered in a splintered wreckage. In the last phase, Cubism paradoxically went flat. The three visible planes of the cube, by the process of extension, were carried beyond the limits of vision—to the frame of the canvas—ceasing to function as indications of solidity and becoming automatically three flat tones. The head, needless to say, disappeared. Representation was annihilated. Art at last was pure, perfect, abstract, and absolute.

The disciples and backers of Picasso have attributed to him the subtlest philosophy, the most profound imagination of modern times. He is supposed to view the world with compound eyes, like the Spanish fly; to behold in a single act of vision the multiple aspects of life. He does not traffic in mundane emotions; he deals with invisible essences and Platonic absolutes; he has succeeded in expressing the inexpressible—the ultimate realities transcending the ebb and flow, the growth and decay, of organic life. But in art, as in all fields of endeavor, a man's capacities must be gauged by his objective achievements; and Picasso's cubes and cones—give them as many pretty titles as you please; disguise them, if you can, by esoteric riddles and psychological balderdash—remain cubes and cones, congested particles of dead matter.

On the other hand, his more spiteful competitors, dashed by his greedy appropriations, have spread the story that Cubism is one of his practical jokes. The charge contains a grain of truth; for there is, in Picasso, a streak of frivolity that is disconcerting to his solemn admirers. Did he not publicly state that art has no past and no future? Did he not paint a lozenge and call it the portrait of his mistress? Did he not paint a number of packing cases, and call them the portrait of his father? And was not the master convulsed with laughter when he saw, at the next Independents' exhibition, innumerable pictures of packing cases, each one labeled, *Portrait of My Father*? But despite his sallies, his Cubism was not intended as a practical joke.

Picasso is rude and illiterate, but a painter of incomparable cleverness—perhaps the cleverest man in the history of art. In esthetic theory and the philosophy of art he is a greenhorn; he was, at the beginning of his fame, and is today, totally unacquainted with the metaphysical interpretations placed on his agglomerate forms. He raises cunning to the pitch of genius; but his intelligence is shallow and his interests are one-sided. In his first experiments in cubic structure, nothing was more distant from his thoughts than the founding of a school or the creation of a new art. He did not get his ideas from a study of Spanish landscape, nor from the study of Plato, nor from deep meditation on the infinite. He is incapable of deep meditation. He got his ideas from Cézanne—from the planes and distortions evolved by the Provençal solitary in his struggles to make his forms more massive. Though playful at times, his ventures into Cubism were serious enough; and his experiments, considered as such, were legitimate and beneficial. Artists have always been concerned with structure and organization—the abstract side of their business. They have to be; it is part of their equipment—but only a part. Most of them, in their studies, have subordinated nature to the pattern; and

181

some, Dürer and Hogarth, for example, have reduced natural forms to geometrical equivalents. But they did not regard their studies as finished pictures, nor exhibit them as works of art. It remained for Picasso to hang the pattern on the wall. He was not interested in what was put together, but in *how* it was put together; and proceeding from Cézanne's unconcealed planes, he developed the geometrical poster known as Cubism, and found himself, unexpectedly, the prophet of a new school. In other words, for the first time, he made the abstract pattern the end of art, concentrating on method to the exclusion of content.

But Cubism would never have reached the exhibition room; would never, in fact, have reached the stage of the framed picture, had it not been for the political maneuvers of Picasso's friends. It might never have been heard of; but coming, as it did, at a time when art was bound up in problems of structure, it would, in all probability, have enlisted the passing attention of painters, have served a certain educational purpose, and then have been discarded, like other technical flurries. The politics behind the movement cannot be ignored. Max Jacob, an apostate Jew, sold it to the dealers—but not for his own personal gain. Jacob is a gentle soul and one of the most generous of men—willing to go to any extreme to help a friend. A poet afflicted with a fear of realities, it is quite possible that Picasso's diagrams ministered to him in some occult way. At any rate, he made a thousand visits to the dealers, and, as we say, put Cubism across. Apollinaire introduced it to his court, preached its gospel—a gospel of his own fabrication—to the gullible louts of Montparnasse, and wrote tomes of lyric drivel on its spiritual message, giving it an exalted esthetic tone. Gertrude Stein peddled it among the expatriates and shipped it across the Atlantic as light to the barbarians. Jean Cocteau carried it to the snobs, and as soon as it became the smart thing to talk about, it was embraced by the homosexuals and cultural experts plying their trade in Paris. It grew into a cult, a contagion; and once the dealers had accepted it, into an international industry.

No one was more surprised than Picasso at the swiftness with which his lacerated forms caught on, or at the impressive effect of his trifles when framed in gold and displayed, with the craft of the Parisian dealer, in the fashionable galleries. The burden of the continuance of the cult rested upon him, and he was equal to the burden. His fertility of invention seemed to be inexhaustible; he plundered and quoted his predecessors with amazing ingenuity; he began to take himself more seriously; to listen to the senseless chatterers surrounding him, and on one occasion he tried to be articulate. Today his majesty is fading, and he may yet live to see himself deposed; but he is still king, and his pictures are still appraised in terms of old masters. For twenty-five years he has ruled the abstractionists. He has, it is true, produced figure compositions—mothers and babes, and huge nudes adroitly piled together—but they have no earthly significance; his book illustrations are patterns in line; and his designs for ballets, his best work, appropriate paraphernalia for choreographic spectacles. A few years past, when Cubism was on its death bed, he was persuaded to lend his prestige to the worst of the Modernist cults, Sur-Realism. This cheap transaction is the only chicanery he has practised; for he is not honestly equipped to enter the nether world of introspective idiocies, and he knows it. There were plenty of demented candidates for the position of leader; but the election of Picasso was good business, and the authority of his name has pulled Sur-Realism into the galleries and made it a marketable nightmare. His latest work has been in this vein, and it is the ghastliest claptrap ever bound in gold. It may be that the little master has flaunted the last of his tricks; but he may hold yet another in reserve; and we may find him, one of these days, exhuming Bouguereau, or Burne-Jones.

Picasso owes his fame, not to a general appreciation of his work, nor to the production of work which has satisfied human needs and requirements; but to the esthetic theories erected in defence of his laboratory equations. His admirers, when pressed for intelligible criticism, stammer in a strange lingo, endowing his pictures with unique properties, and themselves with a special receptive apparatus denied to ordinary mortals. Setting aside, for the present, the mysteries attached to his abstractions, and the psychological interpretations rendered obsolete by recent discoveries, I find that the main obstruction to the clear understanding of his art lies in the separation of method from meaning. Let us analyze this question; first, as it pertains to art in general, and then as it bears directly on Picasso's objective achievement.

The art of painting, like the other arts of human life, weds the past to the present and conceives the future. The vitality of art depends on the coexistence, or more exactly, the interfusion of the three temporal elements. The past furnishes the method which, crystallized in forms, communicates its meanings; the present, seeking new forms to express its own meanings, draws upon traditional method which, by analysis, may be learned and mastered; and by the process of modification—by changes and additions—adapts it to new conditions. When art is a functioning activity, closely related to life and bent on communicating the meanings of life; when the need for expression is vigorous and forceful, new forms inevitably occur. But the only guarantee of a new form is the modification of method under the pressure of current meanings. Painting, through ages of development, is an exceedingly complicated instrument; and to alter inherited methods, thereby creating new forms, the artist must proceed from an extraordinary interest in his subjects—in the ideas and tendencies of his own times. Picasso, preoccupied with processes, and abjuring experience, has spent his life readjusting old forms. His art is wholly traditional. That it appears to be new and original and strange is the result of his having reduced the old forms to their structural components. That it has no vitality and no bearing on modern life is obvious even to those unfamiliar with the vitality of his forms in their original settings.

The forms of the present, the new forms arrived at by the modification of old methods, contain the potentialities for further meanings and future usefulness. The art of tomorrow will be affected and, in part, determined by the force and originality, the vitality or want of it, in the generating art of today. In art considered as a living organism, there can be no possible separation of method from form, or of form from meaning. That combination of factors producing the form also encloses the mean-

184

ing. It follows then that the vitality of method, and the resultant vitality of form, depend upon the nature of the factors subject to combination. When the constituents are taken ready-made from the art of the past, we have eclecticism, or the rearrangement of pattern; we have new alignments and arbitrary relationships imposed upon forms which, in their original context, were combined naturally and logically, and welded into an harmonious structure by conditions and meanings existing at the time of their discovery. To change the relationship of these factors, though it may produce odd and unexpected effects, does violence to the whole train of significant creation. In place of vital method and forms that are fresh and alive and exciting, forms springing from the will to integrate the living stuff of art which is found in the needs of present life, and which, by the unceasing change of life, cannot be found in the past, we have the playing of a little game, an ingenious bit of puzzle-making— entertaining to pundits to whom the factors played with are historically known, and to neurotics who habitually read esoteric meanings into tidy concatenations.

Eclecticism, in its objective manifestations, is a form of rhetoric, an irrelevant gesture, a shell without substance, an engine with no function. It seems to be the predominant art activity of weak or decaying civilizations in which the drift of life fails to release the creative impulse; or of those civilizations in which art is cultivated either for social display, or academically as a mark of special culture—a class mark indicating superior attainments. The art of the modern School of Paris, an eclectic school, is the last gasp of a dying culture. A truly creative art, as Taine so magnificently demonstrated, is indissolubly united with the fundamental drives of a civilization; its forms are born of the labor of artists to embody and communicate the meanings embedded in that civilization. When meanings are not derived from life, but are trumped-up and affected, as in the upper classes of our capitalist civilization where pretense is the basis of culture, art is forced into eclecticism.

Art depends upon and reflects the life of its supporters; and it is a significant fact that all the intrinsically valuable art of modern times has

185

been the work of men discountenanced by the dominant social classes and by the dealers and collectors representing those classes. Hogarth and Blake, in England; in France, Delacroix, Daumier and Cézanne; and in America, Albert Ryder—were all without the support of the art fanciers. Every worthy French artist of the past century was treated with contempt, publicly insulted, and critically condemned. In modern times the good men have managed to do their work in spite of snobbish vilification and the lack of patronage. They have made no connections with, and derived no inspiration from the fashionable centers of art; they have gone to the larger centers of interest—to the life of the people and the background of their own experiences. Cézanne would have nothing to do with the fashionable Parisian art, and returning to his native landscape, discovered in nature materials demanding a new form. What he had learned of the past from his studies of the old masters in the Louvre—what he had derived from them in method—was transformed by the impetus of his direct discoveries in nature.

The real artist, being a free agent, that is, free to criticize and illuminate any condition, creed, or form of behavior, is an intractable person, socially unorthodox, and inclined to revolt. We have come to expect the spirit of revolt in the artist; but this spirit has been debased by the little men who comprise the great body of the profession, and who have none of the courage of the leaders, into a repugnant convention known as the artistic temperament. Our bourgeois society has tolerated the artistic temperament—so long as it has remained in its own circles—and the Parisian French, more tolerant than other peoples of human frailties, have set aside a special quarter of their city for its maintenance and propagation. To this quarter, this Bohemia of Paris, flock the artists of all nations to receive instruction in temperament. These Bohemians have one characteristic in common with the social aristocrats: their lives are based almost entirely upon pretense and the cultivation of illusion. Most of the art of the present day, and of many years past, as I have shown at length in an earlier chapter, has originated in Bohemia.

The cult of art has reached its height in the Gallic capital, where,

PICASSO: *Abstraction*

besides maintaining a playground for temperament, it has provided thousands of canny Frenchmen with a good living. Into this Bohemia, where, in former times, youth was merely stripped of wildness and prepared for a conventional after-life in a politer world, modern commerce has flung its tentacles; and, by exhibiting sensational foolery to jaded intellectuals and wandering rakes, has made the cult of art a profitable business.

Bohemia, in so far as it condones and takes into account the spirit of youth—ignorant, experimental and emulative youth—is a gracious prelude to the life of an artist. It is natural and proper that youth should be concentrated on method; that it should be seriously interested in how things have been done. In every field of art, the novice, with his meager experiences and his unformed personality, attempts to make new forms by imitating the styles of masters congenial to his temperament. There was a time when the Bohemia of Paris served a larger educational purpose, offering the beginner instruction in the traditional methods of his craft, with some of the healthy play of life into the bargain. But that was long ago. Since the middle of the last century, about all that the young artist has been able to absorb is the stage play of Bohemianism. He remains in the world of make-believe, not only during his student days but for the rest of his life. There is, however—you would never believe it from the childish posturing of Murger, Du Maurier and Stein—in certain circles of Bohemia, a serious aspect of life; just as there is a serious side to the college and the university. Bohemia has kept alive, in spite of the death of technical traditions as they were related to the expression of life socially shared by large units, that interest in method without which no effectual artistic performance can exist. By fostering a competitive interest in methods, it offers, even today, a training ground, of a sort, for talent.

But this interest, by the very nature of the Bohemian environment, is bound to be scholastic, or academic. No matter how serious it may be, it is separated from the run of life—directed to no social function. In its most intelligent aspects, it is directed to the archeology of art, to the study of method as revealed in past performances. Bohemia is the natural field for eclectic experiment. Though it cannot be compared, as a training ground, to the shops of the old Italian masters, it affords, nevertheless, the possibilities of reasonably adequate instruction. In any case, it promotes the understanding of ways and means which no artist can acquire in isolation from his fellows.

The great evil of the Bohemian system is that it trains artists to read illusory values into their performances. This is particularly true since the internationalization of Bohemia into the playground for the youth of the world; the common center in which the nostalgic conceptions of youth are pooled, and by the very weight of massed numbers, made to seem real. In this international rendezvous, where exaggerated values are read into everything from the possession of, or share in, a prostitute, to the discovery of the ability of certain African tribes to carve entertaining images, the artistic youth of the world severs its connection with life—with the various localities and environments in which it was psychologically molded. And when we remember that in the great periods, the times of abounding vitality, art was always rooted in local conditions, in the psychology of specific peoples—in life as it is lived under the pressure of a dominant social idealism—it becomes apparent that Bohemia affects art deleteriously by separating youth from the natural habitat. For this organic background, with its allied interests and pressures, it substitutes an atmosphere of nurtured illusion which, so far as life is concerned, is as academic as the conventional academies supported by polite society.

Picasso is a perfect specimen of the artist reared in the atmosphere of international Bohemia. He is neither Spaniard nor Frenchman; his art reflects no environment, contains no meanings, carries no significance beyond the borders of the Bohemian world of its birth. The content of his art, where any is to be discerned, pertains to those vague generalities by which youth unconsciously betrays its ignorance of life.

Like Gertrude Stein, his friend and imitator, Picasso has not risen above the childish play with materials. These twin exotics are prize exemplars of the infantilism of Bohemia: their greatest delight is to play with bits of material, and, then, as an afterthought, to attach meanings to their wilful combinations. Such play is possible only in segregated corners of the world where the artist, like the child, is free from economic and social responsibilities—where, in truth, he is not above life but beneath it. Picasso, like a spoilt child, tears pictures to shreds and patches—the good art of the past, anything that pleases his fancy—and pieces them together again. This has been his lifelong occupation. As a crowning insult to art, he paints, with deadly photographic accuracy, purely material fragments—grained wood, linoleums, newspapers—shuffling them into neat patterns. His only contact with life, his sole connection with reality is to play the photographer! And this in a movement founded on Cézanne's doctrine that "art should not imitate nature, but should express the sensations aroused by nature." For the last word in materiality, for childish play carried back to the infancy of dabbling, we must behold the "composed reality" of Picasso's followers, who, taking their cue from the master, actually paste upon their canvases material substances such as door-bells, clay pipes, handbills, playing cards, oilcloth, and fecal matter.

The commercial exploitation of Bohemia has made the playing with materials a profitable industry; and the organized agents, cackling over sales and balances, have circulated the impression that their merchandise fulfills a genuine social need. Undoubtedly this is excellent salesmanship; but the apparent social functioning of Bohemian art is reduced to a myth by the fact that all its customers are groups, cliques, or individuals living, as the artists live, apart from the pressures of environment—the sheltered museum directors, and the economically protected art fanciers and collectors. The art of Bohemia has no function in life for the good reason that it is not based upon an interest in life but upon an artificially nourished interest in art.

This "pure" interest in art, the esthetic obsession of the Bohemians and their dupes, boiled down, resolves itself into an interest in method. It is no more than that, although anything may be read into abstract method. Boiled down, it becomes primarily a concern with the way in which things are done. Now everybody knows that the forms of art, in one sense, are determined by the way in which things are done. But ways must operate with subject-matter of some sort—with something besides other ways and processes. Methods have no life of their own, no function unless applied to first-hand materials; and when the materials, or subjects, are culled from the dead past, or from an environment removed from the concerns of life, they evoke no meanings save those which may be encompassed by the rearrangements of old forms, by eclectic combinations. And the only meanings—if they may be so termed—to be gathered from such combinations are the pleasurable recognition of mechanical dexterity and the momentary delight in effective novelties.

I suppose we should all agree that love, birth and death are fundamental realities which may occur in Bohemia as well as in any other world; and also that they have been the great preoccupations of art. But in dealing with these universal realities, art has found it necessary to bind them to specific situations. Raphael, Rubens, and Rembrandt, in painting the Madonna and Child, did not try to depict immaculate essences or the concepts of the scholastic philosophers; more humbly, and sensibly, they painted their own wives and mistresses, and their children, as they had observed and studied them, with manifest and affectionate interest in their physical charms and characteristics, thus bringing human significance to a religious ideal. The holy label on their pictures means nothing, the figures, created from special situations, everything.

Bohemia has never painted itself. Picasso, in pictures called *Maternity* and *Life*, has touched upon the deep realities; but his forms are without substance—vague generalities which, it appears, he may have heard of but has never experienced in any of the specific situations connecting such conceptions with life. His picture called *Mother and Child* was inspired, I have been informed, by his own wife and son. You would never guess it. The woman, a swollen effigy, has enor-

PICASSO: *A Nude*

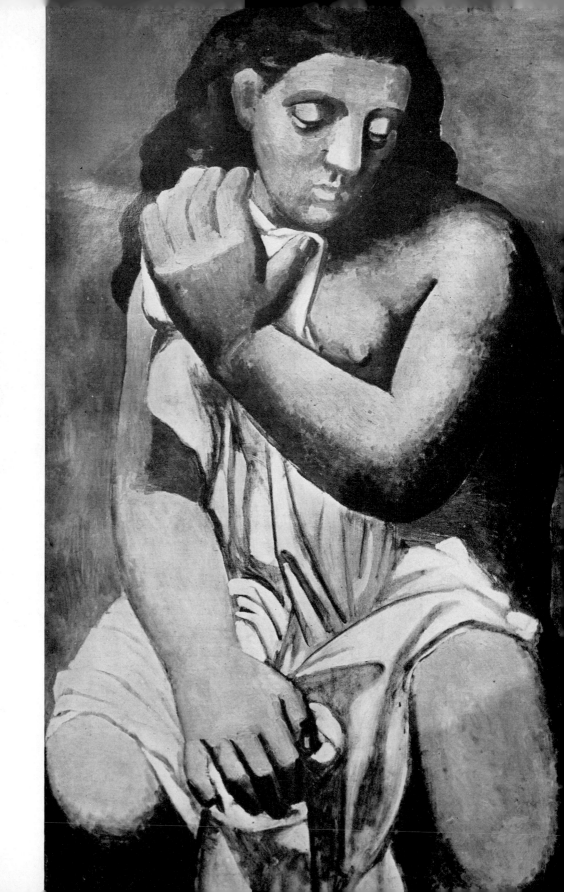

mous hands—ludicrous affectations intended as compositional stabilizers —and the dumb visage of an archaic Greek mask. The child might have been copied from a Graeco-Roman tomb. "But," exclaim the esthetes, "what architectural unity!" Yes—that of the stonemason. "What sense of form!" The archeologist's sense of form. "What sense of line!" The line of the surveyor. The lifelessness of Picasso's art is not to be explained by a faulty base of experience—he has lived and therefore could not have escaped all the human relationships—but in his single-minded approach to art, his Bohemian habit of denying experience in favor of eclectic play. His Cubist pictures have no more vitality than jigsaw puzzles; the works just mentioned, and all his subject pictures, have the odor of the past, of things dug up from the burial ground of some old world. They are combinations rather than creations; loose-jointed in form—held together by no compelling logic; antique borrowings arbitrarily selected and contiguously placed.

But it would not be just to say of Picasso that his career has been wholly worthless. His great technical ability, his unrivaled inventiveness, and his exhaustive research in processes leading to the most extraordinary combinations in painting, have stimulated artists in all parts of the world to the study of method. He has played with all the historical ways of handling space; he is the master of every instrument known to painting. If he had not been sanctified; if he had not been foolishly sold to the public and to students as a miracle man; if he had been accepted for what he is, the foremost experimenter in processes; he might have become the greatest art teacher of modern times.

Slowly Picasso's followers are beginning to realize that processes alone do not produce significant art. Original forms are not thought up nor mathematically calculated; they are the result of imperative human needs, both intellectual and emotional; of the irresistible pressure of living materials, of those things which, rising from life experience, demand their own internal relationships and call for their own methodology. A knowledge of historical processes adds to instrumental power in the construction of such relationships and facilitates the integration of the elements of experience; but it is the reality of the experience that is important in the making of original forms. The impulsion of experience is the only force capable of counteracting habitual usage, of modifying old methods so that new forms can be fashioned. Eclecticism merely plays on the surface of this psychological fact: it brings into combination forms ready-made, old and second-hand materials, things gathered from what may be called hearsay, not from life.

The art of Picasso is without meaning, and its forms, in consequence, without true originality.

Indeed, in those very combinations of geometrical integers into which all the plastic arts may be finally resolved—those relations established between the cube, the cylinder and the cone—the most complex of Picasso's inventions fades into child's play when compared to any small division of a composition by Rubens. Ingenuity, operating for its own sake with pure abstractions, cannot approach, even in the field of abstract values, the formal complexities accruing from representational needs. The representation of experience, limited though it may be, as in Cézanne, to a small section of Provençal landscape, is indispensable to any kind of original construction.

Picasso, as king of the international Bohemia in which whim and the lazy cultivation of illusion take the place of life, is exempt from representational needs. He is at the service of nothing—and accordingly, save for his purely academic achievements in processes, produces nothing.

9

MODIGLIANI

DURING the first decade of the present century, the most popular pastime of the French intellectuals was baiting the Jew. One summer night in the Place du Tertre, when this vicious preoccupation was at its height, two royalists sat in a crowded café publicly expounding the anti-Semitic doctrine. They were in high good humor and insulted the chosen people so that all might hear. At a table close by, a young man, accompanied by a seductive blonde who paid for his pile of saucers, listened to the tirade with an impatience that swiftly rose to fighting indignation. He was a youth of striking appearance, spiritually and physically irresponsible—a son of Montmartre. One could tell from his long untidy hair and his clothes that he was an artist. Instead of a tie he wore a handkerchief of red silk; instead of a coat, an old jersey, a gift and much too big for him; and his corduroy slacks were spattered with paint. One could read in the unnatural luster of his eyes, and in his sunken cheeks, the marks of a pulmonary affliction which had been aggravated by a diet of cognac and hashish. The amorous blonde watched, in admiration, the rising anger of her man, smiled and gave him courage. Suddenly, with all the pride of his race, he jumped up and shouted. He spoke with a strong Italian accent.

"I am a Jew! I answer your insults with battle! I challenge you to stand up and fight! I kill at the same time two cowards!"

The youth was lean and underweight, but he spoke with inspired ferocity and with an insolent conviction that meant bloodshed. The crowd stood up and waited hopefully—but the two royalists sat still.

"Long live the Jews!" shouted the youth.

He was prepared to kill, but the blonde, satisfied with a moral victory, led him to the door. Outside she whispered sweet things about his manhood, and he smiled gratefully—he was weak where women were concerned. She took him to one of those dives frequented by forlorn artists and cast-off women, where world-sick wretches, who have never the price of a square meal, manage somehow to pay cash for narcotic relief.

Amedeo Modigliani was born in Tuscany, the cradle of western art, in 1884. His mother, a native of Leghorn, believed that she was descended from the family of Spinoza; his father's people had migrated to northern Italy from the ghetto of Rome. In his fourteenth year, during a severe illness, he conceived a desire to paint, to the great joy of his mother who loved the boy with an idolatrous affection. He studied first with a landscape painter at Leghorn; but in 1900, having developed signs of tuberculosis, went South with his mother for his health. He attended an art school in Rome, which did him no good, and then went up to Venice to study in the academy there. He remained in the courtesan city for several years, intolerant, from the beginning, of formal discipline, and only moderately interested in Venetian art. Returning to Tuscany, he lived for a time in Florence, a restless youth filled with feverish longings and ambitions roused within him by his discovery of the Italian primitives. He had vague notions of a new art which he would make as simple and clean and moving as the religious pieces of the early masters. His mother followed him with unconcealed delight as he roamed the galleries of Florence. The first to recognize his talent, she saw in her son the hero of a new generation of painters who should revive the glories of old Italy. But the son dreamed of Paris, and after much pleading and many tears, departed, in his twenty-second year, for France with his mother's blessing on his head.

Modigliani in Montmartre! He was young and handsome; he had talent and a little money in his pocket. He had the exuberance of the Latin and the ardor of the Jew; a prodigious memory and an independence that defied all conventions. But, on the negative side, he was poorly trained, of uncertain health, and utterly without will-power or the capacity for study. He went up and down the Hill talking of Shelley and Oscar Wilde, and when drunk at the Lapin Agile, reciting scraps of Dante and looking for trouble. In complete sympathy with the Modernist movement then hatching in Montmartre, he found a niche in the ramshackle building in the Rue Ravignan where Picasso and his poor associates, with their poorer women, were dissecting Cézanne and negro sculptures. He was known as the boy with the eyes of fire, and everybody loved him; for he had a purity of spirit and a tenderness with women which none of the Bohemians possessed. The women were mad about him—he treated them with respect, an attitude foreign to the Bohemian ménage, and he had money. He carried off Picasso's girl, the lithe blonde, laughed, coughed, drank and worked a little.

At first, he drank only wine, and with such resolution as was in him, made an effort to conserve his strength and to work regularly. But it was no use. The disorderly life of the Butte tempted his wayward soul and debauched his nobler impulses; the fire of accomplishment which impelled him to periods of brief but brilliant application, was soon extinguished, leaving him in a state of indolence and despair. From a momentary admiration for Whistler, he passed to Toulouse-Lautrec, attracted by that master's subjects and his acid philosophy of corruption. From Lautrec he was drawn to Picasso's anemic studies in blue—the hags, harlequins and morphomaniacs which the Spaniard had taken from the blue-blooded dwarf of Montmartre. He imitated Cézanne but very feebly, and having accumulated a few canvases, exhibited with the Independents in 1908, and again in 1910. But he had not found himself and his pictures were hardly noticed.

Modigliani's introduction to his own small, but unquestionably original, talent came through the negro carvings which the radical artists were beginning to collect and imitate. One look at the black statues and his imagination conquered his indolence. He saw in them the foundation of the formal vision he had longed for; their curious distortions and expressions of childish fears and pathetic innocence corresponded to his own distorted existence—his despairs and his morbid sentimental-

195

ity; he had at last a structural device adaptable to his pure and wistful conceptions. If, in modern painting, there has been an artist who turned naturally and without affectation to primitive forms, who found in them a spirit congenial, in a measure, to his own, and who established a kinship, however faint, between his forms and human feelings, that artist is Modigliani.

He acquired an African mask, hung it on his wall, and set out to construct a formula to enclose his tragic experiences. On friendly terms with Brancusi and Epstein, he tried his hand at carving. He had, to a certain extent, the sculptor's approach to form: his drawings resembled a sculptor's notes; that is to say, he reduced the figure to a balanced arrangement of geometrical units; and his paintings, one and all, were based on the style of the negro statues. He was hard up now and marble was expensive. He would hang around the stone masons until they gave him a block of ordinary building stone which he would cart off to his studio in a wheelbarrow. But he soon abandoned sculpture—it was too laborious to suit his spasmodic enthusiasm, and the dust was bad for his diseased lungs. However, in his few finished heads, slight as they are and very African and with only a vestige of reality, Modigliani proved himself the most individual of the modern sculptors following the negro convention—the Negro-Plastic, as the doctors called it.

He was penniless—nothing for the landlord; no food. Thrown out on the street, he was taken in by a group of destitute artists who were living, rent free, in a dilapidated warehouse. One of them was a sculptor and a kindly fellow, but Modigliani could not stand his work. In a fit of rage he broke a statue to pieces and fled. Depressed and hungry, he let himself go, accepting food and drink from painters almost as poor as himself but not so improvident. The girls took pity on him, feeding him brandy and drugs. He fell into a long illness; the girls nursed him until he was strong enough to travel and he went back to Italy. Under his mother's care, his health mended, and he longed for the life that was killing him. His mother begged him to remain in Italy, but he was

stricken with a much more dangerous malady than the white plague—
the pox of Bohemia—and he returned to Paris.

His case was hopeless. His personal charm endeared him to all who
met him; his illness and his foolish pride made him an object of compassion—but his habits were incorrigible. He hurried from bar to bar,
from friend to friend, from one girl to another; and at intervals, excited
by some young creature whom he regarded as a fallen angel, he painted
excessively. In an old garret he executed, from memory, a number of
delicate portrait sketches in line, which he sold for a few francs; but the
commercial aspect of the business revolted him, and being an Italian
and fond of discussion, he quickly tired of the confinement of the studio.
In 1913, when his companions, led by Picasso who had quarreled with
the beautiful Fernande, deserted Montmartre for the left bank, he
joined the colony in Montparnasse. At the tables of the Rotonde and the
Closerie des Lilas, the garrulous protagonists of the new art—Maillol,
Matisse, Picasso, Vlaminck, Carco, Salmon, Soutine, Derain, Kisling,
Léger, and Gleizes—assembled to air their theories and to take in each
other's wash. The most eloquent of the tribe, and perhaps the most
uncompromising in his conviction, was Modigliani. "He had taken the
wrong road," as Max Jacob expressed it, "and had to begin the funeral
all over again."

The War came, disbanding the colony and making havoc of the art
life of Montparnasse. Lonely and unfit for military service, he tramped
the quarter, drinking more and more to forget his misery. Early one
morning, dead drunk, he staggered along the street to his garret, stopping
now and then, to serenade the sleeping inhabitants with sad Italian lulla-
bies. The police nabbed him and demanded his papers. "Papers!" he
exclaimed, "papers! Here are my papers—my passport to immortality!"
He went through his pockets and pulled out a messy packet of drawings.
They locked him up, but friends interceded and he was released. He
painted portraits of his comrades in crime—one of a Mexican named
Rivera who looks like a slippery Oriental—and peddled them among
the dealers. "Take them away!" they all cried. All but one, a sagacious

197

young entrepreneur named Guillaume who befriended him and acquired for practically nothing some of his choicest canvases. He consorted with crooks and jailbirds to obtain drugs, and doped himself into insensibility. Half-sentient, he raved and suffered from visions, conversed with imaginary people, and discovered devils in street cars. His mother tried to save him, sending him heart-breaking letters and money for clothes. He read the letters aloud in the cafés, and was persuaded by an English girl to dress more decently. Once decently clad, he returned immediately to his old ways: he sold his overcoat, tore the lining out of his hat, and shortened his jacket with a pocket knife. He was on the verge of starvation when an English poetaster took him under her wing. She was dying to love a genius and found one, of a sort, in Modigliani. She supported him for two years, and succeeded, for a while at least, in convincing him of her purity and her selfless devotion. He painted her pert face many times, and worked like one inspired—"with the audacity of a young god," so she said. But when he found that "the English" was promiscuous, with a taste for the lowest forms of vice, he cursed his angel and ran out. She too had chosen the downward path that leads to salvation, and some years later, encountered again, on that path, her old lover. She was in the last stages of depravity, and the young god was not so well— but his pride was greater than ever.

"My love," he said gravely, "you are a prostitute."

The Bohemians enjoyed Modigliani's heedless disintegration. He went to the dogs with a grand air; there was dignity in his self-destruction and generosity in all his impulses. He was an aristocrat in rags. The others rotted prosaically in the conventional fashion; or became merchants; or sold out to merchants; or collaborated to debase the art of Cézanne into garniture for boudoirs. He had a little of the fire of genius, and some of the humanity that lifts art above craftsmanship. The others, in stiff-necked obeisance, drank tea with rich Americans; when a tea was given in honor of Modigliani, he dosed himself with hashish, set fire to the tablecloth, and rejoiced as the blaze terrified his outraged exploiters. He might live off a woman, but not without giving in return a gallant affection, not without a high-principled regard for his art. Picasso might have helped him, but Picasso was too busy feathering his own nest; the others of his own race—Rivera, Soutine, Kisling, Jacob and Guillaume —were more charitably inclined but too poor to contribute more than the price of a drink. So he took his life in his own frail hands, and his convictions, and his art, and challenged the gods to strike him down.

Modigliani was incapable of playing the game with the dealers—too proud, for one thing; too honest for another. They did not like his work, but they were eager to get hold of it on the chance that it might eventually strike the collector's fancy. On one occasion he offered a series of drawings to a gallery, and the dealer, from force of habit, began to haggle over the price, a trifling sum. Without a word, Modigliani gathered the drawings together and tossed them into the water closet. In desperate straits, he contracted with a gallery to paint for a daily wage, like a laborer, pledging himself to produce pictures for forty francs each, and a bottle of cognac. Imprisoned in the dealer's cellar, and stripped to the waist, he kept his word for a week, most of the time in a state of semi-intoxication; but when his employer ushered a party of visitors into the vault to watch the performance, Modigliani cracked the skinflint on the head with a bottle, and ran screaming into the street. His exhibition with Mademoiselle Weill, who would show anything, created a small scandal. Shopgirls, clerks, milliners and messenger boys jammed the place and stared at the strange chaste nudes. The police closed the gallery until the pictures were taken down, and nothing was sold—after the artist's death, one of the canvases went for 22,000 francs! Francis Carco fell in love with one of the nudes, a blonde girl with flesh of milk and orange, and wanted to buy it, offering little but all he had. Modigliani gave the picture to him.

"You love my painting?" he asked, drunk but none the less appreciative. "Why, what, how so? You understand it? You love it as you love women? So—so—that's it! Take it along!"

By the end of the war his best energies were spent, but it did not matter—his best work was done, and he was repeating with minute variations, the haunting formula he had evolved from the black statues. What distinguished him from his fellow Modernists was his interest in his subjects, his spiritual concern, fleeting though it was, and dissipated by tuberculous passions, with living beings. The rest were wrapped up in formal relationships: Matisse was a pattern designer, Derain a manufacturer, Van Dongen a pander in the newfangled style, and Picasso a compositor. Modigliani, so far as his intelligence and temperament permitted, endeavored to study people, to penetrate their souls, and to show, in their warped faces and attenuated bodies, the fever of living and the little tragedy which, with the prevision of the diseased and talented, he knew was all that awaited him. He never painted a portrait unless bound to the sitter by feelings of affection; never used professional models; never painted a picture merely as the solution of plastic problems. I grant that his penetration did not go very far; that he had no great depth of feeling; that his experiences were all of the same order, without range or variety; but these strictures notwithstanding, his art is extremely personal and real, and if not profoundly moving, then always touching, and in its own sphere, singularly complete.

Modigliani's work falls into two divisions, portraits and nudes, both of which have been indiscriminately extolled for their design and plasticity—qualities for which they are in no respect remarkable. Structurally, his work follows the negro fetish, with accentuated planes borrowed from Cézanne and the Cubists, and with color schemes reminiscent of the clear-toned Italian frescoes. He limited his designs to the single figure: an ovoid head set at a sharp angle on a cylindrical neck, and an elongated torso with the arms and legs only roughly indicated. It is not difficult, when the figure is reduced to its geometrical equivalents and stripped of annoying details, to construct a compact design and forms that are simple and plastic. But it is no mean accomplishment, when adhering closely to the pattern of a sculptural grotesque, to fashion an individualized object expressing the character of the sitter. This Modigliani effected, casting his faces in the same mold, but at the same time retaining and exaggerating, to the point of caricature, the essential features and proportions.

It is not the formal side of his art, but his psychological insight into character that interests us. His portrait of the painter, Morgan Russell, will serve as an illustration. In this pallid face, Modigliani, fifteen years ago, divined the ignominious destination of a promising American who remained in Paris. And through all his characters he revealed the disintegration of his own personality. It is a sad family he created, and a little monotonous—some are sickly with a morbid sweetness; some are overborne by the pathos of futile sentimentality. His nudes, slender, elongated girls of virginal innocence, were girls he had slept with; but he managed, despite the rigid African formula he practiced, to catch them in attitudes of unexpected purity, and to bring out, in face and figure, the delicacy of his own feelings. In all his work, portraits and nudes alike, poor though it may be in vitality, we find the neurotic charm of one of the most hapless souls in modern art.

About 1917, he met a girl, very young and homely, the ragamuffin daughter of unforgiving grocers. The two were united immediately in a noble, but squalid, attachment which nothing, not even death, could dissever. The girl loved Modigliani with an intensity that became a sacrificial mania; and in her he found the perfect compatibility of mind and body. Save for a painful mistake with a treacherous lady of quality, he remained faithful to his mistress to the end. The girl ran away from home to be near him, and to share his life—what was left of it. They lived together in the most dreadful circumstances, a homeless pair, sleeping on the ground, in bars, and in the studios of artists who had nothing to give them but floor space; they lived in cafés, accepting crusts from charitable waiters and hawking their pictures on the pavement; they roamed the Quarter, begging, sponging, suffering—the girl doing the begging.

A Polish poet, Zborowski, undertook to save them. There has been a great flow of talk in the cafés of Paris about the Pole's high-souled generosity; and no doubt he had it. He never lost faith in Modigliani's genius; he gave his friend the shirt off his back, and ran his legs off to convince the dealers of the value of his treasures; and he did sell a few pictures. But Zborowski was down and out himself: he owned nothing but an empty apartment, an itch to write poetry and a wife. He had the spirit but not the means to do Modigliani any real or lasting good; the money he collected was not enough to change the situation, and the painter, realizing this, promptly spent it for stimulants and drugs.

Modigliani's illness had completely undermined his health. He had no strength for painting and not much desire to paint. His old enthusiasm returned when his mistress had a baby, a daughter, and he talked hopefully of going to Italy in the spring with the girl and her child. "I have my mother there," he said proudly. But he did not go; he declined rapidly and walked the streets alone, coughing and drinking more and more. Sometimes he finished a picture and carried it to the door of Zborowski's apartment, and then hurried away. In 1919, he began to spit blood, and the Pole arranged somehow to send him down to Nice for the winter. Having barely enough to live on, he lodged in a hotel for prostitutes; and the ladies, discovering that he was a poor consumptive artist with no money for models, posed for him in his room after their clients had gone. In his paintings the ladies came out clean and pure. Destitute and ready to die, he longed for Paris. Zborowski sold fifteen canvases in Marseilles for 500 francs, and took him back to the capital. In January, 1920, he lay in bed with a high fever, and was ordered into a hospital by the doctor. On the way he fainted, and all night lay in a delirium. The next morning he died in a charity ward, babbling something about his beloved Italy.

The news of Modigliani's death spread from one quarter to another. The artists volunteered to defray the funeral expenses, and while passing the hat, received a wire and a money-order from Modigliani's brother, deputy for Leghorn and official orator of the Italian Socialists. "Give him a royal funeral," the wire read. The funeral afforded the Parisians a grand holiday. Everybody turned out; all Montparnasse; all Montmartre; writers and artists and their women; models, cocottes,

MODIGLIANI: *La Femme aux Bandeaux*

FROM THE CHESTER DALE COLLECTION

children, soldiers, and shopkeepers. The cortege moved slowly across Paris from Montparnasse to Père Lachaise, and the crowds drifted into the cafés talking mournfully of "the last great Bohemian." The procession passed a group of artists, and one of them, Picasso, pointing to the hearse where Modigliani rested under a mountain of flowers, and then to the police who clicked their heels and stood at attention, remarked:

"You see, Modi gets even with the cops at last."

On the night of Modigliani's death, his mistress, Jeanne Hebuterne, pregnant the second time, killed herself by leaping to the ground from a fifth-story window. There was enormous indignation among the artists, when it became known that the Catholic parents of the girl refused to allow the body to be buried by the side of a Jew.

10

GROSZ

He will tell you, in his quiet way, that there are many Groszes; he will say this with scrupulous modesty, with a self-analysis containing no egoism. One Grosz is in the cellar, skeptical and faithless, buried in the litter of a senseless world; one is a romantic traveler, a Gothic visionary in line and in verse, treasuring sentimentally in distant lands the memories of a happy boyhood in the Fatherland. There is the terrible Grosz whose fame has gone round the world—the scourge of Junkers; the most explicit and pitiless satirist of the social habits of man since Swift. There is yet another Grosz: methodical and humorous, domestic, unafraid of bourgeois emotions, incessantly industrious and very kindly—the Grosz you may meet one day among the riff-raff of Sixth Avenue, or prowling in Central Park, note-book in hand, observing the aimless vitality of unoccupied Americans. It is necessary, in order to understand the man, to examine the various and contradictory facets of his character, but it is not necessary to reconcile them. Together they constitute the complex personality of the most distinguished artist of modern Germany.

George Grosz was born in Berlin, in 1893. His father owned a restaurant and a second-hand bookshop, lost his savings and his property during a financial crash, and moved to the village of Stolp, near the Baltic Sea, to become the steward of a Freemason's lodge. In 1900, his father died, and the family returned to North Berlin to a life of squalor and sullen poverty. The cruel suffering of those dark days infected the boy's spirit, leaving a wound which, in the hideous upheavals of post-war Germany, broke out afresh with unmitigated virulence. There was

204

little bread in the house; his mother took in lodgers, and worked far into the night as a seamstress; when, on strange occasions, he went with his sister into a bakery or a beer-garden, he felt that he was a trespasser in a land of fantastic abundance. After two years of this hand-to-mouth wretchedness, his mother found work as housekeeper for the military Casino, at Stolp, and the family returned to the Baltic.

The rest of Grosz's boyhood was peaceful and healthy. "Beautiful times!" he will tell you. "Woods and rivers, fishing and swimming; my mother busy at the Casino all day long, and I, as we say in German, 'on my own fist' from my earliest recollections. I read Mark Twain and Cooper, and the dime novels of the Wild West—Buffalo Bill and Nick Carter—and cheap German magazines reflecting, with blood-and-thunder illustrations, the frontier life of America. There can be no doubt that my first experiences, and my first efforts to draw and paint, were strongly colored by my interest in the New World. Nor was I alone in that interest. To most of my companions, America was really and truly the land of the free. We believed in that phrase and repeated it with childish fervor; and what was more important to my young imagination, America was the land of adventure, rich in romance and savage excitement. The little river which ran through the town became the Mississippi; we were pirates and Indian killers, cowboys, desperadoes, and trappers. I made my cousin pose for me, and tried to depict him as that immortal vagabond, Huckleberry Finn; in a more sinister mood, I painted, in black oils, a picture of an electric chair; inspired by a description of a lynching in Alabama, I called my gang together, and persuaded them, with true Southern eloquence, that we must take the law in our own hands. We captured a poor old darkey who had been accused —rightly or wrongly I do not know—of cruelty to animals, bound him to a tree, and threatened him with a beating. The poor negro howled with fright and his cries brought us quickly to our senses. We unbound him, after he had sworn not to tell on us, and sneaked home, and for a long time were very obedient little German boys.

"Sounds very American, does it not? America, let me say again, was the land of my dreams; I believed it to be the most interesting and the most astonishing of all countries, and for the artist, the most fertile; and I still think so—much to the disgust of my Marxist friends. I remember when Barnum and Bailey's Circus—the Biggest Show on Earth—came to town. I painted the fat lady and the wild man from Borneo, and General Tom Thumb. I wanted to travel with the circus, to go out into the world, to get to America. And I discovered, as I began to see things a little more clearly, that the Pomeranian world in which I lived was far different from the world of books, and from the romantic America I had read about. I had to make a living, and I was determined to make it by means of art."

Grosz did not think of his ambition in terms of art—die heilige Kunst, the sacred stuff of esthetes and professors, had no meaning to a healthy boy with blood in his veins. He looked upon drawing and painting as a natural and absorbing business; he could not remember the time when he was not busy with his pencil, often late at night, in bed in a cold room; and he was in swaddling clothes when he formed the habit of filling note-books with sketches. He has preserved these note-books, hundreds of them, all filed away in beautiful boxes as neat as a pin—a graphic autobiography of a real life. "I was a great admirer of American art," he says, "or what I took to be typically American: political cartoons, those of Thomas Nast in particular—and what an artist he was!—and the comic sequence. I have in my scrap-books a complete history of the comic sequence, the comic strip I think you call it, from the men who worked for the old Puck—to your national hero, Mickey Mouse."

In his first efforts, Grosz produced the usual romantic concepts of the child: Indians, blockhouses, cowboys and fights—always fights—illustrations for his American dreams; and from nearer home, hussars, castles and heroic legends. His work was distinguished from the ordinary run of children's drawings by its conscientious execution and by its observation. He used a sharp pencil, working with tireless application to make everything clean and clear, and training himself to seek out and emphasize significant details. Blood was the main ingredient of his

early pictures, just as, in a later period, blood was to be the main ingredient of his cartoons—his own blood and that of his slaughtered
countrymen. In his eleventh year, excited by the Russo-Japanese War,
he painted, in water-color, a duel between two battleships, a painting
which would make Monsieur Matisse moan in his beard. Not that it is
very remarkable; it is genuinely naïve and very modern in technique—a
spontaneous emotional overflow which, the Frenchman, a slave to
oriental precedent, has never been able to acquire.

Then he suffered a bitter mortification of the spirit—he discovered
High Art! A friendly bookseller from whom he bought his meager
stock of materials spread before him a collection of prints of the old
masters, and talked on and on, drooling and weeping, of the sublime
style. "I was convicted then and there," Grosz remarks. "I was following
the wrong trail; I was a great sinner. My pictures, which had brought me
so many happy hours, seemed to be not only worthless but injurious to
the soul, half-criminal and half-erotic. I walked home with a sinking
heart and destroyed all my masterpieces." But he soon recovered his
good sense, and continued to draw according to his own lights. "I knew
that I was right. I was not sublime; I was interested in people—in adventure and modern life. I had a born instinct for illustration and I
meant to indulge it. The old masters would not be offended. They
would be waiting for me when I was ready to understand them."

He was constantly changing, beginning to think a little, moving from
fanciful conceptions to realism and invective. His talent marked him
from his fellows, and when he entered the local high school, he was regarded with some esteem, and some suspicion—he was supposed to be
different. "I was not different," he explains. "My interests were stronger,
and I had already learned the value of hard work. The school discipline
was very severe—military education, the Prussian ideal. The slightest
infringement of a rule meant five slaps on our tight pants—and no doubt
some of those thick-headed Pomeranians needed it. One of the teachers
was a terrible bully—pot-belly, eye-glasses, loud neck-tie—typical Prussian—you know the sort. He hated me and told my mother I was demoral-

izing the whole school. He hated me because my caricatures had made
me popular among the students. I could stand the slaps on the behind;
but one day, he turned the signet of his huge ring to the inside of his
finger—it was like using an iron slug—and let me have it in the face.
I socked him back, and out I went. Out for good—expelled, fired!

"I found my mother in the kitchen crying. She thought my life was
ruined forever, and my dear sister thought so too. I did not wish to hurt
my mother—she had been very good to me, and she worked so hard—but
I would not give up my drawing. Two stubborn Germans opposing each
other, I guess. I tried to comfort her, and told her I could make money
by my caricatures. She had no faith in art, and my sister was with her.
I would show them. So I bundled together a number of my best comic
things—joke-drawings they were, with my own dialogue which I thought
extremely funny—and sent them to Berlin to a humorous weekly. They
all came back again, like a bad pfennig; and my dreams went into vine-
gar, went sour, as you say. I was only fifteen years old.

"I was as dejected as a boy could be—the faithless Grosz who lives in
the cellar—and I made symbolical pictures of Grief, Misery, and Despot-
ism. A local artist named Pabst restored my spirits. This generous painter
went to my mother and said, 'Your son is very talented. He will bring
honor to Germany, and you must send him to an art school.' My mother
gave in, and it was decided that I should go to the academy at Dresden.
The worthy Pabst prepared me for the entrance examinations, and under
his instruction I painted two copies of a bust of Lessing, profile and full-
face. These were submitted, together with a drawing of an old boot
which I threw in for good measure. The boot, a light-and-shade drawing
done with infinite pains, won the hearts of the examiners. It was their
idea of draughtsmanship, and I was accepted. Proud and happy, and a
little afraid, but on my own fist again, I went to Dresden."

Looking back on his two years of formal training at Dresden, Grosz
confesses that he learned nothing of much value. The effect of the
academic system was to kill or abort originality, and to make reproduction machines of all the pupils. There was the stupid copying of dusty

plaster casts, followed by drawing from living models—drawing of abominable accuracy in which the hairs of the head were numbered and the eyebrows recorded with microscopical precision. At first, Grosz took the academy seriously: he had an exaggerated sense of responsibility, and he knew that his allowance, small though it was, cost his mother many hours of drudgery. After a day spent in the composition classes, he hurried home to his little room for which he paid fifteen marks a month, ate his supper of sausages, salad and cheese, and under a kerosene lamp, struggled with his "imaginative pieces." "They were pretty sad," he says, "too grotesque, too ornamental, too arty. I was very lonely, and sick of phony compositions; I went to the other extreme—grew introspective and sentimental."

Friendships came, and the society of the more talented and independent pupils. He read widely in history and philosophy, and studied in the libraries and galleries. He made the acquaintance of Daumier, Degas and Lautrec, and their successors, Cézanne, Van Gogh, Gauguin and Matisse, men whose influence had not penetrated the thick walls of the academy. His teachers were all pedants, and one of them, an officious, conceited windbag, choked with rage when Grosz mentioned the name of Van Gogh. "So you have found a Gogh," he thundered. "Gott, a Gogh! Who is this Gogh? A crack-pot who tried to paint the sun! For one half-hour, he made exercises at the sun—but I work two years on one painting." Daumier and Lautrec made a profound impression on him, chased away his romantic illusions, returned him to the dramatic stuff of everyday life. "My work was bad," he says, "but in the right direction—closer to the real world than anything I might hope to do in the classroom. I was on the way I was supposed to go." Grosz won two prizes at Dresden, sold one picture, made a name for himself, and was awarded a scholarship in the School of Arts and Crafts, at Berlin.

The atmosphere at Berlin was much more liberal; the teachers more tolerant and intelligent. He enjoyed the croquis classes introduced from Paris, and painted manfully in oil and water-color, at the same time attending to his extraordinary gift for satire. His individuality was beginning to appear—the famous Grosz-Stil; he studied the Italians,

Rembrandt, and the Flemish painters, above all, Bruegel who was to become his favorite artist and his most influential master; and though he had not, as yet, directed his talent into political fields, he found himself in the company of rebellious youths opposed to war and the rising horde of Prussian goose-steppers. But his scholarship expired, and he had to earn his own living.

"I sent drawing after drawing to the magazines, and one memorable day a note of acceptance arrived. How proud I was! At seventeen a professional artist, a paid worker! I received twelve marks for the drawing, and immediately bought a pair of patent leather shoes—wonderful shoes imported from America! I waited and waited for the drawing to appear, and at last it was printed, much reduced, but O.K. I sent the magazine to my mother, with a letter boastfully reminding her that art was not such a bad occupation. But it was still a long way to Tipperary! I submitted a hundred drawings before I sold another. The trouble was with the text: I had no skill at making jokes." He turned his hand to many kinds of work—book-jackets, decorations for menus, lettering, designs for wall paper—saved his money, and in 1913, went to Paris to paint nudes at Colarossi's. In Paris he weighed and tested the dogmas of the Cubists and Futurists, but in other respects, he will tell you, his year among the beauty specialists was a waste of time.

Grosz does not dwell on his experiences in the War. He has no apologies for his conduct, and no regrets; but the great shambles wounded his spirit and the sore will never be healed. Like most intelligent Europeans, he was opposed to war; not as a shrinking pacifist; not with the hysterical lamentations of the unfit or the aged; not as a dreamy prophet insulting a party predestined to defeat; but as a young man of iron courage who, years before the march to the western front, had declared himself for humanity and the preservation of the noblest elements of the German civilization. He was twice discharged and three times condemned. On his first release, in 1915, he was awarded, not the iron cross but the badge of shame—a certificate of good health which he calls his first Grosz-Mappe. In a collection of poems published in Berlin he tried

GEORGE GROSZ: *Sunset*

to show—not very successfully, I think—in huddled images without syntax or continuity, that the whole world was reeling in a dance of death, a jazz war dance of madness and desolation. The poems admitted him to the literary circles of Berlin; but a book of war pictures made him famous.

At the age of twenty-three, he was acknowledged to be the most powerful artist in Germany; and he was also one of the most hated of men. Some of his later social studies will turn your stomach; but these war pictures will turn your soul, revolt and sicken and exalt you, and leave you wondering how an artist of such implacable bitterness could pause long enough to control his emotions. Grosz fought against war with a weapon more deadly than the sword; and his conception of the crucified Christ wearing a gas-mask condemned him to the firing squad. The young Catholics and Quakers rallied to his defense, and the war lords mercifully transferred him to the front-line trenches, trusting the French sharpshooters to do their duty. But the Lord protected him, and on his final discharge, inspired him and guided his hand through a series of Grosz-Mappes which will remain, in the archives of the anthropologists as well as in the albums of art, as permanent records of the social animal debauched by war into the social brute.

In the uprising of the masses, the social revolution following the War, Grosz perceived the dawn of a better day. "I was romantic again," he confides. "I believed in such forbidden metaphysical concepts as Truth, Justice, and Humanity—these in spite of the Versailles treaty. I had no economic program and no party affiliations, but my leanings were toward the extreme left. It was soon obvious, however, that nothing would be changed, or more exactly, improved. I had no faith in the Royalists and none in the Fascists, and I attacked both with all my strength, with an old skepticism sharpened by the War."

Assisted by a number of disillusioned young Germans, he promulgated a philosophy of negation, an artistic or semi-artistic nihilism. Influenced by that facetious Parisian flurry called Dadaism—the practical joke of a group of defeated painters who, instead of decently committing suicide, ridiculed all effort, artistic and humanitarian alike—he turned ferociously against the existing order of all things. "We were deadly serious; we had no humor—and what self-respecting man could have laughed at our country, bleeding and beaten, the spoil of soldiers and hypocrites? We had lived through the War; we had no hope; we were against everything. We would scrap the past; we had no tears for Greece, and none for our Gothic ancestors; we did not believe in art for art's sake, or Germany for the warrior's sake."

During this dark period, a curious Futurist mania was at work in his art. His drawings were kaleidoscopic scraps—murderous in implication; his huge paintings were symbolical confusions; forms seen through forms; soldiers, priests, pedagogues; judges, prostitutes, thieves, beggars, and plutocrats, truncated and distributed among filth and falling buildings, the idea being to reveal simultaneously the actors, the scene and all the dismal wreckage of the chaotic Fatherland. Esthetes prefer the work of this period, prating in their own lingo of the ectoplasmic vision, dynamic organization and plastic purity. Grosz himself is not deceived. "I was so full of hate that I was, maybe, a little insane. But this work purged my system of much poison—the poison of war and the poison of art. If it has any other value, it is as a reflection of the utter demoralization of post-war Germany."

Thus unburdened, Grosz abandoned Futurism to his compatriots who pursued the creed with Teutonic diligence, tunneling through the quagmires of Expressionism into the sunless caverns of lunacy. On his feet again, healthy and clear-headed, his style mature—hardened by fire and anger and punishment into the most effectual cutting instrument in modern art—he produced *Ecce Homo*. You may never see this book, and more's the pity; for it stands among social chronicles as a work of unapproachable realism. The Americans, I fear, despite our relaxed morality and our disingenuous exploitation of nudity and sex, will never permit it. Even the Germans, who accept the physical facts of life more frankly than most peoples, could not stomach the book; and the snoopers succeeded in suppressing parts of it. Grosz himself, today, is a little appalled by it. "All I can say," he remarks, "is that I was once capable of it. My people were like that, and I had neither the tact nor the detachment nor the pity to hold off and say, 'Forgive them for they know not what they do.' "

Ecce Homo may be termed The Anatomy of Degradation. It is neither erotic nor obscene; it is profoundly and surgically explicit. In line, the more incisive because of its economy; in water-color of acid strength, the book presents a culture gone hog-wild; a society, once composed and cleanly, abandoned to its most ignoble instincts. We might say that the only cure for such a society is to let it die of its own excesses; but Grosz thought differently about it; he was aware that the wallowing vitality of the Germans was not decadence but stupration—and capable of satire, he was not without hope. We must remember too that his exposal is essentially metropolitan—largely the life of Berlin; the sorrows and fortitude and lingering decencies of the provincials and pious country folk do not figure in the picture. It is a dreadful picture, a world of fleshly corruption in which the spiritual side of man has been battered to extinction; in which men and women leer and roll and snicker; but there is no gaiety in their lives and no rollicking laughter; not even levity, nor satisfaction—only the fulsome grunts prodded out of them by the coarsest physical stimulation.

There are scenes from the café and the brothel, the bed-room and the officer's boudoir; the park, the garden, the ball-room and the sewer; scenes from public and private life—and so far as Grosz is concerned, it was all conspicuously public. There are dumpy old matrons grinning prominently in the throes of an unexpected sexual reawakening; men with annular faces and turnip heads lunging in bestial embraces; old lechers avidly handling the acquiescent bulk of their hired women; young lovers energetically forgetting themselves; women with snouts and broken tusks; women with enormous breasts webbed and bitten— monstrous women, part snake and part sow, naked and unregenerate, conscious of nothing except the periodic relief of their tumescent organs; maids accommodating their mountainous rumps to the gazes of dress-coated connoisseurs; guzzlers and drunks, young and old; street-walkers, gluttons, vampires, homosexuals, and always in the background, with searing irony, the legless soldier, the beggar, the starving and innumerable poor. One might think in viewing this picture, that the German ideal, if it may be so denominated, was universal and unproductive copulation. And when I say that Grosz is explicit, I mean that he does not scruple to set down everything necessary to a complete record; not only the human body in any attitude or situation, but all its parts, minutely studied and drawn, and organically functioning. Behold the man!

The record is truthful, as those historically informed will certify. Knowing the period, you will say, "That is Germany!" Knowing art, you will say, "That is Grosz!" Imaginatively conceived and bearing on every page the stamp of an individual point of view, *Ecce Homo* passes from biological satire into the realm of art. For art is interesting in proportion to the richness of the personality behind it, and the personality is formed from direct and integrated experiences. The meanings of art are not unchangeable; they vary with specific environments, depending on the character and quality of the personal experiences and on the process of integration. Grosz's experiences, as we have seen, ranged from poverty and romantic play to the horrors of war and social demoralization. He faced death unwillingly but without tears; he faced social madness and brutalized passions without blushing. The formal side of his art—his constructive method—is not classical, it is Gothic; but we have advanced, I believe, far enough beyond Modernism to understand that there were many good men before Cézanne, and that not all of them came out of Italy or out of the East.

You will not find in Grosz's art those large generalized masses employed by the Italians in religious murals and vitiated by schoolmen, like Poussin and Picasso, into empty abstractions. His art is essentially illustrative, and realistic, with fantastic ornament and decorative inventions derived from his own traditions. But it is illustration in the broadest sense: not merely a trenchant description of an event, but a personalized interpretation of German life. It has, of course, its own peculiar furniture and its own point of view. The furniture, more often than not, is grim and disquieting; but even his most ruthless pictures—those brilliant water-colors exposing some exceptionally hideous vanity or carnal engagement—are relieved by passages of great delicacy and gentleness of feeling. He has a marvelous eye for character, setting down in a few lines and a wash of color the telling details—a sticky sensual mouth, a maudlin eye, an alcoholic nose, a wrinkled neck, a sagging overweighted ankle, the budding posteriors of a young girl, the gross protuberances of greedy women, a snarl of pubic hair, a beckoning grin, and a tragic stoop. And with the same spirit that induced his remote ancestors to weave flowers and stars and hundreds of little things in their manuscripts, he seizes upon odds and ends—street-hydrants, fussy chandeliers, garters, labels—and turns them into decorative properties.

In water-color, Grosz is the foremost of living painters. He undertook the medium when he could not afford oils and canvas, and has attained in it a technical mastery that makes bunglers of our leading practitioners. He does not make flimsy sketches, nor random planes, nor melting smudges into which critics may insert mysterious values; he makes pictures; for the most part, people, but occasionally still-life from studies of delicatessen displays, and symbolical landscape—the romantic Grosz again—which does not appeal to me. His nudes in this medium are among the few in modern art that have any meaning. They are not bored models groaning for a dinner—he does not use professional models—they are women he has observed and understood, enjoyed or despised; and they are painted in relation to German life and behavior. In former years, his nudes were sullen chunks, but recently they have begun to smile—lusty German girls, pink, meaty and marriageable. Nudity is not a pose in Germany, and if Grosz approaches it less professionally than the French artists, he approaches it more naturally.

Steadily, since 1920, Grosz has gone forward in his art, increasing in wisdom and in tolerance. Not that he has surrendered a single one of his convictions—in everything he has drawn or painted you may readily see where his sympathies lie—he has been on the side of humanity and he will remain on that side to his dying day. The violent hatred of the War days he has conquered; his grimness he will never conquer, but the grimness is now tempered with one of his strongest assets, his humor. His art has continued in the same central direction—social studies and satire—but he has enlarged its scope and ventured into other departments—stage settings for Reinhardt, lithographs for book illustration, portraiture, and oil paintings expressing, in one or two figures, and in more generalized terms, Germanic traits and feelings for which, in his earlier work, he needed a specific scene and many characters. He has traveled in most of the European countries and has had the satisfaction of seeing his famous style imitated by young cartoonists everywhere. It has been imitated in America, and parodied, but the parodists have only degraded it. Grosz has made peculiarly his own, and used to intelligent purpose, the Modernist device of treating opaque substances as if they were transparent, in order to reveal forms that are naturally covered or hidden from the eye. For example, he has a drawing of a strumpet passing a group of men in a café. By uncovering a certain part of her anatomy, he not only shows what the woman has to offer and establishes the focal point of interest, but conveys instantaneously the one thought in the minds of all the men. It is an effective device, but one that is, in his own hands, often no more than whimsicality. Adopted by his little parodists, it has become an offensive trick.

In 1932, Grosz came to America in response to an invitation from the Art Students League, of New York. The obscurantists of that institution opposed his election, contending, in their ignorance, that he was a fiendish creature who would plunge the League into a bedlam of anarchy, and destroy the respect for High Art. They were shamed into silence when the man arrived and entered upon his duties, a reserved and considerate man, with the interest of every pupil at heart, determined to train his classes to work and to think, to use their heads as well as their hands, and, as we should expect, to study the American environment. He is happy here and intends to make his home in America; he has taken out his first papers and brought his family to New York, a charming wife and two fine boys, Martin and Peter.

Grosz's coming to America was a natural step, the consequence of his ambitions and his development; he belongs here, and he would have come, even though he had not been an artist. He has no desire to conquer America on the strength of his European reputation; all he requires, as he puts it, is "a little room in the social scheme of things, just about as little as remains nowadays, to do his work." He does not pretend to know all about us; he is willing to learn; he takes the bad with the good, and goes on his way, constantly sketching. He does not drink tea for a living; draws no crazy skyscrapers in the Cubist pattern—he is much more interested in what goes on behind these brownstone fronts; does not rave over our beautiful girls. The girls do not look so lovely when he has finished with them: he brings out certain characteristics which American men discover after marriage. If he were a showman, he would advertise the fact that books of his drawings were burnt in Hitler's bonfire; and he would capitalize the publicity he has received from the Nazis. During the past year, using him as a horrible example, the Nazis have exhibited specimens of his work—paintings and drawings stolen from German dealers—with catalogue notes of damnable misrepresentation. And as a further mark of execration, they have persistently listed him among the Jews. Grosz is not, and never has been, a Jew. And he would tell the world that the French—he has a considerable following in France—are using, without his consent, his social studies as propaganda against the Germans. But he does not complain. "Why should I?" he asks. "After all, Hitler and I have been sworn enemies for a long time. Ten years ago, when he was a Royalist demagogue, I made pictures of him as a fanatical war cub. I do not expect favors from my enemies."

11

CUBES AND CONES

MODERN painting, since the death of Cézanne, runs amuck through a succession of cults, and ends, exhausted and impotent, in the present School of Paris. These cults, with their pompous denominations, are merely technical schisms; today they are all dead, and for the most part, forgotten; a few years ago they were screamingly active, and any one capable of enunciating their special mysteries, or even of distinguishing one sect from another, was esteemed as a critic of enviable penetration. Cubism, Futurism, Orphism, Synchromism, Purism, Expressionism, Integralism, Vorticism, Dada-ism, Sur-Realism —what an agony of effort, of rampant conceit, of swollen sensitivity! There is nothing to be gained by discussing them individually; for they may be grouped into two general tendencies which, for practical purposes, shall be called Methodism and Expressionism. A review of these tendencies, if not edifying, will, I think, give us an idea of what happens to art and to criticism when painting has no place in the world.

The exponents of method, of composition for its own sake, were consolidated under the name of Cubism, with Picasso as leader. This school numbered among its practitioners, Léger, Gleizes, Metzinger, Marcoussis, Lhote, Marcel Duchamp, Braque, Delaunay and Gris. Minute distinctions may be drawn between the methods of the various painters, but the distinctions are immaterial: the Cubists, in a body, denied the value of direct experience, of representation, of all the meanings of art as they relate to the behavior of man in any specific environment. They produced abstractions and geometrical posters; in plain words, ingenious patterns, some flat, some in relief, all testifying to a very

218

BRAQUE: *Abstraction*

FROM THE CHESTER DALE COLLECTION

thorough acquaintance with historical ways and means, but all devoid of any meaning above and beyond the technical exhibition of processes. It would seem, in the face of such purely objective things as conic sections or assembled pieces of matter, that one should have to talk sensibly, without recourse to metaphysical fustian or the devious theories of psychology. But such is not the case. Round Cubism and its attendant cults, there has accreted a literature so vast, so full of confidential valuations and subterranean apologies that the intelligent layman shrinks away in abhorrence, not only suspicious of modern art but of all art. It is said:

That Cubism has restored architectural form to art, and that the meaning of art lies in its architectural order. It seems unnecessary to point out that architecture has no meaning apart from its function; that its forms and internal relationships, from the troglodytic cave to the Gothic cathedral and the New York skyscraper, are organic growths determined by the domestic, social, religious and economic needs of man; that, when functionless, it loses its meaning and becomes a tomb, a shrine for tourists; that past forms, literally duplicated and plumped down in a modern environment such as the Lincoln Memorial in Washington or the classical court house in Denver, are expressionless and absurd.

That Cubism—and all Modernist art—far from being an upstart concoction, is allied with the great traditions, a derivative of the art of the past. This is true, but it proves nothing. All the modern arts are traditionally rooted—past forms and conventions modified by the pressure of contemporary civilization into new creations. The prosody, syntax and vocabulary, and many of the colloquialisms of American literature, may be traced back to the Elizabethan writers and even to Chaucer. But it is not because of this fact that American literature is entitled to respect. Nor do we admire Ring Lardner because the language he uses has a remote ancestry. Modernist painting is so subservient to traditional styles and methods that it ignores the meanings of contemporary life.

It is said that abstract art is analogous to music; that Modernist painting, relieved of representational baggage, has attained to a state of naked purity, of harmonic perfection. Furthermore, it is claimed that all good painting is visual music, appealing to the emotions, not through what it represents or symbolizes, but through its rhythmical pattern; that is to say, a canvas by Rubens is a symphony of abstract forms and colors, and one of Cézanne's peasants a fugue. This specious parallel is a recurrence of the Neo-Platonic theorizing of Walter Pater whose famous dictum that "all art constantly aspires towards the condition of music" has ruined many a critic. The synesthetic fallacy—the identification of colors with musical tones—has been exposed again and again and has never been seriously entertained by normal artists. The structural fallacy—the notion that the meaning of painting lies in the harmonic relationship of its parts—has been voiced largely by innocent writers and museum directors who, having just discovered the abstract basis of painting, jump to the conclusion that painting must be close to music, since that art has no natural scale and no need to imitate the buzzings of mosquitoes.

The advocates of pure harmony in painting and music never pause to consider the relation of these arts to the experiences of the composer. Because music does not ape the measures of nature, they assume that it has no connection with life; because painting has a pattern basis, they assume that it must, like music, dispense with representation—with everything that resembles natural forms. You may, perhaps, have noticed that the purists steer away from literature, carefully avoiding any attempt to reduce the significance of the verbal arts to formal relationships. The reason is not far to seek. Literature is still in a pretty healthy condition: its medium is the language of current speech; its meanings refer directly to the author's experiences and may be shared and enjoyed by every one. Thus it is less susceptible to esthetic humbug. It has, of course, its lapses into infantilism—the lispings of Stein and her nurslings—but they are of no consequence.

The arts are united in a common purpose—the integration and communication of experiences—but each art employs its own ways and means. Painting, from Giotto's first efforts to relieve forms in space, Leonardo's chiaroscuro, Rembrandt's achievements in tone, down to

Cézanne's painful experiments in cubic structure, has constantly striven to increase its representational power; not to imitate nature but to make plausible reconstructions of nature; to make forms that are real and convincing, that strike us with the force of life-experiences. And since the conception of reality varies from age to age, new forms are needed to represent, at a given period, the meaning of reality. Harmony is neither a force nor an end—it is the accompaniment of art. We have had, of late, so much harmony in painting that we are all sick of it, artists included; we long for substance, concrete subject-matter, something bearing upon life as it is actually lived.

The tendency to isolate, and to extol for their own sake, the components of art has led to the appraisal of painting in terms of physical properties such as density, solidity, and plasticity. These material properties are not peculiar to art; they are to be found, in greater degree, in natural forms, and are of no importance in painting unless directed to expressive ends. Volumes have been written on Cézanne's plasticity, and on the plasticity of the flat art of Matisse—a contradiction in terms. One might just as well speak of plastic ribbons or plastic wallpaper. The term has become a positive menace, as great an obstacle to clear thinking as "significant form," or that old hack of yesteryear, "tactile values." The modern critical method is to dismember a work into plastic scraps, to collate the scraps, noting, with an imposing array of technical terms, the presence of color, light, mass and line, and then to trace the ancestry of the scraps to the old masters, or better, to the negroes.

It is said by esoteric writers, who are fond of quoting Plato, that abstract art goes beyond ordinary human experiences, and expresses, by its own stark symbols, infinite values and intangible essences. As Apollinaire put it, "The Cubists discovered an esthetic use of form so unknown that only a few poets suspected it." They forget that Plato had no use for artists; that he recognized their limitations, their inability to depict the "divine reality beyond life"; that he accused them, quite properly, of dealing with the inflammable passions of mankind, the vulgar, troublesome human weaknesses which he ruled out of his ideal state; and that he relegated them to a low position in his Republic.

Instigated by abstract painting, certain critics have reduced the creation and appreciation of art to physical reactions. It has been written that lines and colors in certain combinations produce "significant form" which arouses within us—that is, within the favored few—a unique emotion. The notion of significant form is a crude by-product of the outmoded psychology of Grant Allen, Lipps, Lee and Thompson, a bigoted notion restricting all art values to materiality, confusing processes with meanings, and considering form as the simple result of psychophysical responses to objective stimuli. It makes the history of art nothing more than mechanical expansion—the mechanical evolution of technique; it does not penetrate into the intimate connection between form and the antecedents of human experience; nor does it consider how deeply and inextricably bound to one's whole nature are those impulses which take form in the conventions of art. When it was discovered that the forms of machines were also significant, and that our physical reactions to abstract painting were not different from our reactions to mechanical diagrams, the esthetic emotion was invented.

The esthetic emotion is that peculiar state into which the highbrows of art are transported by the perception of formal relationships. It is not to be confused with mere swooning, with the neurotic dizziness of the Pre-Raphaelites, nor the psychosis of the Expressionists. It is an intellectual ecstasy, the privilege of the elite, the last stage of cultivated arrogance. I can understand most of the esthetic emotionalists: their snobbery is transparent; their pursuit of art a retreat from vulgarity. But what shall we say of a man who declares that when he stands, open-eyed, before a picture by Rubens or Masaccio, he sees only formal relationships; that he is not conscious of figures, scenes or anything representational—only of structure? In whom "the recognition of formal relations produces this profound emotion, self-supporting and self-contained"? Shall we say that Roger Fry is a fraud, a humorist, or a nut?

I hasten to answer that he is none of these. For much of Mr. Fry's writing I have only the highest admiration; though he is, perhaps, the world's worst painter, his knowledge of painting is profound; he has lashed and irritated the Philistines relentlessly, and has outclassed them in scholarship; he wrote so wisely, once, of Giotto; and defended Tolstoy's ideas of universality in art—of art founded upon strong, simple human impulses as opposed to the artifices of the intellectual voluptuaries. But when he confesses that "Chardin's bottles arouse in him the same feelings as Michael Angelo's frescoes"—that the growth and turmoil of humanity mean no more to him than the plastic relations of old tinware—I fear that the worst has happened: that his prolonged interest in abstractions has atrophied his powers of appreciation; that the adulation of his lit'ry friends has gone to his head; that he has taken seriously the bleating of his Bloomsbury flock.

When the art of the Methodists began to bore the world, and it was deemed necessary to find in it more substantial meanings than Platonic absolutes, witnesses for the defense made bold to declare that abstract organization was the reflex of a machine age, that the pseudo-scientific technique of the Modernists was the natural result of mechanical forces. It is open to the credulous to believe this; but it happened that abstract art was deduced from Cézanne, a Provençal recluse for whom the machine age never existed. It is also a matter of record that the Bohemians are poorly educated in modern life, and are avowedly hostile to the machine age, living as far from it as may be, preferably in the romantic quarters of Paris. And it is no more possible to symbolize the dynamic energy and movement of modern machines, by arbitrary combinations of lines and masses bearing no discoverable relation to the machine, than it is to symbolize the strength and grace of the human body by abstract designs. The effect of the machine on man—how it has altered his conceptions of speed, power and space—awaits the mind of the educated artist; but it cannot be rendered by the simple trick of reducing both man and his instruments to a common abstraction.

It is said that modern abstract art, which has unquestionably been stimulated by primitive forms, is a psychological necessity, the protest of ill-adjusted souls who, unable to identify themselves with their surroundings, withdraw from society and build up an imaginary inner world. It is further maintained that "primitive races live in perpetual fear, and that their geometric and decorative art symbolizes a desire for order and control and escape from the uncertainties and terrors of life." There is truth in this German postulate, but it cannot be accepted unreservedly. Again we are confronted with the fact that all primitive forms—tattooing, weaving and handicraft, as well as the carved fetishes—as Professor Boas has shown, were religious symbols, perfect communal expressions of the experiences and ideals of tribal units, not the esthetic production of a few cowards; whereas, modern abstract art had its inception in method, was at no time inspired by religious motives or spiritual needs, and remains, as it began, an eclectic business—an exploitation of art for art's sake.

In an effort to view Modernist art comprehensively and in proper perspective, philosophers warn us that the movement is the last convulsion of the corpse of modern civilization; that its poor weak scribble is the handwriting on the tottering walls of the modern social structure; that its very unreality expresses the obsolescence, if not the doom, of the existing order. This portentous reflection we shall leave to the Spenglerians of the future.

Picasso and his co-workers staked everything on method—the deep meanings and hidden mysteries came as afterthoughts; the Expressionists, going to the other extreme, repudiated traditional methods, and professed, from the first, to reveal psychic states by blotches of color and zigzag lines. They did not, of course, abandon traditional practice, not even in those whirligig pieces which contain no signs of intelligence. The movement was introduced to Paris under the name of Futurism, a cult manufactured in Italy and promoted by Marinetti. On its practical side, the cult borrowed from Cubism the idea of trying to illustrate simultaneous aspects of movement. "The plastic interpenetration of matter" was the fine name given to this quirk. Theoretically it was a derivative of Croce's Expressionism; it had propaganda to offer and drove it home in the most sensational fighting style. The argument, condensed from its numerous manifestoes, was as follows: "The language of the old art is dead. Traditions are dead. The old subject-matter is a thing of the past. The nude is rotten. We have a new and more exciting idiom, a set of personal symbols compounded of anything and everything. We will express the dynamic energy of modern life; we will translate into plastic form live states of the soul, we will jerk your sensibilities into the most acute responses. With our shocking emblems of brilliant color and free line, we will make you feel art against your will." The argument captivated callow students and defeated professionals: to break with the past, to abolish tradition, to step forth like a child into a world of freedom, to invest life with fresh symbols, to see, feel and burst into song—thus to create art. Everything was art so long as it was inspired by true feeling.

The influence of Futurism has been of a cryptic nature. As a school it is extinct—I can think of nothing so dead as a Futurist picture—having been absorbed by Expressionism, a movement which has played havoc with all the arts. Like the other sects, Expressionism has cried a far-fetched esthetic, but at bottom, its creed is fairly simple: "Our contacts with nature—the facts of the visible world—for creative purposes are more important than any amount of learning or traditional knowledge. Given a genuine insight into the world of every-day experience, it is possible for the artist to dispense with old forms and to create directly, trusting to the pull of such impulses as follow his sensations. So working, the artist inevitably produces new forms. The burden of dead learning which stultifies academic practice is overthrown by an earnest and truthful expression of experience."

Again we have "the purity of direct sensation," the direct transfer of sensations to canvas without the intervention of the mind; the happy notion that "true feeling makes true art"—the Expressionist war cry which has become the painter's panacea and his silencing answer to the layman. This notion lends authority to that brand of self-satisfaction posing as genius; allows for every imaginable kind of stupidity and lack of knowledge, and raises children, freaks and incompetents into the ranks of the masters. Hence its popularity. But, like many of the ideas of faith-healers, it holds a grain of truth. It states unequivocally that the artist must have a natural and not a forced interest in his subjects; it orders him to look, if only superficially, into his surroundings, and condemns all virtuosity and academic precedent.

The Expressionists, painting intuitively, with warm hearts and small minds, were strongly influenced by Van Gogh—who worked himself into a nervous collapse in his efforts to acquire a sound technical knowledge. They were also influenced by Matisse and the Fauves; but the Wild Animals, let us not forget, while advocating free, or proportional design, were exceptional students of tradition. The world has been flooded with blobs and tangles put forth in the name of pure expression. This puerile stuff is a disgrace to art; it has no more claims on adult attention, and no more right to be considered as art than the bawling of a child—also pure expression.

One of the most mischievous influences in this direction is Henri Rousseau, a customs house official who took to paint in his forty-first year, bundling together, in an amusing, infantile style, his exotic recollections of Mexico where he had spent five years as horn-tooter in a band. Rousseau was admired for his genuine and continuous childishness, his naïve vision which was his birthright, and which, as his admirers found out, could not be acquired by an act of will. In many ways, he was a true primitive, without modern equipment in technique or intellect; and his charming pictures calling up the naïve fancy of the old illuminators have unbalanced many a painter of talent. He is a curious exception in art, a delightful idiosyncrasy; but his work has neither technical nor philosophical merit, and painters who have read those qualities into it have ended in ludicrous imitation. Rousseau has nothing to offer the mind; his art as a source of knowledge is sterile, and as a source of pleasure, quickly exhausted. He has the charm of a blind fiddler playing sweetly by ear, or of an untutored old man lisping in the musical numbers of a child. Because of his "true feeling," and his quaint, rambling

ROUSSEAU: *Tropical Landscape*

integrity, the Expressionists point to him as living proof of the value of intuition in art.

Expressionism runs into cracked symbolism and pathological trances, and abetted by Freudian research, winds up in Sur-Realism. You have seen it in the galleries, each picture a gruesome manifestation of some private and incommunicable agony; and you have seen the spectators, little knots of serious folk seeking in each picture the special key without which no entrance into the soul of the artist is possible. That the artist is sincere and "original" is no recommendation. His originality is of no higher brand than that of the nutty girl in "Huckleberry Finn" who revealed her yearnings graphically in a picture of a maiden with six arms. "Two reaching up toward heaven, two crossed on her breast, and two stretching out before her." That is good Futurism.

The cult of true feeling flourishes among sorrowing and humorless artists. There is Chagall, a Russian Jew, who paints jackasses with visions in their heads, and topsy-turvy villages shot through with memories of his childhood. His disorderly conceptions would be ridiculous if they did not convey a little of the vagabond poetry and the pathos of his uprooted soul. There is Soutine, a Lithuanian Jew, whose mind is afire with something mystic and inexpressible. A shy, kindly, poverty-ridden man, he paints in solitude, with an intensity worthy of Van Gogh, and with an impasto as thick as plaster, figures distorted beyond the bounds of reason; and landscapes which might be the slag heaps of hell. About all that can be said of his work is that it indicates some sort of tragic experience—what, I do not know. His art is supposed to be rich in plastic values.

There is Kandinsky, a gloomy Pole, whose psychic smudges were exhibited, in the company of the more clever smudges of Picasso and the Sur-Realists, at A Century of Progress, and were duly admired by visiting cognoscenti. Kandinsky talks of spiritual harmony—he spins a button on a thread and sings to God. He paints loose, irregular patches of violent color round which lines are coiled like wire. He does no more than that—his work is not even good pattern. The rest is talk, unintelligible talk. He is not an impostor—he is the victim of abnormal synesthesia; that is he has got himself into such a state as to believe that colors symbolize the spiritual life. Because color nuances affect, in a slight way, our moods and feelings, it is easy for morbidly sensitive souls to worship tonal combinations, and going further, to believe that loose pigment can express the deepest emotions. Investigation has shown that the sensational aspects of color are too fluctuating to be of any significance; that the moods induced by color schemes are shadowy and uncertain; and that the positions of these schemes in deep space are never positive.

The idea that unrelated color, or form in the abstract, can be identified with specific factors in our psychic life has no basis in experience. A blob is a blob, and a triangle a triangle; when either becomes the carrier of spiritual meanings, the emblem of metaphysical spasms, or the portrait of the soul, it is an aberration. The abstract forms of Modernist art are eclectic patterns or free decorations—free in the sense that they are not symmetrical; they have, in many cases, taste, tact, and acute feeling for the organization of sensuous elements; but like the designs of other periods, they contain no meanings and no vitality unless they stand for something—for the facts of experience. In that event they require no special interpretation—the key to their significance lies within the work itself.

The last of the horrors is Sur-Realism, a diminutive sect which in its nameless beginning included Chagall, Chirico, and Klee; and subsequently under its own banner, Roy, Ernst, and Miro, the acknowledged leader recently deposed, for commercial purposes, in favor of Picasso. The aim of this sect is to provide a place in art for abnormal perception and neurotic sensibility; to express by symbols the inner world of dreams and fantasies—the debris of the unconscious mind. The accomplishments amount to nothing: incoherent tags and strings; scrambled colors, headless forms, silhouettes, circles and dispersed knick-knacks, which, as symbolical references to the world beyond our experiences, may mean anything. "But," these addled painters insist, "hallucinations too are experiences. They are our own original discoveries, and they are very real." True enough, but discoveries only to the warped minds that make them.

And inasmuch as reality is distorted to fit the pattern of the neurotic mind, they cannot be called real experiences. The validity of experience can be checked, and tested; and no experience is valid in art unless it can be recognized, shared, and connected with reality.

The Sur-Realists, as a whole, are a sincere lot; but Picasso's contributions to the cult are rank frauds. I remember the night when a museum director, a pallid young man, born and raised in the Fogg Plant and top-heavy with old lore, undertook to perform before an intimate group of art-fanciers—the esthetic old ladies who backed his museum and their bored husbands who, for some obscure reason, furnished the money. The young director, fresh from a jaunt in Europe, was chock-full of Sur-Realism. He politely ordered his foot-page to place a Picasso on the easel. The picture was almost pure abstraction, but with a little peering, one could detect, in the swipes of loud color, the suggestion of the upper part of a dead woman—two curves for arms, a circle for a breast, and a face in silhouette, the eye sticking in the bridge of the nose. It was poor pattern; it was not clever enough to be a good hoax; it was framed rubbish. The director began confidently, talking softly of the design—the dynamic organization, the plastic purity, the organic relationships—and trying to adapt his generalizations to the object on the easel. It was tough going. There was a glaring discrepancy between his memorized esthetic slang and the thing on the easel, and for an instant he floundered. He gulped some hydrant water and began again, this time on surer ground. I never saw a young man work so hard. He talked of spiritual values, plastic symbols, sublimation of reality, extra-pictorial metaphors, superhuman compensations, and the psychological insight into states of the soul "so unknown that only a few poets suspected them."

He finished faintly, and the old ladies cosseted him. No one understood or believed him; and yet no one quite doubted him. The old ladies felt that some day they would see it all very clearly; the men, hard-boiled old capitalists, were resentful and ashamed—the young rascal was giving their wives something they could not offer. While they were secretly convinced that the picture was not worth a dime, any one of them would have bought it on his wife's recommendation. And one like them did buy it for an enormous sum. Seances of this sort occur daily in all the museums of America. No wonder the French in their comedies invariably characterize the Yankee as the international fool.

When artists have no purpose in life; when they struggle and suffer for an ideal, only to discover that the ideal is not worth the having; when they possess just enough intelligence to acknowledge the futility of their own efforts; they grow cynical and abusive. Sometimes they are base enough to burlesque and ridicule all attainment; sometimes they band together for the express design of destroying the ideals of others and degrading every form of art. In 1920, a few bemerded cynics founded the cult known as Dada-ism. The cult is extinct, and its members are now reduced to silent vagabondage.

There are a number of artists who do not fall into any rigid classification, and many more who might be classified if it were worth while. One of the most popular of the Bohemians is Derain, a schoolman, like Picasso, and a master of methods. Derain paints with extraordinary muscular control, but his canvases are eclectic rehashings and studio exercises. With his shrewd, fourflushing talent, he can swagger in the manner of any great man; his pilferings range from the Italian Primitives to Poussin, from Chardin to his Parisian contemporaries; and he has made Cézanne acceptable to juries. He belongs in the theater where his décors and designs for ballet have won him wide and deserved acclaim. Modigliani put Derain in his place, once for all, when he called him "a manufacturer of masterpieces." Vlaminck, with the method of Cézanne and the violence of Van Gogh, painted, in his more enthusiastic years, city streets and landscapes of considerable power. But he has painted the same street over and over again, and the same black landscape, and the dramatic interest has been consumed by processes. A much finer painter of streets is Utrillo. This unfortunate artist whose extreme sensitivity was debauched, from youth, by constant drinking, painted the Bohemian background that was too much for him—the damp, moldy walls, the dirty alleys, the rows of disreputable houses, not picturesque as they appear to expatriate fledglings, but contaminating—his own personal version of the romantic ruin of Montmartre.

The smarter side of French life has its spokesmen in Van Dongen who has applied the tricks of Modernism to cheap portraiture; and, very faintly, in Raoul Dufy, a milliner in paint. Dufy came out of the shops; his clever sketches are designs for stuffs and ceramics, but in a movement in which anything goes, he has found it profitable to frame his mincing patterns. One of the most gifted of the Bohemians was Pascin, an American of Italian, Spanish and Jewish blood. He was a born tramp, affectionate, fond of riotous amusements, of children, the picturesque and all shades and forms of lasciviousness. He loved the Bohemian life and lived it to the full, painting it, with the tools of Cézanne, according to his mood —now with the greatest delicacy of feeling, as in his portraits of children; again with unblushing carnality, as in his nude prostitutes. He was a great illustrator, capturing in brilliant sketches of line and tone the movement and character of the exotic scenes that tempted his fancy. He squandered his life, his talents and his money, and died by his own hand, mourned by thousands.

Modernist art, both in criticism and production, has been engaged in the hopeless task of erecting a pure esthetic by the separation of technique from meaning. Its aim has been to place the artist in a world of his own, and to grant him by legislation the unique individuality which all of us in our vainglorious moments would secretly possess. And it has come about that the one who appreciates—the amateur, the collector, and the critic—is as important as the creator; that one has only to understand a work of art in order to win a seat among the privileged coterie. The artist, to his astonishment, has discovered, on arriving at his high and unique position, that his supporters have tagged enviously after him. This is only natural: defenders of an aristocracy have always esteemed themselves as aristocrats.

The machinery involved in this esthetic business is simple: it is only a matter of restricting the range of the significant elements in the production and appreciation of art. By confining the elements to those whose understanding rests upon special training or unusual experience, the number of the elect is satisfactorily reduced, and the prestige of the chosen few correspondingly enhanced. That part of creative work which is removed from ordinary human conflicts, or which can be made to appear so, becomes the very center of significant values. Technique, essentially a matter for artists or a handful of specialists, is a field already prepared, and this field, when judiciously fenced in, is soon completely isolated from vulgar understanding. It only remains for the aristocrats to drag into their exclusive little province the values belonging to the whole of art, and to attach them to minor technical issues. Furthermore, any technical expedient, when disguised in terms of physiological mechanics or psychology, can be magnified to an appalling degree. I have reviewed, in detail, the various ways in which technical interests are presented as reflections of experience. Some years ago the psychological critics, using the terminology of William James, analyzed the artist's stream of consciousness; today, the same critics are writing of Matisse's conditioned reflexes. When we take into account the egoism of man and his climbing instincts, it becomes clear that the most acceptable theory of art is the one which magnifies the difficulties of appreciation—which, without making any demands on hard sense, may be paraded as evidence of superiority.

The separation of technique from meaning, of the material factors from the imaginative content of form, was the outcome of an abnormal interest in abstraction. The steps from experience to expression are not fundamentally different from those in other fields of mental activity, and abstraction is the first step. Its normal direction is towards something objectively useful. That is its biological function—it is merely a means to an end. Art divorced from its teleological basis is comparable to any one of those perversions of normal processes which make for insanity. When the means, for instance, of sexual gratification are removed from actual experience, the victim wanders in a world of fantasies and ineffectual visions. The parallel in art is the separation of technical procedure from experience on the one hand, and from intelligible meaning on the other. When this happens, the artist reads arbitrary and subjective values into his useless efforts, and throws himself upon the mercies of the psychologists. This perversion of talent is accompanied by a steady decrease of creative energy; and we find today that many of the champions of abstraction have passed off the stage, cynical and impotent. And the evils of abstraction are not confined to the artists themselves. It is the tendency of our galleries, universities and museums to employ as directors and teachers excessively esthetic young men who are specialists in fads, historical or current; who, having had no healthy experiences in life, and protected from the harsh pressure of the modern environment, disseminate the notion that art is the luxury of the precious few, that in its highest and purest forms it is never soiled by the grime of reality; and whose mischievous erotic habits alienate from our public institutions all self-respecting members of society.

The strangeness of Modernist art—its obsessional interests and eccentricities—has convinced a large public that the whole movement was a charlatan mutiny organized in Paris for notoriety and profit. This erroneous impression is far too flattering to the artists: as a class, they are too unintelligent to conceive such a scheme, and too ignorant of practical affairs to put it in execution. The exploitation of some of the cults has not been on the level, and there have been cases of individual corruption on the part of artists, critics and dealers. In a society with no solidarity of purpose, with no unifying religion and no general idealism; in a world which encourages pretense and factitious achievement—anything, in fact, that looks important—it is to be expected that art too should be polluted by snobbery, inanity, and commercial cunning. In one respect, at least, modern art resembles modern life: it includes in its ranks the parvenu, the cheapjack exhibitionist, the politician and the virtuoso, together with the deluded visionary who sees a new world where there is only chaos. But the artists, taken one with another, have been sincere and pathetically long-suffering; and most of them have paid a heavy penalty for their devotion to a dying cause.

Modernist art, in its origin at any rate, must be estimated as a natural uprising; and in its broadest aspects, as an educational measure. It is natural in that it is a cry of despair, the assertion of the artist of his right to exist even though he can discover no happier niche than the Bohemian igloo. It is an old cry; it has echoed down the centuries, but never before has it been so insistent and hysterical. Remember that since the Renaissance the artist, with an occasional mighty exception, has been nobody, a superfluous nuisance living anyhow, half his life devoted to persuading himself and the world that he is needed, the other half to the search for a social connection. What social changes will restore him to an honorable position, I do not pretend to know—the claims of the Communists for a better world will be considered in a future chapter—but this I do know: so long as art exists as a thing apart, so long as it continues to feed upon itself, just so long shall we have these internal ructions, these wild controversies and vicious manias, these profound interpretations of trivialities, these heated esthetic spats between Picasso's crowd and the partisans of Juan Gris over the introduction of the guitar into painting.

As an educational measure, the Modernist movement can hardly be overestimated. It has given the death-blow to naturalism; it has destroyed —I trust forever—the old superstition that art is the mechanical imitation of nature. That, in itself, is sufficient excuse for its existence; that alone is worth all that it has cost the world in the devotional pains and defiant self-absorption exacted of the artist, and in the exaggerated pictorial values which the public has been petitioned to accept, admire and purchase. Nothing, it seems, would have slain the curse of imitation except concerted violence and the wholesale slaughter of the photographers; nothing would have cured art of its most ancient sickness except a purgatorial dose of Modernist medicine. Remember that since the Renaissance, save for the work of a few intractable souls such as Rembrandt, Goya, Hogarth and Daumier, art has subsisted on its interest in natural phenomena. From Dutch and Spanish schools of tone, through Manet and the Impressionists, painters have been occupied with the appearance of things, with the rendering of the effects of natural light and shade. The Impressionists took the mind out of painting altogether

234

PAUL KLEE: *Romantic Park*

and made it a form of chromatic photography. The interest in atmospheric effects, while it saved art from total decay, deprived painting of almost every quality which, in its flourishing days, lifted it to a position of power and respect.

The Modernists exposed the shallowness of Impressionism, and at the same time, the academic fallacy that the emotional elements of art—its "beauty," its perfection of form, its majesty, and all the rest—reside intact in nature, and that the artist has only to seek out these natural forms and duplicate them in paint in order to create a work of art. The old business of mechanical imitation again! The formula is not so simple. The emotional elements are the perceived and experienced facts of life; they are transformed by the mind of the artist, an imaginative act involving hard, constructive labor and an indefinable factor called genius. How it is that certain minds seize upon materials which to most of us are commonplaces, remake and dramatize them, and invest them with the magic of a rich and unique personality, is as mysterious as life itself. But the transformation of experience, as Van Gogh's heart-breaking trials bear witness, calls for knowledge—the more the better—of method. The Modernists laid great stress on construction, on the necessity for design, organization, and coherence of statement. By destroying Impressionism, they removed the last artificial stimulus to the life of art. For imitation they substituted structure; but the imperative now is an imaginative content for structure. Unless this is discovered, old Cézanne's purpose has gone wrong, and art is doomed to the nothingness of abstract form.

One of the charges most frequently leveled at the Modernists is that they have never learned to draw, that is, to draw in the conventional manner, and that they have resorted to subterfuges and unsightly distortions to conceal organic deficiencies in draughtsmanship. And I have heard this charge answered by apologists for Matisse in the following remark: "Yes, but he really can draw, you know, when he wants to." The remark is equivalent to the admission that Matisse is merely capricious, that he is mystifying or fuddling the public for some ulterior purpose, when he might be doing beautiful work. The "correct drawing" of

Matisse is of no more value than the academic studies of Gérôme, Sargent or Puvis de Chavannes. The fact is that all the Modernists, Rousseau excepted, were rigorously trained in the conventional system, many of them star pupils and prize-winners. I think we may reasonably conclude, when so many sorts and conditions of men renounce their academic training, that something is wrong with the training.

"But," you may ask, "did not the academies teach the methods, the ways and means, of art?" They did, but by rule of thumb, and with only one end in view—the imitation of nature or the imitation of the externals of the masters. They followed the method of David, drawing the figure by precedent and tight prescription, without reference to its true structure, and conforming to arbitrary or ideal proportions supposed to be pure Greek, but actually handed down from Graeco-Roman copies by French Prix-de-Rome scholars. The Modernists, aided by the enormously increased collections of early art-forms in the museums, have been the most diligent students of method in the history of painting. They have studied the negroes, Asiatics, Mayas, and the Occidental masters, and have studied them for creative purposes. They have discovered that the carvings of the African tribes are more expressive than the public monuments of Paris; that the relatively simple forms of Giotto are incalculably more moving than the modern academic murals painted with naturalistic methods developed from centuries of imitation; that the childlike Rousseau is more of an artist than Besnard or Bouguereau; that art, in its wayward descent into the reproduction of nature, has lost its emotional power, and hence its true meaning.

The Modernists ascribed the emotional power of art to its abstract organization. Holding to this fixed principle, they have explored and experimented with every structural device known to art. They have examined the problems of equilibrium from the simplest forms of balance to the most intricate allocation of weights about a center; they have tested the value of symmetrical and free, or proportional design; the use of distortion; the recession of forms in deep space; the effects of pure color; the resistance of weight and mass; calligraphic line; plasticity and flat decoration; the violation of natural perspective; the intensification of black and white contrasts; the geometrical basis of natural forms; the rendering of objects by the utmost economy of means—all these, not for the sake of imitation, but for new schemes of co-ordination. The net result, however, is not an increase, nor a recovery, of emotional power, but an enlargement of the instrumental resources of the artist. The young student of today finds himself in possession of an instrumental equipment that would have terrified the early masters. This is not an unmixed blessing. To those with nothing to express, it means no more than a boring repetition of idle combinations; to artists of real ability, it means freedom from academic bondage, a swifter realization of their powers, and, it may be, in the hands of genius, a more dramatic art than anything in the past. The fatal mistake of the Modernists was the conviction that, because they had diagrammed and analyzed the structural methods of the masters, their own abstractions contained the emotional properties of the originals. Evidence of structure is no crime—it is often a mark of individuality—but processes, as I have reiterated, must deal with something besides other processes; and method—whatever method —pursued for its own sake, leads back to the Academy.

The tactics, employed legitimately by the Modernists to unmask the academic painters, have reacted on themselves. Abstract composition, which has reduced all forms of imitation to zero, has stripped its own practitioners naked, showed them up, exposed their barren personalities and their feeble mental habits; it has proved that one cannot create art by subjecting forms to the tyranny of processes; that true composition is not an extrinsic equation evolved from the styles of others, but the final form, the personal tone and order assumed by materials experienced at first-hand.

The Great Modernist Movement has come and gone. It went over in remarkably short time; it was interesting, exciting, salutary. Personally, I find its structural vagaries—its ingenious combinations and abstract relationships—far more interesting than anything produced by mechanical imitation: they are, at least, a beginning, the first step toward the making of new things. It was popular with artists because it was primarily addressed to artists for their advancement and edification. Purged of all disturbing realities, it was also popular with certain groups of lay people; its tasteful patterns were appropriate decorations for those geometrical interiors designed and furnished by Frenchmen for Americans devoid of personality. Matisse, himself an interior decorator, and damned by his own utterance, expressed its philosophy in a sentence: "It is an escape from reality."

To many artists, the passing of Modernism is a calamity. Rob them of their cubes and cones, and their pretty theories, and they become nonentities—more miserable than capitalists whose assets were all paper. It has been said that "Cubism is to art what a check is to money"—a check with no funds behind it, or a check to be redeemed in the minted coin of experience. The time has come for the redemption. Modernism has destroyed Impressionism and imitation in all its forms; and it has also destroyed itself. It has removed from art all artificial stimulants and restoratives, including its own. It has carried art back to first principles, cleared the way for a new order. It was a concentration on method to the exclusion of content. The next move of art is a swift and fearless plunge into the realities of life.

12

AMERICA: THE BACKGROUND

THE country was lovely in the spring. The uplands were green with fall grass, the ponds were full, and the whole valley bursting into life. Wheat was everywhere: miles and miles of it in all directions, an inland sea, an unharvested sea waving in the wind. Wheat was the major crop—the State was the wheat field of the world. You had only to sow it, complain about the weather, and cut it. After the fall sowing, the farmers prayed for snow to protect the tender grain against the cold; in the spring, too much or too little rain, or hail or wind, destroyed the crop—so the farmers said; but the harvests were unfailingly abundant.

It was a country of sudden and fearful changes of weather. In June, a stretch of glorious days, and then, one morning, a greenish sky and the stillness of death over the wide valley. The air was stifling, with a watery haze dimming the sun. Early in the afternoon, black spongy clouds boiled over the northwestern horizon; and a little later, clouds of the same hue, but swiftly moving, came out of the southwest. The two masses made for each other, as if guided by divine vengeance, met, and out of the concussion sprang several twisting clouds, full-formed and ready for action. The spiral offspring coursed over the valley, always in the same northeasterly direction, moving forward, concentrically, and at the same time, dancing up and down. Sometimes they dissolved peacefully into thin air, effecting nothing more serious than to put the fear of God in the hearts of the farmers; sometimes they scooped up an orchard or shaved a wheatfield as clean as a ribbon, or disemboweled a house; always they played fantastic tricks with the laws of nature; and once, I remember, they wiped a settlement of Swedes off the map. After the tornadoes had vanished, great chunks of ice dropped down from the heavens, and beat holes in roofs, and beat down the fields. A marching army could not have made a more thorough job of it.

Windmills were never silent; and in the summer, the southwest wind blew its hot breath over the land. The wind blew perpetually, and there was never a cloud in the glittering sky; the only clouds were the dust storms which whirled through the streets and sifted under the rattling windows. The streams dried up; the corn shriveled on its stalks and flapped in the wind; the faces of the women were like wrapping paper; farmers—next-door neighbors—drove ten miles to town to stand on the street corners and discuss the drought; and at the close of each day, my father scanned the horizon for signs of change. The heat lightning flickered over the distant hills, but the rains would not come. In the winter the flat valley was the playground of blizzards; but the autumn was a season of golden days. Swallows gathered over the shocks of corn, and the wheat stubble—before the ploughing began—rolled out like cloth of gold; and the hills swooned in a purple haze. At dusk, in this wide prairie land where, not so long ago, the Indians hunted the buffalo, and where, within my father's memory, the last buffalo was killed, there was grandeur and desolation, the freedom of vast distances, and the loneliness of an uninhabited world, an infinite loneliness stretching back into prehistoric eras when those cretaceous hills were the coastline of a gulf dividing the American continent. I used to tramp those hills at night, addicted to a form of nature worship which broke out in verse, my first trials at expression. As a boy, I was not conscious of the extremes of heat and cold, nor of the effect of the climate on the people. We all ran wild and no one was the worse for it.

The town was settled by Northerners, some coaxed from their New England homes by Eli Thayer, others from Pennsylvania and Ohio. My people, on both sides, were from the South, the only rebels in the town, but no one gave a hang about our slave-holding ancestors. The caste system had not yet developed and distinctions based upon wealth, birth or breeding did not exist. There was almost a perfect communal spirit among the settlers: all worked for the common good; every deserving soul was given a hand; and if a man turned out to be a cheat or a sponge, he was ushered out of town on a rail. There was color and pomp in the little town: men wore plug hats and tail coats, and carried handsome walking sticks; the leading citizens drove spans of chestnut horses; and the favorite recreations were gambling and drinking. On one occasion the grand jury returned indictments against every man in the community, including its own members and the judge of the court. The judge arose and addressed the county attorney: "The grand jury, in its infinite wisdom, has seen fit to indict the court." Whereupon, with mock indignation, for he was a brilliant speaker, he proceeded to try the cases. One by one the men appeared before him, pleaded guilty, and were duly fined and sentenced to jail. At the conclusion of each sentence the judge delivered a sermon on the "pernicious evils of poker playing." The fines were never collected; nobody went to jail; and the gamblers returned to their cards.

My father, one of the pioneering graduates of the University of Missouri, went west in a stage coach in his twenty-first year, with a copy of Thomson's *The Seasons* in his pocket. He was a grave, high-tempered, sensitive man—a lawyer with a strong sense of humor and a will of iron. Though unmistakably an Anglo-Saxon, he bore, in his pictures, a striking resemblance to Dante Rossetti; and when I called attention to the likeness, he was as proud as Punch, for he had modest literary ambitions and was the author of a book of poems, privately printed. He was a great reader: he knew his Shakespeare by heart and quoted the bard on every subject; he was an authority on Dickens and Mark Twain, and an admirer of Bill Nye, Eugene Field and Bret Harte. He held women in chivalric esteem, so long as they were content to be women—in the field of business, or politics, he regarded them as eyesores. "In all my life," he said, "I never met a woman who would do business like a man. Women are constitutionally incapable of observing rules."

He was a fine father. He never put me to work, or suggested that I

241

become a real estate agent, or a man of law, or endeavored to curb my vagabond propensities. And he kept his faith in me in all my adolescent wanderings, and whenever I returned home, gave me a hearty welcome. He respected my love for books and made it possible for me to buy as many as I could hold, some of them rare volumes imported from England. I grew up on Mark Twain and Swift, and the British poets. He was proud of my poetic symptoms, but my leanings toward art excited his gravest suspicions—he looked upon painting as a low pursuit, all right for Europeans and effete Easterners, but for one born west of the Mississippi —by God, no! I heard him swear for the first time—he used neither slang nor profanity—and he was slow to forgive me. When I came back from Paris, full of big talk about the French, and Bohemia, and the cosmopolitan spirit, he rebuked me solemnly.

"Your grandfather," he said, "and Mark Twain were bosom friends. One night, in a hotel in St. Louis, after the great Missourian had become a world figure, the two men were drinking juleps and talking of old times. They quarreled because Mark Twain defined a Southern gentle-man as 'a mossback who hides behind a tree and shoots his neighbor in the back,' and was promptly called a traitor. 'That sounds like the animadversion of a Yankee,' your grandfather retorted, 'a Yankee with European refinement. You're nothing but a mossback yourself, Sam.' 'I guess I am,' Mark Twain replied, and primed with whisky, he sailed into the French. Remember how he took the hide off Paul Bourget?" asked my father, rubbing it in.

"Liberty, equality, fraternity, and adultery," I answered, "a provincial joke."

"Missouri wit," said my father with a smile.

" 'The French have their good points,' Mark Twain went on, 'but in the ways of Bohemia they haven't had my training. I was the original Bohemian. When little difficulties compelled me to move on, I moved fluently. All that I had to do was to —— on the fire and call the dogs.' "

My father loved the plains and the sunburnt women and the long golden autumns. He was not unhappy, but there was an unfathomable loneliness in his heart, the sadness of the pioneer. He was always gazing beyond the horizon, a far-away look in his eye, dreaming of something which, through pride or reticence, he never mentioned. In the evenings he would sit on the front porch, smoking innumerable Key West cigars, and talking of the prose style of the old English jurists, of poetry, and in a reminiscent mood, of his own youth. His grandfather's place had been raided by the James boys, and he had brought with him a collection of tintypes of the border outlaws—Frank and Jesse James, the Quantrells, the Fords, the Youngers and Bill Anderson, who, in his opinion, was the worst of the lot. This collection was my pride and joy, and I would exhibit it, when we played circus, on the walls of our carriage room. It was my first art gallery. When it was reported by western papers that Bill Anderson was alive and running a ranch down in Texas, my father nailed the fiction with first-hand evidence.

"When I first saw Jesse James," he said, "he was nineteen years old. He was a fine-looking lad with the makings of a good citizen, one you would never suspect of villainy, but he had got off on the wrong foot—he was the son of a hardshell Baptist preacher. He had been engaged in crime for several years, but his exploits had been confined to local stealing. During the month of August, in '64, the border counties of Missouri were overrun with bandits. Bill Anderson, who had been in business with the Quantrells across the border, had organized a gang of his own, and was riding roughshod over the country, plundering and killing; and the James brothers, on a smaller scale, were following his example. One afternoon there was a hot fight between Anderson's men and the home guards, or volunteer militia. Jesse James had witnessed the skirmish, but for once, as a spectator, and observing the strength of the home guards, decided to change his hunting ground. He came galloping down the highway with three of his men, turned into the lane, and stopped at my grandfather's place to pick up a few horses. While the men were going through the stable, he hurried into the house to see if there was anything else he might borrow. But inside he found a scene that made him pause.

243

"My grandmother was in her last illness—she was very old but her beautiful auburn hair had not lost its color—and when Jesse James saw the group at her bedside, all of us very still and terrified, he looked sick and ashamed. I was only a boy, but I remember the Baptist piety in his face. He had deep blue eyes, and a complexion as smooth and clear as a young girl's. It was a hot day, and he took off his weapons, a belt with two pistols, and laid them on the bed; but he kept his rifle in his hands. He stood there leaning on his rifle, and glancing, I thought, with real compassion at my grandmother. Then he said:

" 'Well, old Bill won't bother you folks no more. They plugged him in a hundred places.'

"That," my father said, "we all felt was a help. He told us that when the bushwhackers, after their custom, tried to storm the militia, Anderson, like a fool, left his men and charged straight through the home troops. His men did not follow him; he started to turn back, and the local boys filled him with lead.

" 'They dragged old Bill's body through the streets of Richmond,' Jesse James said as he left the house.

"He looked mighty sad," concluded my father, "but just the same, he took our horses and our guns. What could you expect from the son of a hardshell preacher?"

The town is a little city now, but the color and individuality are gone. The tornadoes are gone, and the cattle, and the horses—they have riding academies now, with gaited nags and young girls breaking their pelvic bones. The pioneers are gone. My father is one of the last: though he reached years ago what Mark Twain called "the scriptural statute of limitations," he walks as briskly as a youth, growing stronger, it seems, with time, and more implacable. The pioneer spirit lives in the twilight of Willa Cather's prose, but the artists, crammed with Cézanne and Picasso, have not touched it. The change from the buffaloes to the cattle, from the cattle to the wheat—who shall paint it? Who indeed? They are building golf courses on the hillsides, and exclusive districts of manor houses with formal gardens. One of these days the pioneer spirit will return suddenly in the form of a tornado, and blow those houses to smithereens; and the sons of pioneers will wonder why the hell they planted English architecture on the prairies.

The pioneer spirit was in me, and I was soon off and away. I went to Paris, but the fortunate discovery that Frenchmen were born and not made, returned me to America before it was too late. I voyaged down the Mississippi from St. Louis to the Gulf—a dream come true. I passed Cairo in the night, like Nigger Jim, but my freedom lay somewhere down the River; I saw the bluffs of Memphis recede and the country flatten out behind the levees; I tramped through villages in Arkansas where hogs wallowed in public mud-holes; and when the boat stopped at some planter's woodyard, I sat in the bar and watched the nigger gals, gorgeous in striped calico, come aboard to buy gin, a black drink in those days. I loitered under the pepper trees of Mississippi towns with the painted daughter of a St. Louis brewer—the girl was going down to Vicksburg to join her fiancé. When we pulled up at Vicksburg, the fiancé was not there, and the girl screamed so loudly and so impenitently that the whole town flocked down to the wharf. I left her sobbing in her paint, for I knew she had not been faithful to her man.

New Orleans was in an ugly frame of mind. It was the day on which Jack Johnson had knocked out Jim Jeffries at Reno, and the negroes were afraid to show their faces. They had attempted a celebration, and had been clubbed and driven across the River. The white folks were stunned by the news—what kind of trash was it that would permit a nigger to fight a white man? Yet many of them had bet on the fight and had lost heavily. Tin-horn sports who had gambled on Johnson, collected their money and swarmed the streets behind the station for a revel with the mulatto girls. But that night the mulattoes locked their doors and cowered alone in their dark cribs; and the French ladies on the other side did a land-office business. I loved New Orleans despite the dirt: I have never believed in dirt, even when it is old and picturesque and acceptable to artists. It was far better than Paris; the people were a little shiftless, but their friendships were real—not those professional alliances of the Latin Quarter which, at bottom, were an excuse for indecency. They were not always acting or selling their sordid stageplay to outsiders in the name of art. I found scholars there; and men and women whose dignity did not interfere with their joy of living. I expected to make my home in New Orleans, but a fever caught me and sent me to the mountains of Colorado.

Denver is a clean town a mile above the sea. The people there are among the best in the land, truly and typically American—the sons of miners and cowpunchers. Normally they think, act and disport themselves in the cultural tradition of their fathers, with frankness, intelligence and the memory of the gala days at Central City. When they turn to the fine arts, they forget the gods of the mountains and chase after false prophets. They build classical court houses and Italian villas, and hire smug European sculptors—bedroom Modernists with smooth tongues—to carve dead images for their extravagant temples; they bring the dregs of abstraction into their art classes and teach the immortality of the tulip and the odalisque, while the ghost of the Red Indian haunts them day and night. Why should the men of Denver be interested in Picasso? Fortunately, most of them are not; and when I was in Denver, the first time, no one had ever heard of Picasso. I expected to make my home there, but the fat city editor of the sheet for which I was reporting hold-ups and minor crimes, decided that I could not write in the style of his red-letter requirements, and fired me. He did not know what a blessing he conferred on me; and I boarded a train for New Mexico without going through the formality of buying a ticket.

The artists had not yet descended upon New Mexico, and the great State was not suffering from the cult of Lawrence and the worship of the Indian. My destination was determined rather unceremoniously by the night watchman at a division point on the Santa Fe, and I had no choice but to try my luck in a little town partly enclosed by mountains and looking down on an illimitable expanse of mesa land. But I did not regret my forced landing. The watchman, on closer acquaintance, was touched by my tale of woe, and introduced me to the station agent; and at the end of the week, I was working on the railroad as night billing clerk. The hours were long—from seven at night till seven in the morning—but the work had its social compensations. My duties were to weigh and tranship coal, to send fast, or red-ball, freights out of the yards within the allotted half-hour, and to have the waybills ready when the conductors had been rounded-up by the call boy. At intervals, when there were no freights to be dispatched, I had nothing to do but to listen to the Homeric talents of the train crews. The freight conductor is the toughest of all God's creatures. My lot has been thrown with farm hands and threshing crews, with Sicilian stokers, Cuban procurers and dealers in art; as a duly enrolled drudge in His Excellency's navy, I have been quartered with the lowest of blue-jackets—but all these are babes and sucklings compared to the freight conductor. Every one had a new and more scurrilous version of *Casey Jones* which he sang as he examined his waybills. To this day, whenever I hear the whistle of a locomotive, my ears ring with obscene corruptions of that imperishable ballad.

I spent most of my spare time in the mountains, sketching, or in the Mexican quarter known as the old town. I loved the old town with its neat adobe houses, its plaza, its priests, goats, and babies, its dark-eyed girls, and its luxurious saloon kept by a German. I met people who were at peace with the world, contented with the simplest pleasures—to drink a little and to dance; to bask in the warm sun and contemplate the clear blue sky and the mountain ranges. I met Penitentes, who, at Easter time, stripped themselves to the waist and lashed their bodies into insensibility with the blades of yucca plants—a great theme for an artist with a religious turn of mind. And I met Luciana. She was sixteen but fully grown, with a high bosom, a thin waist, and a foot that would have nestled comfortably in a beer glass. She was a handsome girl, despite the pockmarks. In her amorous moods, the blood would rush to her cheeks, the scattered pits burning a deeper red, and she would burst into Spanish expletives. I learned Spanish from Luciana, in her own home, surrounded by I never knew how many brothers and sisters, all shy and respectful; and watched eternally by her mother's eagle eye.

247

My boon companion was a car-whacker. Now car-whackers, as an economic unit, are played-out mechanics, greasy dogs who, when a train pulls in, poke their heads under the cars looking for hot-boxes, broken draw-bars and couplings, and defective air transmission. But this car-whacker was a young chap with the face and figure of a half-back. He might have been a college boy, for all I knew, but he refrained from mentioning his personal history and I was not inquisitive. Six months before my arrival, the yard master had found him lying in the sand-box of the round house, and had summoned a doctor thinking the boy a victim of t.b.—a natural inference since many lungers found their way into the town. But it was only a case of starvation and the strain of riding the rods. The boy was soon in perfect condition, and jobs being few and far between, had taken what he could get and had made no complaint.

The young car-whacker had an overmastering weakness for women. Every morning, at daybreak, after he had inspected his last train, he would hurry down a winding road to the mouth of the canyon to a house called the *Three Nines*, open a window, and drop into some girl's bed. The personnel of the house was continually changing and he was never certain who his bed-fellow would be—that, he assured me, was part of the fun. He was very popular with the girls and the madam, dined with them regularly, and paid them by the week, handing over his checks like a devout husband. It was money well invested, he said, and he was very happy. The wise old madam, to insure the proper functioning of her girls, and to keep them in good spirits, sent them out in the afternoons for a breath of air and an hour or two of wholesome relaxation. Well mounted and garbed in fancy riding habits, they would gallop hilariously up the main street and out on the mesa, to the unspeakable discomfiture of the good people of the town. The car-whacker told me which of the horses belonged to the mayor, and which to the hotel keeper; who paid for the girls' outfits; the gross revenues of the house; and other intimate matters pertaining to the *Three Nines*. He seemed to think that the house was a good joke on the town—and perhaps it was.

The young fellow was buoyantly satisfied with the world, until he fell in love. One morning, when he let himself through the window and tumbled into bed, he encountered a girl who won him completely. It was love at first sight, or more exactly, love at first conjunction—though it was pitch dark in the little room, "he could tell," as he expressed it, "from the feel of her that she was different." I would not have called her pretty but she had neither the appearance nor the manner of a professional. She was bleached and thin and not very bright; but she had a sweet face, and she was mad about the car-whacker. The love affair upset the whole house, and the madam plotted to undo it. Her first rule was to discourage the girls from falling in love—a real passion aroused their jealousy, made them shirk their work, and always ended in disaster. The girl, instead of riding out with her companions in shame, journeyed far up into the canyon with her lover. Sometimes I accompanied them, but it was no fun for me. Perched on a rock, the wind whispering among the pines, and the waterfall echoing down the canyon, she clung to him, desperately in love and desperately unhappy.

The complication cost the madam her best client. From some strange notion of fidelity, the girl refused the car-whacker what she bestowed—now all unwillingly—upon the men of the town. And the car-whacker, inspired by equally chaste motives, severed his relations with the other girls of the house. The madam raged and overworked the girl. The young man saved his money and consoled himself in his plans for the future—they planned to get married in the spring, and to beat it for California. But the girl broke down with t.b., and being no longer useful to the madam, had to be removed. Not a family in the town would take her in, and I found a bed for her in a Mexican house. The car-whacker attended her like a Sister of Mercy and called in the best doctors and paid them all his savings, but the girl died before the winter was over.

I left New Mexico in the spring, bound for New York, and traveling, this time, on a pass. I thought it advisable to travel while I was eligible to a free ride, that is, before I was found out. In weighing a string of loaded coal cars, I had neglected to ascertain the tare weights, an error I did not discover until the coal train was well on its way to Albuquerque.

A makeshift occurred to me, and I stamped on each ticket the first tare weight that entered my head, subtracted the tare from the gross, and filed the net weights of the loads in the freight office. From my experience with railroads, I knew that if I confessed my crime, I should automatically cease to be an employee of the A. T. & S. F.; and that, if I said nothing, it would take at least a month and a thousand telegraphic communications from Chicago to track down the source of the irregularity.

My train departed in the night and the car-whacker came alongside to say good-bye. He was on duty as usual, and had only a moment to wish me luck. He was a tough young man, but I noticed that he wiped away a tear with his oily glove. "I never go there any more," he said, pointing toward the house at the entrance of the canyon. As he knelt down to inspect the journals, the light from his lantern shone upon his face—the saddest face I have ever seen.

Whoever, in his youth, has lived in the Lincoln Arcade, at Broadway and Sixty-fifth Street, has experienced all the miseries of the artist's struggles for recognition in New York. That old building, not only to myself but to countless artists of every creed and aspiration, is the symbol of the mockery and degradation which the young man with ideals and hope in his heart must endure in his battle for a place in the metropolitan world. You rose above it and conquered, or you died in one of its hovels, alone and unremembered. Could we have foreseen the long dark road we were destined to travel, with the penury, the snubs and the lost illusions, we would have said in one voice, "Let us go back to the mountains and the ranges, and marry the women of the soil, and tell our people that in New York art hides her face in shame." But we were very young, and we pooled our miseries in a common fund of forced jocularity and hard work. A blow for one was a blow for all, and we laughed it off together; and good luck for one was food for many.

The Arcade housed an unsavory crew: commercial artists, illustrators, starving students, musicians, actors, dead-beat journalists, nondescript authors, tarts, polite swindlers, and fugitives from injustice. The commercial artists occupied the best studios and lived elsewhere. They were

JOHN S. CURRY: *Roadmenders' Camp*

good fellows—on better terms with New York than the rest of us—but fundamentally they were money-grubbers innocent of the meaning and purpose of art. The few of us who had been in Paris and had been caught in the snares of Modernism were eventually ostracized. We had ourselves to blame: we flouted the hacks with the cocksureness of youth and made ourselves generally obnoxious. There was Thomas Benton, a Missouri boy just home from Paris, with giant ambitions. Nothing daunted him and he was a glutton for work. And S. MacDonald-Wright, altogether the most brilliant young man I had ever met. He could do anything, that fellow, and do it with the ease of a master. He never had to learn; he was born mature, and the variety of his gifts was embarrassing to every one but himself. His smaller abstractions remain, both in color and composition, superior to the best that Picasso can put together. He spoke French perfectly; he could out-think and out-talk anyone on any subject; and he dressed like an English lord. But poverty bore down cruelly upon Wright. He had been reared in luxury, and in Paris had lived in style; he had, in his early twenties, founded Synchromism, and had exhibited at Bernheim-Jeune's and in Munich. Landing in New York with a bale of cosmic symphonies—huge abstractions which today he uses to wipe his feet on—he expected a sensational reception. Nobody remarked him and he languished in the Arcade, a neglected master. He despised New York. Finally he gave up the fight, confessing that "he was tired of chasing art up the back alleys," and retired to the somnolent air of Santa Monica. From the French and Italian influences of his youth, he has strayed into a world of Chinese philosophies, and in that world we shall leave him, for I have no key to its mysteries.

Adversities came thick and fast and we were obliged to go our separate ways. It was each for himself now, and the devil of art take the hindmost. Recalling those squalid years, I am tempted to view the present depression lightly. I began to think that the artist had always been depressed, that it was his fate to live in a state of chronic depression. The loneliness of New York settled in my soul, that crowded isolation compared to which all other forms of social hunger are interludes of tranquillity. As I walked up and down Broadway, I remembered De Quincey's youth in London, and his apostrophe to "stony-hearted Oxford Street," which my father had read to me when I was a child. Stony-hearted Broadway, the stamping-ground of gregarious enemies, the national highway of cut-throat rivalries! I yearned for the pleasant loneliness of the prairies, for the companionship of high mountains. I have been penniless in many corners of America and in the West Indies; but to be broke in New York, with artistic ambitions and no aptitude for making money—that is real poverty, supreme and beyond compare. I might have returned to my native town and lived in decency, but I would not have acknowledged defeat for all the comforts in Christendom.

I lived in cock-lofts and subcellars from Spuyten Duyvil to the Village; above coal yards by the East River, and above saloons on the West Side. But I learned, from bitter experience, something of the magnitude of New York—and the misery, and I learned the habits of the various populations. I have never learned to love the city, as the Frenchman loves Paris, but I find myself always coming back to it, attracted by a multitude of interests. The attitude of the artists puzzled me from the first—even those who were to outgrow their French predilections. Most of the artists secreted themselves in their foul studios and painted still-life or things far away from their environment; the others thought they had painted New York when they had converted a skyscraper into a congeries of abstract forms. Never an attempt to show the effect of the engineer's colossal handiwork on the people; never a hint that the artist, who called himself a Modernist, was living in the most modern of cities.

I wrote poems and managed to sell a few lyrics, but I soon cured myself of this evil. I was a minor poet, and minor poetry is worse than still-life painting. I wrote three novels, one a ferocious, and immature, satire on New York entitled *The Paradise of Fools*; I tutored the good-for-nothing scions of plutocrats in Latin and Greek, but one fell day, when the headmaster was called to the hospital where his wife was childing, the boys made a bonfire of some of the choicest pieces of furniture—and my resignation was accepted. I rewrote manuscripts for established authors; I coached young Jewish stenographers in Spanish; and I taught Spanish in one of the high schools until I could stand it no more, preferring routine wretchedness to that form of living death. The Navy commanded me: Seaman Second Class, four on and eight off, holystoning the deck, polishing brass, days of coal mining. A hitch in the Navy prepares a boy for three walks of life—the night watchman, the laundress, and the janitor.

There seemed to be no end to my precariousness, but a chance meeting with Clarence Britten, one of the editors of the reorganized *Dial*, proved to be a smile of fortune. Britten, besides being a sagacious editor, had the soul of an artist and the magnanimity of a saint. He talked with me at length, ploughed through my accumulated trash, and sent me a book on Brangwyn to review. I had never reviewed a book, and having nothing to lose, gave Brangwyn the drubbing of his life. I could not do so well today, even though my dislike for the Welshman increases with each wall that he bespatters. The review was more than an analysis of a poor painter: it was the expression of the compacted fury and hate and misery of my eight years in New York. There is no such thing as detachment in criticism. That outburst put an end to my anonymous preliminaries. Scofield Thayer, of *The Dial*, opened his pages to me, and allowed me to range untethered. When I defended Modernism against all comers, hammering home the truth that the movement was a salutary return to first principles, he was delighted; when I became impatient with the trend of the new art—its retreat from reality—and challenged the painters to produce something in their own right, or go back to France, he was not so enthusiastic. But he respected his men and printed my stuff. I owe a debt of gratitude to *The Dial*.

During those hard undergraduate years, I contrived, by hook or by crook, to relieve my homesickness for America. Three times I took to the open road: the Middle West again and New Orleans and the South. A winter in Mobile improved my spirits immensely. Voluble old gentlemen, and their frail wives all in black with fichus of handmade lace, who

253

lived sedately in the ante-bellum past, welcomed me to their dilapidated mansions—after I had submitted my family credentials. They fought the War again and talked alarmingly of the freedom of their grandchildren. The third generation had forgot the War and sectional hatreds—as one young man remarked to me, "I have no prejudices against the North, but I would never marry a Yankee girl." The changing South, the new South, the South of Stribling and Wolfe—what a subject for the painter!

In the early spring, we sailed across the Bay to a shoreline of semi-tropical beauty. There, amid ripening oranges and magnolias in full bloom, I enjoyed the charm and gaiety of the South. The boys were very courtly; the girls, in their organdie frocks, ready to be wooed. The girls with names out of Poe—Annabelle Lee, Virginia May, Ardelle, Eulalie, and Nadine—and one enchanting Jewess, Aline, who played the violin. We drank whisky straight, with milk chasers, and at night swam in the warm waters of the Bay. I hated to leave Mobile, but the spell of the sea was irresistible. I roamed the water-front, watching the fruit steamers, manned by canoodling squareheads, discharge their cargoes of bananas: and sailing vessels come into port with coffee and linseed from South America. The captain of a schooner took advantage of my restlessness and signed me up as an apprentice; and I sailed in his three-masted lumber wagon to Puerto Rico, a voyage of thirty-two days, and my first real acquaintance with the sea.

Puerto Rico, the pearl of the Antilles, deserves a better fate than to be the spoil of politicians; than to be harassed or despised by yokel governors and picayune commissioners appointed in Washington. The Portorriqueños are a peace-loving people; they suffered the Spanish tyranny without a single revolution, and they ask of the nation that conquered them only an honest government and intelligent consideration. They have suffered hurricanes, abject poverty and industrial ruin —they are entitled to a new deal. I spent one of the happiest years of my life in that fair Island. My classes in the University were composed of the most courteous students I have ever engaged to help, and the most diligent. In no other part of America is education so ardently cherished:

254

the Puerto Ricans have the highest regard for the profession of teaching; and more—they accord the teacher the rights of a human being and do not expect him to wear the mantle of righteousness.

Footloose for three months, I wandered from one end of Puerto Rico to the other, and found the Island the flower of hospitality. In the homes of friends or strangers, in the mountain huts of peons and the village fondas, the house was mine as long as I cared to linger. The people have the fine pride and the warmth of the Spaniard, and none of the arrogance. I cannot say much for their passion for cock fighting. Pop Hart, alas, now no more! loved the game, but his pictures of it are far more dramatic than the real thing. I must accuse him of loving the spectacle more than the combat. On Sunday mornings, the peons come down from the mountains carrying their birds in bags. The pit is placed among the cocoanut palms in a natural amphitheater, and round the wooden enclosure scores of fighting cocks are leashed to stakes. The excitement exceeds anything to be seen at prize fights, and for the reason that the owners wager all they possess on their birds. I have seen peons go raving mad as their hopes are cut to pieces; I have seen them leap into the pit, lift a dying fighter in their arms, suck the blood from its wounds and blow a red spray into the bird's mouth to revive it for one more attack. There is no sport in cock fighting, it is a duel to the death between pets that have been trained to kill or be killed—but, being a game of chance, it is popular with men who do not care for other forms of bloodshed.

New York is an inspiring city—when one returns to it after a long absence—the metropolis of inestimable attainments and despairs. I have often exhorted artists to pluck up their courage and explore, as a respite from their soul troubles, the hinterland where the madness of paint is unknown. But you cannot budge them from their Manhattan roosts. Living in insecurity at the beck and call of the dealer; prying into the sales and styles of their competitors; and eager for the stale crumbs of journalistic praise, they depend upon the galleries and the latest European fads for their inspiration, and produce pictures which are no more than nominal allusions to the life of New York. The time will come, I

255

dare to hope, when we shall have local schools of painting in America, self-supporting and ministering to genuine communal needs. When that golden day arrives, we shall bury the New York racketeer without benefit of clergy. And the artist, delivered from the seductions of the metropolitan exhibition, which draws him to Fifty-seventh Street as it draws the playwright to Broadway, shall paint for a steady local market, and for a reasonable wage. A dream? Perhaps—but at any rate, not a Freudian dream.

Southern California boasts an exceptional interest in art. This interest, at present, is unintelligent, showy and superficial, but it is not wholly a pose. I am inclined to believe that it springs from environmental conditions which will bear watching. As I stood, in the house that Frank Lloyd Wright built, disciplining a rowdy audience of native sons, counseling them to paint their splendid open markets if they must paint still-life, it occurred to me that there was ground for hope in southern California. Domestic architecture, for the most part, plastered shacks of hacienda lineage, is improving rapidly, and has reared habitations that are comely and appropriate; men and women alike take pride in their streets and gardens; dwelling out-of-doors, they are easy-going and healthy, with a sensuous response to life that is not characteristic of Americans, a pagan joy which may occasionally be distinguished from the physical indulgences of strapping youth. It is conceivable that some day: when they have built a Chinese wall round Hollywood, and have left that naked cancer to its own proliferations; when the cult of athletics, and the other cults, have been suppressed; when an earthquake has erased most of the city of Los Angeles and shaken the builders into a more seemly notion of architecture; when the riffraff from the Middle West has been absorbed and silenced—this sensuous joy of life, informed by a spirit of humility and intelligence, may give us a native school of painting. The sons of San Francisco do not go in for art. They have a mediocre academy, a couple of depressing galleries, and an inaccessible museum. Northern California, esthetically, is virgin.

But I can imagine no richer field for the historical painter than the northern part of California, the scene of the gold rush of '49. The emigrant trains and prospectors; "the steel-shod cavalry crossing the Sierras," as Joaquin Miller expressed it; the settlement of San Francisco and the last extension of the pioneer border—there indeed is epic material. And I can imagine no more efficacious antidote to the poison of New York than a long sojourn in the Siskiyou Mountains. I lived there in a flimsy hotel among people who grow tall and indolent. The background was nature on a grand scale. The shadow of Mt. Shasta fell upon my window, and that purple mass with its snowy peak, became my Fujiyama. I painted it many times, but I did not exhibit my pictures.

At the hotel I fell in with a modern cowboy, a sleek, ashen-haired young knave who had forsaken the herds for art and the rodeo. He was a born liar—a native of those parts—a superb horseman, and an able crap-shooter; a deputy sheriff, he carried a gun, but, at home, his major occupations were riding about the country in full livery, and painting pictures which ranked with the whimsies of A.E. He had drifted back to California because of his insane interest in the mistress of the mountain school. The girl was a Portuguese with a slightly negroid cast of features, but very stunning and melancholy. She loathed the cowboy, but he was incredibly vain and hung around her convinced that he could break her down. Two years before this, he had been the rival of a young Portuguese rancher for the girl's favor. The rivalry grew so intense that, in the dead of winter when the snow lay deep on Mt. Shasta, the suitors agreed to end it by a contest in physical courage. The one who excelled in mountain climbing would be the better man, and would return, in triumph, to claim the prize. What happened on that expedition will never be known, but late in the day, the cowboy appeared dragging his rival through the snow at the end of a rope, like a sled. He told a mournful tale of how the Portuguese had played out, how he had tried to revive him and could not, and how he brought him down the mountain as swiftly as possible. The Portuguese had been fearfully used and died from his injuries. The cowboy stuck to his story and was never brought to trial. After all, what was the life of a Portygee to the Californians?

257

At night the cowboy and I would stroll over to the baggage room of the station for a friendly game of dice. In the navy I had been liberally educated in crap-shooting, but I was no match for that cow-artist. He beat me at every throw, and his victories were humiliating; but his fulsome ballad singing and his art talk made me despondent, and I was glad when he went off to a show in Wyoming. Last summer, at the Chicago Fair, I met him again. Dressed to kill, he was on exhibition, with four other cow-gentlemen, at the doors of a building erected by the makers of a celebrated mouth-wash. He was a professional artist now, and had painted a mural for the mouth-wash king. While he and his fellow actors were criticizing John Charles Thomas's rendition of *Home on the Range*, I went inside to survey the mural. I took one look at the western scene and fled—it was inferior to the cheapest form of magazine illustration. Here, I told myself, is the other extreme of American art. At one pole we have the artist who is trained to death; at the other, the cow-artist, the hick painter, the dog walking on his hind legs. Cow-punching is in its decadence now; the boys are showmen—rodeo performers and instructors at dude ranches; they go in for balladry and painting; they are at home on the radio but not on the range.

I have passed happy summers in New England—in Maine and in the sunshine and fogs of Martha's Vineyard. Torn between the western mountains and the sea, I have had to compromise and live in Long Island within reach of New York. But the West is closer to me than any other part of America, and when I cross the Mississippi at St. Louis, I begin to feel at home again. Some day I hope to return to New Mexico to live—when the Bohemian artists have abandoned that great State. My experiences have given the lie to the popular notion that America is a standardized country. If you believe that it is everywhere the same, try North Dakota in the winter and then the green fields of Virginia; contrast Seattle with New Orleans, Galveston with Minneapolis; Kansas City with Boston, and San Francisco with Chicago. It is a country of endless variations, and no one man shall know them all. There are many Americas which, in time, I trust, shall all be revealed to us in art. In

Oregon, I met an extraordinary character, a man who had been an Indian fighter and sheep rancher, and who, in his declining years, was living in comfortable estate in the hills above Portland. He knew a thing or two about art, this formidable old gentleman, and had been in Africa when Matisse was there, and had observed the Frenchman's passion for shapeless Moorish women.

"Why is it," he asked me, "that our artists can discover nothing in America worth painting? Why do they everlastingly paint studies and not real things? And why, in the name of God, do they kowtow to the French?"

Those are fair questions and I shall do my best to answer them in the next chapter.

13

THE SNOB SPIRIT

W<small>E CAN</small> no longer turn away from the significance of the sub-ject-matter of art. America lies before us, stricken with economic pains, but eager for the voice of criticism, and in desperate need of spiritual consolations. Shall we face the situation like honest workmen; or shall we hide in the dark tower and paint evasive arabesques on an ivory wall? Again and again, with all the temper at my command, I have exhorted our artists to remain at home in a familiar background, to enter emotionally into strong native tendencies, to have done with alien cultural fetishes. And at this critical moment, I repeat the exhortation.

I make no plea to jingoistic madness; I do not ask for national flattery, nor for the cackles of patriotic duplicity; nor is it my wish, presumptu-ously, to thrust advice upon initiates in the craft of painting. Like many other sentinels, I have observed the rise and fall of French Modern-ism in America, viewing with indignation the snobbery and the facti-tious refinement of our professional painters; and, searching for new issues, I have discovered in the undercurrent of American art the direc-tion of emerging tendencies. And I have noted in these tendencies a close resemblance to conditions of the past: I am reminded continually of the trials and achievements of Ryder, Homer and Eakins, and of hundreds of extant prints—woodcuts and illustrations which are not only of genuine artistic merit, but which, in their character, are true reflections of the American spirit. Against the annual crop of chlorotic plants nurtured in the Bohemian slums of Europe and transplanted in America, this homegrown stuff stands out vigorous and healthy—crude

260

perhaps, and a little naïve, but real. Better one Ryder than a dozen Whistlers; better the nameless illustrators for the old Police Gazette than an army of imitators of Matisse and Picasso.

American painting suffers from over-refinement, a disease common to most of our cultural activities. All the argument in the world will not make America old in spirit. To this day she has preserved a semi-barbaric physical frontier—and the frontiers of her mental life reach out darkly into Voodooism. Granted the inflexible, second-hand, British culture of Boston, there is, on the fringe of this culture, rural New England with its folkways and superstitions, and industrial New England with its immigrant slaves, half-starved and illiterate. If you doubt the existence of the semi-barbaric culture of the South—the whole of Dixieland from the huts of the hill billies to the ramshackle mansions of lecherous colonels—you have never lived in the South, and you have never read Thomas Wolfe's great novel *Look Homeward, Angel*. The substance and staple of Western novelists from Mark Twain to Dreiser, Cather, Anderson and Lewis, is the pioneer spirit struggling against or enmeshed in the shams of refinement.

On the culture of the Middle West I speak with authority. I was born and raised on the plains among migrating cow-gentlemen, hysterical politicians, abolitionists, prohibitionists, cranks, gamblers, and ignorant wheat farmers; I remember vividly how poor folks in covered wagons returned sadly from Oklahoma, the victims of sooners at the opening of the Cherokee strip. And my experiences were not exceptional. The American family has always been on the move, advancing frontiers and carrying the spirit of the frontiersman into our cities, our religions, our government, and our international conferences.

Thus it has happened that barbaric religions and primitive habits of thought flourish profusely in America. Mormonism grows numerically stronger year by year; quacks abound; the screech of the Holy Roller echoes in the suburbs of our great cities; in New York City, the testimonials of the Uranian Society, and the mystery worship fostered by the Roerich Museum, would shame the witch doctors of Hayti; senators and stock-brokers consult female astrologers; and cults based upon faith healing and the amulets of medicine men multiply beyond calculation. Refine upon these cults; put them in dress coats; smear upon their uncouth ceremonials the transcendentalism of Boston or the false mysticism of the Orient, and they become Christian Science or New Thought. They develop into powerful social and political organizations, invading the privacy of our homes, framing fool laws, taking away the liquor of our fathers, and playing into the hands of gangsters who, in true frontier fashion, subvert the law of the land with the shooting iron. But keep the frontier undefiled by cultural pretensions; let it develop naturally within its own limits; and it produces not only valid art forms but the beginnings of an organic tradition of art. It calls upon God in sublime rhetoric; it breaks out in folk songs, ballads and spirituals; and until a few years ago, dealing with things it loved and understood, it produced pictures: chalk-cuts, woodcuts to embellish sheet music, almanacs, and illustrations for popular sentimental magazines and sporting journals which frequently touch the realm of masterly composition.

From this I do not wish to imply that the artist should retain the characteristics of a hill billy. By doing so, he would only restrict the range of his perceptions and consequently the range of his art. The charm of primitive, or folk art, is centered in the genuine character of its meanings. But because it is genuine, folk art, which is essentially poor and limited—inferior indeed to folk music in variety, intricacy and emotional power—has been exorbitantly praised by esthetic faddists. Its forms are simple, and its meanings, as I have said, limited; but for these very reasons it is a convenient illustration of the inseparability of form and content.

As a matter of truth, the popular engravings and illustrations which I have cited were not wholly indigenous products of the New World. A certain amount of education and tradition was involved in their production—in the Currier and Ives prints a very considerable amount—and European education at that! My point is that the heritage was submitted to the influences of a new environment; that old forms and conventionalized methods were not repeated habitually for their own sakes but put to work in new situations; and that traditional practices were radically modified by the exigencies of new situations. It is the old story of survival by adaptability. Art, like all biological growths, adjusts itself to new conditions or dies in a world of perpetual change.

If there is anything in art that may be set down as a certainty, it is the fact that participation of some sort is indispensable to appreciation. To know and understand a work of art, one must be able to enter into it, to participate in the spirit that created it. One cannot remain apart, especially above it, and appreciate its values or measure its appeal. In this sense, art may be compared to true Christianity where pride and caste have no place, and where simple vulgar honesty is more likely to afford the key to salvation. Art is a social phenomenon, or it is nothing. It proceeds from special habits intimately related to ways of living; and as an activity it is subject to the vagaries of living. Let us look into this matter as it pertains to the growth of American society.

Let us take, for example, the indentured servant of pre-Revolutionary days. Having served his term, or deserted his master in the night, he takes to the backwoods and establishes a homestead. He is a rough fellow—he was rough when he came to the Colonies, and in his new environment, engaged in the struggles for self-preservation, he has acquired no polish. He had no position in the motherland: he was an underdog when he sold himself into bondage. Swiftly and naturally he adopts the psychology of the American frontiersman. His sons and daughters are rough—their cultural accretions are confined to ways of invoking the mercies of the Almighty God and singing rather mournful songs. As time goes on, these accretions, under pressure of a new environment and a new psychology, begin to assume a unique character. Despite an inherited technique, they are shaped into new patterns. The far-off European background of the indentured servant with his sorrows and tribulations is obliterated; and his descendants, unconsciously perhaps, find themselves in possession of the stuff of art. It is crude and simple

263

stuff, but it has this in common with the ingredients of the greatest art: it is formed of direct experiences with living materials.

Let us suppose that our homesteader had the good luck to fasten upon a piece of land which in due course proved to be strategically situated with reference to inter-regional trade; and that his great-grand-children, in consequence, amassed enormous fortunes as traders, manu-facturers, or middlemen. Here we arrive at a momentous turning-point in ways of living—and incidentally in the growth of art. For the first generation which carries an economic burden only moderately lightened, local display is sufficient. Exaltation of the plain self—without formali-ties or blushing—is entirely satisfactory. Such art as is practised is not esteemed as a means to social advancement, nor as a mark of superiority, but as a simple delight, a natural appetite to be vigorously indulged. Give any share-cropping fiddler or untutored hill singer, a little leisure, even today, and he does not question his art—he indulges it.

In the next generation, however, this forthright attitude begins to disappear, and in succeeding generations it is lost altogether. Cities are built; social distinctions are more closely drawn; wealth is centralized; the wheels of education are set in motion; huge sums of money are de-voted to the business of mass refinement; people begin to put on airs and to affect nice ways of behaving. Now nothing could exceed the ob-vious refinement of the kitchen girl transformed into a lady. And the example of the kitchen girl, during the process of transformation, offers an exact parallel to conditions which have prevailed in American paint-ing. Ignoring the original and brilliant contributions of our novelists and architects; following year after year the predatory trail of Whistler through European schools and masterpieces; the American painter has endeavored to put on the elegance and style of the Continentals. His achievements, on the whole, have been glittering dexterity and pathetic imitation. Ashamed of his heritage and his environment, he flaunts the exaggerated niceties, the polite mannerisms of cultures which, being most remote from his own social roots, seem to be, by the magic of distance, most worthy of imitation.

A few parvenus can do no great harm—they may indeed be very amusing—but when the parvenu spirit becomes a national attitude, the condition may be properly described as calamitous. From the very beginning our students are taught that painting is essentially a European attainment; our museums, particularly the newer foundations with their rich endowments, to win social distinction, buy Old Masters—usually unworthy examples—and the smarter specimens of French Modernism, and become dumping grounds for dealers, and the dupes of sharpers known as experts; the owners of the new Waldorf-Astoria Hotel, planning congenial decorations for their parvenu diners, shell out $100,000 for the bombastic capers of a second-rate Spaniard; and our cunning dealers employ as provincial agents men and women socially prominent in communities where the art fad is momentarily raging, and where art, like cold creams and beauty lotions, gains prestige by the endorsements of the elect. Thus the parvenu spirit has developed into a national characteristic, and the painter can hardly do otherwise than reflect this spirit, and cater to it, and feed it with shams and masquerades in the European manner.

Art in America is an affectation of caste. It has ceased to be work and has become genteel behavior; it has ceased to function as a social need and has become the property of dilettantes. In subject-matter and in form, it is polite and mannered rather than robust and creative. It has abandoned the riches of American life for a parvenu, or false, environment. For the essence of American life is not to found in Newport and Southampton, nor at the Ritz Bar in Paris, nor among the pajamaed gamblers of the Riviera. The only outlet, the sole means of escape, for the American painter, lies in the discovery of the local essence, after which we may hope for a viable native school and eventually for a sublimation of its forms.

No one, not even the most condescending of British lecturers, would call Henry Thoreau a yokel; nor would the angriest apostle of Internationalism call Henry Ford a village tinker. Yet the forms, literary and industrial, accruing from the work of the two men rose originally from

the homeliest and least adorned of realities, from typically American
realities. The painter, of course, must be an educated man in the true
sense of the term—educated as the great painters of the past were educated in the civilizations producing them. He cannot, and call himself
an artist, be a disgruntled, anti-social beggar, nor a parvenu, nor an ignorant worshiper of an imported estheticism that has no place in the
realities of American life. He must also be educated in the language of
his craft. For all art is composed of a language which must be studied and
mastered, a language embodying not only technologies but human meanings, social and psychological assessments—the infinite surmises and
experiences of the soul of man. But the language of the plastic arts, in
spite of its long period of currency, is still extraordinarily flexible, lending itself to new combinations and new units of expression to meet the
demands of new environments. Here I must emphasize again the fundamental kinship between form and meaning, and show how procedure—
the formal instrument of art—is modified and vitalized by subject-
matter.

Renouncing subject-matter, the average painter returns what appears to be a devastating rejoinder. "It makes no difference what one
paints," he says. "The form is the thing. If the objective characteristics
are not of the first importance, then no subject, however exciting, can
redeem the failure." In some respects he is right. But like the common
run of professors and critics who bolster up his position, he overlooks
the fact that the forms of art are the direct offspring of experiences, and
that any experience, whether new or stereotyped, produces its equivalent in form. The form may be, as in stereotyped experiences, a pretty
low grade of art; it may be, as in the work of Picasso, whose experiences
—to stretch the meaning of the word—are confined to the analysis of
technical methods, an abstract pattern. But in any case, the form reflects
unmistakably in its objective characteristics the mental habits of the
maker—his poverty-stricken emotions, his dependence on others, and
the whole background of his existence.

By the word form, I mean the integration of the elements included

266

CHARLES BURCHFIELD: *November Evening*

in an expression, the cohesion, in the plastic or graphic arts, of line, mass, volume, tone, and color. Psychologically, the way in which these elements are successfully put together is the result of habitual modes of action which, by repetition, become expert and automatic.

In plain language, the artist, by persistence and repeated effort, learns and masters his technique. During the process of learning, the tendency to do things in his own way gradually becomes a matter of routine, and when he has mastered his tools, he handles them more or less automatically, proceeding in well-defined channels of action. By force of habit, if he is at all expert, he uses his technique as easily and naturally as the pedestrian uses his bones. If he is timorous and conventional, or a believer in art for art's sake; if his notion of art is to approximate the qualities he admires in the work of others; then his mental and technical habits will be formed entirely upon precedent, and the best that he can achieve is eclectic combinations. On the other hand, if he is a man of originality—one in whom performance is a means to express interests residing not in art but in life—the technical equipment left to him by tradition will be radically modified, and precedent will play only a minor part in the formation of his mental habits. With the first, form is necessarily repetition; with the second, by the very nature of the compelling interest, it will be, to a considerable extent, original expression. Originality in art is proportionate to the power of interest to communicate itself; and by communication I do not mean the simple process of recording a fact, as the snapshot records it, but the creation of a new and appropriate vehicle—a new form.

All of us, after our modes of action have hardened into fixed habits, find that we have created for ourselves a very congenial atmosphere of personal judgments and valuations which, in turn, fortify and rationalize our habits. The parvenu spirit with its exaltation of the status quo is a perfect example of crystallized habits, of proper and correct behavior pedestalled and reverenced. It constitutes, therefore, the ideal background for our lazy-minded art dealers and the pushing artists whom they exploit. It is also their livelihood and often a source of wealth, and as such, justifies the rationalization of villainous habits.

Forms—objective manifestations of behavior—are inseparable from habits, and the psychology of their development is identical with the psychology of other activities. Our modes of action, to a large degree, are based upon traditional observances. "Man," Havelock Ellis says, "is a bundle of inherited tendencies which come he scarcely knows how or whence." It is not only natural but inevitable that we should do things as we have learned to do them until a situation of vital importance exposes the inadequacy of routine ways. Then, and then only, is the inertia broken and the revision of habits possible.

But formal habits cannot be revitalized without first-hand experiences and fresh interests. To imitate or borrow the code of another does not make for new forms except in the most restricted personal sense. The common American custom of affecting European forms—after their canonization—unquestionably stimulates individual effort, but once we apply an objective criterion to such effort, the true state of affairs is revealed as hopelessly parvenu. The parvenu artist is afflicted with sub-merged feelings of inferiority—which explains his snobbish adoration of European manners. How easily he forgets the realities of American life in his ambition to behave properly! How quickly he rationalizes propriety, or conduct established by centers of good taste, into intelligent behavior! How arrogantly he seizes upon everything which, in its essentials, is most distant from the common local environment!

The parvenu spirit in its most repugnant form is generally associated with the hard determination of the arriviste to be successful. This is a grave error. To desire success and to be successful are marks of plain sense. What is really pernicious is the disposition to scorn conditions and realities responsible for success because they do not seem to correspond to accepted patterns of living in the station arrived at. If all successful people were cursed with parvenu instincts, life would be intolerable. The parvenu, like the snob, is secretly ashamed of himself. To this we must attribute his veneration of social customs most remote from those which produced him. And to this is to be traced the motive which impels the American painter to imitate the latest European fashions rather than attempt to deal with local materials. He has been taught by the snobs who dominate the art schools that Europe offers the standard of values. In terms of technique this is obviously true—for there is no classic American art. But he is taught nothing of the foundations of technique, nothing of its true nature as an acquired and developed habit dealing with and modified by human meanings and local environments. He is taught only to imitate—to duplicate externals. A sensible historical view would show the student how the objective facts of art are conditioned by the varieties of social pressure; whereupon form, as an *activity*, would emerge and be distinguished from form as an isolated object.

Art, to the creator, is not a finished article but an activity, not a commodity but a continuous labor. To the parvenu and his backers it is something else: the badge of a higher caste, or refined merchandise. To the dealer and collector it is an investment, a negotiable object, and by the etiquette of display, a precious object. Inasmuch as the standard of the fine and precious is erected on scarcity values, it happens that common realities can have no value unless sanctified by time and distance. Cézanne, for example, one of the homeliest and earthiest of painters, during his lifetime was the most despised of men, an utterly worthless artist, and a creature of contempt in the refined circles of Paris. But today he is a valuable painter—a rare Old Master. He has, you see, by the connivance of critics and dealers, become a sanctified artist, and extraordinarily high priced, and acceptable to the society that once howled him down. Today the standard of appraisal is so corrupt and disingenuous that the value of contemporary art is gauged by its similarity to objects which, being rare and precious, are coveted by people of sudden refinement. Thus original contemporary forms are ruled out of parvenu society.

American art, in all probability, will continue to be a branch of the occidental tradition. Technically, it derives from European schools just as modern European art derives from the old art of Italy. The wise painter, aware that a mastery of procedure is his first concern, cannot afford to neglect his forerunners. In the formation of the basic habits of his craft and in the forging of new tools and methods, he must draw upon his vast European inheritance. An extensive and thorough investigation of past methods would tend to check the formation of facile technical habits, enable him to avoid fashionable snares and makeshifts, and to measure the psychology underlying current interests. Our art schools should be purged of academic rot, classic and Modernist. There is too much talk about Art—the holy and precious property of collectors and parvenus. What should be taught is the practise of art, its history and psychology—the development of forms as molded and conditioned by the mental habits of the painter and his environment. More of that, and art would take care of itself—in spite of the academies.

In the United States we enter a new background for the growth of art, and in one respect a unique background. The American is born and bred with no cultural memories in his heart. He is the child of a civilization in which things are built for service, to be scrapped and replaced by more efficient models when the day of their usefulness is over. It follows that he cannot, unless he is a parvenu, be expected to practise art for art's sake, or beauty's sake, or for the sake of any abstraction whatever. But it does not follow that he is left with nothing to paint, and that he must go to Europe for his inspiration. For the genuine artist, America holds an unprecedented variety of experiences, an untilled field of overwhelming richness. The spirit of the frontier, with its semi-barbaric morality and lawlessness, is fused and intermingled with the most complicated industrial technology in the history of the human race. The result is that man everywhere, but particularly in the industrial centers, has become a curiously alert and nervous organism. Men make machines and machines make men; and the interaction of the two, in specific environments, has evolved a psychological state and a background which are uniquely American. It is the painter's business to provide an appropriate form for this curious condition. To accomplish the task he must have first-hand knowledge, the *knowing* of things, common knowledge born of experience and sustained by observation and habitual intimacy with American life. For the things we have observed closely and are driven to express by interest, curiosity, appreciation, or love, will assume their special form and character, provided our mental habits have not hardened into inflexible conventions.

There are, at present, American painters who, by trial and error under the stress of genuine interests, are recasting their habits and producing evidence of new forms. But they are few and far between, and assuredly not popular. The majority are content to copy the current mannerisms of Europe, and to sell their souls to international dealers. It is true, I suppose, that in the course of human events, the American environment and its psychology which are happily absorbing the best energies of our historians, critics and novelists, will capture the interest of our painters and force them into useful activity. But this, I fear, will not occur until the interest has become an ingrained habit, a natural approach to native subject-matter. The love of art, no matter how sincere or profound, will not suffice. As perfect illustrations of the ineffectualness of the love of art as a stimulus to new forms, I may cite the art colonies of Woodstock, Provincetown, and Santa Fe. Working in typically American—in unique environments—but working servilely from European forms and without organic interest in their subjects, these rustic Bohemians produce only imitations. Even the local color escapes them. The American scene is perverted into a technical pattern. Instead of surrendering to the scene and allowing it to modify the pattern, they impose an imported pattern on indigenous materials, with the result that the New Mexican desert resembles the Provençal landscape of Cézanne, and the Indian is chopped into the cubes and cones of Paris.

It is not enough that the painter, equipped with a technical apparatus manufactured in Europe, should sit before an object and record it unreflectively, like a machine. Art is not merely communication through a given instrument. The creative act consists first, in the discovery of the situation to be experienced; and second, in the discovery, or invention, of the appropriate expressive instrument—the form which, by reason of its unique qualities, shall be equivalent to the special characteristics of the situation. When life, American life, develops in painters, interests stronger than the interests aroused by canonized art, we may hope for a native American school.

14

AN AMERICAN ARCHITECT

IN THE words of Frank Lloyd Wright, "The artist is always a pioneer, and America cannot afford to believe that great art, as her interpreter, is moribund." The pioneer spirit of America, driven suddenly from its conquest of the land into industrialism, finds expression today, at the pinnacle of its recklessness, in architecture. Its bold and youthful disregard of consequence is embodied in stripped forms of towering steel. Say what you will of this architecture—and it is fashionable now to condemn it—words can only weave a superficial garland round the fact of its existence. There it is; and the truth remains that the architect, more than any other artist, has participated in modern American civilization.

Unlike the affiliated arts of sculpture and painting, the architecture of our industrial epoch is a direct reflection of social impulses, an automatic outcome of ways of living. It flaunts no assumptions about life—it is the child of life. Its highest values are those of pure function; it is simply a frame for human activity. Whatever reservations the architect may hold individually, his work, if successful, is acquiescent. It testifies with varying grace to the ideals of those in power, meeting their conceptions with unconscious compromise. It accepts life without comment; its references to life are implied and open to interpretations which are as valid in the stock salesman as in the literary playboy.

Our industrial civilization has produced, if not the greatest, then beyond a doubt, the most astonishing forms in the history of building. It has also, with its brutal contempt for human rights, pushed architecture into the realm of abstract science; and it has subordinated the artist

273

to the engineer. The architect is no longer an artist—he is a business man, the servant of utilitarian needs. The great exception is Frank Lloyd Wright of Wisconsin, who rises above his contemporaries as their own skyward projections rise above the squat forms of the past. One of the first to practise functionalism; the first advocate of the machine; a trained engineer, a lifelong student of the abstract side of his profession, and the father of the modern style, Wright has never mistaken material conveniences for spiritual values. A fearless man, he has resisted by word and deed, and by the force of his powerful personality, the modern tendency, as he puts it, "to create out of machinery nothing but a machine." His architecture is more than a frame for human activity, more than an inclosure for domestic contentment or industrial toil. It is an expression of and an incentive to the best living; and an expression of his own philosophy of American life. The Europeans gratefully pay tribute to his genius; in America, he is regarded by his own profession as a conceited outlaw and a paper architect. He is the most original of American artists; and we may say, I believe, without exaggeration, that no architect, past or present, has surpassed him in individuality.

Wright is a pioneer not only in the daring of his creative discoveries but in his relation to the frontiers of American life and thought. He has the loneliness of the pioneer, and the restless vision—the will to search, explore and conquer; and he has the pioneer's independence of Old World cultures, that insolent suspicion which, he says, caused him, as a boy, "to hate instinctively the empty, pretentious shapes of the Renaissance." And he has the courage of the men who ventured into the western wilderness to found a new civilization: of domestic tragedy, private misfortune, public scandal, and professional abuse, he has borne enough to send a score of lesser men to their graves. Today, in his sixties, though he complains grievously of his poverty and his lack of commissions, he may be counted a pre-eminently successful man. He is a world figure, and save in America and France, is recognized as the foremost architect of modern times; he has designed and erected a hundred and eighty buildings and conceived, on paper, seventy more; his home in Wisconsin is one of the wonders of American art and the goal of visiting European architects; he has made and spent large sums of money; he has lived opulently on the fat of the land, with the means to gratify his extravagant tastes in art and in material goods; his *Autobiography* is a masterpiece; his impassioned writings on architecture are permanent additions to the literature of that subject; he has never truckled to anyone or sacrificed a conviction for a job; he has never designed a Gothic skyscraper; his career defies imitation, but his example fortifies the ideals of the youth of America. And he is still healthy and belligerent, more confident than ever of his powers, and full of schemes and projects. Soon, I trust, we may behold in living form one of those shining structures of glass and sheet-copper which he has designed for the city of the future.

Wright was born in southern Wisconsin, in 1869. His mother's family were Welsh pioneers; his father was a morose New England preacher and amateur musician. He writes eloquently and with great affection of his mother's people, but has little to say of the misfit clergyman and his dour ancestors. As a boy he lived and worked on the land which his God-fearing grandparents had wrested from nature. They were heroic souls, those Welsh pioneers, men and women of character and intellect, and of tireless energy. From them Wright inherited his capacity for work, his integrity and his love of nature which have figured so prominently in his philosophy of building. The life of the farmer boy is hard, and he was overworked. He will tell you that, but with no vindictiveness in his heart; and today, viewing with blasting disdain the callow, city-bred youths who aspire to the international style, he dwells magnificently on the intrepidity of his boyhood—the long hours, the physical hardships and the grimy contacts with the soil; and to shame those who believe that fame and esthetic attainment should efface the fundamental vulgarities of life, he sings hymns in praise of the bull and the sow and the procreative facts of the farm.

But Wright was no ordinary farmer boy. There was joy in his life and the counsel of a wise and understanding mother. He grew up with books and music, learned to play the piano, and, without instruction, to draw and paint. And unconsciously in his daily chores, he studied the configuration of the landscape, the growth of trees, the sites of buildings and the ground-plan of nature. The poetry of the prairies was in his blood, a communion with nature which, in after years, augmented by Oriental influences, became a form of religion. He knew, he says, from the moment he was able to know anything, that he was to be an architect; and in his fifteenth year went to the University of Wisconsin to study the art of building. The University offered no courses in architecture, and Wright, with the foresight of genius, entered the school of engineering. He was restless under academic discipline, and in the spring of his senior year, without waiting to take his degree, departed abruptly for Chicago.

He found work in the offices of Adler and Sullivan, proved his originality in his first designs, and remained with the firm for six years. Among the builders of that horrible period, Sullivan stood alone in his ideas of "organic architecture." He was a master of ornament, an exponent of American democracy, and the inventor of the steel-cage construction which was to convert the masonry skyscraper into a material unit. There can be no doubt that Sullivan shaped Wright's career, and no one acknowledges the fact more generously than the pupil to whom Sullivan was always "Lieber Meister." The two individualists quarreled over a technicality and parted company, the master slipping into neglect, the pupil going his independent way to fame; but the estrangement was eventually healed and Sullivan, a lonely pioneer and in his last years, incurably afflicted, wrote, for an elaborate Dutch monograph on Wright, a beautiful tribute to the Imperial Hotel. Adler and Sullivan were metropolitan architects and the domestic problem was assigned to the young man from Wisconsin.

American habitations, at that time, were overladen with European tags and thefts; "unique in their impudent confidence," to quote Lewis Mumford—"and uniquely hideous." They were indeed so hideous in their high-storied pretentiousness, their dislocated gables and dormers and their scroll saw embroidery, that our painters, of late, have been putting them on canvas as records of a barbaric culture. They were the abodes of parvenus, and as such, seemly and consistent; just as the sterilized Modernist apartment is the appropriate exhibition room of the parvenu fanciers of Picasso. Wright was twenty years old when he entered this wilderness of horrors. There was no precedent to guide him: the refined eclecticism of Stanford White was, in his eyes, as odious as the provincial garblings; Richardson had designed some excellent houses in the English tradition—but Wright was an American; and Sullivan's principle that "form follows function" had not been applied to domestic building. From his twentieth to his thirtieth year, Wright conceived and developed an absolutely new type of building, as original a form of architecture, I venture to say, as any man has ever brought forth working alone. How did he do it? Largely by sheer genius. He worked from an ideal of organic simplicity and unit fabrication, and inasmuch as the motives and principles governing his designs are applicable, with minor variations, to all his work, I shall enumerate them as outlined in his Princeton lectures.

"1. To reduce the number of necessary parts of the house and the separate rooms to the minimum, and make all come together as enclosed space—so divided that light, air, and vista permeated the whole with a sense of unity.

"2. To associate the building as a whole with its site by extension and emphasis of the planes parallel to the ground.

"3. To eliminate the room as a box and the house as another by making the walls enclosing screens, the ceilings and floors and enclosing screens to flow into each other. To make the proportions more liberally human, and the structure appropriate to the material. Extended straight lines or stream-lines were useful in this.

"4. To harmonize all necessary openings to the outside or inside with good human proportions and make them occur naturally—singly or in a series.

"5. To eliminate combinations of different materials in favor of

277

mono-material so far as possible; to use no ornament that does not come out of the nature of the materials.

"6. To incorporate all heating, lighting and plumbing so that these systems become constituent parts of the building itself. These service features become architectural and in this the ideal of an organic architecture is at work.

"7. To incorporate as organic architecture—so far as possible—furnishings, making them all one with the building and designing them in simple terms. Again straight lines and rectilinear forms.

"8. To eliminate the decorator. He is all curves and efflorescence, if not all period."

In the first years of the century, Wright attained to complete mastery of his Prairie Architecture—to use a label that is now historic. Nothing like it had ever been created, and such examples as the Coonley House, Riverside, Illinois, must, without qualification, be called the perfection of building. The characteristics of the Prairie Style are universally known: low block forms of brick, or wood and stucco, strongly emphasized horizontal masses, a long roof-line, a low-pitched, or flat overhanging roof, windows grouped as compositional units, a sparse but cunning use of ornament, and the whole beautifully related to the landscape. These houses, judged as works of art, represent a perfect mean between abstraction and experience, a balance between Wright's geometrical science and his knowledge of the requirements of American living. Much has been written by Europeans of his plastic form, his three-dimensional organization of planes and his cubic structure. Wright, from the beginning of his career, has given profound consideration to these abstract elements; but years before Cubism was ever heard of, he designed and constructed architectural forms, which, as abstract units, are enviously regarded by the Modernists. But he has had nothing but contempt for pictorial Cubism in architecture, and has never been influenced by the European "functionalists"—the borrowing has been the other way round.

Wright has always believed that form follows function—not only in basic plan but in ornament—and he has approached each commission as a discoverer seeking a new form; but he has never been deceived into thinking that a structure, because it functions properly, like a machine, is an architectural achievement. The grain elevator, for example, which is often cited by the Germans as the finest type of organic American architecture, is to him only the admirable solution of a mechanical problem. The architect must refine upon the naked structure, ornament and individualize it, and adapt it not to the service of the functioning robot but to the needs of humane living. When he was twenty-five years old, Wright boldly raised his voice in behalf of the machine—the machine as an esthetic tool, mastered and employed by the artist-builder. This, in the wake of the Ruskin-Morris movement when "the tyranny of the machine" and "the death of the beautiful" were on every one's lips, was greeted with jeers. Heedless of denunciation, he vindicated his ideas in practical works—in poured concrete, machined ornament and pre-cast cement blocks—and the world took notice. Today the home is a machine, with all the furnishings coldly mechanical and prophylactic, and the pictures turned out with a lathe—and Wright is sorry that he spoke.

In the placement of a building—the joining of man's work and the work of nature in holy matrimony—Wright is without a peer. I doubt that he has ever been rivaled in his ability to make a house live and grow in its surroundings. Perhaps it was because of his ability in this prerequisite of architecture that he was excluded from A Century of Progress. There were other reasons: he is not so easy to work with— and he would have thrown that cardboard Modernism into the Lake. If you would understand the genesis of a work of art, how it develops from the experiences of the maker into the formal structure, read Wright's description, in his *Autobiography*, of the building of Taliesin, his home at Spring Green, Wisconsin. It is told in vigorous, poetic English, not in the language of the trade; and as light on the dark problems of esthetics, will rank with Conrad's prefaces.

"When," he writes, "family life in Oak Park in that spring of 1909, conspired against the freedom to which I had come to feel every soul entitled, and I had no choice but to go out, a voluntary exile into the uncharted and unknown, and live, if I could, an unconventional life—then I turned to the hill in the Valley, as my Grandfather before me had turned to America—as a hope and haven.

"Architecture, by now, was mine. It had come by actual experience to mean to me something out of the ground of what we call 'America,' something in league with the stones of the field, in sympathy with 'the flower that fadeth, the grass that withereth,' something of the prayerful consideration for the lilies of the field, that was my gentle grandmother's. Something natural to the change that was 'America' herself.

"And it was unthinkable that any house should be put *on* that beloved hill.

"I knew well by now that no house should ever be on any hill or on anything. It should be *of* the hill, belonging to it, so hill and house could live together each the happier for the other. That was the way everything round about was naturally managed, except when man did something. When he added his mite, he became imitative and ugly. Was there no natural house? I had proved, I felt, that there was, and now I, too, wanted a natural house to live in myself.

"I wished to be part of my beloved southern Wisconsin and not put my small part of it out of countenance. Architecture, after all, I have learned, or before all, I should say, is no less a weaving and a fabric than the trees. A beech tree is a beech tree—it isn't trying to be an oak. Nor is a pine trying to be a birch, although each makes the other more beautiful when seen together.

"The world has had appropriate buildings before—why not more appropriate buildings now than ever before? There must be some kind of house that would belong to that hill, as trees and the ledges of rock did; as Grandfather and Mother had belonged to it, in their sense of it all."

Wright fully intended to find the house and did find it. He relates all that the land meant to him—its material riches, its memories, the things that had formed and made him. With these in mind, he built the house, and it came out of the hill like a living fabric. It was a grand house, "an

280

architect's workshop, a dwelling as well for young workers who came to assist. Around the rear court were farm buildings, for Taliesin was to be a complete living unit, genuine in point of comfort and beauty, from pig to proprietor. The place was to be self-sustaining if not self-sufficient, and with its domain of two hundred acres, shelter, food, clothes and even entertainment within itself."

When the work was finished, a deranged negro servant murdered seven of the occupants, and set fire to the house and Taliesin was burned to the ground. Wright rebuilt it; the lightning struck, and again the house was destroyed. And again Wright removed the dust and ashes and spread his handiwork over the brow of his beloved hill. It is Taliesin III now, not one of his most perfect buildings, but a great one, growing out of the hill, as he wished it, a living plant of the rambling order.

It has been objected that Wright's domestic architecture is not uniformly successful; that the interiors, "although carefully thought out and excellent on paper, are sometimes dark and monotonously cluttered." There is truth in the objection, for he has proceeded by trial and error, rather than by formula, and his accomplishments have not always fulfilled his expectations. He has traveled alone, and in his earlier houses built when he was very young, what appeared to be right and ample in the graph was not always satisfactory in the material form. The problem of lighting, for instance, which he endeavored to solve by using windows as integral groups, not as random perforations, cost him many sleepless nights. The general plan was as perfect as man could make it—"organic architecture," to use his favorite term—but the admitted light was insufficient. And there was no remedy—his structure could not be altered. He must build again, and better—a new design, more window space, more light. But even his least successful houses, his failures, if you choose, have an integrity of structure and purpose that casts an obliterating shadow over the flimsy eccentricities of his Modernist imitators.

The objection that his houses are not for the small builder is also true. Wright is a lavish soul by nature and by deliberation, lavish in his demands on life, in his conception of a civilized mode of living, and lavish in the honesty of his efforts. No mean abodes for him; no cramped cells or cheap, deceptive real estate; no grimacing ornament to hide intrinsic shabbiness; no glib compromising to win a client. He is more than a builder—he is an architectural evangelist. He has told with a smile the valiant struggles of some of his clients to live up to their houses—I can imagine what a holy show a Kansas politician would make of himself in one of Wright's houses—and he has told with his famous irony how a client "has turned her American home into a gallery for antiques." A humanitarian first and last, Wright has given years of attention to the housing problem of slum-dwellers; he has designed unit cities, regional communities and decentralized cities, but there is no money in his ideas, and promoters are not public-spirited.

The objection that Wright's imitators are the most reprehensible of practising architects is also warrantable. Wright never intended that his own style should be imitated. He has said, "Principles of construction employing suitable materials for the definite purposes of industry and society, in living hands, will result in style. The changing methods and materials of a changing life should keep the road open for developing variety of expression, spontaneous so long as human imagination lives." He has set a standard, and when more architects of his courage attack the problem of a native style, we shall have the variety and the truth of expression which he exemplifies. The objection that his buildings have a "foreign look" is totally untenable. Why they should look foreign to Americans who have demanded, or endured, nothing but conglomerate European styles is too much for me. Perhaps they are only foreign to critics whose idea of an American home is the multicellular apartment house. Wright has not created *the* American style, but certainly he has created a style of his own, and as certainly a distinctively American form of architecture.

Having conceived and mastered a new domestic style, Wright turned his attention to other departments of building. In 1903, he designed and constructed the Larkin Administration Building, at Buffalo, a landmark in the history of architecture. There was nothing in Europe to compare

1903

FRANK LLOYD WRIGHT: *Larkin Administration Building*

with this amazing structure; "a simple cliff of brick and stone," it marked the beginning of the New Tradition, the Order of the Machine Age; it was an unprecedented and successful effort to carry his principles of building into the field of modern industrialism. "It was," in his own words, "a genuine expression, in terms of the straight line and the flat plane, of power directly applied to purpose in architecture—in the sense that power and purpose are united in the ocean liner, the airplane and the motor car. And it is fair to say that it had a profound influence upon European architecture for this reason." In 1904, he was commissioned to design a church, and the result was Unity Temple, at Oak Park, a poured concrete edifice and the very first example of monolithic building.

From this time to about 1920, Wright exerted an enormous influence upon the Europeans. It is only fair to say that we owe to him the best tendencies of contemporary building, and to him also must be attributed the primary impulse to the functional development of architecture. The secondary impulse came from the mechanical genius of the American engineers, and from the pictorial abstractionists of Europe, a school despised by Wright on the ground that "functionalism without human values is not architecture." His European imitators are no better than the American copyists; his influence has been fruitful and salutary when architects, working humanely on the problem of local needs, have studied the simplicity of his masses, his flawless sense of proportion, his clean and stately walls, and have applied his principles with freshness and originality.

Wright was also a pioneer in the use and extrusion of ornament. We need not insist that the impressive nakedness of the Empire State Building and the Daily News Building is the direct result of his influence; but it is true that his unencumbered surfaces, and his theories, gaining authority in America after their acceptance abroad, have played a conspicuous part in the elimination from our skyscrapers of useless cornices, Renaissance façades and medieval ornament. When he first gave thought to the matter, architectural ornament was a branch of distorted classicism, a more or less ingenious eclecticism. It is unnecessary to go into its history, or into the psychology of its various defenses, to understand its obvious falsity as esthetic expression. Ornament, in its relation to building, meant embroidery, an embellishment laid on without interfering, in theory at least, with the larger rhythms of architectural structure. Originally, its office was symbolical and more human, but this office had disappeared, and it had become an excrescential pattern struggling to adapt itself to changing mechanical structure.

With the appearance of the skyscraper, decorations intended for stone and marble, the old masonic mass, were transferred to the delicacies of sheathed steel. The results were preposterous; they are still preposterous, quite apart from the fact that the old masonry ornament was an archeological hangover. Recently, an attempt has been made to invent more appropriate decoration, but the fundamental difficulty of significance, or meaning, cannot be overcome by ingenuity, and the cleverest embroidery of the Modernists, at second glance, is pretty sterile stuff.

Ornament is one of the most trying of architectural difficulties. The Greeks, bent on having sculpture at any cost, cluttered the pediments of their temples with carvings, of all situations for figurative decoration the most awkward and cramping. And worse; they used marble to simulate wooden beams, and painted their statues and surfaces of natural stone in vivid colors—a barbaric practice that kindles Wright's finest indignation and makes him undervalue their just achievements. The Gothic builders, the ancient Americans, and the Orientals, working from religious motives, produced symbolical ornament which, in addition to its architectural fitness, carried human connotations; the modern designer, impelled by no religious convictions, in plain words, is up against it. How to decorate the modern skyscraping shaft is a debatable question —it may be that the skyscraper, like the poker, is better unadorned.

Wright, from his youth, has wrestled with the problem of ornament. His first decisive step was the wholesale scrapping of Beaux-Arts filigree, bridal cake curlicues, pseudo-classical veneer—every motive, in fact, employed by architects merely because it had, at one time or another, a decorative purpose. For this he merits unstinted admiration. His next step was to discover, in the materials used, the kind of ornament consistent with the nature of those materials; the third step was to relate the pattern to the architectural mass. We may say that in his exteriors he has been, on the whole, victorious. He has designed, and related with consummate skill to the wall spaces, leaded glass, pre-cast slabs, and patterned concrete blocks. His interiors, where ornament has been applied with caution and simplicity, are also successful, if not distinguished. But Wright, like all artists, is capable of illogical procedure. He condemns classical and Renaissance derivations, but does not hesitate to draw upon Eastern sources. And he is capable, as the Midway Gardens testify, and the large rooms of the Imperial Hotel—to judge from photographs—of exoticism, fantastic protrusions, and decorative accessories at variance with his laws of organic unity. In general, though he is susceptible to Eastern symbolism, Wright uses ornament abstractly to relieve the bareness of the wall and to accentuate architectural rhythms, erring on the side of simplicity rather than in redundance. Theoretically, he believes in the collaboration of the plastic artists, but to my knowledge he has never permitted a painter or sculptor of individuality to tamper with his walls.

In 1913, in an exuberant mood, Wright designed the Midway Gardens in Chicago, a remarkable work which the inconsiderate burghers have allowed to be effaced. This beer garden, excellent in ground plan, revolutionary in its machined ornament and patterned surfaces, outstanding in its adaptation of form to purpose—and not so pleasing in its meaningless geometrical statuary—had a large and not wholly commendable influence on the recreational architecture of Germany. From 1913 to 1917, he was at work on the Imperial Hotel at Tokio. I know this celebrated building only from photographs, and they are not particularly impressive: the elaborate interior ornamentation is not to my taste, and the general plan, which is admitted to be of unsurpassed excellence, is not revealed by the camera. Nor can I speak with authority on its value as "a poem addressed to the Japanese people." Sullivan described it as "Wright's masterpiece, the high-water mark thus far attained by any modern architect; superbly beautiful, a noble prophecy." The Imperial Hotel is memorable for other distinctions. In ground area, it is 300 x 500 feet, or two and one-half times the area of the Chicago Auditorium, an unanswerable reply to the charge that Wright is essentially a domestic and small-scale builder. It is also a monument to his engineering genius. He erected the Hotel on a flexible foundation devised not to oppose but to distribute earthquake action. The test came, in 1923, in the severest quake of the last fifty years. The Hotel behaved as it was supposed to behave, throbbed on its floating base, absorbed the shock, and settled into position again, without a fissure—the only building to survive the shiver.

The Barnsdall House, at Los Angeles, built in 1917, is heavy and sculptural, and only in one respect—its relation to the background—worthy of a place among Wright's best work. In justice to the architect, it must be said that his duties in Japan prevented direct supervision of the execution of his plans. The Millard House, Pasadena, 1923, an inexpensive dwelling and an object-lesson to the Neo-Spanish romantics, is the work of a master builder. It would seem to be a far cry from the low-lying Prairie Architecture to this upright form, but the constructive principles are not dissimilar. In California, Wright was building for a different environment—and how inimitably he unites house and landscape!—and building with different materials—pre-cast blocks with steel re-inforcements in the joints. The ugliest of materials, the concrete block, in his hands becomes a thing of beauty.

Of late years, Wright has devoted himself largely to municipal architecture. He has designed a plaster model for a Mesa City, near Denver, and has made plans for cantilevered skyscrapers with glass and copper exteriors and machined ornament. He does not object to the skyscraper as a legitimate modern form, but as a congesting mania and a feudal compromise—a structural absurdity, a steel skeleton to which heavy, non-supporting masonry is anchored and punched full of holes. The "solid skyscraper," he maintains, is an anachronism, and he talks magniloquently of the organic forms he is ready to build when the capitalists recover their senses—glass from ground to summit, crystal or opaque, light, clean and iridescent, fabulously beautiful.

Wright has written extensively of the viciousness of the existing city. "The architect's immediate problem, as I see it," he says, "is how to mitigate the horror of human life caught helpless or unaware in the machinery that is the city? How easiest and soonest to assist the social unit in escaping the gradual paralysis of individual independence that is characteristic of the Machine-made moron, a paralysis of the emotional nature necessary to the triumph of the Machine over man, instead of the quickening of his humanity necessary to Man's triumph over the machine?"

He has a remedy: the decentralized city, which, with our modern methods of intercommunication, is, or should be, the natural line of progress. He would build the "Broadacre City": an acre of ground for each family; all the refinements and comforts within a radius of 150 miles; luxurious motor-buses traveling over magnificent landscaped highways; no grade crossings, billboards or telegraph poles; trees and flowers along the way, and fields for the safe landing of safe, noiseless airplanes; rural factories and power plants; the buildings varied with the topography; tall co-operative apartment houses standing free in natural parks; "charming homes and schools and significant public gathering places—architectural beauty related to natural beauty."

"When the salt and savor of individual wit, taste, and character in modern life will have come into its own, and the countryside far and near will be a festival of life—great life—then only will Man have succeeded with his Machine. The Machine will then have become a Liberator of Human Life." There is something visionary and Utopian in Wright's Broadacre City. That passion for humanity, that pioneer courage and faith in himself which have driven him to the realization of his noblest architectural dreams, blind him, at times, to the inhumanity of man. But given the funds, he would set about building it tomorrow—and

I, for one, should rejoice. But I fear that it would not work. Cities, like the course of human life, cannot be so logically predetermined. The idea may be economically and esthetically sound, but it ignores certain unreasonable and ineradicable human instincts—Wright has some of them himself—the overweening aspirations, the mad desire to rule and to bully, the joy in deliberate cruelty, the immoderate indulgences, the will to wallow and decay—the contradictory colors composing the white light of personality, the utterly inexplicable forces which made Michael Angelo carve like a god and live like a pig.

Wright has said that "it is an inflexible will, bridling a rich and powerful ego, that is necessary to the creation of any building as architecture, or the living of any life in a free democracy. Call it individual. It was ever so." But the rich and powerful ego, which has sustained him through his architectural labors, and through financial reverses and domestic pains, has also made him temperamentally difficult and unduly suspicious. Unconsciously he dramatizes his superiority and assumes the master's prerogatives; he is inclined to see only the weaknesses in the works of his fellow practitioners, and to suspect them of forging his ideas; he inveighs with evangelical fury against our parvenu tastes—our pseudo-classical eclecticism, our period houses, our French pictures, and our foreign decorative fads—yet he finds no incompatibility between his own truly American home and the Oriental objects of art which he collects and uses as ornamental properties. Theoretically, he would employ the talents of painters and sculptors, but in practice, he would make them dance to his own tune—which means that he would make them ornamentalists and not artists. Painters and sculptors of individuality and power have never danced to the architect's tune, and cannot, at this late day, be expected to obey the flourishes of Wright's baton. They regret that so influential a man should make no provision in his buildings for interpretations of American life which, presumably, might be as valid and interesting as his own.

Frank Lloyd Wright is the highest type of American artist. And he is living proof of one of the oldest truths in art: the man who knows the

FRANK LLOYD WRIGHT: *Design for Skyscraper in Glass and Sheet Metal*

psychology of his people, who has lived with them and loved them, fought for them and with them; who, from his own experiences and independent conceptions of art, builds for local needs, also builds for immortality. Not only that—he removes provincial barriers and passes into world-wide usefulness. Wright has waged a lifelong battle for an American ideal. Nothing can intimidate him; nothing can restrain the expression of his convictions. Two years ago, the Museum of Modern Art, in New York, held an exhibition of designs and models to educate the public in the notable developments of modern architecture. Wright sent an exhibit, but when he discovered that he had been lumped with the international stylists—the "specialists in spectacle" and scenic designers calling themselves architects, the foreign mechanics who have stolen his style and returned it, up-ended and meaningless, to America, the pictorial abstractionists who compose buildings as they compose Cubist patterns, and the machine-mad Le Corbusier and those of his stripe—he broadcast his repudiation of the show in a philippic that drove the stewards into temporary retirement.

"Architecture was made for man," he wrote, "not man for architecture. And since when has the man sunk so low, even by way of the machine, that a self-elected group of formalizers could predetermine his literature, his music, or his architecture for him? . . . The methods, materials and life of our country are common discipline to any right idea of work. Allowed to exercise at our best such whole-souled individuality as we find among us, the common use of the common tools and materials of a common life will so discipline individual effort that centuries forward men will look back and recognize the work of the democratic life of the Twentieth Century as a great, not a dead, style. The honest buildings from which this proposed internationalist style is derived were made that way. We can build many more buildings in that same brave, independent, liberal spirit."

15

TWO SCULPTORS

BARNARD

O N ARMISTICE DAY, 1933, an American sculptor celebrated the
completion of the plaster model of his great memorial to the
men who died in the World War. No holiday was declared in
his honor; the celebration was private, and as the sculptor surveyed his
handiwork in an abandoned power house by the Harlem River, he
remarked, "I have paid a debt to humanity." For exactly fifteen years he
had labored on the memorial, without cessation, and had paid in monumental coin; with a faith that had moved mountains of clay, he had
modeled fifty-three heroic figures, each nine feet, or more, in height,
and had grouped them in their appointed places on the shafts of a
hundred-foot arch, an undertaking worthy of the masters of sculpture.
The event received a poor press. The news reporters, in good American
style, described the magnitude of the work, and commented respectfully
on Barnard's idealism, on the strange faith and energy of a man who,
in this sordid modern chaos, had not only conceived and executed on a
grand scale his uncommissioned monument, but had financed it entirely
from his own earnings.

The art reporters were dumb or non-committal—afraid to risk their
reputations with a man of genius. They hinted that the recluse of Washington Heights was old-fashioned; and so he is, with Michael Angelo for
company. They said that his sculptures were not architectural, forgetting
that the same objection might be uttered, to no purpose, against the
reclining nude figures of the Medicean Sacristy. They let it be known

290

that the artist was a fanatic; and he is indeed—in his verbal soliloquies; but when it comes to the art of carving, he speaks a language to which he was as truly born as any man who ever lived. So they reserved their panegyrics for a fashionable European, a prayerful brass-polisher whose rubbings were on display, at the moment, in Fifty-seventh Street.

Barnard himself was not perturbed by the niggardly attitude of the critics. He no longer needs the stimulus of public acclaim, and he was never concerned over success or failure in the worldly acceptation of those terms. Having practised the most difficult of arts for fifty-seven years, in the beginning under desperate handicaps; having, in his twenty-third year produced one of the most impressive works since the Renaissance; and with great achievements to his credit in every branch of sculpture—colossal single figures, group compositions, wood carvings, portraiture, formal studies, reliefs, and symbolical nudes—he finds himself today with but one interest, an interest amounting to an obsession: the translation of his war memorial into marble and mosaic. This little job, he estimates, will take about eight years. "I'm a known sculptor," he says. Which means that as a boy he incurred the jealousy of Rodin; that the French have stuck ribbons in his coat; that the Germans have written about him; that he has been rejected by the British, alternately honored and ridiculed by his own countrymen, and shamelessly defrauded by the State of Pennsylvania. And it means that his material recompenses have been enormous. "I have made nearly three-quarters of a million," he says, "with my chisel and these stubby hands; I made $260,000 from my statues of Lincoln alone. And I am putting it all into my monument." Idealism, fanaticism, genius, whatever the name, it drove Barnard to sculpture and it has held him to his art with a resolution and a nobility of effort that should hearten the youth of America.

If ever a man was predestined to one art, and one alone, Barnard is the man. He sees, feels and thinks in masses of stone. And in addition to his instinctive ability to handle his medium—his definitely sculptural gifts, he was endowed with great physical strength, the will of a pioneer, the zeal of a Christian martyr, and a propensity to dissipate his fine imagination in exalted allegorical visions which, it may be, cannot be successfully expressed in sculpture. Born in Pennsylvania, Barnard passed his boyhood in the backwoods of Iowa. He calls himself a Westerner, and I am not one to refuse him that superlative designation. He lived among the men of the frontier, shared their hardships and sorrows, saw them struggle to advance the borders of civilization. Those early impressions of struggle, physical courage and spiritual groping remained with him; and roaming the banks of the Mississippi, self-reliant and most of the time, alone, he was troubled by ambitions. He collected birds and animals and, to preserve his specimens, stretched their skins over clay models. His facility with clay made him a local phenomenon, and when, at the age of thirteen, he modeled an astonishing portrait head of his sister, his career was signed and sealed. At seventeen, he entered the Chicago Art Institute, and by incredible economies, lived a full year on the sum of eighty-nine dollars! The miserable instruction at the Institute was mitigated by his study of casts of Michael Angelo's statues which, by special privilege, he was permitted to enjoy behind closed doors. The following year, a portrait commission netted him $300 and he departed immediately for Paris.

Barnard, a voluble talker, does not discuss the privations of his twelve years in Paris. He knew that the lot of the sculptor was hard, but the career was self-inflicted and he does not expect hero-worship for his poverty and his rectitude of principle. An artist intimately associated with the youthful sculptor has confided to me the trials of those starvation days. "There was no one in Paris like George Barnard. He was divinely inspired, impelled by a purpose he could no more escape than he could slave as a ghost artist for academic celebrities. The rest were mechanics, Bohemians and shopkeepers. I can best describe him in Balzac's tribute to Daumier: 'There was much of Michael Angelo in that boy.' Barnard knew it, and talked about it—he had the greatest confidence in his ability; and by temperament and deliberation, set out to rival the old Florentine. He talked in a language we could not understand —I don't believe he understood it himself—the fiery language of a prophet. But when the chips began to fly, he was a different being, the finest carver in Paris. Rodin was aware of that fact. The old satyr groaned with envy when he saw the *Two Natures*; it was inconceivable that a boy of twenty-two could carve such a masterpiece. 'The American is too ambitious!' Rodin exclaimed. 'He cannot go on; he will kill himself with his giants! But my God, what stupendous sculpture!'

"Barnard had little respect for his French contemporaries, Rodin excepted. 'Fol-de-rol decorators,' he called them. Nor was he tempted by the Bohemian life of Paris. He stayed in his studio and worked—sixteen hours a day with nothing to eat but a little rice! He would thaw out his fingers over a cup of steaming coffee, drink the beverage to warm his insides, and work all night in the cold. How he continued to work when he was hungry, I don't know. He said that hunger didn't matter, if one had faith. But his poverty never embittered him, nor perceptibly reduced his energy. It did hamper him, however, for he was naturally a carver, and could not afford the huge blocks required for his dreams. Sometimes, to test his skill, he would choose a marble of irregular dimensions, see a human form buried in the block, and without modeling a preliminary study in clay, carve one of his exquisite nudes. They were much closer to the Greek than Maillol's heavy figures. He demanded vitality and movement as well as architectural unity. He was well known in his early twenties; commissions began to come his way; he went on working, and his exhibition, in 1894, established his fame."

Barnard admires Rodin, but he has not been influenced by the Frenchman. The resemblance between the two sculptors is incidental, both deriving from Michael Angelo and adopting, to their disadvantage, certain practices, such as leaving figures attached to a roughly chiseled background. Barnard, though he talks like a Manichean priest of the mystical properties of light, was never an Impressionist. He models from knowledge transformed by an imaginative vision, not from light effects; his anatomy is truly sculptural—the development of sequences of planes running up and down and round the figure to carry the conviction of unity. Rodin exaggerated and intensified appearances, polishing his surfaces, and modeling by the play of natural light. In no other sculptor can one discover such perfect representation of atmosphere. Light seems not only to flow over his marble, but to be caught within it and to radiate from it. The difference between the two methods may be observed in the Metropolitan Museum. Barnard's *Two Natures*, poorly lighted, conveys its power and unity from any point of view; Rodin's nude carvings, in the most favorable lighting, are by comparison, fragmentary and worm-like.

Barnard's French exhibition was a sensational success. He was, beyond peradventure, the greatest living master of his craft, and his spiritual powers apparently were unlimited. He might have remained in Paris, opened a fashionable studio, received lucrative commissions and led a soft life. But easy living was the last thing he desired. His *Two Natures* had exhausted his American experiences; and the rest of his work in France, though vigorous and original, was more or less experimental. He needed the harsh realism of his own country to balance the abstract side of his genius. "I am going home to work for my people," he said.

For forty years he has worked for his people, and not always with their appreciation or gratitude. Technically and in his striving for monumentality, he carves in the tradition of Michael Angelo, but the inspirations and driving force behind his art are the direct result of his American experiences and his belief in American ideals. He is a poor philosopher, and his idealism, as he expresses it in words, runs from the sublime to the ridiculous, from the democratic chants of Walt Whitman to the sentimentality of the pioneer with his dreams of suffering *Motherhood* and the *Burden of Life*. But a strong sense of reality saves Barnard from barren allegory on one hand and from mere decoration on the other. He is always a sculptor, and the weight of lofty conviction has saved him from the conventional pieties of that prolific hack, Daniel Chester French; from the effusive window-dressing of Frederick Mac-Monnies; from the engineering bombast of Gutzon Borglum; and from what Epstein aptly calls the "tea-party Buddhism of Paul Manship." And

294

it has imparted to his work a vitality and connection with life which are conspicuously absent in so distinguished a sculptor as Maillol, whose sedate and beautifully poised figures seem to be isolated effigies exhumed from an old civilization, or shop statues of armless immobility and sluggish perfection carved in emulation of the Olympians.

In an ecstatic mood inspired by Whitman, Barnard said to Isadora Duncan, "I see American dancing. I will carve a symbol of the dance of the Western world." Isadora was delighted to pose as the spirit of the dance, and, disguising her corybantic impulsions under the quaint eugenical notion that genius begets genius, she incontinently begged the sculptor to accept the gift of her body. Barnard refused to be seduced. The refusal was a blow to the dancer's amour propre, and being a woman who offers and tells, she publicly charged the artist with "carrying virtue to the point of fanaticism." Barnard was indeed a fanatic when his art was at stake, and he was also different from the ordinary run of artists. He had his own ideas of the improvement of the race, and he saw no necessity to turn a working contract into a studio intrigue simply because a woman happened to be promiscuous.

In 1903, he was commissioned by the State of Pennsylvania to design two sculptural groups for the Capitol, at Harrisburg. "I was glad," he says, "to put together what I had been thinking and studying about for a lifetime. Michael Angelo carved only nineteen figures in all his life. The plan agreed upon called for sixty-seven." The State set aside $700,000 for the project; the contract was signed; and Barnard went off to France where he could be assured of skilled labor. Quartered in a huge studio in a suburb of Paris, with fifteen assistants, he proceeded with his studies, paying his men out of his own pocket. But no money came from the State commissioners. The original sum, by systematic malversation, was cut in half, then reduced to $80,000; and he was unable to collect a penny of the final appropriation. His personal funds were exhausted, but his men stuck by him and he promised somehow to pay them. A profound student of medieval art, he mounted a bicycle, and traveled through southern France, searching for pieces of Gothic sculpture buried in ruined monasteries, farmhouses, and churches. His rummagings were extraordinarily fruitful, and by selling the sculptures to the art dealers of Paris, he managed to pay his assistants and to finish his symbolical groups. But not as he had first planned them: he was compelled to limit his conception to thirty-one figures, all nudes—at that time a terrific shock to American moralists. Barnard was the only man connected with the building of the Harrisburg Capitol who did an honest job. As a reward for his integrity—and his artistry—the official thieves eventually paid him less than the physical cost of his materials!

Continuing his excavations in Languedoc, Barnard amassed one of the most valuable private collections of Gothic sculpture in existence. To appease the French, who were nettled because an American artist had outwitted their own archeologists, he presented the French government with some of his choicest pieces. The rest were shipped to New York and installed on Washington Heights, in a monastic setting of his own designing and built by his own hands. The treasures and the background were recently acquired by the Metropolitan Museum for a nominal sum. Barnard might have realized a huge fortune from the collection, had he cared to dispose of it by the piece. There was no limit to the man's idealism!

In 1917, his great statue of Lincoln, intended for Parliament Square, was rejected by the British. That pontifical ass, Sir Claude Phillips, had the impudence to tell the American "what a monument to Lincoln should be." He said that the statue was "crude." What an adjective to hit upon! For sheer constructive skill, for subtle characterization rendered by modeling of the highest refinement, the Lincoln is worthy of a place among the works of another crude sculptor, Donatello. The solitary protest against the calumny was raised by Epstein who not only praised Barnard's art in the most generous terms but attacked the politics behind the campaign for the rejection. But, as Epstein says, "naturally no one would listen to a sculptor's opinion."

Barnard's work is inspired by ideas which, in the medium of words, are philosophical states expressing himself in relation to his perceptions of the struggles of humanity. These verbal labels, and in fact his own redundant explanations of them, are no more than cryptic generalities; but when the idea is imaginatively treated, that is, referred to actual conditions of his experience and infused in human figures to represent those conditions, the result is sculptural form communicating emotions common to every one. When the idea is separated from the flow of life experience, becoming the end as well as the generating force, his figures are visibly more abstract and his meanings more ambiguous. But his far-fetched abstractions with their intimations of nebulous soul states, are not to be confused with the geometrical shapes of the brass polishers, egg layers, and makers of book-ends. Barnard uses sculpture as a communicative instrument; he is never an ornamentalist, and if, in some of his allegorical conceptions, he fails to realize his intentions, he has at least discharged the sculptor's duty in constructing plausible human figures with which emotions of love, power, sorrow, and freedom are legitimately associated. He does not spend years on a simple ovoid form, smoothing and caressing it with maternal pride, in order to pretend that he has reduced the structure of the universe to its eternal symbol—the egg.

The great work of his youth, bearing the slightly pompous title, *I Feel Two Natures Struggling Within Me,* is a representation of the Platonic duality of man—the conflict of the physical and the spiritual, of body and soul. "The vision came to me," Barnard says, "in my first days in Paris when I saw so many of those statues of victory with raised arms and symbols of triumph. 'What victory?' I asked myself. 'What triumph?' Then and there I decided to create a symbol of the two forces planted within man, the symbol of my own struggles as an artist and the struggles of every living soul, the symbol of civilization as it always has been and will continue to be." By his idealism, his deep feelings, his years of appalling effort, and his technical mastery, he was uniquely fitted for the task. The whole of his youth, indeed, the whole of his life is epitomized in those nude giants. Such a conception, unless perfectly controlled, would slop over into sentimentality, or destroy itself in fantastic illustration and virtuosity.

No one, I imagine, will see in this sculpture all that Barnard himself finds written there; for he naturally associates it with his own agonies and aspirations. But no one with eyes to see can escape its power, or the everlasting struggle conveyed in the strained muscles and facial expressions. As a piece of carving, the merits of the work cannot be exaggerated. Not since Michael Angelo has an artist demonstrated such knowledge of sculptural anatomy, or used it to a more creative purpose. The two figures are infinitely more plastic than those Modernist objects designed for no other reason than to exhibit the quality of plasticity, and the purity and freedom of sculpture made after the formula of the negroes. Barnard's work is neither pure nor free in this sense; but his technical knowledge is used to create an emotional power which far exceeds anything aroused by the mechanics of geometry. In his nude carvings, he has never surpassed the *Two Natures*; but in his huge single figure called *The Hewer*, perhaps because the influence of Michael Angelo is less prominent, he has achieved a more individual form.

The two groups at the entrance of the Capitol, at Harrisburg, are worthy of all the praise bestowed upon them by the Europeans when the models were exhibited in Paris. The individual figures are magnificent; the grouping of them is another matter. From one point of view, the figures seem to be without organic connection; from another, they are huddled round a core of unused marble. In this work, Barnard attempted the most difficult of sculptural problems—the relating of forms separated by actual space—a problem that has never been successfully solved. Michael Angelo considered his groups as a single unit, holding his figures within the block; the bas-relief admits of a limited lateral extension but of no depth; Barnard endeavored to hold together forms which, to the eye of the spectator, are severed by measurable gaps. A more harmonious arrangement might have been worked out, but it would not have conquered the difficulty which, apparently, is insoluble. For sculpture, while it occupies space literally, does not use space as a constructive element. Space to the sculptor expresses nothing—it is merely a void in which voluminous form is organized. But painting, by defining and

GEORGE GREY BARNARD: *Head of Lincoln*

(*Plaster*) COURTESY OF THE ARTIST

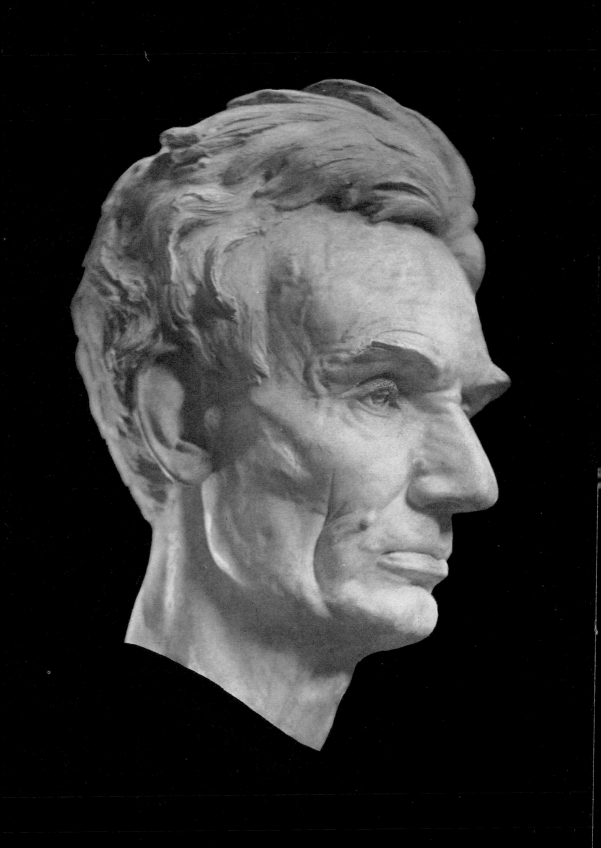

limiting the contours of masses, by considering masses as contours in relation to space, may project its forms to any desired depth.

Barnard's masterpiece is the statue rejected by the Londoners, and the source of anguish to Americans who believe that Lincoln should be immortalized as the great Sunday School Superintendent. Here we have in the rocky road of sculpture, a road cumbered with large clock ornaments, gravestones, and sulky personifications supposed to be classical because they are void of significance, the rarest of coincidences—a great subject and a great artist. Barnard was the man of destiny for a Lincoln memorial. As a boy, the character of Lincoln had been impressed upon him by his father who had known the rail-splitter personally; his early life on the frontier had acquainted him with the physical struggles of the pioneer and the curious mixture of idealism and practicality which Lincoln incarnated; he too had brooded on the afflictions of his people, and, in his fifty-third year, could honestly say that he had devoted his life to a noble purpose. The subject pinned him down to a concrete reality, at the same time allowing ample scope for his imagination and challenging him to create both a likeness and a symbol. Before beginning the task, he gave a year and a half to historical research, living in the environment where Lincoln had lived, and talking with men who remembered him, examining documents and all the extant portraits, and finally, by good luck, discovering a Kentucky mountaineer whose gaunt features served as a perfect working model for the head.

Barnard was not afraid of Lincoln—not afraid of the uncouth visage, the long legs, the big hands and feet, the ugly frock coat. Nor did he, like Rodin in the statue of Balzac, produce the effect of monumentality by modeling a head and submerging the rest of the body in a bulky draped pedestal. He did not tone down the uncouth face, nor exaggerate the features in the direction of the soft holiness of the conventional man of sorrows. The man of sorrows is there, a positive, powerful, tragic man held to earth by the huge feet; a lonely leader, a symbol of what Barnard believes to be the ideal of the pioneer civilization in America. I know of no happier illustration of the effect of the subject on the artist. Here

Barnard forgot his Michael Angelesque visions, laid aside the burden of traditional examples, and out of a grotesque subject with figurative attributes despised by the followers of classical beauty, created a work of undying grandeur—the most original statue in American art and one of the most forceful portrait monuments ever conceived.

Since the completion of the Lincoln, the sculptor has labored in deep seclusion on his War memorial. His retirement from the world has not impaired his vitality or good spirits; at seventy he has the enthusiasm of youth and the strength and agility of an athlete in his prime. His energy is simply staggering—he handles daily more than 500 pounds of clay and is never tired! But his seclusion has removed him from every contact with the facts of life. Today Barnard is a fanatic living in a world of abstractions. He is utterly oblivious of external circumstances, of the existence of his family, of everything save his allegorical vision. The canny Litvinov, who wanted the Memorial for Russia, got at the root of the matter when he said, "A grand work, Mr. Barnard, but where are the warriors?" The criticism does not mean that Barnard should have depicted a gruesome war scene, or that he was not within his rights as an artist when he elected to build a symbolical monument of nude figures. But it does mean that he has relied on his vast technical knowledge and his science, to the exclusion of living experiences without which no abstract idea can be made convincing.

It is too early to pronounce final judgment on a work which is still in the plaster. I wish that some of the pictorial appurtenances had never occurred to the artist. The mosaic rainbow running over the bridge of the arch, and the mosaic between the shafts, a scene in color depicting rows of crosses in Flanders Field, are fantastic, pictorial and incongruous with the dignity of the nude figures. My guess is that the idea, in marble, will be unintelligible—but the arch will be redeemed and raised to distinction by individual figures beyond the talents of any other sculptor of the day. Barnard belongs to the breed of heroes. The conviction sustaining him in his great works has at last exiled him to a world which exists for none but himself. His wife, who has companioned him in all his undertakings, has said that "his work and fame will go down in history, but his indifference to his family will never be recorded."

EPSTEIN

A man of totally different cast and breeding is Jacob Epstein. A Russian Jew born in New York, in 1880, he decided in his youth to enter the arts—to accept the difficulties of the artist's position in modern society, and to bring honor to the profession. His first work was in book illustration, but he was, from the beginning, by temperament and ambition, a sculptor. To escape the irritations of a family of unsympathetic merchants—he was the first artist in the family—he went to Paris; but Paris did not satisfy him, and at the end of two years he moved to London where he has since resided. In London he is a celebrity, and the controversies aroused by his exhibitions and memorials have received international publicity. His career is a record of high purpose and strong individuality substantiated by extraordinary achievement.

That Epstein has won, in London, the hostility of the academic crowd and the Bloomsbury esthetes alike, is a compliment to his independence and originality. That he has forced Philistines and snobs, Jews and Gentiles, lords, financiers and shop keepers to take cognizance of the existence of sculpture, is nothing short of a triumph. That he has revived public interest in the rarest of the arts, is proof that a man of sufficient power can always get a hearing. And to his great credit, throughout the protracted campaign of ignorance and accusation, he has kept his head and continued to work. He is the most forceful of modern sculptors and one of the most distinguished of living artists.

Epstein has not sought the loud-voiced notoriety which, pursuing him from his first commission—the statues for the British Medical Association building—has made him the most discussed sculptor since Rodin. But he has never been without the pugnacity, or the ammunition, to strike back at his accusers and to expose their vulnerability to the world. His spoken and written utterances show him to be a critic of superior knowledge and intelligence. His views on art, ancient and modern, abstract and representational, are not only sound, but expressed with exceptional clarity, a pleasure indeed in these days of fine distinctions and transcendental theorizing. He scorns the irrelevant erudition of the sciolists and the shallow dogmas of the Anglo-French purists. I have not the space to enumerate his critical virtues, but, as a sample of his good sense, I must mention that he has, by an authority confirmed by his own good works, demolished the notion popular at the present time that direct carving is a much more exacting and artistic performance than modeling. All great sculptors, he declares, have done both; the distinctions are faddish and academic.

"The greatest mistake that Americans can make in the future," Epstein says, "is to look to Europe for direct inspiration. . . . Art must take firm root in some definite country." On the face of it, this statement would seem to be contrary to his own development, but actually, it must be said, he has taken firm root in a very definite country—he has become thoroughly British. He lives, writes, talks, and acts like a native; he is imbued with British culture, and his portraits bear witness to his grasp of the psychological attributes of the English people. His status may be explained by the fact that, in America, he remained an unassimilated foreigner, and that in England, after thirty years of residence, he has acquired a nationality. The resentment provoked by his sculpture in England is the price he has paid for his artistry, originality in the plastic arts being so rare and upsetting as to create a furore whenever it appears. He has not surrendered his individuality to British standards: Epstein, to all intents and purposes an Englishman, has cherished his racial inheritance and submitted to its influence, without humility and without arrogance. As a Jew, he inclines naturally to oriental traditions in sculpture; and without pressing the point too far, we may say that his own migrations and those of his family, and his reflections on the woes and persecutions of his race have profoundly affected his art, both in theme and in emotional content. This is as it should be, and when he tells us that he finds "heroic expression and eternal verities" in primitive sculpture, we may credit his conviction and not accuse him of merely falling in line with the archaistic carvers and Modernist negromaniacs.

Epstein, physically powerful, has produced a large and diversified collection of sculptures. His work may be grouped into three divisions: abstract, or semi-abstract conceptions of a symbolical nature; architectural, or mural, carvings; and portraits in bronze. His ultimate rank as an artist, I am sure, will not rest on his efforts in the first division. I do not know how seriously he takes his abstractions—artists have a weakness for the poorest of their offspring—but I have never heard that he attaches exaggerated importance to purely formal arrangements. One of the first to collect African fetishes and to analyze structural relationships, he has undoubtedly profited by his essays in abstraction. His *Venus*, a faceless epicene standing on a pedestal formed of a cock treading a hen, is a monumental absurdity; his *Genesis*, though not without dignity, is a tour de force; his *Rock Drill*, intended, in some inexplicable way, to symbolize man and the machine, fails of its purpose for the good reason that its naked mechanical components have no relation to the functioning machines of our experience and only the remotest suggestion of the structure of the human body. But Epstein, in his less representational works, differs from the purists in that his masculinity and good sense, have, sooner or later, brought him back to humanity, preventing him from a quest of the absolute.

The search for the absolute is one of the most curious aberrations of artistic talent. Balzac understood this form of diathesis and presented it beautifully in *The Unknown Masterpiece*; but the hero of his story was a crude realist compared to the modern perfectionists in art. The quest for perfection tends to sterilize and limit creative capacity. It is analogous to the Puritanical search for righteousness in which the most minute affairs of conduct are subjected to and measured by some unattainable ideal, to the detriment of expansive living. It tends to concentrate energy on minor issues and leads to the microscopical scrutiny of details which, like the trifling moral codes of the Puritans, have only imaginary significance.

The sculptor Brancusi typifies, among contemporary artists, the obsessional pursuit of an ideal. Out of the great field of life experience he selects a few geometrical shapes, and fixing his attention on the interplay of textures, rubs and polishes his eggs and spicules into surface effects of marvelous delicacy. But in the attainment of his little ideal, he has manipulated the communicative and expressive aspects of his art completely out of existence—all that is left is faint rhetoric. It is true that his rhetorical surfaces have the element of originality: as concerns textural perfection and ingenuity, his work is unrivaled in the mechanics of sculpture, past or present. But, one asks, what of it? Textural perfection does not constitute living sculpture, and Brancusi's productions, large or small, cast in shining brass or carved in radiant marble, remain in the category of paper cutters, door knobs, and bathroom appliances—exquisite objects but spiritually closer to the vagaries of the decadent Roman poets than to the drift of modern life. The esoteric meanings supposedly expressed by his objects are read into them by irresponsible fantasy.

These meanings, when intelligible, assume that sculpture is frozen music. And here we meet again one of the popular fallacies of modern art—the belief that a tangible analogy exists between music and the arts of painting and sculpture. Music, being non-representational, is the ideal art, the one to which, in its abstract perfection, all the others aspire. But sound differs from visual phenomena in that it has no fixed boundaries. A sound wave has the property of indefinite extension; that is to say, it is limited only by hearing capacity, and within the radius of hearing can be checked only by the entrance of another wave. In consequence, musical form deals with constantly, and literally, active elements which move and flow in aerial space. Furthermore, the reverberations of sound, unorganized sound, are emotionally more poignant than the stimulations of the other phenomena of the physical world. In the whole range of visual experience, there is no single sensory unit—no combination of colors, no geometrical shape—which, without the aid of associative factors, can be compared in emotional effects to a unit of sound. Color, the nearest

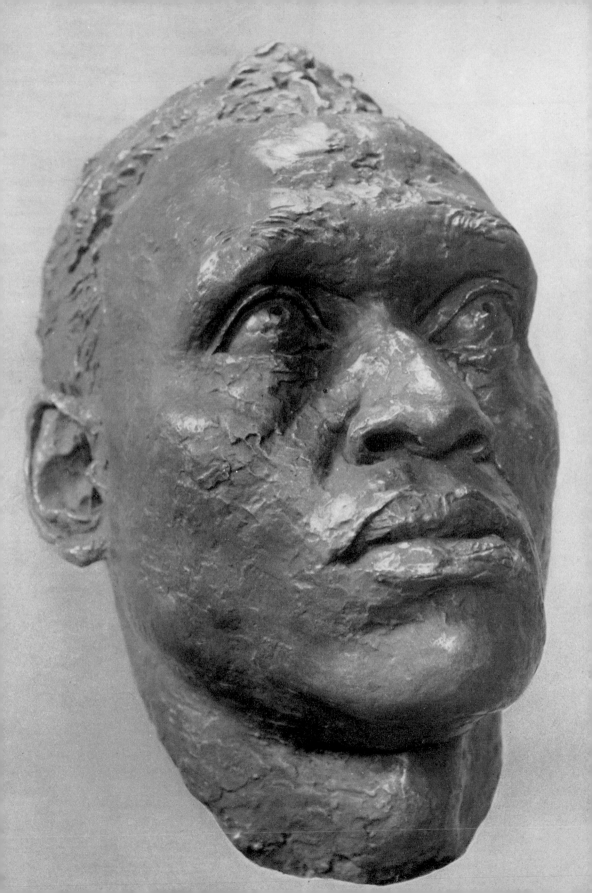

JACOB EPSTEIN: *Robeson*

equivalent, never enters the soul with the power to move deeply; never enters, that is, alone, but must be associated with and related to representation of some sort to be effective.

The difference between musical form and the forms of painting and sculpture is not one of esthetic procedure—both aim at logical and rhythmical structure—but of material ingredients. Musical sounds, emotionally effective in an unorganized state and incalculably moving when composed, are independent of representational symbols; whereas the materials of the plastic arts become emotionally alive only in an organization implying or openly presenting an associative context. Thus, when painting and sculpture transcend mere embellishment, they must connect their materials—color, line and geometric shape—with common human experiences, the emotional content of which is recalled by representation. Without this connection, they remain in the field of surface decoration which, however graceful and charming, cannot produce the responses of great art. This does not mean that music is created in a spiritual vacuum; that being the purest of the arts, it is independent of time, locality, and life experience. It means that music has the power to communicate emotions without referring to the situations, or conditions of reality, inspiring them; that it has no need of the associative symbols indispensable to the plastic arts.

The confusion of processes with values is responsible for most of the theories erected in defence of the modern effort to make the plastic arts pure. Brancusi is a purist. He has chased the illusion of human values in dissociated geometrical shapes for many years; and while it is presumptuous to say that he has accomplished nothing in sculpture, it is an incontestable fact that he has labored sanctimoniously in a field which historically has produced only ornament. Against ornament, as such, I have not a word to say—certainly the making of decorative objects is a necessary and legitimate branch of art. My quarrel is with those who, rhapsodizing over Brancusi's work, read into it meanings which it does not and cannot possess.

Brancusi reminds me of one of my aunts—now in heaven, poor soul!

She belonged to that unfavored class of women locally referred to as old maids, but the term, I fear, technically speaking, was inaccurate. The fire of Santa Teresa flamed within her, but she was not very strong and far from personable. Toward the end of her girlhood, she had an experience —an unmentionable one in the community—which sufficed to fill the whole of her life. Nothing else happened to her, or needed to; she spent the rest of her days nursing, caressing, polishing the memory of that short-lived dispensation. She retired from the world, remaking and re-living, in every waking hour, an adolescent ecstasy. It exalted her spirit, made her unapproachably virginal, and she died, in sanctity, a martyr to a single circumstance.

Representation in the plastic arts is not a sin. It is utterly different from the mechanical reproductions of photography. As in poetry and the drama, it calls for mental activity, controlled thinking, selection, emphasis and order. Instead of becoming poorer, as the abstractionists assume, the plastic arts become richer by association. Painting and sculpture, in emotional content, are closer to the literary arts than to music; and it is only in matters of structure that analogies to music may be sustained.

Epstein has never been interested in mere embellishment, but his mural sculpture raises the question of architectural fitness and human significance. His large figures in high relief, called *Day*, and *Night*, carved for the office building of the London Underground Railway, are, among the hideous public monuments of the British Capital, veritable masterpieces. Considered in relation to the building—as architectural accessories—and as sculptural masses divested of all meaningless detail, they are superbly designed. But having said this, my enthusiasm ceases. I am not bothered by the abstract qualities, nor by the distortions; nor does the departure from the classic tradition offend me—had they been in the pseudo-classic style, however poor, the British would have admired them. The carvings, for all their vigorous personal touches, lean too heavily on ancient styles; the types and distortions and the facial expressions —the forms—were not dictated by experiences with living things, but by

306

Epstein's knowledge of the Assyrians and Chaldeans. Edgar Wallace, writing in praise of the groups when most of the Londoners were crying in horror, voiced a pertinent criticism in his remark: "If these works were dug up by some archeologist they would immediately be hailed as masterpieces." They would indeed, but is the greatness of contemporary art to be measured by its resemblance to archeological deposits? The Hudson Memorial, as pattern, could hardly be improved on—and it is more than pattern. It suggests symbolically the wildness and strangeness of the unearthly heroine; but it too has an archaic quality, the look of something dug up from the past.

Epstein, in common with so many modern artists who have recognized the integrity and remarkable formal qualities of primitive and ancient sculpture, has fallen into the illusion that it is possible to incorporate the special character of such art into modern design. His architectural reliefs like the works of those nondescript sculptors contributing to the puerilities of Rockefeller Center, have the appearance of stage properties, of archaic exhibits intended to evoke a sense of the mysterious and bizarre. While his carvings are serious, and impressive in their mural fitness, they must be classed with the recherché patterns of Picasso—they are resurrections rather than creations.

It is possible, beyond a doubt, for a sculptor to return to ancient forms and to profit thereby; but he gains nothing and adds nothing to art by the imitation of appearances. The conditions producing ancient art—the physical and spiritual needs determining the specific character of its forms—are gone forever; and it is not reasonable to argue that modern life can be expressed in the signs and symbols of the Assyrians. What is valuable in the old art is not to be found in the imitation of Mongolian faces and Egyptian sphinxes, but in a study of the instrumentalities of organization—in an analysis of the various ways in which the technical problems of crest and hollow, mass and resistance, plane and counter-plane, were solved. In this study there are many discoveries to be made, but in order to vitalize his discoveries, the sculptor must put them to work, not as exhibits of ancient styles, but as tools to facilitate the organization of his own experiences.

Modern sculpture is afraid of modern life; in practically all its manifestations, it attempts to re-live the life of another period. Thus, the most powerful of the arts, and in some respects, the most apprehensible, is, in its current images, the most negligible, the least worthy of any one's attention. Epstein, in one division of his art, overcame the fear of life, and created works which are almost the sole excuse for the existence of sculpture today; but in his architectural efforts, he has not been so genuinely modern.

Epstein's pre-eminence in portraiture is attested by a body of work which, in volume and emotional power, entitles him to a place among the greatest masters of this branch of sculpture. That is high praise, but there is no reason to withhold it. Through some universal inhibition, the modern world is reluctant to acknowledge greatness in the plastic arts; novelists, architects, historians, and even poets, receive their meed of glory, but when it comes to painters and sculptors, the incredulous public refuses to be convinced—the great men are all dead and gone. True, most of the great sculptors lived long ago, and their art today is a poor thing; but now that we have a great sculptor, alive and not disposed to hide his light in a tomb, we should all give thanks for his incomparable gifts.

Epstein has produced more than a hundred portraits in bronze. Some, naturally, are better than others, but there is not a dead one in the lot, not one that does not shine out as a living, sentient being; and the best make those ancient masterpieces—excelling in monumentality and the "large generalized masses" so beloved by critics—seem a little costive and sleepy, in plain words, a little boring and over-rated. For this transplanted Russo-American Jew, this self-made Englishman, has wrought miraculous effects in bronze, has somehow instilled into dull metal a vitality of flesh and spirit that no one would deem possible, if it were not a living fact, a vitality compared, and rightly, to the magical achievement of Rembrandt. How has he done it? I do not know. By genius, of

JACOB EPSTEIN: *Miriam Patel*

course, but the answer explains nothing. By technical skill and that strange ability of the artist to express and dramatize his own personality by interfusing it with the personality of another.

Epstein's mastery of his craft, his technical resourcefulness and knowledge of ways and means, are so vast and disconcerting as to lead many to believe that he has gained his ends by illegitimate methods—by grotesque expressions, clamant distortions, and Impressionist tricks of modeling duplicated in bronze. The answer is that no other sculptor has succeeded by such tactics; and that the appeal of his art, which is to the spirit, could not have been created by deception. The field is open to every one; nothing is so easy to make as a dead image in clay; the world is full of photographic modelers, and ingenious hacks—but there is only one Epstein. If his heads were not the work of a true sculptor, and a great one, they would not hold the attention for more than a casual glance. He has, to be sure, used and made personal, various technical devices which, in his imitators, are no more than violent mannerisms. He places his sitters under a strong light, the head raised to receive the full force of the light; he models roughly, and translates the broken surface into bronze, not for the sake of creating the atmospheric illusions of Rodin, nor to preserve that looseness, and sketchiness which is cheaply thought to be artistic; but to hold the light, to insure the sharpest contrasts of plane and mass necessary to the construction of expressive anatomy. But these technical processes are neither forced nor borrowed; they are part of the man —his own way of making visible his probings into the soul of man.

Epstein, always individual, has built up one of the most original styles in all sculpture. There are traditional influences at work in his art —plenty of them—but they are submerged in his own personality. Originality in art does not consist in the coinage of new words, but in putting old words to new uses. In his portraiture, he has shaken off the tyranny of past styles: he is bold and independent; he has no fear of modern life; no fear of representation, sentiment, psychological insight into character, the dramatic interpretation of moods. He has portrayed servant girls, black and white, lords and ladies, dukes, soldiers, authors, and children, and in all he has seized upon and accentuated the unique physiognomy and the specific character of his subjects. And he has gone far beyond external face-making; he seems to have read the inmost secrets of his sitters—to have made them symbols of the various classes of humanity. And beyond that: he has impressed upon them his own brooding personality. There is no doubt about it. One would know an Epstein anywhere, though it be labeled Conrad, Lady Gregory, the Duke of Marlborough, or Christ.

The members of this large and increasing family of Epsteins are, in their emotional effect on the beholder, stronger and more incisive than the flesh-and-blood individuals of real life. They contain, you see, not only the personality of the subject heightened to the last degree, but added to it, the personality of one of the most exceptional of modern men. The combination shocked the British. It was, after all, the Epstein in the statues that unsettled their equanimity. Here was a man who was not afraid to bare his soul, an outspoken man of deep feelings and deeper reflections, a man who put the touch of sorrow, a weeping doom, the curse of God, a magic wretchedness in every face he modeled. It was not meet in a land where reticence is the test of gentility for an artist to make his convictions so overpoweringly truthful, much less to express them in public.

There is no reason why Epstein, who has exemplified his originality in a hundred heads, and in larger works, such as *The Visitation*, and *The Madonna and Child*, should not conceive public monuments equally free from archaic influences. It is not necessary that he should do so—he has already done more than his share to make modern art worthy of the name. But he is in his prime now; and we, who have welcomed his art and admired his rebellious spirit, have come to expect from him, as a crowning achievement, a heroic monument which should stand, in relation to the modern age, as a symbol of man's battle against the forces threatening to destroy his individualism. That has always been the battle of the artist.

16

THE NEW GOSPEL

IN THE opening years of the century, many Americans returned from Europe with stirring ideas on art and life. Among them was Alfred Stieglitz, the photographer. But Stieglitz was not one of those cultivated travelers who had gone abroad in quest of further cultivation: he was a workman, and while his particular notions of art had no possible bearing on American life, his position as practitioner, as worker with the camera, made him hospitable to the young talent of his own country. He entertained many preposterous theories, but his general attitude toward art was sound. He conceived it as an activity, not a collector's plunder, as a worker's job. In Europe, he had watched and been impressed by the revolutionary movement in modern art; and in America he proceeded at once to champion the cause of young artists who, like himself, saw in that upheaval the promise of a golden day. It is not beyond probability, in the general assumption of the time—the belief that the new tendencies were to conduct painting away from the field of representation—that Stieglitz also saw a golden opportunity for photography which, as a reproductive agent, might usurp the time-honored position of painting in rendering the real world.

However that may be, Stieglitz, with insuppressible energy, threw himself whole-heartedly into the march of the painters toward "purity" —toward an art unimpeded by what were supposed to be the irrelevancies of representation; and his laboratory at 291 Fifth Avenue, became at once the center for the pullulation of advanced ideas. His remarkable photographs—their supremacy has never been seriously contested— were over-ridden in the stampede of painters, critics and connoisseurs

311

who gathered at 291 to view and discuss the "progress" of art. In those discussions the voice of Stieglitz was constantly ringing. In the bedlam of half-baked philosophies and cockeyed visions concentrated in 291, he shrewdly managed to hold the position of arbiter, to maintain a reputation for superior acumen. He did this, it seems, by an intuitive sense of the fundamental weaknesses in the gabble that enveloped him. By no means an intellectual and untrained in the handling of ideas, he had a talent for re-assembling notions and presenting them in a prophetic style which, veiling their inherent weaknesses, made them more inspiring and important in his own mouth than in the mouths of the original purveyors.

In addition to this talent, Stieglitz possessed the most efficacious of all instruments of power—an absolute faith in his vision. Like Mary Baker Eddy, Evangeline Adams, and the yogi, he could gaze into space and receive affirmative blessing for whatever his ego dictated. This psychological gift operates with curious force, not only on naïve susceptibilities but on minds trained in the critical processes of thinking. To those infected with vague idealisms; to the loosely educated and those unable to integrate their knowledge and experience; and to the unguided yearners who turn to art to find themselves; it is irresistible. The fortunate possessors of such power are born leaders of men.

Stieglitz, a Hoboken Jew without knowledge of, or interest in, the historical American background, was—quite apart from the doses of purified art he had swallowed—hardly equipped for the leadership of a genuine American expression; and it is a matter of record that none of the artists whose names and work he has exploited has been noticeably American in flavor. All have had talent; some, like Marin and O'Keeffe, a touch of genius; but their abilities, for the most part, have performed in a vacuum of ambiguous spiritualism where the discovery of meaning required the psychic powers of a medium. For this task, Stieglitz was almost divinely endowed. The office of seer and medium agreed perfectly with the nature of his ego and his visionary habits; and his seances, with Marin and O'Keeffe as subjects, became famous, casting a hypnotic spell on the followers and patrons of art. But of late years, Stieglitz's prestige has steadily declined. Young artists, under the influence of a new conception of art wherein form is definitely allied with and dependent on content no longer listen to his hieratic monologues. In spirit, his present gallery, *An American Place,* is a dwindling continuation of the spirit of 291—alien to the current drive for an explicitly native art. The new trend of painting, following Benton's pioneering example, is toward strong representation and clearly defined meanings which may be shared and verified by large groups of people; and in this movement the elusive apparitions of the Stieglitz group have no function.

Yet Stieglitz is an important factor in modern American art. He may have mistaken the direction it was to pursue, but certainly he was not mistaken in advocating the cultural necessity of native expression; and he was the first Modernist impresario to draw distinctions between American and European art. His crusading energy inspired and impelled, yes, even shamed, people to buy pictures which, but for his insistent talk, they would have scorned. He made collectors and collections. And had he been avaricious, he might easily have made a fortune; he had in his possession, and still has, pictures of high market value—works of the most celebrated and negotiable Europeans—which he introduced to America, and exhibited, not for profit, but as illustrations of new activities. He has driven sharp bargains for his artists, but himself has remained poor. When he opened his gospel rooms at 291, the critical world, under the influence of the conventional dealer, had come to regard art as a rare object, and to appraise it in the language of the lapidary and the jeweler. Stieglitz brought plainly before the critics and the public the value of art as human activity.

This is the one fundamental value arising from his erratic career, the one enduring contribution—and its importance cannot be overestimated. In the confusion of fanatical ideas whirling in his mind, it stands as evidence that, at bottom, something of the worker's solidity persists in him, something even the spiritual purities of High Art and High Talk cannot destroy. And there is his photography which, despite the absurd

313

claims obscuring its genuine merits, is proof that the man can do, as well as spout. A picturesque figure—now past seventy, in ill health but remarkably active, still talking, exhibiting, proselytizing. I have quarreled with him for many years, but he has never allowed differences of opinion to disrupt friendly relations; and he has always welcomed me to his seances with disarming cordiality. Others disagreeing with him have had, I think, the same experience.

Stieglitz must be credited with the introduction of the new activities in art to the American public. To keep the records straight, I list the following exhibitions selected from a bulletin prepared by the impresario himself.

Europeans—Drawings and water colors by Picasso—1911; Sculptures by Matisse—1912; Sculptures by Brancusi—1914. (These three individual exhibitions antedated all European showings.) Drawings by Rodin—1908; Paintings and Drawings by Matisse—1908; Paintings and Drawings by Rousseau—1910; Designs by Gordon Craig—1910; Water Colors by Cézanne—1911; Lithographs by Toulouse-Lautrec—1909; Paintings by Picabia—1913; Paintings by Severini—1917. (These exhibitions were the first to appear in America.)

Americans—Alfred Maurer—1909; John Marin—1909; Marsden Hartley—1909; Max Weber—1911; Arthur G. Dove—1912; Alfred J. Frueh—1912; Abraham Walkowitz—1912; Elie Nadelman—1915; Oscar Bluemner—1915; S. MacDonald-Wright—1917. (These were the first individual exhibitions in America.) Stieglitz discovered, developed, and married Georgia O'Keeffe, and first presented her in 1916.

To complete the catalogue, it must be noted that Stieglitz was the first man anywhere to exhibit the drawings and paintings of children; the first in Negro Sculpture; and the first to bring color photography to America.

The crusading spirit of Stieglitz strengthened the confidence of young Americans converted to the new gospel, and led, in 1913, to the historic Armory Exhibition. This cosmopolitan circus, displaying European and American examples of the latest tendencies in art, was adroitly adver-

JOHN MARIN: *Maine Landscape*

tised, and provoked a unique hullabaloo. One picture, a mediocre specimen of French Cubism, mysteriously labelled *Nude Descending a Stair-
case*, sped the issue from esthetic circles into the field of popular ridicule, and at one stroke lifted the exhibition into national prominence.
Most of us remember those vociferous and ill-mannered times: the
orgies of indignation, the bravado of nondescript painters intoxicated
with publicity, the protests of dealers and antiquarians, and the piteous
bleat of academic retainers trembling for the safety of their little jobs.

The immediate effect of the imported ideology was heartening. The
more sanguine critics were elated, and prophesied, if not a renaissance,
at least an efflorescence of native genius such as had never before appeared in the Western Hemisphere. Strange as it may seem, the spirit of
art was alive again, and under the stress of French ideals, an inspiring
burst of vitality shot forth. Galleries devoted exclusively to the modern idiom were founded; eccentric magazines containing hateful manifestoes and bewildering illustrations, were born overnight; and Green-
wich Village emerged as the locale of the new movement, the Bohemia
where starving painters, the addled and sincere together with the charlatan, subsisted—not, unfortunately, by art, but by catering to the romantic
appetites of up-town idlers. Another exhibition was hung, an exclusively
American affair certified by five experts who made bold to declare that
the assembled art was genuine and ennobling—the selected canvases of
men capable of sustaining the new impetus. With this exhibition the
Modernist forces were consolidated and the several painters hurried forward with hope in their hearts: a little sympathy from the public, the
cooperation of the dealers, the proper exploitation in the press, and they
should soon be on their way to fame and fortune.

What fine old American families were represented in this assault
on the fortresses of academic culture! Benn, Bouché, Bluemner, Dasburg,
Halpert, Kuhn, Kuniyoshi, Lachaise, Stella, Sterne, Weber, Walkowitz,
Zorach—scions of our colonial aristocracy! There were other painters of
true American lineage—Benton, Burchfield, Chapin, Coleman, De-
muth, Dickinson, Hartley, Marin, McFee, O'Keeffe, Sheeler, Wright

and Yarrow, but most of them at this time, thanks to Stieglitz and the French, were alien in method and in point of view. The men of the old order—Henri and Luks, but particularly, Bellows, Hopper, Sloan, and Robinson—who had done work of unmistakably American flavor, were looked upon as outmoded, as relics of a school that was all very well in its way, but illustrational and unesthetic.

Since that memorable uprising of 1913, much has happened. The sensational tenets of Modernist art are dead and buried; the zest for discovery and for battle has been exhausted; the creative stream runs thinly, if at all. The majority of the men enumerated above, and their associates, have gone the way of all hacks, settling down into the rôles of scheming jury painters or studio virtuosi, without a program and with no excuse for exhibiting. Very few have anything of public interest to say; some keep up a front and drink tea for pittances; some are teachers; others live wretchedly by feeding the whims of western museum directors; or the uneducated fancies of collectors, who, now that Modernist art has grown stale and academic, are beginning to buy it. When all is said and done, it would seem that artists flocked to the new gospel for precisely the same reasons that have lured young intellectuals to the red flag: incapable of thinking for themselves, they adopted, with unquestioning alacrity, European plans and specifications which, besides giving them something to do and to talk about, held the promise of security and superior position in an unfeeling world. But it is well to remember that their art, bad as it is, is no worse than any other form of bad art.

We need not deprecate the Modernist uprising in America, but we may regret, with all our powers of recrimination, the direction it has taken, and its debilitating effect on native talent. After all, it was a movement, and that was something. It called attention to the survival of the art impulse in man; and by spectacular expedients—concerted screaming, quarrels, vilification and outlandish exhibits—called attention to the worthlessness of what passed for art in the modern state. For centuries art had lingered on without any kind of social office, an aristocratic plaything kept alive by a single interest, the preoccupation with optical phenomena. Toward the close of the nineteenth century, this interest had culminated in the Impressionist recipe for recording natural appearances, in the clever deceptions of salon painters, and in the sloppy sentiment of the official decorators—all of which was structureless, pointless and photographic.

The new movement, in theory, aimed to destroy the conception of art as a brainless transcript of nature; to strip the artist of photographic sleights and to force him to reveal his spiritual kinship with the world; to return art to a truly expressive basis; to supply traditional knowledge, but at the same time to discourage imitation of past styles; to offer the artist a complete set of working tools, a familiarity with structural methods, so that he might proceed at once to the ordering of his experiences. It offered the American artist the example of Cézanne who, to the best of his ability, had applied his knowledge of ways and means to his findings in the real world; and it offered him a technical equipment of overwhelming richness. But the American artist, through lack of intelligence and through false upbringing, was so awed by the French trade-mark on his instruments and so captivated by his possession of them, that he used his tools, not to disclose and to sharpen the meanings inherent in native subjects, but as exhibits of themselves.

The failure of the American painter to raise his profession to the level of creative distinction enjoyed by the other arts is the result of his inability to overcome two difficulties. First, his education tends to make him suspicious of his background. Whether trained at home or abroad, he is taught to imitate European paintings; and thus can discover no connection between his acquired technique and the materials which America affords his experience. His education kills his initiative and makes him timorous; fears constantly beset him—the fear that he is not really artistic, that he is not proceeding properly, that he is not like his European models. As a consequence, he either closes his eyes to the world about him, or sneaks back to his studio where he is in no danger of seeing anything.

The second difficulty goes hand in hand with the first. The custodians of American painting, the collectors, critics, connoisseurs, and highbrow appreciators, look to Europe for their cultural norms. It seems to be impossible for cultivated Americans to admit the existence of American talent in the plastic arts. Their attitudes and actions, psychologically examined, indicate a state of mind in which the admission of superior ability in a compatriot would be a reflection on their own position, an affront to their self-esteem. We are living, you understand, in a democratic country, and though it is probably true, even today, that some lucky rascals have more money than honest toilers, it seems to be decreed, by popular opinion, if not by legislation, that no one, outwardly at least, shall have more genius than his fellows. In the early days of the republic, this was a healthy belief. It was born of pioneer independence, and acted, especially in politics, as a check to hero-worship and the establishment of dictatorial controls.

It would still be a healthy belief, if the growth of cultural snobbery had not made it the fashion among the elite to look to Europe for standards of taste, the affectation of which lifts the parvenu above the vulgarities of democratic life. I would agree with the average American that it is a good thing, in a democratic society, to create no heroes or superior beings, but I find it hard to stomach the notion of his cultivated brother that it is fitting and proper to import them. But whether I, or those of my kind, like it or not, snobbery brings in its heroes. For some of the importations are heroes indeed—the works of real genius are numbered among the fads and vagaries of those who indulge in, or profit by the indulgence, in art. But the habit of appealing to Europe for permission to practice the art of painting, of bringing in every Jean, Jacques, or Judas whose reputation has been made by venal French critics, and setting him up as a model for American youth, has wrought irreparable damage and very little good to the development of an indigenous art-culture.

Art cannot mature in an environment which grants it no cultivation; and the indigenous plant which might be strong and lusty in natural soil, is vitiated into an exotic growth when transferred to the collector's hot-house. There are in America many cultivated men and women who express a desire to encourage a native school of painting, but to win their approval, American art must conform, in subject and style, to the imported variety: "Art is art," they blandly tell you, "existing beyond the boundaries of nationalities." This is true in the abstract; but particular works of art are produced within nationalities, and in their most flourishing state, are conditioned by local influences.

17

PRACTISING AMERICANS

I<small>N THE</small> present economic crisis, America, more conspicuously than
ever before, stands out as a separate part of the world. If the nations
of Europe are united on any one thing, it is that America is a pretty
distinct place—a country of rude and unseemly practices which by no
standard of comparison can be termed European. It is reasonable to
suppose that some of these characteristics must appear in any genuinely
American art; it is also reasonable to suppose that from the Continental
point of view, and in the eyes of Americans obsequiously adopting that
point of view, such an art should be branded as inferior and of small
importance. That is precisely the case. Those Americans who have acquired abroad a new set of attitudes and habits, look down upon their
countrymen with grinning scorn, basing their self-esteem upon the illusion that they are original and superior because their manners are different. Our patrons of art, taken as a whole, are of this stripe. When they
buy an American work of current vintage, they select a picture done in
the accepted European style; they award prizes only to works which,
aping foreign mannerisms, confirm their own pretensions. In officialdom
the blind lead the blind.

A survey of the course of art, great art or small, decorative or representational, reveals the trail of local characteristics. The life of the
artist—or the life of any one, for that matter—is not a philosophical system embracing the whole world; it is the growth of an organism reacting
to environment; it is a combination of the self and those factors existing
outside the self, the perpetual readjustment of habit to the procession
of changing facts. Such apprehension of the stream of facts as leaves a

320

mark deep enough to affect the personality occurs within a limited range. The most distinguishing, indeed the inevitable sign of great art, is the mark of this limited range—the mark of environment, the impress of a special civilization. Even the most vehement partisans of International Art—or simply Art, one and universal—even the most rabid opponents of American art as such, are continually talking and writing of French Art, Italian Art, Chinese Art, Mexican Art, and Negro Sculpture. They deny their faith in acclaiming it.

American art has borrowed its constructive apparatus from across the seas. Its technical instruments are derived from the Occidental tradition of Western Europe. There is nothing derogatory in the fact: tools have always passed from civilization to civilization. The working tools of American literature may be traced back through our British colonizers to the ancient Greeks, and further, to the cradle of the human race. American literature is distinguished from its British parent by local variations, by new forms created from the exigencies of a new environment. The essential thing in the formation of any art is that tools shall be applied to situations at hand—to the expression of actual experiences; the unfortunate thing, especially in painting, is that tools, in most instances, are used merely as demonstrations of mechanical instruments, that is, as exhibits of themselves. But however stereotyped the patterns of art may have become, they have their remote origins in human activities—in ways of living and in the interpretation of life. Let us examine the matter a little more closely.

Throughout the ages, permeating one civilization after another, we find two kinds of art which, though of common ancestry, have proceeded in divergent channels. The first is the art of adornment manifested in dress and in the decoration of arms, abodes, and utensils. The second is the art of more complicated emotional meanings, essentially representational and impregnated with human values. The art of adornment among primitive peoples was bound up with religious ceremonials; and its forms, in consequence, were largely symbolical. It was by nature abstract, but the meaning of its symbolism, let us bear in mind, was a direct outgrowth of social observances and responses to the facts of life. In this it differs from the abstractions of the Modernists who, aided by ingenious literary gentlemen, have projected absurd metaphysical values into works which are no more than exercises in pattern-making.

The art of adornment, in the course of its historical journey, lost its symbolical attachments and passed into the limited field of pattern-designing, or pure decoration, as it is known today. This brand of art traces arabesques on pottery, weaves patterns into rugs, and only a few years ago, ran an exuberant jigsaw over American architecture. Its abstract nature and lack of meaning which Modernist cults prize as the criterion of purity do not prevent its degeneration into complete vulgarity, a fact to be remembered by any one attempting to penetrate the theoretical background of modern art. Yet the art of decoration is not to be despised. It is, in truth, of inestimable importance in the development of painting. It is the first school of art, the kindergarten of appreciation. To those incapable of appreciating the quality of good pattern, the underlying theme, the physical basis of great art, is lost.

For the highest types of representational art, such as the canvases of Rubens and Rembrandt, are also forms of pattern-making in which certain relations of line and shape—by suggestion and by their equivalence to visual experiences in life itself—stand for, say, the human figure, a tree, a house, or a flower. These relations, intrinsically patterns of more or less complexity, and the outcome of long evolution, become the units of design in the art of representation. It is more difficult, of course, to control such units than to master the simple units of pure decoration; but in both departments the manipulation of forms tends to become automatic, or habitual. In decadent periods of representational art, the units of design and their relationships arrive at the stereotype. The stereotype, the child of habit, like all other habits, is broken only when new factors and new meanings engage the artist's attention—meanings that could not be represented by old and exhausted forms.

I mention these technical matters to make it clear that in art, as in more practical activities, it is the new, or different situation that breaks

322

inertia and sharpens the wits of man for further discovery and invention. Thus it is plain that all vital art proceeds from a physical basis, that true creation springs from fresh interests and deeply rooted attachments to native subjects. I must also point out that to appreciate art one must have a realistic mind—the ability to see things as they physically are. To the gentleman of business who is accustomed to regard art as the sublimation of dreams; to the hard-headed man of affairs on whose ideals reposes— alas, now in ruins!—the structure of modern life, this will no doubt seem preposterous. For it is to the name reality that he makes his most reverential bow. But a little investigation of the nature of his interests, of the elaborate and involved symbolism of his technique, will dispel the illusion of his claims to the title of realist. One has only to follow the pronouncements of our political and industrial high priests during the last few years to understand how easily the "ought to be" of symbolical reasoning usurps the office of fact.

The ability to realize physical conditions would appear, at the moment, to have no place in the system of practical affairs. Intricate technical graphs and codes, verbal formulas, and numerological charms are accepted as facts instead of the actualities to which such abstractions are normally related as instruments. The gentleman of business tinkering with his motor, or practising his golf strokes, is more essentially a realist than the master mind at his desk rationalizing his apparent interests. In the one instance, he is forced to the observance of fact, for the success or failure of his efforts is immediately perceptible; in the other, the logic of his symbolism is sufficient to produce the mirage of truth.

In art we have an analogous situation. In the minds of most painters, technique, or ways of doing, is a substitute for experience; in other words, the logic of construction assumes greater importance than the thing constructed. Of late years, the artist has managed to rival the man of affairs in extravagant supposition. The insidious habit of theorizing on instrumental relationships is responsible for the evil, just as it is responsible for the absurd interpretations of conditions in the world of business. Method is confused with the end, or purpose, of method; it

323

becomes the goal of art, and when it does not square with obvious fact, it is the fact that is distorted. The creative spirit departs when the artist ceases to be an explorer in the world of reality; it returns when some unusual situation arises which cannot be taken care of by habitual action; when strong environmental pressure forces the artist to modify his practice in order to enclose the meaning of his experience.

To the beginner in art, the process of learning is similar to that of the amateur inventor engaged in evolving a new type of engine. At first, it is simply a process of discovery, and, as concerns the beginner alone, a creative process. But the results, except to the individual, are unimportant and remain unimportant until a special situation arises which so stimulates his inventive powers that a new form is produced. This calls for unusual aptitudes, for capacities beyond the average—for genius of some sort. It is one of the characteristics of engineering genius that it is constantly confronted with unusual and challenging situations—the most potent stimulus to the new alignment of mechanical functions. This characteristic separates creative energy from the lethargy of the average mind which hardens into habitual action and would almost seem to shun enlivening experiences. The great majority of artists are afflicted with the lethargy of the average mind.

Unless the artist finds in experience the stimulus to a new alignment of his materials and to new functions for his instruments, his discoveries remain purely personal. Thus it happens that the average artist is an amateur, or an academic hack. He may attribute deep meanings to his aimless repetitions, but the true nature of his work cannot be disguised.

We have in America a number of painters who are not fooled by European conventions, who understand that a painting-habit, even though it has been acquired abroad, is none the less a habit, and that its apparent originality is simply the effect of a new setting. To this group, life and experience are more important than art, which is as it should be; for any man who is absorbed in art, to the exclusion of living experiences, is on the road to the madhouse or the academy. With these painters instruments and methods are directed rather than exhibited, and therein lies the secret of such originality as they possess. It will be observed that all of them are concerned with subject-matter—with representation—and in all we have evidence of sensitivity to environment. Their forms—the relations established between the parts of their works—are plainly affected by their experiences with things. They have the characteristic American interest in facts, social and physical. They are not hot-house products. They fulfil at least one of the preliminaries to great art: they are an organic part of the society in which they live, and their art reflects the color and character of that society. They are active participants in life; they are free from the esoteric nonsense of Modernists who are unable to cope with realities; they are forceful individuals whom the history of the period will have to take into consideration.

Of the two thoroughbreds from Stieglitz's purified stable, Marin and O'Keeffe, there is little to say as relates to the general unfolding of American art. Neither attempts the representation of American life; both are conventionally reticent, painting still-life and landscape fluently, but with esoteric leanings and a delight in cryptic suggestion. O'Keeffe makes large patterns out of small flowers, paints them beautifully, and brings to her work a love for the subject which separates her, at once, from the ordinary still-life specialists to whom a bowl of flowers is only a burst of color or a pretext for an abstraction. Her smaller pieces place her in the company of the Oriental flower painters whose intense interest in their subjects impelled them to represent the specific character of flowers, and to vitalize their forms instead of using them as decorative accessories. Certainly, of all the women now painting, O'Keeffe is the most artistic.

Marin, with his astonishing talents, is apparently capable of anything; but he lacks the one essential quality of great genius—the power of self-discipline. Before a landscape he makes magnificent skirmishes, develops richly characteristic sections; but unable to carry a suite of forms to a logical conclusion, he resorts to compensatory flourishes of a decorative nature, beautiful in color and tastefully arranged, but witnessing a spirit of play rather than that determined research into the structure of natural phenomena which we associate with great landscape painting. I sometimes think that if Marin had lived in an age when artistic genius was esteemed as something more responsible than anarchic self-expression, that if he had escaped the encouragement lent to that notion of art by the persuasive personality of Alfred Stieglitz, he might well have been the first landscape painter of our time. Such speculation, of course, is idle; but Marin has both the poetic insight and the talent necessary to fill the place. What he needs, and what he may, perhaps, yet acquire, is the discipline to drive his divisions through to their logical ends, instead of exploding his forms all over the paper when they refuse, at first trial, to come out in the desired way. Technically, he is one of the world's master water-colorists, but in looking at his work, I cannot help recalling the remark of a young painter to whom I had put the question, "What do you think of Marin?" The answer was, "I have been looking at Marin's water-colors for years—and I can't find anything to see."

Totally different from Marin in temperament, but sharing some of his explosiveness, was the late Pop Hart who, practically unknown during most of his life, has now won deserved recognition. This extraordinary figure shunned the dreary art atmosphere of New York, and the cliquish painters dominated by Stieglitz—he was an independent adventurer in art and in life. Undisciplined, like Marin, he was saved from capricious estheticism by his intense love and appreciation of the world and its inhabitants, his rambling, insatiable curiosity in the types, faces, habits and amusements of the lower orders of society. His water-colors and drawings, though light in structure, are vivid representations of real experiences. Hart was a knight of the road, a romantic hobo with a strong stomach and an alert intelligence. He wandered into the strange corners of America and the West Indies, always observing, drawing, and having a good time. His art is a truthful account of his nostalgic peregrinations and his realistic vision. His fame will continue to rise.

Of Hart's generation is the old war horse, John Sloan, draughtsman, painter, and the most distinguished etcher of modern times. Sloan is an American, primarily an American of the great city. In his etchings and paintings of New York life in the early years of the century, he is in a

JOHN SLOAN: *Sculpture in Washington Square*
(*Etching*) COURTESY KRAUSHAAR GALLERY

class by himself; and none can doubt that his work will live and hold the interest of all who love America. He matured before Modernism had plunged art into a searching analysis of structure—a tendency which has begotten an enormous amount of sterile and stupid experiment, but which, at the same time, has established the close alliance between form and the matter it encloses, or expresses. He matured when painters were laboring under the misapprehension that art is the product of undiluted and unconditioned seeing; when the dexterity of Manet, or of Sargent, in the reproduction of surfaces, was overpoweringly influential. But Sloan was an artist moved by the human aspects of life—a social radical and a deadly realist as well. He followed some deep-seated impulse which shunted him out of the studio, where false illusions are easily nursed, into the life of the people. There he was forced by the varied nature of things to reorganize, to design, to keep clear of photographic appearances. It cannot be said that he is a great composer, but he is unquestionably the best of his generation, with the exception of Boardman Robinson.

But the facts of life, which Sloan faced so admirably, are stubborn things; they do not readily yield to formal structure—to an orderly arrangement. In the necessary compromise between design and observable fact, he was inclined to neglect the structure, to preserve realistic fidelity at any cost. Beholding the work of the Mexicans—he was the first Yankee to give them a hand—and of the rising younger men headed by Benton, he must have felt the inadequacy of his design, its structural uncertainty and incompleteness; for he set out, a few years ago, to develop a style that would atone for his deficiencies. But his late expeditions into Modernism have produced nothing to compare with the richness of his earlier work which, at its best, by right of intelligence and execution, ranks with the social studies of Hogarth. His latest efforts consist of experiments in tempera—conventional conceptions covered with cross hatchings. Sloan's interest in style seems to have smothered his interest in life: like any hack, he paints old nude women in whom there is not even a flicker of sensual suggestion—which is about the only excuse for nude-painting anyway. An ugly wench, full-clad, is bad enough; stripped, she is intolerable. If the artist must paint nudes, let him follow the example of the old Venetians, and paint one that fits pleasantly between sheets.

But Sloan, despite his late nudes, is an artist, supreme among modern etchers, assured of a high position in American painting. He is also a valiant warrior who has waged many a battle for social decency and for American art, and will wage many more before he calls it a career. Once he has finished with his wenches and his search for style, he will, I am confident, return to his studies of metropolitan life upon which his fame so solidly rests.

Boardman Robinson, associated with Sloan on the old *Masses*, and reared in the same atmosphere of social commentary, is one of America's great draughtsmen. The cartoons and drawings of his news sheet days have been envied by a long line of imitators and successors. He is also the first modern American of genuine artistry to execute a large mural. His *History of Commerce* in the Kaufmann Department Store, of Pittsburgh, though strongly influenced by Benton, is a landmark in American mural painting—the first practical challenge to the silly, outworn conventions of the Beaux Arts, conventions known by every one, outside of Rockefeller Center, to be as dead as their embalmers. Robinson, in the old powerful days, went into the world of general experience for his motives, but the spirit of discovery seems to have forsaken him. He is a better designer than Sloan, but he too has succumbed to the draped nude, hoping, I take it, to find in conventional subject-matter greater freedom for experiment with form and color. But like Sloan, and all who, seeking personal freedom, retire from the world, he has become the victim of his own doubts. His nudes are a little more gracious than Sloan's, but hardly more interesting as pictures. His drawings, however, still retain the remarkable vitality of his best period; and it is probable, I think, that if Robinson had been able to continue his work in mural decoration demanding the incisive study of facts, his reputation as a painter would have steadily improved.

Charles Burchfield, an artist of brilliant promise in his first exhibitions, seems, as the years go by, to stand aloof from his materials—from the Main Street he made famous in paint. A little too clever to submit to the discipline essential to the formation of a new and valid style, he trusts, with alarming frequency, to theatrical expedients. But Burchfield, to do him justice, was one of the first of the modern artists to utilize the physical background of America. He has not received the credit he deserves for his part in deflecting the attention of our painters from the French school, with its concentration on mechanical ingenuity, to the native environment. He proved, with the utmost clarity, the gorgeous possibilities of the physical scene, while other painters of similar aims were turning out stationary characters in a world of abstractions.

John Steuart Curry, of Kansas, is a painter of that typically American phenomenon, the Middle West. He is a true artist, extremely sensitive to his environment, and suspicious of quackery in all its isms. He is self-taught; he has been painting only a short time; he is as free from traditional borrowings as a man can be and paint at all; yet he has already produced the most original genre painting in American art. No other painter has been so deeply affected by the poetry of the West. Curry deals with the life that moved and made him—he has neither the glibness nor the inventiveness of the jury painter—and when he ventures outside his experiences, he has nothing to give. He paints the barnyard, the wheat fields, the tornado, rustic burials, and baptisms in the open air; the sultry Kansas wind blows though his cornfields; and in his characters, all drawn with strange tenderness, there is the pathetic loneliness and the sinewy courage of the pioneer. He is poetic, but he does not shrink from homely scenes, nor does he idealize his people. But the good people of Kansas—those, I mean, whose cultural smatterings make them ashamed of their background, and whose meager knowledge tells them that art is something remote and inaccessible—are loath to admit that he is an artist. If he painted with a French accent, if he made all the women lovely and all the men heroic, and transformed those arid plains into picturesque nooks for romantic lovers—he would be the pride of the Sunflower State.

As a composer, Curry has much to learn. In his Kansas pictures, he managed somehow—by sheer conviction and intensity of purpose—to get his experiences together in coherent style. But he is ambitious and bothered by his technical limitations. His most recent exhibition, a series of circus paintings, showed a marked advance in construction but a corresponding decrease in poetic power. His difficulty, I believe, will be lightened when he discovers in his Eastern environment, interests as compelling as those Western interests which inspired his best work.

Reginald Marsh, another young man of great ability, has been influenced by the robust Americanism of John Sloan. He has the same eye for significant detail, and the same inclination to slight the design for the sake of truth to fact. He is a man of even temperament, with none of Sloan's fighting rage with life or the propensity to take sides in social and political issues. But he is an observer of life, or of that very real slice of it extending from the shop and subway to the dance hall and Coney Island. Marsh is young enough to develop better control of his instruments. There are, in all his pictures, magnificent parts, pieces and sections; but he has not yet learned that an artist's experiences, however vivid and exciting, cannot be satisfactorily presented unless he has command over the relations and stresses binding a work into a unit. In this modern day, when artists do not fit automatically within any tradition, some scholarship is indispensable. Ways and methods of working have to be mastered even though such methods, later on, are profoundly modified by the materials treated. Marsh is a stubborn fellow; he has great gifts, but he refuses to see that his reliance on the camera—obvious enough in the details of his recent pictures—is only retarding his development as a composer.

It is in composition, in the establishment of clean relationships between forms, that American art, as a whole, comes to grief. Owing to the popular growth of photography which, mechanically, furnishes an effective conglomerate, and owing to the common American habit of falling back on make-shifts before difficulties, the American artist has never disciplined himself in the art of design. He trusts that haphazard arrange-

REGINALD MARSH: *Texas Guinan and Her Gang*

ments can be put across by dexterities of one sort or another. John Marin is the arch offender against law and order; but Marsh and Curry, who are much more responsible to their subjects, have, at times, the same loose-ness of purpose. Thomas Eakins, also a poor designer, was saved by his devotional interest in the substantial nature of things, and by confining his efforts to the simplest of forms. His whole art, one might say, was directed to getting the most out of a face or a hand. But Eakins, notwith-standing his sincerity, was something of a pedagogue; he has not the stature of a Renoir, much less of a Titian or a Tintoretto, and I cannot agree with the critics and artists who are trying to raise his art to the skies.

Marsh and Curry, reaching out into a world of more varied phenom-ena, attempt more than Eakins, but they must find some means of integrating their experiences before they attain to greatness. And inte-gration is to be found in the technicalities of the arts of design, the study of which, with our galleries, libraries and collections providing a com-plete historical review, is within the grasp of every one. But weaknesses aside, men like Marsh and Curry represent the New Deal in American art. They have broken with Europe; they have turned their backs on the hot-house estheticism of Stieglitz and on the hosts of dealers whose notions of art he helped to mold; they are working in the healthy field ploughed by John Sloan before he became "artistic"; with Benton, they are forming the new generation. Another artist who has spurned the shelter of the studio to chart a definite course in modern life is William Gropper, cartoonist and painter. With more scholarship for the sake of a richer assortment of tools, Gropper should develop into an artist of remarkable power. I have seen from his hand some of the most poign-ant drawings of human misery that have ever been made.

There is hope for American art. There is hope in spite of imported isms, manners and habits which have no connection with American life; in spite of Rockefeller Center, and the maneuvers of the dealers to liqui-date their frozen assets—their investments in the worthless securities of the Left Bank.

331

18

BENTON

SOME twenty years ago, as I have faithfully recorded, I came to New York from the Southwest, ready to fight and to die for the arts. In the old Arcade at Lincoln Square, that nest of youthful genius and dying failure, I ran across Thomas H. Benton, fresh from Paris. He was a sight, with his tight French clothes, his flat French hat, and his Balzac stick—the antithesis of everything American. He talked of abstract beauty and the subtleties of Gallic philosophy; of Platonic visions of art, and French poetry, an interest which, in the light of my own aspirations, was most impressive. The nostalgia of Verlaine, the perverse sadness of Baudelaire, the attenuated dreams of the Symbolists— those neurasthenic imaginings of the French genius of the period which today no one would associate with Benton's life and thought, seemed to compose the fabric of his being. He was only twenty-three, but he looked old and sad: his face was deeply lined and drawn, and I cannot remember that he ever laughed. He was, I felt, the victim of some strange irregularity of development.

In his nineteenth year, Benton had broken away from the Middle West and the frontier traditions of a political family to enter the insurgent art movements of the Paris of 1908, and the impact of the sudden transition was written upon him. He had been pushed from boyhood into manhood without that intermediate play of adolescent experience which acts as a stabilizer in the current of mature life. He was capable of the most infantile behavior, of an impossible naïveté that stood out, I soon discovered, in sharp opposition to his sturdy common sense, and

332

to the true nature of his thought which, even at that time, showed considerable integration and logical power.

Benton was born in southwest Missouri, in 1889, of a family famous in the West since the rule of Andrew Jackson. His great-uncle, after whom he was named, was the great Missouri senator; his father was a criminal lawyer, United States District Attorney under Cleveland, and for many terms a member of Congress. The country of his childhood can hardly be appreciated by the youth of today. It was a land of raw and buccaneering individualism, in essentials not different from the environment of Huck Finn and Tom Sawyer. From this community of hill billies and tobacco-eating politicians, he was removed in the winter months to the more polite and pretentious society of Washington. Travel and the meeting of all sorts of people were a part of the routine of the Benton family, and he learned to accept, as a matter of course, the divergent and contradictory ways of life. In the Congressional Library he acquired the habit of reading, a habit which fed his passion for making pictures. To his father's profane disapprobation, he began to draw, not occasionally but all the time, with an inherited stubbornness of will that cannot be ignored in the criticism of his relentlessly driven paintings. There was no stopping him; he studied at the Chicago Art Institute for a year and a half, and then went to Paris.

The collision between Benton's thoroughly American boyhood and the artificially stimulated life of the Latin Quarter was reflected in everything he attempted; and from the day that I met him to the end of the War, I do not believe that he painted a single consistent picture. He had enormous energy and determination, but his productions were not his own—nor were they frankly of any school. He made his bow to the current isms, but without grace or that ease of mind which lends the illusion of conviction to imitation. For ten years his painting was so labored and unpromising that most of his confreres were secretly of the opinion that he was outside his field. His most courageous defender was Mac-Donald-Wright, who steadfastly maintained that buried in his halting, badly imitative, and crude performances, were the seeds of genius.

It was Benton's studies, not his paintings, that interested me during this period. He would translate classic works into geometrical figures, a proceeding not unlike that of his friend Wright who turned classic compositions into color suites. I remember thousands of formal analyses—Assyrian, Egyptian, Greek and Renaissance. Night after night, month after month, he devoted himself to the various schools and masters, to Michael Angelo, Rubens, Piero della Francesca, El Greco and the Orientals, absorbed in sculptural form; and poor as his paintings were, that type of form was manifested in all of them. His essays in Cubism and abstract art were invariably tempered by the influence of the classic past. And, as was natural in one addicted to scholastic analysis, he indulged in theory, constructing philosophies of form and supporting them by heavy reading. Some years later, the fruits of his speculations were published in *The Arts*, in a series of articles which are still discussed by students, although Benton finds them immature.

From 1912 to our entrance into the War, I followed Benton's progress pretty closely. Every time I returned to New York, after one of my periodic excursions into the provinces, I found him more American—less retiring and better equipped for an active life. I saw him shed the worn-out rags and fripperies of French culture; I watched with amusement the animosity he aroused in his contemporaries who clung to the Bohemian idealism of the Left Bank—his wide reading in psychology made him skeptical of the fragile theories upon which Modernism fluttered, and his critical manners were distasteful. He was tactless and out-spoken, and his blunt condemnations did not become a painter whose own work was technically uncertain and experimental rather than expressive. He had not found himself as an artist, but it was plain that he was beginning to find himself as an American. He had returned to the athletic youthfulness which had been suspended by his trans-Atlantic flight. The last vestiges of French influence disappeared in the War. Benton's naval service, in contrast to my own, was a southern holiday. He was ordered to Norfolk where, on Saturday nights he boxed as a featherweight for the entertainment of old sailors and war-bride ensigns.

During the week he was free to train and to paint; and he left the service with eighteen pictures which clearly indicated an original style of art.

Benton's career since the War is the story of the reciprocal effects of extraordinary experience and extraordinary technical knowledge. Having readjusted himself to the native background, and recovered his youthful ability to participate psychologically in the life of America with its emotional ties, prejudices and sentiments, he began, step by step, and scene by scene, to build an art of and for the American people. Year after year, he has traversed the country, a knapsack of drawing materials on his back. On foot and on horseback, by motor, train and river boat, he has explored the United States from the great industrial centers to the furthermost corners of the backwoods. People of all kinds pose for him, put him up for the night, share drinks, stories, and gossip with him. His pictures have grown out of a rich experience—they represent, not hearsay, but life. His expeditions are not those of the traveler or sightseer, the social reformer or the statistician; they are in the nature of the return of the native to the country of his youth. He understands the rank and file, and more than any artist I know of, has the ability to fit automatically into the various patterns of American life.

Benton, mural painter, draughtsman, anthropologist, and interpreter of the American civilization, falls into none of the neat categories of modern art. To the conservatives, he is a Red; to the radicals, he is a chauvinist. His art is too specifically real, too deeply impregnated with what I shall risk calling *the collective American spirit*, to touch the purists, methodists, and doctrinaires—those whose idealism kneels to international panaceas and European formula. Yet his reputation somehow increases, and he is esteemed by the younger generation of painters as a master. Discerning foreign visitors are startled by the power of his native style—for Benton is American. He has the rawhide individualism, the cynical laugh, the rough humor, the talent for buffoonery, and something of the typical Westerner's sentimental slant on life. And he has, to the full, the American's distrust of ideas divorced from facts, a healthy realism which, whether our social soothsayers like it or not, may carry us safely into a better society.

Benton's art, apparently, is a direct and unblushing representation of American life. The average person regards him simply as a reporter of his time, and is attracted or repelled by the subject-matter which, according to temperament, is true or false, in good taste or bad, commonplace or exceptional. So pronounced and factual are his representations that even those conversant with the intricacies of formal structure tend to overlook his power as a designer. From a strictly lay point of view this is an advantage; for it is through content, through the materials represented, that art performs its initial function of social communication. But in a critical examination, the character of his structural machinery cannot be avoided—Benton's realism is inseparably bound up with his conception of form. What appears to be so conclusively the effect of mere observation, what coincides so truthfully with the layman's own experience with visual reality, is actually the product of a complicated technique arrived at slowly by years of experiment. Among artists and students, his three-dimensional murals are discussed as structures; to practitioners, it is evident that he has gained intense relief by diligent planning.

The violent contrasts in Benton's designs, the uncanny palpability of his forms, and his realization of great spatial depth, have wounded the sensibilities of critics who insist, with most of the architects, that a mural should be a flat pattern preserving intact the plane of the wall. On this question Benton himself has spoken explicitly in the catalogue of his Whitney Museum murals; and it is worth noting, so far as the ethics of criticism are concerned, that his argument has not been answered. Bias and habit have preferred simple denunciation.

"This means," he writes, "that significance should be subordinated to a convention; for only that which has no challenging qualities of its own can exist without radically affecting its surroundings. As the fetish of purity must inevitably fall when life enters, so the purity of architectural form cannot be maintained when painting enters, unless that

THOMAS BENTON: *History of Indiana—The French*

painting is so pallid, so much a convention, that it is unnoticeable. There is plenty of painting, of course, sufficiently conventional to have no marked effect on its surroundings, but the architect, though he uses it frequently enough, certainly holds it in contempt. The call for meaning, for significance, is strong in all men, and even the architect must tire of empty gesture and sickly archaic affectation."

The notion that painting should not dislocate the plane of the wall is a cliché which does not square with practice: no artist with anything to contribute has respected the architect's neutral surfaces. Even in the case of Puvis de Chavannes, the high prophet of the convention, the wall is divided and the plane broken. Any combination of color and tone, in fact, will cut the mural space and impair its architectural purity. The question becomes, then, one of degree—of the power of the painter to assert himself—and in the robust art of the Renaissance, from Masaccio to Rubens, the trend of painting was toward a more convincing relief, toward an all-inclusive representation of the conditions of reality.

The understanding of Benton's technical aims is simple enough, once we have rid ourselves of the esthetic slush accumulated in the last twenty years. He believes, with Leonardo da Vinci, that art is a study and representation of life, and with the Greeks, an "imitation" of life, the term imitation, in distinction from modern usage, implying conscious co-ordination—the bringing of experienced facts into harmonious relationship. A little familiarity with the classic mimetic will clear away most of the critical confusion surrounding his work. He is theoretically sound, and his efforts to find a form equivalent in intensity to actual experience have the sanction of the masters of the past, and for that matter, of Cézanne. True, he breaks radically with the past; but as the terms of Greek thinking must be adapted to modern usage, so must the terms of the plastic arts be cast in new molds.

In three major works—the murals in The New School for Social Research and in the Whitney Museum, and the colossal history executed for the State of Indiana—Benton wields a style that is practically mature. In each his classical affiliations persist; he maintains, that is, the classic attitude, but has developed new terms and instruments to support that attitude. In this he has proved his genius: the form that he has developed is almost a perfect equivalent of the realities of American life. The tumultuous forces of America, its manifold dissonances, and its social anarchy, are perfectly expressed in the restless counterplay of his forms. The common criticism that his work is without poise or serenity is an unwitting affirmation of its truth, its connection with its time and place.

The affected, Neo-classic simplicities of Picasso and Chirico have no bearing on modern life, and like the Neo-classic works of the crumbling Renaissance, are decadent and unfruitful. Benton is no Neo-classic; he has allowed his classic derivations to take a course in harmony with his direct experiences in life. No canon of perfection, or of what habit has decreed to be in good or bad taste, has obstructed his path. He has found an appropriate form for the things he has seen and known, at whatever cost to the conventions of technique. That his forms are often hard to grasp has led many to the conclusion that his pictures, like the photographs of the tabloid and the rotogravure supplement, are merely haphazard assemblages. This criticism springs from shallow observation: beneath his contrasting subjects, all deliberately planned, runs a counterplay of mass and volume that has no structural parallel since Rubens.

But it cannot be denied that his complex designs occasionally break down: in the murals of the New School, for example, the right angle turns were, at the time, too much for him. But we must remember that his painting is not an art of flat pattern, of surface against surface, but of volume against volume, the most formidable of technical problems. His conceptions are three-dimensional, precluding by their nature the use of the silhouette with which anything can be done and on which such distinguished mural decorators as Orozco and Rivera so largely depend. Where sculptural bodies are projected into deep space and volume is overlapped by volume, disturbing situations arise, but the consistency of his designs is retained in spite of the flaws. The Indiana mural is a complete vindication of his method. The volumes weave rhythmically in and out of the wall, and back and forth, in an unbroken flow; and the

338

right angle turns are faultlessly executed without the aid of arbitrary patterns at variance with the rest of the structure. Here too is vindication of Benton's theories of the value of high relief in wall decoration. The realism obtained thereby is overpowering, and the History of Indiana seems to be a living occurrence, a drama unfolding before the spectator.

To explain without diagrams the anatomy of Benton's designs is next to impossible. Generally speaking, we may say that he sets one movement, or unit, of block-forms against another—a few large blocks against many small ones, a dominant rhythm balancing several minor strains—and all circulating round poles or centers of interest. But it is unnecessary to go into such technical details: the dynamics of his art can be apprehended without exact knowledge of the principles involved. In his pictures, beneath the striking appeal of character and scene, one feels the sweeping rhythm, sees and feels the infinite variety of line and volume, the contrasting forms, the violent action and counteraction of masses. Perverse, or superficial observers, have professed to find this style chaotic. The themes, to be sure, by selection and particularly by juxtaposition, frequently depict social chaos, and the forms sustain the disorder; but the relationships are controlled—if anything, too rigorously controlled —by an organizing power unmatched in modern art.

What is chaotic in Benton is his modern America, and who can deny the factual and spiritual truth of this aspect of his work? It is my guess that in a more sensibly planned and orderly society of the future, this great drama of lawless change, which he has painted, will stand as one of the supreme arts of the transitional period, and will be valued because it is veracious experience and not futile prophecy. He has painted our capitalist America and the America of the pioneer and the individualist —its history and its current phenomena, all of which he knows and understands. The rushing energy of America, the strength and vulgarity, the collective psychology, are embodied in his art. The subordination of artistic tradition to actual experience with American life has enabled Benton to create the outstanding style in American painting, perhaps the only style.

339

But this original, ambitious, and comprehensive art is burdened with things difficult to digest. In the first place, Benton's intellectual and technical struggles are disturbingly visible. One receives the impression of tense muscles and tight lips in all that he undertakes. There is never a pause, never a feeling of relaxation; everything is strained and accelerated to the last degree. In his latest work, the Indiana mural, the tightness and glaring emphasis have been subdued, and he has painted with uncommon ease; but in his work, as a whole, every form, movement, and facial expression is fiercely driven—the art of one who works by will rather than for love.

The next obstacle, and until recently the most forbidding aspect of his painting, is his color. Benton uses color to reinforce projections which have been pre-established in tone—in black, white and grey—and insists that each color shall be the exact equivalent of the established tone. The most important factor in his processes is tone; and, in consequence, he has for years practically disregarded the equally important element of color harmony, holding, it would seem, to the idea that any color corresponding to his tone, and forcing his form into relief, is good color. It is only right in this connection to point out that he has always argued that fundamentally his color relationships are satisfactory, but defying conventions in their unusual correspondence to tone—to light and dark —they offend or shock the inexperienced eye. This argument is not to be scorned: the young artists esteem Benton as an effective, if not a gracious, colorist; and judged strictly by function, his color does what he intends that it should do—adds to the relief of his forms.

There remains, apart from technical issues, the controversy over the social content of Benton's art. Slowly, in this modern world, our attitude toward the esthetic is changing, with the promise that art may become once more, as it was in the past, the exponent of social ideals. The Mexicans, Orozco and Rivera, are enrolled in a militant Communism, and their views of the world are colored by the notion of the inevitable rise of the proletariat to power. Benton, on the other hand, holds aloof from any fixed pattern of ideals. Despite his tremendous vitality and his massive knowledge of American life, his art, so far as meanings are concerned, seems unfailingly to end with a question mark. Even in his Indiana mural, the great historical progression reaches the modern world and explodes in anarchical contrasts from which almost any meaning may be gathered. Radical criticism stresses this point and asks what significance his art may contain for the future. His work, as already noted, is so thoroughly attuned to the actual conditions of the present age that it will stand, I believe, as its perfect representation. It might become, however, in the event of great social changes, by the very reason of its representational truth, a horrible example. There is admittedly such a possibility.

Benton neither idealizes nor satirizes one aspect of society in preference to another. His art, as it partakes of a social point of view, is an enigma—not liberal, radical, or conservative. He depicts the antics of a chorus girl with the same gusto and dramatic power which he bestows upon a momentous historical episode; to him a night club and a strike of workers are of equal importance as social documents. As concerns meanings, his work is apparently inspired by no beliefs, no conceptions of relative value in the kaleidoscope of facts. Were he only a painter of little scenes, or lolling odalisques in diapered interiors, like Matisse, no exception would be taken to this characteristic of his work; but he presents vast mural suites and juxtaposes masses of socially significant facts in such an exciting fashion that one searches immediately for an underlying pattern of thought—and searches in vain.

Benton is critically assailed by two factions, the purists and the propagandists. The purists, subscribing under one guise or another to the fallacy of art for art's sake, resent alike his subject-matter and his form. Bohemians by trade, they classify him as low, common and vulgar, brutally forceful, but wanting in discrimination. They either deny his originality altogether, or assign it to the tabloid and the comic strip. The second faction, restricting the function of art to revolutionary propaganda, refuses to admit the significance of any work, however rich in human values, which does not proclaim the ideals of the Third International.

Benton has no interest in the malicious carpings of the purists, but naturally, from his record, is interested in the critical attitude of the Marxists. He was the first modern artist in America, and with the Mexicans, the first in the world to emphasize the importance of the subject in the growth of an original art. He published his views on form and subject in *The Arts*, June, 1924; but as early as 1918, he had turned his back on the cults emanating from France—the abstraction, the still-life, and the playing with materials—and had resolutely set himself to the painting of a great history of the United States in which, to use his own words, "form should meet the exigencies of event and cease to distort meanings for the sake of trivial patterns and pretty surfaces." From that day to this, he has explored the social geography of America, historically and in current phenomena, and has directed the whole of his experiment to the communication of social fact. Now that the tide has turned, and the battle for meaning is won—theoretically, at least—Benton finds himself renounced by the very artists who, having helped themselves to so many of his general ideas, should be his henchmen. They agree with him that the world can no longer be visualized as still-life, that the art of surface and technical gesture is dead; but they are unable to distinguish between a socially significant art and one sold to social ideals; they imitate his style and borrow his methods right and left, but scorn his completed statements because, they complain, his art does not elevate the working classes or coincide with revolutionary conventions.

Benton is in accord with the radicals in his belief that the art of the future will be no ivory-tower pastime but a form of social communication: to interest men the artist must go into the world of men for his materials. He also believes that original expression springs from the pressure of environmental interests, from experiences which, owing to their insistent individuality, cannot be warped into old patterns. He objects to Communist art on the ground that it too, like purism, is saddled with conventions which, with reference to the actual substance of life, are mostly illusory. While art, historically, has been the servant of various idealisms, it has drawn its vitality, not from the ideal, but from the exploration of the ways and habits of people. Christian art was not produced by the painting or carving of an ecclesiastical concept, but by the representation of life disregarding dogma in favor of experience— a point which I shall air thoroughly in the next chapter. Today, as in the past, it is the artist's business to see the world clearly, and to allow no convention of ideology or technique to obscure his vision or stand in the way of representational truth. This, needless to say, is the approach of the realist who demands substance instead of dreams. But if you squint at the world in the red light of a social ideal, or see it as the field for the cultivation of delicate sensibilities, you will, like the Communists and the dilettantes, shrink away from Benton's art, finding it uninspiring or underbred.

But it is possible, unless a revolutionary change utterly destroys social continuity—a condition neither imminent nor probable—that future historians will point to Benton, and not to the Communists as the more authentic product of the present upheaval. By his fidelity to his experiences, by his historical knowledge and his sense of the country, he has built up an enduring reality instead of a bodiless concept. The murals in The New School for Social Research will illustrate my contention. Visitors, turning from the Orozco Room, ostensibly the revolutionary expression, to the Benton Room, which is dedicated to the existing phenomena of a capitalist society, are unprepared for the variance. "The Mexican is calm and severe!" they exclaim. "The Benton murals are a riot!" The implications are clear, and while they do not invalidate Orozco's fame as a painter of walls, they do make questionable his insight into the social development of America. Orozco is the one great idealist in modern painting, but his whole art, in contrast to that of the little radicals and hang-dog intellectuals who merely corrupt or evade the facts of life, is a combination of symbols. Like Blake, he does not represent the actual world, but an imaginary world abstracted from his meditations on the

343

human predicament. His symbols, as they relate to facts, are poetical, and in the best sense of the word, religious. Benton, penetrating the collective American spirit, has fashioned an art in keeping with that spirit, and as contradictory in its appearance.

From time to time, one hears or reads the criticism that Benton debases America, that his painting is ignoble caricature, an insult to our high ideals and sterling sentiments. These strictures, as a rule, have their origin in the cliques of New York—the indoor esthetes and neuralgic professors to whom art is an excuse for verbal exercise, the display of dead learning, and the cautious manipulation of "advanced" attitudes. Truly, Benton's America is not their world; their America is the sidewalks of New York, the gallery, and the high tea. They will never know anything about America, for they are incapable of entering into any form of American life outside their own little circles. Benton, at home anywhere, goes happily about his business, adding to his fund of knowledge and painting America as he understands and enjoys it. He has not slandered our country, but by the volume, truth, and power of his art, he has done more than his share to discredit the East Side-Harvard school of esthetics.

Benton is one of the few living artists, in any department, with a first-rate mind. He has not only the ability to live and to create but to think; and a painter with the ability to think is something criticism has not had to reckon with for many a day. No wonder his defiant forms and dramatic conceptions baffle the professors! He is, like Dreiser in the novel and O'Neill in the theater, a pioneering force in American art. He has battled with academic stupidity for twenty years, and his murals announce the doom of the pseudo-classical antiquities disfiguring the walls of our state houses and municipal buildings. His History of Indiana, beautifully mounted by architect Hibben, is a work of the first magnitude. But in the face of all his achievement, I feel that Benton's best work lies before him, that he has not yet arrived at complete maturity. He is still experimenting—searching for more intense relief,

THOMAS BENTON: *History of Indiana—Politics and Education*

deeper space, unprecedented contrasts of form and subject; in almost everything he paints, I find passages which I wish were otherwise—mawkish clashes and unrealized intentions. Given the co-operation of the architects—for he is essentially a mural designer—he should become the most influential of American painters.

19

THE MEXICANS

"I was not one of those fools who are capable of producing something rather graceful but entirely without significance."—*Cellini*.

THE four men who first repudiated the philosophy of Modernism, a French method which, under the dominion of Matisse, Picasso, Brancusi and their idolaters, separated art from the living world in a scourge of abstractions and conventionalized studio subjects, are George Grosz, in Germany, Thomas H. Benton, in America, and the Mexicans, Diego Rivera and José Clemente Orozco. These four painters, dissimilar in temperament and variously trained, may be held accountable for the changing direction of art—a new movement which, winning the allegiance of the young, is leading art into the communication of experiences and ideas with a social content.

While Grosz was exposing the demoralized passions of post-War Germany, and Benton, virtually unknown, was struggling with a social history of the United States, the two Mexicans, grasping the opportunity afforded by the revolutionary turn of events in their country, developed the first significant mural painting of modern times. From the turmoil of their own people, from living subject-matter, they produced a living art of the wall. This initial impetus, destined to play havoc among the citadels of American culture, not only placed in bold relief the possibilities of a mural revival but raised the whole question of the relation of art to society and to the promulgation of ideas. It also trained the spotlight on two diverse personalities about whom those who elect to sit in critical judgment are in constant disagreement. Of the two, Rivera, with

346

DIEGO RIVERA: *Self Portrait*

(*Original lithograph*) COURTESY WEYHE GALLERY

an ingratiating innocence which conceals his cunning opportunism, is the more prominent. It was he who precipitated the popular commotion.

Rivera appeared at a moment of apparent complacency, when the mysteries of art, tended by pampered young men and their critical sires, were flourishing in cultivated society; when the ability to talk the cabalistic slang of modern esthetics had become the token of superior breeding and discernment. He announced, by his murals and his published addresses, that the mysteries were only the stage-play of illusions; that the high-toned emotions and delicate sensibilities laid upon the altar of modern art were devoted to something without substantial existence. The trouble began in Detroit. Commissioned to decorate the walls of the Institute of Arts, the Mexican painted a panorama of frescoes which are certainly not flattering to the capitalist regime, nor to preconceived notions of beauty. But Mr. Edsel Ford, having engaged the artist, supported him like a gentleman and paid him handsomely for his audacity; and Rivera departed for New York amid the wails of the obscurantists.

What happened in New York is history. Hired, because of his international fame, by friendly enemies who, two years before, had courted him in a fashionable exhibition, he went to work in Rockefeller Center, did what he was in the habit of doing and what could only have been expected of him; but when the job was three quarters finished, he was, for no sensible reason, suddenly expelled. It is not my purpose to examine the charges preferred against him by his rivals, Mexican or American; my concern is with the issues raised by his murals, and with his repeated verbal challenges to the existing order of art.

The portly Mexican has carried painting from the Ivory Tower into the market-place, from the studio cloister into the news columns of the press, the camps of the Communists and the arena of belligerent social ferments. He has shocked the specialists and their cultural patients with a proclamation reducing their "plastic purities and mysteries" to bourgeois affectations. He has said that "art is propaganda or it is not art"; and his answer to the question *"What is Art For?"* (The Modern Monthly, June, 1933) though crudely expressed, conceited and bombas-

347

tic, has fallen into the chosen ring of art fanciers like a Communist bomb. For nothing could be more painful to the esthetic snob than to be convicted of bourgeois refinements. To compensate social restlessness, the snob had resorted to art, convinced that in Modernism lay the one hope of emancipation from the vulgarities of bourgeois society. By practical necessity, he was, of course, forced to live physically in an unenviable environment; but in art, with its involved and elaborate mysteries, he found glorious escape from reality. By embracing and reciting the new esthetic creed, he proved that he was not just a contemptible bourgeois battening on the miseries of the workers. In modern art he saw before him a prospect for the play of profound thoughts and emotions aloof from the pressures of environment and indelicate physical habits. The distinctions, often exquisitely subtle, between representation and form, between the apparent and the real, offered unlimited inducements to the display of acumen and sensibility.

Then Rivera appeared with the brutal pronunciamento—frightful in its rawness—that all these distinctions and subtleties were but the outcome of a bourgeois psychology, the culmination of an over-refined, peevish, and soulless way of living. And his statement cannot be dismissed as mere ruffian adherence to party principles—the wedding of art to doctrine—though it receives most of its advertising from such connections. Fundamentally, it relates to the eruption of feelings and dissatisfactions much more deeply rooted than political tenets; it springs from the historically recurrent search for overt meanings, for actual order in life—the search attending the breakdown, also recurrent, of the instrumentalities of living. Under the pressure of this search, individual artists, as well as individuals in other professions, rush wildly for the security of some sort of position. A center of orientation seems to be an absolute necessity. Communism, with its well-bolstered doctrine and its social guarantees, affords the obvious support. When the whole world is meaningless and purposeless, here is certitude.

On the face of it, Communism would appear to be the most portentous movement in art since the lords of the High Renaissance robbed painting of its holy office and made it the agent of vanity. For we find, on consulting our records, that art, as a living activity, has been united to dominant idealisms. The great arts of Egypt, Assyria, and Greece, lived and prospered by representing beliefs and convictions shared by large social bodies. The art object—the painting or carving—was a communicative instrument. In calling art to its service, Communism is appealing to that instrument. It has denounced the stupidity of studio art and the empty elegance of schoolmen like Matisse and Picasso; it has demanded the expression of ideals inseparable from daily human conflicts. It has faced the fact that art cannot live on itself alone, and by making form the servant of meaning, has unconsciously returned to the classic attitude. For the first time since the Christian Church, emerging from the Roman wreckage, employed humble zealots to embody its ideals in stone and color, has the artist been called to a social function. I do not exaggerate the case. Let us review briefly the course of painting.

Occidental painting rose to its most splendid heights during the Renaissance, but in its pompous extravagance the seeds of decay were planted. Esthetic interests were isolated; art erected its own culture, and became the handmaiden of riches and aristocratic display. It became the possession of a class which eventually was to lose every real connection with life, to dwell in a world of illusions and memories, a world of fantastic play acting. Since the Renaissance, art has been slowly withdrawn from common life. For a considerable time, in spite of the fierce antagonisms of individual artists, it followed a patronizing aristocracy, removing itself farther and farther from the representation of the ideals, beliefs and habits of the dominant members of society. As long as the aristocrats actually controlled the people; as long as they functioned by directing the machinery of living, the art they fostered retained a certain amount of health and vitality. Rubens, for instance, belonged to an organic social group, not to a sham society, an obsolete class. But with the rise of the bourgeoisie—the result of the evolution of the instrumentalities of production and exchange—the old aristocracy, with its tributaries in art, ceased to function, existing as a social appendage

349

serving no better purpose than to set the standards of gentility and fashion.

Christian mythology had prescribed subject-matter which brought the artist into direct contact with an idealism universally shared and professed. Accepting this mythology literally, the artist, at first, produced only childish concepts or meaningless visions and abstractions from pagan forms; and it was not until skepticism had broken the rigid doctrinaire attitudes of the Church that he was able to connect his subjects with living things and to build an art of human values. By expressing Christian faiths and myths in terms of his own experiences with his fellow men, the artist remade his subjects; nominally they represented Christian mythology; actually they represented current realities. The symbolical use of personal experiences is characteristic of the other great art forms, Egyptian, Assyrian, Greek, Indian, and Chinese. It is the most important element in the relation of art to meaning, and in the answer to the question, "Is Art Propaganda?"

With the revival of learning—the popularization in aristocratic circles of scholarly voyages into the art and thought of the Greeks and Romans—art, as I have said, began slowly to retire from the field of common experiences, and to dally with subjects bearing no relation to life as it is actually lived. In its retirement, however, it managed to retain one vital factor, one redeeming preoccupation which saved painting from utter uselessness and extinction. I refer to the interest in natural phenomena, an interest originating in the efforts of artists to make Christian myths more convincing and lifelike. Leonardo, you will remember, was a profound student of natural phenomena; Titian, in his old age, experimented with broken color; Velasquez was a slave to photographic appearances; the Dutch tone painters achieved miracles of naturalism; Manet followed their example; and with the Impressionists, the analysis of light became a mania and a scientific novelty.

The facts of nature, as presented to the eye, offered a field for fresh investigation which restrained the painter from complete abdication, along with his patrons, into the realm of cultivated illusion. Long after the social function of art had disappeared, the painter, though attached to an aristocratic society consecrated to operatic pretensions and living above the exigencies of plain human affairs; though compelled to deal in Greek and Roman mythologies—subjects above common beliefs, above all beliefs; the painter, I repeat, contrived to produce an art that was not wholly without meaning. The research into natural phenomena was its own reward, a content of a sort, in spite of subject-matter that drove him away from life experience into studio eclecticism, and eventually into modern academic seclusion.

The first decisive step in the elimination of the meanings of art—the separation of form and content—was taken by Poussin, the father of the Academy. Poussin's paintings were originally, have been, and are today the toys of connoisseurs, and the envy of all artists doomed to live and die in the museums. His studious, archeological correctness served as a model for all those stilted, Neo-classic pictures solicited by a decaying aristocracy. Though there have been intractable or revolutionary individuals such as Rembrandt, Hogarth, Goya, and Daumier, who do not fit in the scholastic pattern, occidental painting since Poussin has been segregated from society. Its researches and discoveries have been of no great consequence—the property of small esthetic cults.

Art has lost its historical connection with dominant idealisms—lost its most important function. There is no need to disguise this fact. Its claims, for the most part, are preposterous; its accomplishments negligible. Modern art, the art succeeding Impressionism, which seemed to promise so much, now promises nothing. Its exhibits are stale and nonsensical—of no value whatever save as adjuncts to the vanity of wealthy collectors who find in it the parallel of their own spiritual emptiness. Its obscurities and aberrations still inspire the drivel of the esoteric scribes; but it has no meaning save that which is read into it by the dictates of idiosyncrasy.

Democracy, you see, has provided no mythology adaptable to the symbolical apparatus of painting; its ideals have been continually shifting, have accommodated themselves to the rapid changes in the mechan-

351

ics of production and distribution. Democratic society has created no background of vital belief, no general conviction that behind the shifting dance of expedients there exists a spiritual reality, absolute and unchangeable. Democracy has drained the substance from the old illusions to which art was faithfully united: the illusion that eternal life actually lay beyond the horizon of fact; that the King was divine and his antics inspired. Today the King is not even a figurehead—he is an obsolete dunce; and the Church, like the old aristocracy with its ideals of power, grandeur and gentility, survives as a clearing house for social indulgences.

Enter Communism with concepts which would seem to parallel those of the early Church—concepts treated as realities. It has a fine mythology —emanating from Marxian dialectics; and a program, a celestial vision promising universal participation in the good. And it poses the equivalent of the old functioning aristocracies and priesthoods in its notion of a dominant proletariat, a specifically favored class in whose hands rests the ultimate happiness of mankind. The set-up would seem to be perfect for the symbolical powers of the plastic arts. And the artist is restless, ready for the call. Intelligent young men everywhere are conscious of the fact that their connection with the polite society which supports art is artificial and dependent on vogues—on fashionable whims capitalized by dealers.

Rivera's declaration, therefore, cannot be disposed of with a sneer. As already noted, it goes deeper than party affiliations; it enters into the profound restlessness of the human spirit confronted with inevitable change. By implication at least, it voices the old undying truth that art cannot subsist on itself. And inasmuch as that is exactly what art has been trying to do, it will be worth while to consider a system which, whatever its claims, would relieve art from the ignominy of self-consumption.

The Communists assume that, at last, they have identified art with a general ideal, whereas, in reality, they have done no such thing. They have only bound art to a specific program, using it as the tool for the propagation of economic theories which, though geographically distributed, are far from universal in their application. This, I submit, is the basic error of the new system. There is a vast difference between the kingdom of heaven, as visualized by the early Christian worshippers, and the heaven on earth, as formulated by the apostles of the proletariat. The characters of Communist mythology are living people—obstreperous human beings. And the workers of the world—the proletariat in the best sense—cannot be squeezed into a general concept without the most violent distortions of fact. Nor can they be represented by conventional symbols.

And I must again point out that the great religious art of the world attained vitality only when conventional symbols had been subordinated to the study and appreciation of fact; when religion had lost its intense concentration on spiritual ideals and had grown tolerant of the parade of life. The Church employed art as the tool for its propaganda, but no real art appeared until the artist had disregarded propaganda in favor of the realities of his life experience. The art of Italy, though enclosed in the framework of Christianity, a general ideal which prescribed its subject-matter, was composed of various local schools expressing local psychologies, each dominated by powerful but locally conditioned personalities.

This historical fact should be borne in mind by those artists who, aware of the true condition of modern art, its essential worthlessness and its snobbery, are ready to cast their lot with a political party, a militant organization preaching concepts assumed to be of universal significance, and by nature religious. No art can be enslaved to doctrine. Art, in its proper manifestations, is a communicative instrument; but it communicates its own findings—*not what is doled out to it;* not what an economic theory imposes upon it, but its discoveries in the actualities of life.

The most dangerous aspect of the present situation is this: the artist expects to win salvation merely by transferring his allegiance from one group to another, an act amounting to no more than affixing a different label to the bag of tricks which art, since the War, has become.

Among the intellectuals offering lip-service to proletarian ideals, but

353

living carefully by the pseudo-aristocratic standards sifting down through democracy, one finds as many fakers and opportunists as are attached, on the other side, to the dying powers of wealth. It is true that the dilettante Communists have been spared the most offensive element in modern art—the gigolo and the homosexual playing on the vanities of bored women; but nevertheless, to gain access to their doctrine, one is obliged to brave the stench of affectation and dishonesty. In this field all sorts of artificial standards are erected to authenticate the revolutionary content of works of art. Psychologically, there is no difference between such standards and those erected to determine whether an art is "pure," or "truly plastic." The esthetic intellectuals prepared art for the salons of wealthy society by inventing the correct mysteries; the proletarian play-boys cleared the way for the powers and advocates of Communism by passing on the correctness of the artist's social attitudes. In so far as the artist is concerned, there is little to choose between them. Both are as dictatorial as were the old Church Fathers who not only ruled that art must proclaim the ideal through mortification of the flesh, but also specified the list of symbols. Both demand that the artist conform to a pattern.

But no viable or healthy art can be forced into a pattern. The health and growth of art depend on the artist's original discoveries in life and nature where the logic of a pattern, even when it appears to exist, is but the transfer of an intellectual or emotional illusion. Neither life nor nature contains logical relationships: they must be made, and it is the business of art to make them. Art and philosophy—the "as ifs" of the human mind—are the vehicles through which experience is integrated and the human desire for rational order, or logic, is satisfied. That is their supreme function. But they fail to operate effectually with second-hand material. The man who rearranges and catalogues the thought-forms and systems evolved by others, without referring to the adventure of life, is not a philosopher—he is a professor; the man who rearranges the art-forms evolved by others, or illustrates economic theories, is not

DIEGO RIVERA: *Zapata*

(Original lithograph) WEYHE GALLERY

an artist—he is an eclectic, like Picasso, or a political accomplice, like the cartoonist of the industrial workers.

An art limited to propaganda has no choice but to deal with given material, and to deal with it arbitrarily—to stack the cards in the interest of a political game. The critical questioning of life and along with it, the discovery of the unexpected—of new and exciting things which, fitting no old patterns, must be communicated in fresh terms—this independent exploration, which is the very soul of art, is forbidden by the rules of propaganda. Cartoons, broadsides, and illustrations may be highly useful in the promulgation of doctrine, and may indeed point a very bitter moral; but true art, which is the discovery of a specific world, a personalized world partly of the artist's own making, must penetrate beyond the facts into the emotional beliefs and habits of an environment; must range far beyond the patterns of doctrine into the complexities and contradictions of reality.

If Communist propaganda is to father a new art, its proponents must be prepared to submit to the most ruthless treatment of its doctrine. The true artist is never numbered among the faithful. If Communism should happen to tempt the powers of a young Daumier, it would find itself in the embarrassing position of harboring a heretic. For Daumier, an underdog reared in a radical atmosphere and using his art, at the beginning of his career, as a revolutionary weapon, lost faith in his youthful dreams of the sovereignty of the people, and subjected all political agitators, irrespective of creed or party, to merciless critical examination. He was always on the right side—the side of humanity—but his interest in French life was not consistent with political doctrines.

Communism, instead of linking art with a general ideal, has enslaved it to a specious Internationalism in which meanings and values are regarded as absolute and universal. This form of Internationalism is not more conducive to the growth of art than the international Bohemianism of the esthetes. Art is a local phenomenon. It may find its subjects in ideals aiming at universality, but it must treat those subjects simply as frames for the richer content derived from experience. Great art has never deviated from this axiom. Buddhist art, for example, is so named for historical convenience; intrinsically it is the art of various peoples who, by means of local experiences and psychological attitudes shaped by special environments, transformed doctrine into living expressions. Let us look into the troublesome question of the meanings of art.

Meanings are neither constant nor absolute; they vary from age to age, changing, dying, and reappearing with the different trends of civilization. Nor are they, in the strict sense, universal. Huckleberry Finn is unintelligible to the Chinese; more acceptable to the Americans than to the British; and closer to Middle Westerners than to New Englanders. And the art of China, with its elaborate symbology developed from indigenous beliefs and habits, is, for most occidentals, only an archeological toy—this, in spite of the precious gabble of connoisseurs. I do not say that the art of the past may hold no meaning for the modern man; my point is that the strongest appeal of art—its full content, its specifically human message—is to the civilization producing it. In short, meanings are largely of a contemporary nature—contemporary in the broadest sense, denoting the social life and characteristic mental attitudes of overlapping generations. I grant that the psychological insight of Leonardo may interest the modern American, atheist or Catholic; that we may still be moved by Michael Angelo's brooding athletes; that Rembrandt, closer to Americans than are the Italian masters, appeals to many of us with something of the force of a contemporary. But it is not reasonable to suppose that any past art, considered as a movement affecting the lives of men, can carry the significance of an art drawn directly from an environment in which we are living participants. Most of us—artists too, if they are alive—while we study and admire the deposits of the past, devote the greater part of our interest and discussion to the books, pictures, and buildings of the present. The painful truth is that the major appeal of past art is to the specialist; and no great art was ever founded on the limited attention of specialists. To the artist, if he is more than an academic or a slave to canonized beauty, the old forms serve as disciplinary tools in the ordering of his own experiences.

The forms of art are interesting in proportion to the richness of the personality creating them; and the elements composing the personality are derived from two sources—the character and intensity of experience, and its processes of integration. These two elements in conjunction produce the artist; one without the other is helpless. No matter how poignant or striking the experience may be, if the artist cannot contrive an appropriate form for its objectification, his meanings are vague and unconvincing. And no matter how extensive his traditional knowledge, if his acquired method is not fertilized by experience, his forms will be academic and imitative. What happens with the successful artist is that the realities of environment actually work upon his spirit, forcing him to modify traditional processes and to create a new and personal instrument.

The Communists assert that ideas are indispensable to art. They are right: without ideas, or concepts, nothing would be done—and the cult of sensitivity has become the refuge of quacks and neurotics. But the idea is the generative factor, not the end, of art. An idea may, in itself, be vital, but it will not produce an interesting form unless referred to the actual conditions of experience. It is not the physiological nose or head that is expressive, but a particular nose or head observed by the artist in some significant situation. In the process of construction the head may be idealized, as in Greek sculpture, but its character and meaning are determined by the stuff of life involved with and conditioned by environment. Rubens had ideas—grandiose classical concepts lending their names to his pictures—but his ideas, transformed in the crucible of experience, came out not as goddesses, but as Flemish housewives whose truth and reality were recognized and enjoyed by people totally unfamiliar with the generating idea.

With the Communists the beginning and end of art is the moral idea. The artist is drafted into the illustration of an economic theory, and the best the idea can do is to inflame his moral indignation. No experience, no observation, no discovery, is allowed to interfere with his political duty. He takes a method, preferably the Modernist pattern, and bends it into the service of a verbal idea. Most ideas, I need hardly say, owing to

357

the early conditioning of our communicative needs, are verbal, but the idea, passing through the imagination of the artist, is transmuted into a pictorial form which carries a new meaning. Albert Ryder's paintings were inspired by verbal concepts of the tragedy of man, but his paintings cannot be translated into words. Ryder, poet and mystic, represents to perfection the yearning that runs so easily into sentimentality, the strange sadness underlying so much of American life. He is true to a psychological type which I have met, not only in New England but throughout the Middle West; not only among tenant farmers of the South, but under the conventions of many a Babbitt. In his art is the nostalgia of the roving, groping, bewildered American people.

When art is wedded to propaganda, its content is limited to the expounding of doctrine. Once the moral is pointed, there is no further use for it. I examine and enjoy and applaud the brutal force and savage energy with which our radical cartoonists attack some current villainy; but I do not find myself returning to these diatribes, as I return to Hogarth, the meaning of whose art lies not so much in the specific subject as in the understanding of the psychology of the British people; as I return to Daumier whose best work is not merely an illustration of an evil, but the co-ordinated experiences of a profound personality. The propaganda plays of Bernard Shaw, written to expose corruption or prove a theory, are as stale today as the trumped-up estheticism of Oscar Wilde's dramas. Shaw once said that a knowledge of economics was as necessary to the structure of his plays as a knowledge of anatomy to the structure of Michael Angelo's figures. He forgot that Michael Angelo was not trying to prove anything.

You will have noticed that the propaganda artists display very meager acquaintance with the American background, and indeed, very meager knowledge of the figure and the way in which behavior and occupational interests actually affect human anatomy. Doing what they are told to do, they turn out dreadful concepts—bestial stuffed shirts, monstrous forms so fiercely exaggerated, so remote from reality as to defeat their own purpose. Thus their art runs swiftly into trade symbols and conventions;

358

into stock forms and stereotypes of no more enduring value than the stereotypes of the Bohemians.

Propaganda cannot produce an original art; cannot produce any art, though it may accompany it. I recently asked one of our best cartoonists, a truly radical young man and an excellent painter, why he was not a Communist. His answer was: "The moment I become a Communist, I cease to be an artist. My hands are tied; my independence sacrificed to a system. If I want to paint my wife and baby as I know them—to express what they mean to me—I cannot do so. I must paint them as starving victims of Capitalist crimes. Propaganda is to art what the gun is to the soldier, not an expression but an explosive." There would be no room in propagandist art for a skeptic like Leonardo; an outcast like Rembrandt who shirked every social obligation; a turncoat and a trimmer like Goya; an old tory like Cézanne who lived on inherited wealth.

The learned Mexican, Rivera, was for years a notorious eclectic, a combiner of styles. Well trained in the old and Modernist schools, a jovial soul at ease in the art talk of the Boulevards of Paris, ingenious, able, and filled with European experiences, he returned to Mexico with a technical and intellectual equipment lifting him head and shoulders above his Mexican and American confrères. He developed rapidly a fluent fresco idiom; and tremendous murals literally rolled off his brushes. Facile and brilliant, he won and held public attention. In his own country he was an artist, a most distinguished artist. His native murals, despite obtrusive mannerisms acquired from the forcing of experience into French and Italian molds, have, to a considerable extent, the character of original discoveries welded into forms. At home, he painted pictures containing social meanings which his countrymen, capable of sharing, praise or regret—sufficient proof, I think, of the genuine quality of his Mexican experience.

Orozco, his most notable rival in the Mexican renascence was content to remain in the oppressed land of his birth. He had neither dexterity nor brilliance; he was ignorant of the tricks of eclecticism and of the politics of self-aggrandizement—and he was lost in the flood of praise lavished on Rivera. But as time goes on, Orozco increases in stature; his art, informed by a grim integrity of spirit, begins slowly to stand out as a profoundly original contribution. His Mexican frescoes, in perspective, grow steadily in importance, and perhaps because of his very lack of facility, gain an impelling seriousness. It is he, not Rivera, who brought into modern painting the austere conviction, the deep-plumbing search into religious feelings, and the tragic cry of suffering humanity lost to mural decoration since the early Italians. He has written on the walls of Mexican buildings not merely the external clashes—the violence and bloodshed of the revolution—but the spiritual clashes of a race he loves and understands. One might think, considering the antiquity of painting, its infinite variations on the human figure and the ways in which forms are held together, that every compositional scheme had been discovered and exhausted, that new postures and rhythms were no longer possible. But this man, by genius of course, and untrammeled by precedent, has created works of indisputable originality—new attitudes and astonishing relationships which could only have been inspired by direct penetration into the actualities of Mexican life.

Yet, of late, Orozco's style, like the clever adaptations of Rivera, borders on the cliché. It is my duty to record that the best work of these two painters is to be seen in their homeland. Both are now substituting symbols for the vigorous representations so characteristic of their Mexican frescoes. Neither has shown much perception of the color and psychology of the United States. From the point of view of the purists, of those contending that art exists for itself alone and is sufficient thereunto, this objection is irrelevant. Theoretically and logically, the purist contention is perfectly sound; but unfortunately, the logic of art does not extend beyond the use of instruments into the province of meanings, and the fact remains that that art thrives best on subject-matter and in environments where the artist is emotionally at home.

Rivera's general capacity has enabled him to surpass Orozco in handling the American people and their background; but his efforts in this field, at best, seem to build upon hearsay rather than true experience,

JOSE CLEMENTE OROZCO: *The Barricade*

and for all their ingenuity and prodigious competence, are not convincing. Rivera's trouble is that he has had no real American experiences: playing shrewdly on the sympathies of the workers and on the snobbery of the highbrows, he has not had time to get acquainted. In his American murals he practically disregards experiences. With the help of his assistants, he assembles his data—machines, episodes and properties snatched from industrialism—and skilfully converts them into symbolical space-fillers. He must, of course—and this is an honest conviction—abuse the capitalists; but his huge mechanisms, expressly designed to uphold the worker, have none of the deadly effectiveness of the cartoons of Gropper and Minor. They are crowded with wooden Indians, stock figures, and the insignia of Communism—the result of his determination to press the obvious factors of the American environment into molds developed in the social upheaval of Mexico.

In his Detroit murals, Rivera resorts to a form of symbolism approximating the academic business of Puvis de Chavannes. He attempts to portray concepts such as *Biological Research, Industry,* and *Health,* by scenes which, in the absence of first-hand knowledge of actual conditions, are hardly more persuasive than lists of abstract emblems. The social message embedded in these pictures is almost indecipherable; and Rivera's verbal elucidation has the didactic ring of the class room propagandist.

The good people of Detroit were offended less by the social satire than by the lack of prettiness and graceful allusions to the gods and heroes of conventional wall painting. His last American venture, the frescoes in The New Workers School, of New York, was made entirely out of books—out of historical matter supplied by his helpers and doctored by him for Communist consumption. I am not protesting against the subjects, but against the emphasis placed upon them by the artist. You cannot see the humanity for the indignation. Every fact, every episode, every face, is distorted to prove the iniquity of the capitalist system. From one end to the other, this historical sequence is an expression of ungovernable rage. Its meaning is not to reveal and communicate actual

361

American conditions, or historical interests transmuted in the crucible of experience, but to scream the immorality of Capitalism.

I have heard young Communists asseverate that at last we have a mural painter with the courage to deal with raw facts. Rivera, in truth, does deal with facts, but always as parts of a political movement, always in behalf of an ideal, not a reality. The content of his painting is not directed toward representation as such, but toward the liberation of the working classes, as those classes are internationally construed, and toward the formation of a world Communist state. The purpose of his art is to promote an ideal, not to present the phenomena of life; but inasmuch as he employs phenomena as material for his campaign, his distortions of fact are annoying to those who know their America. Rivera, unlike Benton, cannot paint a face that is unequivocally American. No doubt Benton would be confronted with the same impossibility, if he were to risk his brush with Mexican types, but the American artist never strays outside his direct experiences.

Rivera will try anything, and with his great sweeping talents, nearly always acquits himself with distinction. But he has come to view the world from the bias of Marxian dialectic—as a universal movement headed toward the redemption of the submerged classes. Like intellectuals everywhere—and he is patently an intellectual though a fantastic one—he rides blindly through the vivid world of fact. In his own country, this world of fact, a part of the texture of his life and inculcated into him during an impressionable childhood, persists in his work, imparting to his Mexican murals, notwithstanding his eclectic European habits and his propaganda, the flavor of truth and the substantial reality born of direct experience.

Orozco's work in this country is utterly foreign to the American character and background. Though a resident of the United States for a number of years, he still lives in the sun and shadow of his native land: the types and symbols, the cactus, the ancient Indian pyramid, the sudden contrasts of light and dark, the physiognomies of his people, remain as in his Mexican pictures, unaltered and unalterable. In his Dartmouth decorations, he has chosen his themes from ancient Mexican culture, a wise decision on his part but puzzling to the college boys. An inflexible personality with none of Rivera's facility in adapting styles and contriving superficial resemblances, he has been forced to depend upon abstractions from his life in Mexico. But his abstractions, based upon his own experiences, have an unimpeachable integrity, save in those structures marred by the insertion of copies of photographs. Orozco commands his own style, one of the few authentic styles in modern painting. An avowed Communist like Rivera, he too is capable of ignoring realities in favor of dialectically conditioned interpretations, but because of his very clumsiness, perhaps, never ventures beyond his depth. His symbolical apparatus is not a sudden acquisition nor a Communist mannerism; it is a natural growth consistent with the traditions of his race and the poetry of his imagination.

But Orozco's great art, as I have pointed out, is in danger of succumbing to habitual procedures. It is the tendency of every artist to dwell in the clouds and to rely on old habits and accumulated knowledge; but if the artist is to preserve his strength, he must constantly be brought down to earth. Orozco, I believe, has abstracted from his past all that is pregnant and useful; and unless he returns more frequently to the land of his youth—the only land he really understands—the formation of clichés will ruin him. Originally a profoundly vigilant draughtsman, he has allowed his symbolical abstractions to displace observation, with the result that his figures, taken as individual units, are now almost as empty as purely geometrical forms.

It is obviously less difficult to combine and unify abstractions than realities, and Orozco's years of application to the process of abstracting and simplifying have no doubt contributed to the originality of his style. Certainly he is, at present, a more powerful composer than in his Mexican period. But now that he has his style in hand and the relationships of his forms under perfect control, it is time that he injected more immediate experience into his art; that he returned to the specific character of the things he represents. Symbolism in painting usually leads into nothingness. An art built round an ideal content demanding a verbal structure for its complete expression is ruinous to a painter whose symbols are not vitalized by the flow of visual experience. The painter must observe and study the physical world for what it is. The danger of any art inspired by ideals and propaganda lies not in the generating force but in the tendency of the ideal to separate the artist from the facts of life, and to urge him to employ stereotyped processes in place of experience which is the life blood of all creative work.

But in spite of criticism, Orozco is a great figure in contemporary art, a man of whom we should all be proud. There is none like him. As I have written elsewhere, his achievement, with that of his rival Rivera—as a whole, and in terms of meaning and function, in terms of structure and plasticity, in organizing power and draughtsmanship, in human significance and social criticism—puts to shame the combined efforts of the European Modernists. It may well be that the two Mexicans, with Grosz on this side of the Atlantic instructing our youth, with Benton relentlessly on the American job, and young students everywhere alive to the changing order, are the forerunners of a new art in the modern world. And this new art will not be devoted to the whims of rich collectors nor to the scholastic attention of specialists, but to the needs of large groups of people who, for a long time, have taken no interest in art because art has taken no interest in them.

CONCLUSION

THE day is dead when the ability to distinguish between the various Modernist sects made a man a critic. The day is past when the exhibition of tools entitled a painter to the name of artist. It is no longer necessary for the painter to sacrifice his life to an ideal that has no meaning to the world; it is not incumbent on the American people to believe that the appreciation of Picasso is the mark of cultural emancipation. There is nothing in Picasso for them to appreciate; not a single connecting bond between his barren forms and the realities of American life. His art is all processes, and there is no way in which those for whom art, by its nature, is intended, can participate in processes; and without participation, true appreciation does not exist. Absolved of this mythical obligation, the American people, I should think, should revert to and encourage an art which they can understand and enjoy, an art which, however inchoate, has at least one of the requisites of great art—the appeal to the flow of common experiences.

The lines are definitely drawn; the issues are clear. Either the American people want an art which may be called their own, or they want something else. If they want an art of painting comparable, in indigenous appeal, to the other arts, they will never develop it by the present system of snobbery and hero-worship. If they prefer an art of European patterns and eclectic mixtures—and it appears that they do —then, I say, let them have it. I ask for no embargos or reprisals; no tariff barriers, and no exclusions based on provincial ignorance—and no exclusions, remember, of American talent. Let art be free, and pure too, if that is what is desired. All I ask is that the choice be honestly stated, the preference frankly defined. Those who regard art as modish

365

decoration, as inarticulate embellishment, have every reason to favor French Modernism, and every incentive to buy it. And it is more sensible to buy the original French manufactures than the American imitations. Truly, they order these material things better in France. In the exhibition at the Chicago Fair, the French painters of the modern School of Paris made the American painters attached to that school look seedy and second-rate. So if you like organized smudges, geometrical patterns, abstractions, and particles of color divorced from a context, by all means indulge your tastes to your heart's content, and to the depletion of your purse. All I ask is that you do not lie about it; that you do not pretend that there is a soul in your patterns, or that they contain psychic mysteries and spiritual values. To do so today is not only an impertinence, but a sin against intelligence.

"There's no way of getting good art," Ruskin said, "but one—at once the simplest and most difficult—namely, to enjoy it. Examine the history of nations, and you will find this great fact clear and unmistakable on the front of it—that good art has only been produced by nations who rejoiced in it; fed themselves with it, as if it were bread; basked in it, as if it were sunshine; shouted at the sight of it; danced with the delight of it; quarreled for it; fought for it; starved for it; did, in fact, precisely the opposite with it of what we want to do with it—they made it to keep, and we to sell. And truly this is a serious difficulty for a commercial nation. Try to make your art cheap—a fair article for a foreign market; and the foreign market will always show you something better. But make it only to please yourselves, and even be resolved that you won't let anybody else have any; and forthwith you will find everybody else wants it."

The plastic arts in America have not invited the assistance of our best minds. Our painters, taken one with another, are sincere, disposed to be friendly, and eager to do something worth while; but psychic inbreeding has dulled their wits. Discarded by the world, they have no point of view, little scholarship of any kind, not much practical sense, and no knowledge of the life with which, one would suppose, they

366

should naturally deal. Their sad predicament may be largely attributed to social isolation, to their inability to enter into any department of modern life. No one asks or expects anything of them; no one seems to care whether they live or die.

The painter must cease to esteem himself as only a delicately attuned receptive instrument; he must become a workman again, know the world, draw and present it according to his knowledge, relate his experiences with logic and good sense, and abandon the habit of hiding his deficiencies in a babble of esthetic terms. Let him get down to work; and in possession of all the resources and instruments of his craft, break his back to do something that shall stand in its own right, independent of verbal exegesis. That our painters and their potential patrons are unacquainted with the function of art is confirmed by exhibitions everywhere. It is also confirmed by the recent craze for photo-murals.

The arguments for the photo-mural, and for all photography as an art-form, are based on two fallacies. The first is that inasmuch as painting is a visual art, the camera, aided by new processes of enlarging prints, could more swiftly and economically discharge the duties of the artist. It is true, of course, that painting, as an art of vision, is first presented to the eye, but the material it presents cannot be gathered by the eye alone—not by the artist's eye nor by the eye of the camera. Human vision in so far as it registers any meaning, is not a mechanical operation. All perception is constructive, an integrated effort involving a lifelong train of memories, associations, and experiences. No one, save the idiot and the new-born babe, is capable of viewing an object with the innocence and mechanical detachment of the camera. The optical impact is simply the first step toward knowledge. Good painting is not a mechanical record of things seen; it is a coherent statement of what conditioned human beings know about things. The meaning of the photo-mural differs in no respect from the meaning that we read into the rotogravures of the newspapers. In the photograph, it is the subject, not the treatment, that interests us; in painting, the interest is proportionate to the power of the intelligence to modify and dramatize visual facts.

The second fallacy is that the photographer, by the selection of his materials, by retouchings, focal distortions, and the pitching of his camera at eccentric angles, can compose a picture. All composed painting, and mural painting especially, calls for an absolute control of accent. There must be rhythm—an order of lines, planes, and colors so calculated that the eye is carried easily and inevitably from one form to another. In the rhythm of all art worthy of the name, we find that individual preferences are manifest and active, causing sharp accentuations, dramatic concentrations of energy in prominent forms, variations in size and type with no regard for photographic accuracy or perspective; we find that static uniformity is abolished; and we feel the beat of living materials, of knowledge used creatively to excite our emotions. The photograph, however disguised or altered, remains a mechanical record. It contains no evidence of mind or imagination.

Let us not pretend that the photo-murals of Rockefeller Center have anything to do with art. And while we are in that center of megalomania, let us confess that the Brangwyn mural is a shabby convention; that the Sert is disingenuous and theatrical—a sprawling example of academic virtuosity. Both are a disgrace to New York City. And let us not pretend that Manship's huge sculpture is, in conception, anything more than a boudoir knickknack, or a paper-weight, because it is egregiously magnified. And the doors of the British Empire Building! Ah, those doors! That field of blue, those scabs of gold!

I knew a man in New Mexico who had four sons and three daughters. He was proud and strong, and his children were like him, the sons young giants, the daughters as handsome as they were intelligent. But to his unspeakable grief, his wife gave birth to a fifth son, physically undersized and mentally a half-wit. The old man was ashamed and heart-broken; and to add to his humiliation, the idiot boy was artistically gifted. This dwarfish creature would sit all day in the sun, sticking tiny black and white pebbles into the sand, arranging them in mosaic

JOSE CLEMENTE OROZCO: *Detail Cortez and Malintzin*

(From mural in true fresco) COURTESY OF DELPHIC STUDIOS

patterns of facts and of men riding horses. When the Mexicans were making adobe blocks, he would mold designs in the damp clay—figures in relief, working with unnatural patience and with the skill of a finished modeler. But his designs gave one the creeps; they were spiritually sick—they were silly. . . . I am sorry I mentioned those idiot doors.

I am interested in art as an activity proceeding from and affecting the lives of men and women. I am, therefore, as much concerned with the environment and the experiences of the artist as with the created object—the two are inseparable. Unshorn Europeans tell us that the proper way to criticize art is to view the object as a purely plastic contrivance, a material composition, and that a knowledge of the conditions producing it is a hindrance to formal appreciation. Reading their criticism I can believe them. Such criticism leads into a blind alley of technicalities or into a metaphysical lingo that has no meaning. The multiplication of museums in America does not charm me. Often enough the spirit of the founders is praiseworthy, but the administration of the funds is painful. On the whole, our museums are gilded show places stuffed with inferior old masters and directed by soft little fellows from the Fogg factory who use pictures to titillate mischievous erotic appetites. Some of them support little communities of retainers, traders, and esthetes. They cater to tail coats, bored women, and kept radicals. By the style of their buildings—which is usually classical; by ignoring the needs of the community and the work of valid Americans; by investing wantonly in European goods so as to make an impressive showing on paper, and to advertise the magnitude of their cultural pretensions; our museums foster the notion that art is something ancient and inaccessible, instead of a decent job performed by an intelligent workman for an honest audience.

Today, when the artist has no organic market for his commodity, when the system of buying and selling pictures is artificial and corrupt, the genuine collector is a blessing indeed. But there are not many. I know several collectors to whom art is an unaffected need: they do not buy more than they can consume; as far as it is practicable, they

369

buy directly from the artist, without cheating him, or haggling over prices, if he is reasonable; they have no desire to hoard everything an artist has done, being content with a few choice works representing the different phases of his career; they do not turn their houses into museums but set aside a special room for their treasures—and they do not make you sick talking continually about art. But most collectors are horse traders at heart. Having amassed a fortune in business, they hope to amass a cultural equivalent in pictures, and to expand spiritually in direct proportion to the expansion of their collections. Having monopolized and controlled some article of commerce, they have an insane desire to monopolize and control painters—to own, hoard, and hide, every extant scrap of the artists whom they affect. Their instincts are hoggish and uncivilized. They buy pictures as Mae West buys diamonds, but with a signal difference—Mae West loves her diamonds. She knows their value as investments, and she admits that her tastes are hoggish; but her tastes are genuine—she loves her collection. And unlike the collectors of French Modernism, she has never pretended that there is a soul in her costly gauds. Some collectors, to avoid paying taxes, have succeeded in incorporating their galleries of private stock as public educational institutions—and try to get in them! There is only one cure for collectors who are rich enough to monopolize an artist's work and base enough to withdraw it from public use—confiscation of their plunder.

The hope for American art lies in the tendency now forming. The character of the tendency, and its leaders, I have already discussed. To the young artists of the new movement who must, for the time being, remain unannounced, I can only express my gratitude and best wishes. I have met them collectively and individually, hundreds of them, in every part of America: intelligent and talented young men and women who are not looking to France nor to Fifty-seventh Street for salvation; who understand that the collapse of the French Modernism has not improved the old art of the academy and the mindless art of the Impressionists; who realize that Modernism is a method rather than

INDEX

INDEX

INDEX

INDEX

It would be a fine thing, if we had in America a dominant idealism, a spiritual force uniting artists in a common purpose, making them practitioners again, affording them legitimate markets, and circulating their pictures. But I see no signs of the coming of this Utopia. In the absence of a Utopian scheme, the artist must adapt himself to realities, put living above painting, and do his best in the worst of worlds.

an expression; who are turning to American life for their materials and to local exhibitions for their audiences. During the next decade, before a proper balance has been struck between subject and composition, we shall be deluged with horrible story pictures. I can bear it. They will be better than the dry-bones of abstractionism. And they will be better than that form of painting practiced by professional Modernists, amateurs, doctors, lawyers, and old ladies, to compensate impotence.

The story value of painting cannot be dismissed. It should be remembered that the art of the Italian Renaissance, for example, was called into the service of the Church, not because of its formal attributes, but because of its power to represent collective beliefs and aspirations. And it should be remembered by every one attempting to assess the values of painting, that associated meanings can be, and frequently are, more real than things themselves. Modern criticism has failed to recognize the fact that the picture is a symbol as well as a composition, or thing. Painting comes into contact with society and finds its proper function through associative channels, but in so doing runs the risk of becoming utterly false and conventional. The frightful banality of the murals in Rockefeller Center illustrates this danger.

I have only one medicine to prescribe for the painter—an interest in living. The nature of the interest is his own problem; it may be metropolitan or rural, poetic or realistic; but it must be genuine and exceptional. Unless he has this interest, this intelligent curiosity and relish for life, he will never be an artist. I do not ask him to celebrate America; no self-respecting artist could glorify capitalism. I ask that he have some basic conviction, some point of departure. His business is not to teach, but to reveal; to communicate meanings which may be confirmed, shared, and enjoyed by an intelligent audience. He must preserve his independence. I do not mean that he must be free in the Bohemian sense—that he must live in a state of irresponsibility which prevents him from facing any useful experience. He must be free to question any system, creed or situation.